Before him the prairie spread alight with slanting sun and early grain. For a few miles it fell gently, then with a long slow swell slipped over the horizon. There was a state of mind, a mood ... in which one could skim along this curve of prairie floor and, gathering momentum ... glide up ... and soar away from earth. He succeeded now, borne by a white-limbed steed again. And as they soared the mystery was not solved, but gradually absorbed ... a heartening gleam upon the roof of life to let him see its vault and spaciousness.

'A Day with Pegasus'

There is a brief but revealing moment towards the end of [As for Me and My House]: Mrs. Bentley takes Philip's best paintings and drawings and spreads them out for Philip to view. She's trying to convince him yet once again that he can do it: 'Be detached and fair,' she says. 'Isn't there something there that's important?' Philip makes a deprecating remark. 'I gathered them up then,' says Mrs. Bentley, 'and trying to laugh, said the exhibition was closing for lack of an appreciative public.' Exactly.

Margaret Atwood, *Survival*

As for Sinclair Ross

David Stouck

UNIVERSITY OF TORONTO PRESS
Toronto Buffalo London

© University of Toronto Press Incorporated 2005
Toronto Buffalo London
Printed in Canada

ISBN 0-8020-4388-7

Printed on acid-free paper

Library and Archives Canada Cataloguing in Publication

Stouck, David, 1940–
As for Sinclair Ross / David Stouck.

Includes bibliographical references and index.
ISBN 0-8020-4388-7

1. Ross, Sinclair, 1908–1996.   2. Authors, Canadian (English) – 20th
century – Biography.   I. Title.

PS8535.O79Z86 2005   C813′.54   C2004-905981-5

University of Toronto Press acknowledges the financial assistance to its publishing
program of the Canada Council and the Ontario Arts Council.

This book has been published with the help of a grant from the Canadian Federation
for the Humanities and Social Sciences, through the Aid to Scholarly Publishing
Programme, using funds provided by the Social Sciences and Humanities Research
Council of Canada.

University of Toronto Press acknowledges the financial support for its publishing
activities of the Government of Canada through the Book Publishing Industry
Development Program (BPIDP).

Contents

Preface   ix

Acknowledgments   xiii

1 Wild Rose   3

2 The Housekeeper's Son   10

3 Bank Clerk   26

4 Musician   42

5 Winnipeg   69

6 Days with Pegasus   92

7 *As for Me and My House*   107

8 War Years   124

9 Montreal   139

10 *The Well*   161

11 *Whir of Gold*   181

12 Tourist   208

13 *Sawbones Memorial*   219

14 Literary Forefather   242

15 Suicide   262

16 The Order of Canada   276

Notes   299

Bibliography   329

Illustration Credits   337

Index   339

Illustrations follow page 168

Preface

Students of Canadian literature hardly need to be persuaded of the importance of Sinclair Ross. His short stories about Prairie farmers and their families have long been the stuff of Canadian anthologies, and *As for Me and My House*, set during the 1930s drought and Depression, is regarded as one of the country's classic novels. But more significantly, the fiction of Sinclair Ross, unlike that of his contemporaries Morley Callaghan and Hugh MacLennan, remains central to the ways we are engaged in reading literature. The short stories and *As for Me and My House*, for example, are read in terms of gender and identity formation. In *As for Me and My House* we find a male author writing in the voice of a woman, who in turn is writing about a man – a voice that comes to us across history (the novel was first published in 1941), but also across gender and sexuality. We ask now, how does one read a novel in which one cannot map a stable identity in terms of author and speaker? What, in fact, did it mean in 1941 for a male writer to speak in the voice of a woman, a postmodern narrative strategy familiar enough today in a book like Richard B. Wright's *Clara Callan* (2001), but unique to the realistic novel of the 1940s?

Similarly we read Ross's fiction, especially his last book, *Sawbones Memorial*, in the light of what we might call postcolonial reasoning, for he reminds his readers that there were people living in the small Prairie towns he describes who were outside the colonial, English-speaking mainstream, 'foreigners' from Scandinavia, Eastern Europe, and China, as well as Aboriginal inhabitants. Like many contemporary writers today, Ross describes those people outside of history – ethnic and racial minorities, strangers and migrants – whose presence and difference interrogate the power structures his novels portray. In that light, one can say he wrote about survival in all its aspects – economic, artistic, racial, and sexual.

Sinclair Ross's significance to the literary culture of Canada is clear, but the man himself has been dimly perceived. During his lifetime, he was almost invisible, never reading from his work in public, seldom giving interviews. Shortly after his death in 1996, Keath Fraser wrote a brief memoir about his relationship with the older writer, one that has unfortunately left a bleak and, for some, a sordid impression. Fraser's memoir constituted a public outing of Ross as a gay man, but unhappily associated his sexuality with promiscuity and criminal behaviour. Many of the anecdotes recorded in the memoir were related to Fraser during the author's long illness with Parkinson's disease, when medication would induce wild imaginings. I don't quarrel with Fraser's perception exactly; rather, I have placed it here in the larger context of a life story that emerges from interviewing people who knew Ross from the time he was a small boy, from visiting the places where he lived and worked, from letters he wrote to friends, editors, and publishers, and from my own knowlege of the man.

That larger picture includes a less easily categorized sexuality. While he was candid in conversation about his homosexual experiences, he also talked about his love for a particular woman during his youth, and about his sexual relations with other women later in life. He felt 'comfortable,' as he phrased it, with bisexuality, because it gave him greater range, he believed, as an artist of human nature. He lived alone, but he found himself drawn to close friendships with couples and transferred this to his fiction in patterns of triangulated desire. This biography is not an attempt to 'straighten' the public image of Sinclair Ross, nor to theorize his life, but to provide a record of his experiences and of how he viewed them himself. His understanding was shaped in part by the shifting attitudes towards sexuality in the twentieth century; during the greater part of his lifetime, homosexuality was viewed variously as sin, disease, and criminal behaviour, and only in his old age was it accepted more widely as a legitimate form of human expression. At the same time, he held all his life to the romantic concept of the artist, regardless of sexual feeling, as someone apart from society, for whom loneliness and distance were necessary conditions for creativity.

Although the words of this biography are mine, the book in a sense has three authors. I embarked on the initial research with John O'Connor, University of Toronto, whose boundless enthusiasm for Sinclair Ross and meticulous research methods never ceased to inspire me. We travelled together in Saskatchewan, gathering information and documents from the places where Sinclair Ross had once lived; we visited Ross's brother in a nursing home in northern Michigan; and we spent a week in New York City trying to locate information about Ross's American agents and his first book publisher, Reynal and Hitchcock. We spent many hours in Vancouver discussing our subject and sharing our findings, and that collaboration is deeply embedded in this biography.

The other collaborator is Sinclair Ross himself. He and I had engaged in correspondence for a number of years while he was living in Europe, and then he moved to Vancouver, where he spent the last fourteen years of his life. Here I gradually gained his trust, and he agreed to cooperate if I wanted to tell his life story. Because of his illness, there were many days when interviews, even conversations, were not possible; extreme mood swings in reaction to drug therapies would leave him almost comatose for hours or else in an agitated and hallucinatory state. But there were good days in between, and, once the research and writing had begun, my method was to take him the materials I had found (letters, interviews, photographs), and they would invariably stir his memory and bring more information to light. When I read the first chapters of the biography aloud, he would make corrections and additions, sometimes rephrasing a line for greater accuracy, or for sonority.

In our conversations, I was acutely aware of how sensitive he was to his audience and how he bent his words to his listener. I also remembered something he said to me in a letter dated 5 September 1977, when he wrote: 'If anyone is so ill-advised as to attempt a biography ... with so little to work on, the poor fellow will in desperation try his hand at inventing.' So I have had to ask myself throughout this project, how much was I inventing? How much in our conversations was Sinclair Ross inventing himself? In that vein, I learned not to take seriously those anecdotes he only told once and later could not remember. I reminded myself not to run with a hunch, or make guesses, but to remain, in my subject's words, 'tethered to reality,' anchored by the incontrovertible substance of dates, places, letters, and photographs. Accordingly there are gaps in the narrative where no material evidence has come to light and where the author's memory could provide no pieces to complete the picture. His mother's frequent moves when he was a child created some of those gaps, but more surprisingly there are periods in Ross's adult life (between 1952 and 1954, and 1963 and 1966) when the man and the writer disappear from public view, and no prompting could assist the man to reconnect with those years through memory.

But the larger picture is clear. Sinclair Ross told me about his lonely childhood and about his cheerful but overbearing mother, and about the men and women with whom he fell in love. He told me about his work and about the places where he had travelled. But most of all he told me about his struggles to get published, to make his living as a writer in an inhospitable place and time, and his failure to find an audience. I hope I have composed a record here that is commensurate with the expectations of both of my collaborators, and that this life story will provide further reasons to continue reading Sinclair Ross.

Acknowledgments

My first debt of gratitude is to that group of friends who formed a little community around Sinclair Ross in his last years. Keath and Lorraine Fraser encouraged him to move to Vancouver in 1982, and for the next fourteen years they attended to his physical and social needs and looked after his business affairs. Their friendship was unwavering, and Ross referred to them as 'my family.' Here I thank Keath especially for providing me with copies of letters received from his friend and for folders containing correspondence Ross had conducted in the 1970s and '80s. Irene Harvalias also played a major part in the last years of the author's life; unfailingly attentive to his needs when hospitalized, she made it possible for him to write when he could no longer use a pencil or typewriter. Volunteering as his amanuensis, she typed out several versions of his last two manuscripts and conducted much of his correspondence. Like the presence of the Frasers in his life, Irene's almost daily visits – her attention and interest – guaranteed a quality of life in the face of disease and debilitation. I thank her for creating those optimum conditions in which I was able to visit and work with the author on his life story.

Two young men, Andy Trapnell and John Whitefoot, also greatly enhanced the author's last years with their loving admiration for both the man and his work, and I thank them for sharing with me the stories of their friendship with Sinclair Ross. I thank John Whitefoot as well for contributing archival items he has located in his bibliographical pursuit of Canadian authors, and for reading a draft of this biography and making some corrections to the manuscript.

Interviews made it possible to extend this life from a memoir to a full-scale biography, and I am grateful to those who generously shared their stories, letters, and photographs saved over the years. From Sinclair Ross's years in the area of Prince Albert, Saskatchewan (SK), I thank Ernest Wernham and Albert Pugh; from the Rolling Prairie District, SK: Gladys Olson McLean,

Orville Olson, and Myrtle Doell; from Abbey, SK: Clara Lee, Theodora Dow-sley, Svea Pederson, Harold Braaten, Bessie Cottingham, Emil Pederson, Dwayne Thompson, and Lena Hunchiak Campe; from Lancer, SK: Dorothy and Lorrain Volden, and Marjorie Panton; from Stoughton, SK: Percy Bowes, Vesta Pickel, and Bliss and Florence Kerr; from Indian Head, SK: Bertha Lang, Mavis and Roger Gray, Pat Miller (Ross's great-niece), Margaret and Donald Price, Belva Howatt, James and Dorothy Conn, and Fern Schoch; from Arcola, SK: Cal Ingram, Clarence Samis, Frank Woodbury, Kaye Hawker Murray, Eve-lyn Gordon, and Verna Carr; from Winnipeg: Doris Saunders, Chester Dun-can, Mary Johnson, Robert Savory, Audrey Peterkin, Tora Talgoy Noyes, William Thorne, Roy St George Stubbs, Lillian Downes, and Basil Hunter; from New York: Kenneth McCormick; from Montreal: John Gibbon, Doyle and William Klyn, Molly and William Baxter, Alec Lucas, Mavis Gallant, and Dorothy and Alvin Goldman.

Beginning with the appearance of his early short stories in the pages of *Queen's Quarterly*, academic interest has always been at the centre of Sinclair Ross's career. Professor Lorraine McMullen first introduced Ross to many read-ers in a full-length study of his work; I owe her a special debt of gratitude for helping me to meet the man as well. Several teachers who corresponded with Ross made their letters available for this biography. They include Ken Mitch-ell, University of Regina, David Carpenter, University of Saskatchewan, John Moss, University of Ottawa, Wilfred Cude of West Bay, Nova Scotia, and John O'Connor, University of Toronto. Their generosity has been exemplary. I have also been assisted with items and advice provided by my colleagues Sandra Djwa, Carole Gerson, Kathy Mezei, and Peter Dickinson, and by student research assistant Jes Battis.

Professional interest and institutional cooperation are vital to a project of this kind, and, accordingly, I thank Robert Weaver, Jack McClelland, and William French, all of Toronto, for conversations about Sinclair Ross, and I am grateful to Sheila Kieran, Toronto, Myrna Kostash, Edmonton, and the exec-utors of Margaret Laurence's estate for making letters written by Sinclair Ross available for this project. I thank here the staff of libraries and archives who have provided materials when requested. I acknowledge especially Carl Spa-doni, McMaster University Library, Rachel Grover, Thomas Fisher Rare Book Library, Anne Goddard and Ghislain Malette, National Archives of Canada, Maureen Fox, Saskatchewan Archives, University of Saskatchewan, the 1993 staff of the Saskatchewan Archives, University of Regina, and Nancy Blake at Simon Fraser University Library, who cheerfully tracked down some stubborn items of information through interlibrary loans. At University of Toronto Press I thank my former editor, Gerry Hallowell, who supported the publication of a book of Ross criticism and prepared me for this longer project. I am grateful to Siobhan McMenemy and the readers of this biography in manuscript, who guided me through the complex matter of writing about gender and sexuality at the beginning of the twenty-first century; to Ken Lewis, whose meticulous copy-editing gives high quality to so many University of Toronto Press books; and to Frances Mundy, who courteously supervised the passage of this book through the final stages of production.

Finally, there is the special pleasure of thanking family and friends who have assisted in a project of this kind. For alerting me to the Grant Macdonald Collection at Queen's University Library and for providing items from the Royal Bank's publication, *The Teller*, I thank Jo Marriott of St Catharines, Ontario. I thank my daughter, Jordan Stouck, for helping me to locate some of the Ross letters, and my mother, Winnifred Stouck of St Catharines, for her careful work in preparing many of the illustrations for this volume. Her skill and readiness to copy loaned photographs, in a time before computer scanning, were invaluable in creating a photo archive of Sinclair Ross's life.

Finally, two travelling companions gave me important material assistance with this project: my cousin, Raymond Manson, helped me find my way around Montreal, as I searched out the people and places Sinclair Ross had known there for twenty-two years; and my friend and colleague, Myler Wilkinson, worked with me in the Saskatchewan Archives in Regina, searching for and recording any mentions of James Sinclair Ross in the province's newspapers. Their interest and company were a great assist and a source of much pleasure.

Research for this book was supported by a grant in 1993 from the Social Sciences and Humanities Research Council to travel to Saskatchewan.

AS FOR SINCLAIR ROSS

one

Wild Rose
1908–1915

When James Sinclair Ross was born on 22 January 1908, it was a bitterly cold day in the bush country of northern Saskatchewan, but winter wasn't the only adversity attending his birth. His father had brought home a Native woman, Mary Belle Clifford, to assist with the delivery of his third child.[1] Mrs Clifford was well known in the Shellbrook area as a skilled midwife and a kindly woman, but she had asked for a strong drink – 'a toddy of rum,' she said, 'to warm her fingers.' Peter Ross handed her the bottle and went out to the stable to look after the horses, but when he came back he found the midwife drunk. 'Nonetheless,' the future author would say, 'she delivered me.'[2] But sometimes he gave a darker version of the story wherein, after several drinks, Mrs Clifford passed out, and he came into the world unattended. 'From the start,' he would say in this version, 'never a leg up.'[3] He was surrounded instead, as a new baby, by the voices of his parents quarrelling, the importunate demands of a sister and brother, and the howling of the wind across the prairie, sounds that in his fiction echo still.

Peter and Catherine Ross were homesteaders who had moved to their farm, located twenty-five miles north-west of Prince Albert, five years before Jimmy was born. The Rosses' frame house, set back from the road, had a peculiar appearance to the neighbours because its roof was flat and its sheet metal sides were painted bright red.[4] Jim would remember it, however, with some pride as 'no two- or three-room log shack,' but a substantial two-storeyed house, with four large rooms on each floor, including a lean-to summer kitchen.[5] In spite of the cold admitted in the winter and the intense heat generated by a flat roof in the summer, the house seemed spacious to the small boy, in keeping with his mother's conception of 'living well.' The first house on the property had indeed been a two-room shack, twelve feet by fourteen feet, constructed by Jim's father of unbarked logs and valued at forty dollars.

When she moved out to the homestead, his mother immediately began planning the new house and oversaw not only its design but its construction.

The house is now gone, but Jim described it in a memoir that old neighbours recognize as fairly accurate.[6] Downstairs there was a central kitchen used all year round, but as well a separate dining room where his mother entertained company with silver service at a formal table. This room was heated by a big wood stove with lots of nickel trim, and one of its windows was filled with house plants on tiered shelves – pots of geranium, ivy, and wandering Jew. Kate (as she was known) called this her 'conservatory.' The dining room also served as a sewing room and study.

Seldom used, but with a rather grand aspect to a small boy, was the front parlour, warmed in winter when Jim's mother pushed back the plush, wine-coloured curtains and let the warmth of the dining room penetrate its recesses. The parlour was Kate's repository for culture. There were bookcases for her collection of Sir Walter Scott, Dickens, and other popular British classics from the nineteenth century, and on the walls were lithograph illustrations. A guest could take a seat in one of the wicker chairs; however, Kate would not permit family members to do so because the velvet on the seats was wearing thin. The prize ornament of the parlour was a pump organ, a harmonium Kate called it, which could be heard half a mile away 'if the wind [was] right.' On Sundays she played hymns by ear, but during the week she played old Scottish songs like 'Annie Laurie' or 'Robin Adair.' Upstairs were four bedrooms, including a spare room for visitors 'with starched embroidered pillow shams,' lace curtains, and a picture of St Cecilia playing an organ.

Kate Ross's desire for a nicely appointed home and for furnishings to reflect an upper-middle-class background ran counter to the limited vision and capacities of her pioneer husband. When in 1902 Peter Ross filed a claim with the government land office on a quarter section of land (160 acres), he bound himself, for a three-year period, to break or clear 30 acres, to construct a house worth three hundred dollars, and to reside on the land for at least six months of each year. The terrain consisted of grassland, poplar forest, and a spruce swamp, 100 acres of which was suitable for cultivation. Records for the Saskatchewan land office reveal that he was slow proving up, that it took nearly six rather than three years before the land was fully registered in his name. Later land title certificates show the property burdened with debt and the final foreclosure of a mortgage against the property.[7] By then the Rosses had separated and Kate had gone her own way, taking her younger son with her.

A wife's high expectations and a husband's slow, ineffectual progress towards economic self-sufficiency were elements in a marriage that seemed doomed to fail from the beginning. Divergent family backgrounds were especially crucial to this mismatch. Both Catherine Foster Fraser and Peter Ross were of Scottish descent (although neither was actually born in Scotland),[8] but there the similarities ended. Kate Ross's ancestors were distinguished people, numbering several accomplished and sometimes notorious figures. For example, according to Kate's account, they included Simon Fraser, the first Lord Lovat, who, for his loyalty to Bonnie Prince Charlie, was the last man to be beheaded in the Tower of London. His wife was from the nobility, and William Hogarth painted his portrait.[9] Kate's father, John Fraser, was an ambitious Unitarian minister who had studied in the United States with Theodore Parker, the radical Unitarian theologian, and her oldest brother, John Foster Fraser, was a distinguished London journalist and author who was eventually knighted for his achievements. How did his sister come to live on a rough homestead in what was then still the Canadian Northwest Territories?

The death of Kate Ross's minister father, while only in his thirties,[10] left her mother with five children to raise and little support. Eventually, Jessie Patterson Fraser married Thomas Holmes, a middle-aged bachelor, a locksmith and shopkeeper, whose younger brother, Andrew, had crossed the Atlantic in 1883 and was launched on a prosperous career in the fledgling community of Prince Albert. As a building contractor and later mayor of the city, Andrew Holmes made a distinguished place for himself in the economic and social development of northern Saskatchewan.[11] Tom Holmes was not made of such ambitious stuff, but when he brought his wife and her children over to Canada, he provided them with a steady livelihood by working for the Canadian Pacific Railway. There were only three of Jessie's five children in Prince Albert: the oldest son, John Foster Fraser, chose to remain in Britain, where he pursued his career as a journalist; a daughter had died in childhood before the family left for Canada. Catherine, and two brothers, Stuart and Theodore, made up the Fraser family in Canada.

Catherine, who was born 15 April 1876, was still in her teens when she met Peter Ross, a prospective homesteader from Ontario working in Prince Albert as a drayman. In his late twenties, withdrawn and lacking self-confidence, Ross was illiterate (could barely sign his name) and had no financial resources. Kate's mother was alarmed by this relationship. Even though her family had removed to a remote frontier region, class differences were still important, especially in light of Andrew Holmes's success and rising social position. Kate, an impulsive and headstrong girl, continued the relationship in defiance of her mother's wishes, but it was probably a letter from her older brother, John, admonishing her not to make a fool of herself by marrying a lumberjack, that strengthened her resolve to go her own way. Accordingly, Catherine Moir Foster Fraser and Peter Sinclair Ross were married in Prince Albert in 1896.

Just a few recorded facts outline the early years of the marriage. Records show that a daughter, Effie (named Euphemia after one of her father's sisters), was born on 26 May 1897, and three years later a son, Stuart, on 4 September 1900. In one of his land title declarations, Peter Ross describes himself as 'teaming,' transporting cordwood and other supplies in the area, and also being employed as a brick-maker in Prince Albert. At this time he may have begun making the three- and four-day trips north to Lac La Ronge in winter, hauling oats and other food stuffs to the missionary school there and returning with furs and frozen fish. He filed for a land grant in 1902 and received title 11 February 1908, just a few days after his second son, James, was born. Otherwise the record of those early years consists chiefly in what was remembered by the Ross children and their neighbours, and by what the local newspaper allows us to presume.

Foremost in local memory is Kate Ross, a stout, energetic woman, admired for her superior housekeeping and cheerful social ways, but also regarded with apprehension because of her violent temper. Many of the early immigrant settlers in the district were British (most continental Europeans did not arrive until the 1920s), and Kate enjoyed the social life they created. The Rosses' neighbours included Canfields, Lycans, Wernhams, Heaps, Ormans, Painters, Pughs, and Soles. In that company, Kate was quick to check any unwarranted pretensions, and the story goes that when there was a proposal to call the new postal district Sandringham, Kate asked how many had actually seen Sandringham (a royal estate in Norfolk) and suggested the name Wild Rose instead. But her old neighbours felt she put on airs herself, dressing up in black silks for church services, disdaining farm women's talk of chickens and gardens.[12] She especially liked to entertain the circuit preacher for Sunday dinners. Services were held in what was called the Crystal Plains School with preachers of different denominations, and Kate, with what some thought presumptuous ebullience, would discuss theology with her guests, especially what she, as a Unitarian, regarded as 'the problem of the Trinity.'

A newspaper titled the *Shellbrook Chronicle* began publishing in 1912, and its social columns list Kate in attendance at anniversary celebrations and tea parties.[13] In contrast there are no mentions of Peter Ross in the social columns, nor, more significantly, is he mentioned as one of the 150 winners in the area's agricultural fair. Kate enjoyed social life and indeed did not refrain at times from 'putting on airs,' but children in the area were more likely to glimpse and remember another side of her character. Ernest Wernham, a boy five years older than Jim, remembered coming over to the Ross farm with his brother and finding Mrs Ross in a rage about something. When she saw the neighbour children approach the yard, she threatened to cut off their heads with a butcher knife, and they returned home, shaken. The children heard rumours about a scar across Pete Ross's face; his wife, it was whispered, had hit him with a poker while he slept. Mrs Ross was remembered by the neighbour children as a strong woman with a passion for cleanliness, who kept a nice house 'with fancy curtains and lots of flowers,' but at the same time as a demanding woman with a wicked temper. Pete Ross was a loner and often cantankerous.[14]

Jim's earliest memories were of his parents' quarrels. Most often it was over money – her extravagance on the one side, his failure to earn a better living on the other. The house was mortgaged, but Kate was determined nonetheless to have certain items that, while luxuries to most homesteaders, were to her mind essentials – things like the harmonium, silver service, and a damask tablecloth, separate clothes for Sunday, and a subscription to the weekly newspaper from Regina, which she passed around to other residents in the area.[15] A good cook, Kate refused to skimp on food. At Christmas she regaled family and visiting neighbours with her mince pies, plum duff, and shortbread, even though the ingredients were costly and each year they were sinking deeper into debt. And she made sure the whole family had plenty of warm clothing for indoors as well as out, refusing to huddle up under quilts or blankets as some did when there was a cold spell. She loathed the homely materials she sometimes had to use: "'So what if you bleach flour bags and use them for underwear,'" her husband shouted, "'– do you think you're the only one? You're a homesteader's wife. There's no money for anybody to throw away.'" Pounding the table, she would accuse him of wasting money on tobacco, and he would curse and point to her 'fancy curtains' and to all the tea she drank, at which point the argument would reach its inevitable climax with Kate bursting forth: "'You'd think you'd be ashamed [to begrudge your wife a cup of tea]! What kind of man are you! If you'd take hold and do something – or get somebody to help you – you don't know how to farm – you just keep piling up more debts.'"[16]

But in a memoir titled 'Just Wind and Horses,' Jim describes another kind of climax to their arguments: 'They were always fighting but this day it was worse. He was standing behind her with a butcher knife at her throat. That's what I thought. I screamed and started pulling at his leg to make him stop and my brother came and took me outside. He said I had it wrong. My father was trying to take the knife away from her.'[17] That scene is telling in two important aspects: obviously it suggests the painful confusion of a child caught in a domestic crisis, not knowing what is happening or who is to blame; but it also suggests clearly that in some ways Peter Ross was a match for his domineering wife, that he did not always meekly submit to her abusive tirades or her socially ambitious view of things. Especially painful for the boy were incidents in which he was instrumental in causing a quarrel to erupt. Near the end of his life, he would remember how at age five he fell and gave the underneath of his forearm a deep cut on a handsaw. It bled profusely and his parents feared blood poisoning and amputation. But after they had washed and bound up the wound, they started hurling accusations at each other, Kate blaming Pete for leaving a saw lying in the yard, their quarrel creating a much deeper wound in the boy than the blade of the saw.

Trying to understand his parents' unhappy marriage, Jim focuses in his memoir on an injury his father sustained in an accident with his horses. Exactly what happened is not clear: Was there a thunderstorm and the horses bolted, and he was pitched out of the wagon on his head? Or was he already on the ground holding them by their bridles, and they bolted while Stuart was unhooking the tug? No clear account survives, although both Jim and Ernest Wernham remembered a doctor eventually coming from Shellbrook to assess his condition (there were no cars or telephones), and his being given electric shock treatment to restore movement in his legs. The accident was said to have caused a personality change in Jim's father, his behaviour becoming irra-tional and abusive (although Jim's brother would tell him years later that the accident had made no significant difference in their father's behaviour). When it took place is hard to determine, although it probably took place before 1912 (before Jim turned four) because the *Shellbrook Chronicle*, which started publishing that year, reported myriad property accidents and minor health problems for the area and no account of Peter Ross being injured is recorded.

Jim was remembered by Ernest Wernham as a quiet, introverted little boy, whose doubtful view of the world earned him the sobriquet 'Pouter Ross.' A Wild Rose picnic photo clearly illustrates that nickname. He stayed on the sideline during games and refused a part on stage in the school concerts. At social events, he could always be found huddled beside his mother. His sister and brother, however, were outgoing young people, taking part in the area's social activities, Effie attending church and youth group parties, winning races, and Stuart, also sports-minded, becoming in 1915 president of the local shooting club known as the 'Wild Rose Tigers.' In contrast, Stuart's chief memory of his younger brother as a small boy was that 'he always had his nose in a book.'[18] To Jim, it seemed that his eager, demanding siblings left little room for him in the family.

Jim remembered the house at Wild Rose vividly, and he remembered with a poet's eye certain details about the remote northern countryside of his birth, particularly how in spring snowy masses of pin cherries and saskatoons bloomed along the edge of the poplar bluffs and how clouds of hungry mosquitoes would boil up from the sloughs at sundown. But most of his memories fixed on departures and returns, for at some point in time after the accident with the horses, Kate left her husband and teenage children on the farm, but took Jim off with her. The break, however, was not a simple one. Kate returned to Wild Rose at least twice, trying to make the marriage work, but eventually there would be 'more yelling and shaking the poker' and they went away again. One can only guess at a timetable for these traumatic events in the small boy's life. Jim is listed as being in grade one at the Crystal Plains School in May 1915, but when in July of that year the Painters gave a party in Wild Rose none of the Rosses is listed as a guest. Nor is Jim listed as one of the children present at the Crystal Plains School Christmas concert for 1915. Similarly, in 1916, Kate is not mentioned as taking part in the formation of a Red Cross Society (which does list most of the women in the area), nor is she listed as being a guest or sending a gift for a big wedding in Wild Rose in September 1916. It seems clear, in other words, that by fall of 1915 Kate and Jim had left Wild Rose for good and were never to return. If that calculation is accurate, then Jim never saw his father again after the age of seven.

two

The Housekeeper's Son
1916–1924

Never beg Jimmy, whatever you do never beg. – Kate Ross

To make a living for herself and her son, Kate Ross worked as a housekeeper for the next nine years. The boy's relation to the world was significantly altered; where he lived was no longer 'home,' but a transitory workplace where he was the son of the housekeeper. Sometimes he and his mother shared the same room. The first time they left Wild Rose, Kate worked for an elderly couple in Regina named Forsythe. She kept warning her son not to touch things: 'Remember, they're not ours.' Occasionally he would slip away and play with a couple of small children who lived on the same street. One day they gave him some toys and he brought them back to the house, but his mother became angry and made him return them. She felt he had made himself an object of charity. Independence, the kind she exhibited when she left Wild Rose, was an important lesson to learn. They didn't stay long in Regina because the situation was complicated by another woman working during the day as a personal maid for the Forsythes. She and Kate did not get along. As Jim remembered it, his mother did the cleaning and cooking, but the Forsythes, being frail, needed help dressing and managing at the table. The maid, some years in their employ, was like a family friend, and Kate, feeling the inferiority of her position, decided to return home again.

After she had made a final break with Wild Rose, Kate found work in the area of Indian Head, approximately sixty miles east of Regina. Effie Ross, a spirited, strong-minded young woman like her mother, had left home in 1915 and found work as a housekeeper with the Price family in Indian Head. Although Kate and Effie were often on bad terms, Kate wound up following her daughter to Indian Head. On 28 November 1916, Effie, age nineteen, married Matthew Price, thirty-five, the older brother of her employer. The marriage was reported in the *Shellbrook Chronicle*, with Effie curiously identified as the 'eldest daughter of Mr and Mrs Peter Ross of Prince Albert.'[1]

When Kate came to live at Indian Head, she was employed on at least three different farms in the area. Bertha Brack Lang's memories provide the most vivid glimpse we have of the author in that period. Kate was working for Walter Hill, an English-born widower, and the Brack farm was adjacent. Jimmy was eight years old, roughly the same age as Bertha's older brothers, but they were rough, mischievous farm boys, and Kate wanted a gentler playmate for her son. So she encouraged five-year-old Bertha to come and play games with Jimmy – snakes and ladders, tiddly-winks. But when Kate was not on guard or when Jimmy was at the neighbours' house, the Brack boys would release a particularly aggressive red rooster which chased Jim through the yard, digging its sharp beak into his heels and ankles. Kate was very protective of Jimmy for, unlike her two older children, he was undersize and prone to frequent illness. In the Indian Head area, from 1916 to 1918, Kate also worked for the Livingstons (Mrs Livingston was crippled) and for the Holdens, and Jimmy attended Jubilee School. The specific reasons she changed employers so frequently are not recorded. Perhaps her quick temper got the better of her and she suddenly resigned, confident she could find work elsewhere. Perhaps better prospects beckoned. She may have been known as an opinionated and overbearing woman, but she also had a reputation as an excellent housekeeper, so that mostly she did as she pleased. In his memoir 'Just Wind and Horses,' Jim describes it this way: 'Out working as a housekeeper she would say, in spitfire moments of defiance and exasperation, "I may have to cook and clean for you but I'm better born," and always get away with it, was never told to pack it up and take her blue blood with her. Of course, she was an efficient housekeeper, a good cook, and they may have just shrugged and said let her enjoy herself' (83).

Yet the frequent transfers must have been difficult.[2] When she moved about, Kate took as many of her possessions as possible, filling not only several bulging suitcases but three big trunks containing her favourite books and wedding presents, which included impractical items for travel like a large cut-glass bowl and a coffee pot and cream pitcher that had belonged to her mother. In contrast, when he became an adult, Jim would live austerely, accumulating as few possessions as possible. But like his mother, he would lead a peripatetic life, never feeling there was a place he could call 'home.'

Jim retained two very specific memories from this time spent in Indian Head. While living at the Holden farm, he had his first experience of sex with another boy. On a hot summer day, when there seemed to be nothing to do, the Holdens' twelve-year-old son (Jim was about ten) suggested that they go up into the hayloft together and 'rub.' Jim knew his mother would be angry if she found out what they were doing; it was nothing but sharing a pleasurable sensation, not touching each other, but it was furtively done and he knew she would be shocked and angry. The other vivid memory was from the fall of 1918 when Jim, like so many others, became ill during the Spanish influenza epidemic. For a time his mother was frantic, certain she was going to lose her son, who had become her sole purpose for living. There were deaths in Indian Head as elsewhere, but Jimmy survived. To get iron into his system and rebuild his strength, Kate ordered a basket of fresh grapes when her employer sent to town for supplies, but by the time the hired hands arrived back they had eaten almost all of them.

By 1919, Kate and Jimmy had moved west to Abbey. Her employer was Sid Ketcheson, a burly farmer in his early thirties who owned a half section of land and was not married. This, in fact, would be the pattern for the remainder of Kate's working years: her employers would be single men on farms out in the country. There she could run a house on her own terms and not be accountable to anyone. Moreover, she could fabricate an identity for herself and her son. At first she said simply that she was a widow. Later she went into detail, saying that her husband had been an alcoholic and that one day he'd had an accident with a dray and horses that cost him his life. It happened, she said, while Jimmy was still a very little boy.

Telling stories in which the facts were greatly distorted, or not present at all, was one of Kate's great weaknesses and abiding pleasures. 'She would tell great whoppers,' her son observed many years later, 'for the truth never worried her.' For example, she told of herself being captured by Indians at the age of nine, when in fact she was a child then living in Britain. She amused locals with stories of a mongrel dog named Stubb on the farm at Wild Rose. He had a bad habit of jumping up and biting at the noses of passing horses, causing accidents. One day a man stormed into the Ross kitchen to complain, but she turned him out abruptly for using unseemly language. Her audience always liked that story, picturing the surprised complainant. Then she would go on to tell how Stubb one Sunday stole a roast of pork. Actually, she had already fed the family and was playing the harmonium in the parlour when the dog made off with a few leftovers, but she knew her audience would appreciate a more dramatic version – the meat gone before the family could sit down – and she happily accommodated them. Jim remembered once correcting her and being severely reprimanded for contradicting her in front of guests. She also told stories at his expense; for instance, how once he fell through a trapdoor in the lean-to kitchen into a crock of blueberries (probably saskatoons). His hair, nearly white then, was stained purple, but she went ahead nonetheless and used the berries for pies. Sid Ketcheson enjoyed Kate's stories, but especially he appreciated her efficiency in the kitchen and did not complain overly that she had a boy in tow. His home was big enough and there were chores for a boy on a farm.

Ketcheson operated a half section, sharing equipment and labour with his brother, who also worked a half section. In stark contrast to the homestead in Wild Rose, with its stretches of uncleared bush and its burden of debt, Sid Ketcheson's farming operation – a half section in wheat and a quarter section (on pre-emption) for cattle – had the marks of success.[3] There was a stable, three granaries, and a large barn, which alone was worth an estimated $2,000. Collectively Peter Ross's farm buildings were valued at $180.[4] In part, the difference was geography: Abbey is located in open grasslands, and when rains come at the right time harvests are bountiful. But rains do not always come. Abbey is located in what is known as the Palliser Triangle, a large area of southern Saskatchewan and Alberta (also designated as part of the Great American Desert), where some years there is almost no rain at all. Accordingly, a successful farmer must budget his operations to carry him through the lean years. Sid Ketcheson had that kind of foresight, and, as his neighbours would say, 'he knew the value of a dollar.'[5]

Jim liked the expansiveness of the farm, its well-cared for livestock, and its air of prosperity. He also liked the activity of men working the land and herding cattle, and enjoyed listening to their banter and conversation around the kitchen table. But sometimes their talk, with its irreverent and racy innuendos, made his mother ill at ease, and she warned her son to keep his distance from the men when they were out of doors. She made him feel grown men were dangerous, and that he should remember he had no father to protect him. It was a painful reminder, but he did not feel threatened, for Sid and his farmhands largely ignored the boy; instead, he felt how unimportant he was, how much he was an outsider in the big world of men, to which he had no entry. Kate urged her son to concentrate on his homework, to make something of himself in a world described in books. She was determined he would not be like his father, or like his older brother, Stuart, who, in his unenterprising way, seemed to be following in his father's footsteps. She had never been able to enlist Stuart as one of her allies in the ongoing battle with her husband, and, leaving him behind on the farm at Wild Rose, she grew to think of him as one of the 'monsters' in her life.

For Jimmy, who was eleven and twelve when they lived at Sid Ketcheson's farm, there would be no initiation into the world of men, and the drama of his mother's life held no attraction, but there was an intense pleasure that absorbed his days, and that was his ownership and care for a horse. To readers of Canadian literature, this horse would be known as Isabel, or 'The Outlaw,' but to Sid Ketcheson she was simply Lady, an American Standard trotting horse, a sorrel with a white blaze, who needed more breaking in than Sid had time for. Jim could handle her, and he spent hours in the stable grooming and talking to her. So Kate, with uncharacteristic foresight, decided she would buy Lady, and he could ride her to school. She paid Sid three hundred dollars. The boy's intense feelings for the horse would elicit from the grown author one of the most powerful descriptions in his fiction:

> She was one horse, and she was all horses ... To approach her was to be enlarged, transported. She was coal-black, gleaming, queenly. Her mane had a ripple and her neck an arch. And somehow, softly and mysteriously, she was always burning. The reflection on her gleaming hide, whether of winter sunshine or yellow lantern light, seemed the glow of some fierce, secret passion. There were moments when I felt the whole stable charged with her, as if she were the priestess of her kind, in communion with her deity. ('The Outlaw,' 19)

Going to school had always been difficult because there was seldom any continuity from one year to the next; by the time he was in grade five, Jim had been to at least four different schools. Undersize, introverted, and with no significant connection to the communities in which he and his mother lived, he was either ignored by the other boys or bullied. He seldom took part in games. But riding Lady to school gave him status and a feeling of pride he had never experienced before. He was a good rider and he liked to arrive just before the classes began, so that everyone could watch him dismount, tie up Lady in the school stable, and brush her down. She had a reputation for being temperamental – liked to take the bit in her mouth – but Jim relished the admiration of the other children. The risk was worth it.

His other strong recollection from this time in his life was how hard his mother worked while they lived at Ketcheson's farm. Sid did not provide a generous budget for the kitchen, and Kate had to stretch herself in order to set a good table. She wanted to please her hard-working, successful young employer, but she was now in her mid-forties and going through what was probably a difficult menopause. In 'Just Wind and Horses,' Jim tried in one paragraph to convey that hard time in his mother's life:

> Up to her eyes in extra harvest hands ... harried and irritable, face flushed and sagging with near-desperation weariness, untidy wisps of hair whipped across her

forehead ... killing and plucking chickens along with churning and scrubbing and cleaning just as usual – feet and ankles swollen twice their normal size ... swearing at the dog to get the cows out of the garden – the half-acre vegetable garden that was her responsibility, spring to freeze-up – onions and peas, beets and carrots, a few bachelor's buttons and nasturtiums squeezed in, no time to look at or smell them ... the same as the two-acre potato patch – planting, hoeing, digging ... her responsibility too. (96)

Sid Ketcheson was pleased with her housekeeping, and perhaps he was just as puzzled and sorry as Jimmy when, early in 1921, Kate announced that she would be leaving to take a position on another farm. He agreed to buy back Lady for three hundred dollars.

Why Kate Ross left the Ketcheson farm in the early spring of 1921 cannot be explained (perhaps the work had become too heavy for her, perhaps she had an argument with Ketcheson about the household budget that her son was not aware of; or, possibly, she had grown anxious about the rowdy farmhands and their influence on Jim). We do know, however, that her next employer, Nels Forfang, was someone she had known before, and she may have simply been flattered by an invitation to come and work for him. Forfang, a successful and well-regarded bachelor homesteader in the Wild Rose area, was now living in the Rolling Prairie District of central Saskatchewan, between Chaplin and Riverhurst.

Kate and Jimmy arrived in April, and on their first day they had Sunday dinner with Lewis and Lettie Olson and their young family, close friends of Nels Forfang. Many years later, the Olson children would recall what a fine lady Mrs Ross appeared to be; she was wearing a fur coat that was vividly remembered by one little Olson girl, whose doll was under the coat on the bed, and who was too intimidated to reach under and retrieve it.[6] Mrs Ross, it was understood, was a widow. Even though Forfang was from the Prince Albert area, where Pete was still living, Kate succeeded in convincing the people in her new setting that her husband had died. She would not have liked, however, the joking that would eventually go on behind her back; when Lettie Olson was cross with her husband, the other men would tease Lewis and suggest he visit widow Ross.[7] Kate had no interest in another man. For her, Forfang's austerity and personal cleanliness created exactly the right environment in which to work and raise her son.

Nels Forfang was part of a largely Scandinavian community from Minnesota that homesteaded the area in the early 1900s, turning the expanses of steeply undulating prairie into cultivated farmland. Forfang was prosperous, owning three quarter sections of productive land, yet he lived frugally – his four-room frame house was small and unpainted. But perhaps because he was originally a city man from Minneapolis, and fastidious and orderly by nature, he decided to hire a housekeeper to keep his home clean and cook his meals. He is remembered as sober, well-dressed, mannerly – 'a man of some education, well read, a gentleman.'[8] The Olson family recall a night when their father was lost in a fierce blizzard and how he found his way finally by 3 a.m. to a little house where a lamp was burning – there was Nels Forfang sitting in his chair all night reading. He had a substantial book collection, mostly histories that he sent for by mail. While Kate and Jimmy Ross lived at his home, he would have been, like Kate, in his forties.

In addition to being a prosperous homesteader, Nels Forfang was a photographer of note in the Rolling Prairie district. Some of his pictures have survived in private collections and on museum walls in the Riverhurst area. Notable among these is a photograph taken of a prairie fire that swept through the Rolling Prairie in 1914. Before the fire was halted by a concerted fight from all the men in the area, Forfang took a dramatic photograph which he subsequently sold in postcard form for a dollar a dozen. This photo, not unlike an abstract painting, is a vivid study in lights and darks which reveals a sophisticated sense of composition. His pictures of workhorses in harness and of homesteading families are no less remarkable as photography. And yet, though Forfang was a successful farmer and skilled photographer, he is also remembered as the last man in the district to farm with horses, working with a team of four until he was in his seventies, and when electricity finally came to the area in 1956, he remained one of the few in the community who chose not to be serviced.

Self-confident and often self-absorbed, yet never eccentric, Nels Forfang was a man whom Kate Ross could work for comfortably. Kate's attempts to bully her employer were met in kind. They had some 'furious rows,' Jim remembered, with Forfang going out to the stable to cool off; but both recognized determination and strength of character in the other and for the most part respected each other's ways. To the boy, however, there was something forbidding in the presence of his mother's employer, a man who seemed stern and aloof. While Forfang was equable in nature and fair in his dealings with others, he did not seem loving or generous to a sensitive thirteen-year-old boy. Most of the time, Forfang simply ignored him, although the boy felt acutely his being in the way. Partly this was the result of the physical arrangements; there was no separate bedroom, so that Jim did his homework and slept in an alcove off the living room. Kate was sensitive to Forfang's lack of interest in children and kept Jim in the background as much as possible. Usually, for his January birthday, she would save a few candies from Christmas and place them beside his breakfast on the twenty-second, but that year she let the day pass unacknowledged.

The Forfang farm was twelve miles south from Riverhurst, the nearest town of any size, and it was a further three miles south-west from the farm to the Rolling Prairie District school; this would be one of the most isolated regions in which the future writer would live. If Kate wanted her son to have opportunities, she could not have chosen a more unlikely place. But the drama of an adolescent boy's life will unfold inevitably and indelibly, no matter how mean the stage or unlettered the players. The homesteaders in the Rolling Prairie District were chiefly Scandinavians, with names such as Heieie, Olson, Bergrud, Svaren, Nelson, and Johnson; they had come north for land from the American Midwest beginning around 1908. Men and women with a variety of practical skills, they spent most of their lives on the essential tasks of breaking land and building homes. They built a one-room schoolhouse in 1912, which served not only for educational purposes but as a social centre, a meeting place for picnics, dances, and concerts, even for wrestling matches. In addition, the Lutherans held their church services here and on occasion used the school for funerals. The one room held pupils from grades one through eight, often just one or two pupils in a grade, and the teachers, most frequently young, unmarried women, usually stayed one or two years at the most. Jimmy entered the Rolling Prairie school as a senior student and remembered reading his name in the provincial list of successful entrance candidates while riding in Forfang's wagon from Riverhurst back to the farm. In the fall of 1921, however, there was no high school in the area to attend, and so he returned to the local public school to work independently at correspondence course materials provided by the Saskatchewan Board of Education. The teachers, first a young Englishwoman, Constance Pooley, then a Miss Edmonds, helped him with his high-school work, and he was regarded as a special pupil by both the teachers and his classmates. The only other tuition he received at that time in his life was a few painting lessons from a Mrs Mulholland, a farmer's wife with some artistic skills.

Jimmy Ross, despite his innate diffidence, left a vivid impression on the other young people in the area. More than seventy years later, he was remembered as a good-looking boy with intense brown eyes, well-spoken and well brought-up, 'very mannerly for his age.' He was also remembered as nicely dressed, often wearing a tie and knickers instead of overalls like the other boys. But though he was sometimes different in his clothing and scholastic ability, Jimmy Ross was remembered by the other children as being friendly, in no way holding himself apart.[9] He observed wryly, more than once, that his mother had wanted him to think of himself as better than the other boys, but that it was hard to be a snob when you were just the housekeeper's son.

While Jim was remembered positively by his former classmates, he remembered those days very differently himself. By age thirteen, he was becoming painfully self-conscious and ashamed of his appearance: his stature remained small and he was still underweight; moreover, he had large ears on a narrow head. To make things worse, his mother forced him to wear 'Little Lord Fauntleroy' outfits – frilly shirts and short pants – and he remembered his practice of sometimes taking overalls to change into and hiding his 'good' clothes under a culvert, once beyond his mother's gaze. Late in life, he would sometimes recall being baited by the others boys for the way his mother dressed him, and of attending a picnic once, standing all day beside a tree and not taking part in games because the other boys in dungarees would have laughed at him. His memories of feeling on the margin for breaking the clothing code of a country school would one day be recounted in *Sawbones Memorial* in the painful recollections of Benny Fox sent to school in bow ties and boater.

Going to school and doing chores on the farm (year round feeding the cows and bringing them in from the fields) made up the days – but there were adventures and pleasures as well. Forfang had a gramophone and, although most of the records were of the Cal Stewart 'Uncle Josh and Aunt Nancy Put Up the Kitchen Stove' type, there were two recordings that thrilled the boy and would lie at the heart of a lifelong love of classical music. They were the 'Meditation' and 'Adoration' from the prelude of Leoncavallo's 1892 opera *I pagliacci*. No pieces of music had made such a strong impression on the boy since he played a march tune on a gramophone in Abbey. But chief and most constant among his enjoyments was riding Penny, a gelding that Forfang let the boy take to school. Sometimes he rode horseback through the hills, and he would remember how on certain days banners of light would unfold, creating mosaics across the undulating landscape. But more often he hitched the horse to a buggy and would give a ride to Ruth McVeigh, daughter of the woman who kept house for John 'Arndt' Alstad, a bachelor homesteader on the next section. En route they would pick up Gladys Olson, the oldest daughter of Lewis and Lettie Olson, who would remember with what skill and composure Jim managed the horse and buggy on the hilly trail to school and back. Occasionally he would take the horse over to the schoolhouse on Sunday afternoons to attend the Lutheran church service and Sunday school. But the author's most vivid memory from riding horseback in the Rolling Prairie District was of an early spring day when, on his way to Mrs Mulholland's for a painting lesson, he came upon a writhing mass of garter snakes in a breeding colony. Feeling physical revulsion towards snakes of any kind, he quickly rode away, but the sight was indelible and fascinating.

In the Rolling Prairie, he experienced pioneer life at its harshest. Although his mother would pile several blankets over him at night and put a hot brick inside the foot of his bed, he would be shivering with cold by morning. The contents of his chamber pot would be frozen solid. Outside, he witnessed some of the harsh dramas of homesteading that would form the bedrock of his fiction: a hailstorm destroying crops and buildings, wild horses invading the fields, an electric storm and the sudden inferno of a prairie fire, blizzards and the long winters and despair experienced by some of the settlers–especially by farmers' wives isolated from any social life, and by single men unable some-how to marry and start a family. Still vividly recalled in the Rolling Prairie District is the day when the new wife of long-time bachelor John Alstad tried to hang herself in the chicken coop.

But the chief drama for Jimmy Ross, at the age of thirteen, was being initi-ated into sex by some of the girls he knew at school. 'Let's do it here,' said one girl offhandedly, as they were gathering saskatoons in a high hilly stretch. 'And so I was broken in,' explained the author more than seventy years later, although he was not yet sexually mature. He had no feelings of guilt, just curi-osity and pleasure; nonetheless, he knew that his mother would be unrecon-cilably angry if she learned what was happening. She was already warning him about the danger of girls – the diseases they might harbour, the possibil-ity of their having babies – and in a veiled manner she alluded to promiscuous behaviour in some of the 'immigrant' families. But in the loft of the horse sta-ble at school 'things went on,' and in good weather they took place in a low spot behind the school yard, a willow-lined creekbed. The creek was half a mile from school and they had to hurry, eating lunch on the way, but there Jimmy learned about sex from two other girls who, to his great pride, 'mea-sured' and pronounced him the biggest boy in the school. He took pride too in the rivalry among the girls for his attention. But fifty years later, in *Saw-bones Memorial*, he would tell the story from the point of view of a middle-aged woman, Sarah Gillespie, one of the 'good girls' at school who only heard rumours and caught glimpses.[10] Unlike Jimmy, Sarah listened to her mother, who said a young girl who had sex before she was fifteen would be covered with black pimples and would always have to wear a veil. There is a first-time sexual initiation scene in *Whir of Gold*, told from the point of view of the boy as aggressor;[11] the author, however, never laid claim to this hayloft scene between Sonny McAlpine and Millie Dickson as being other than fiction.

There was, however, an actual incident in the hayloft at school that he would never forget. There, by surprise, he came upon a dull-witted boy –

older than the other children – with one of the girls. She beckoned Jim to come and watch. With the girl's encouragement, the fifteen-year-old was masturbating, and Jim, for the first time, saw a boy ejaculate. A strange little triangle had formed there momentarily, a girl and two boys, and it quickly dissolved, but in some ways it would be a shadowy template for the shapes of curiosity and physical desire to come.

A vivid school-yard drama of a different kind was the merciless tormenting of two Ukrainian boys, the Myketiak brothers Stanley and Mike, who spoke English with an accent. Both boys were good at school work, and Miss Pooley tried to protect them from the rough boys in the school yard. When she heard them called 'hunkies' and being teased for their accented speech, she informed the class that they spoke a more correct form of English than the rest of them and always would be better speakers of the English language. Mike sometimes stood first in the class. None of this made them popular with the other boys, and being small and slim, they were beaten up regularly according to the idle whims of the school-yard bullies. Jim, too, was small and slim for his age, smart in school, and sometimes made to wear different clothing, but he had learned how to blend into the crowd and remain inconspicuous. The plight of little Mike Myketiak would be a germ for the story of Nick Miller in *Sawbones Memorial*, which originally had a working title of 'As Flies to Wanton Boys.'

The future book that perhaps owes most to Jim's experience in the Rolling Prairie District is *The Well*. Something of Nels Forfang's practical yet enigmatic character occurs in the Swede, Larson, and the problem that Forfang had with his well probably remained a significant association. Forfang's well was about one hundred feet deep, and it provided good drinking water; but there was coarse sand at the bottom of the well which quickly wore away the leather plungers in the cylinder, and so the well was often in need of repair. When the plank top was removed, the well gaped; the boy could see the wide wooden cribbing and reflect on how easy it would be to propel someone to an 'accidental' death.

After more than a year in the Rolling Prairie District, Kate was growing restless because the social life in this remote region was so limited; during the long winter, she had found little to occupy herself with beyond needlework. Something of a crisis took place. One day, looking through a bundle of English newspapers sent out to her by an old Scotswoman she had met at the Riverhurst general store, she came across a picture of her brother, Sir John Foster Fraser. He was described as one of the chiefs of the Scottish Clans Association, presiding at a banquet in honour of the singer and comedian Sir Harry Lauder. Fraser's fame weighed heavily on his sister. 'My God it's Johnny!' she burst out, then broke down sobbing. Jim would write in 'Just

Wind and Horses': 'In the thirty-odd years we were together I seldom saw her give way to tears, but that day her apron was drenched with them' (85–6). When she telephoned the store to thank her acquaintance, she was told the old woman had returned to Scotland, and that seemed to depress her further. It made Kate think about returning to Britain herself, but for Jim's sake she decided against it. He would remember: '... she stood at the window a minute looking across the bleak, windswept yard cluttered with wagons and machinery, then said, "I'd like to go ... but it's better here for you. Canada's all right – in a way."'

When the harvesting was over that fall (Jim was fourteen), Kate gave her son a choice: they could stay with Forfang, who had agreed to add another bedroom to the house, or they could leave Rolling Prairie and relocate in a town with a high school. Jim chose to leave, and after Christmas at Indian Head with Effie and her family, Kate found employment in Stoughton, a town of about 250 people in the southeast of the province. For the first time, she took a position in town, keeping house for a bachelor veterinarian, a man in his thirties with a reputed fondness for children. In Stoughton there was a good three-room school, with classes up to grade twelve, and a music teacher available for piano and voice lessons once a week. Kate felt fairly certain that she had made a good choice with her new job. The choice was a significant one for fifteen-year-old Jim because it brought him within the sphere of three men who, for a short time, would have something like a fatherly role to play in his life.

The first of these was his new teacher, Weldon Umberto Pickel, the principal of the Stoughton school and an educator of distinction in the province. He taught the high-school classes in Stoughton, with a special interest in literature, and left a strong and positive impression on the future writer. Pickel was originally from New Brunswick, of United Empire Loyalist descent, and came to the Prairie provinces, where he trained at Brandon College to be a minister in the Baptist Church. By middle age, he was a teacher in the Saskatchewan public school system. Remembered by his daughter and by area residents as a serious, often stern man with no time for small talk, Pickel had a deep and genuine love for poetry and took pains to encourage anyone who showed an interest in literature.[12] He required as part of his English classes that students memorize lengthy passages from *Narrative and Lyric Poetry*. Pickel was a writer himself, producing a short history of the Regina First Baptist Church and a Loyalist history of the Sherwood and Pickel families; and his two daughters, Enid and Vesta, became poets of standing in the Saskatchewan Poetry Society. Seventy years later, Sinclair Ross would still be able to recite with pleasure passages from Tennyson and Longfellow that he had memorized for Mr Pickel's class – from 'Horatious at the Bridge' and 'The Lady of the Lake.' But what was important to the sensitive adolescent with a natural love for reading was to encounter a middle-aged man with a passionate love for poetry who was also a respected pillar of the community. Pickel's encouragement of Jimmy from January to June 1923 was again one of those experiences that left an indelible mark.

Another significant player entered Jimmy Ross's life in the winter of 1923. Kate decided that Jimmy should have music lessons of some kind, and inquiries led her to call on Frank Woodbury, an energetic and strikingly handsome young musician who gave piano lessons one day a week in Stoughton. Frank Woodbury, who also taught the Pickel sisters, remembered Mrs Ross bringing the boy to the studio he rented in a private home in Stoughton and arranging for lessons. He remembered his crowded schedule – there really was no room for another student – but at the same time there was Mrs Ross's determination. He agreed finally to add Jimmy 'after hours,' at 9 p.m., when normally he would be driving back to his parents' home in Arcola. From almost the first lesson, he recognized in Jim an unusually sensitive student and quickly forgot the inconvenience of the late hour.[13]

Frank Woodbury, who would appear again later in Jim's life, was a glittering instance of talent, energy, striking good looks, and social charm in combination. As a young man, he earned his teaching degree from the Regina Conservatory of Music and went on to build a successful career as a music teacher and adjudicator in Saskatchewan. By the late 1920s, he was in charge of organizing music festivals in the southeast part of the province. But there were temptations along the way. In 1920 while he was a student and taking part in local theatre productions, he was offered a starring role in a Hollywood picture being filmed in Regina. It was exam time, and after much agonizing he decided to turn the offer down, but more than seventy years later he would still reflect on the 'road not taken.' Frank Woodbury had a distinguished career as a musician in both Saskatchewan and Ontario. He composed sacred music which was widely performed (some of his hymns were published by the Frederick Harris Music Co. in both Canada and England), and in his later years he was made an honorary member of the Royal Canadian College of Organists. He knew and influenced many people, including another future writer, W.O. Mitchell, when the latter was still a boy living in south-eastern Saskatchewan. The sense of excitement he brought to the arts was not lost on Jimmy Ross at fifteen.

Yet another man in Stoughton would engage the future writer's imagination. Kate's employer enjoyed a reputation as a successful veterinarian and farmer, as a good-natured man with a special way with children. He had come to Stoughton from Ontario, a bachelor of some means, and he did not marry until he was in his late thirties. In 1923 he was thirty-three years old. It was his custom after the noon meal to lie down in his bedroom, and sometimes he would invite Jimmy to lie down beside him. On those occasions, he would frequently hug him or press him against the wall. Kate, cleaning up in the kitchen, knew nothing of these encounters and freely gave permission when the doctor asked for Jimmy to accompany him on his calls at outlying farms. Sometimes on those trips, the older man would slip his hand between the boy's legs and fondle him, teasing him about girls and the kind of man he would some day be. Years later, the author would reflect on the veterinarian's behaviour, reluctant to call it abuse because the older man's attentions were not entirely unwanted by the fatherless boy. But this experience was confusing because he was pretty certain society held such conduct to be wrong; it would, in turn, colour the relationships of boys and men in his fiction. It is suggested perhaps in the complicated relationship between Philip and Steve in As for Me and My House, and assumes criminal manifestation in Ross's last published story, 'The Flowers That Killed Him.' Late in his life, Ross would link his experience with the veterinarian to the stories that emanated from Newfoundland's Mount Cashel orphanage in 1989. He said he would like to write the story of a boy who has no father and seeks out the company of older men, but is eventually taken advantage of. 'A boy without a father is a pitiful thing,' he would say more than once. If he were younger, he ventured, he would try writing a cycle of stories about boys from an orphanage – 'the subject holds terror but fascinates.'

The Stoughton Times for 5 July 1923 lists pupils who wrote the exams set by the provincial Department of Education. James S. Ross was promoted to grade eleven with honours, standing second in his class.[14] The disappointing news for Jim was that Mr Pickel had resigned;[15] he had been an exemplary teacher. Moreover, if Jim really was 'sweet on Enid,' as the teases had it, he would be doubly sorry to see this family leave town. When school was closed for the summer, Jim worked on the veterinarian's farm, hoeing corn and pulling out wild mustard and other weeds that invaded the grain crops. His companion in the fields was Hughie Adams, the only son of the Presbyterian church minister. Young Adams was a spirited, good-looking boy and possessed the self-confidence of a much wanted and indulged son. From the time he was a small boy himself, Jim dreamed of having a perfect friend, someone he could share his time and all his thoughts with. That figure lived in his imagination, but for a few months that summer he savoured for the first time the rare pleasure of an actual friend; they worked on the farm together and chummed around town. But Hughie Adams would die prematurely, of heart failure, before the year was over, like the farmer's son in As for Me and My House; and his death, like the attentions of the veterinarian, would not be forgotten. The departure of an inspiring teacher and the death of a friend were all part of a yet greater upheaval for the boy that year.

Sometime in the summer months, Kate made up her mind to move again. There were rumours in Stoughton that her employer consorted with prostitutes and that he had a venereal disease. Not taking any chances, Kate contacted Sid Ketcheson and arranged to return to his farm for the harvest season.

Yet another move, but the consolation for Jim in this return to Abbey was being able to ride Lady again. This was the first time that he worked in the fields in earnest, stooking grain. Although he was only fifteen and of a slight build, he gave a credible account of himself and felt no small satisfaction in being able to work alongside the other hired hands. One incident seemed to measure his new maturity: in the fields one day, something shot up inside the leg of his pants and lodged itself between his trousers and underwear. He was certain it was a snake and could barely keep from screaming out. But with his composure intact, he managed to get to the house, where he found that he was simply harbouring a mouse inside his overalls.

Jim stayed at the Ketcheson farm until the end of harvest, and then it was decided that instead of going to school in Abbey he would take grade eleven at Indian Head, where there was a bigger school (110 students in the high school) and more teachers with special skills. Jim and his mother travelled to Indian Head at the end of October 1923, and Kate arranged that he would board for the school year with the McKenzie family, who lived in the very centre of town, across from the Presbyterian church. Effie Price and her family lived six miles north-east of Indian Head in the Sunny Slope area, which in winter seemed too long and risky a distance to travel every day. The McKenzies, a genial couple and relatively prosperous, had two school-age children, Bruce and Cora, and in their large home Jim would have his own room. To their parents' dismay, the McKenzie children were not very diligent at school, and not wanting to cause jealousy, Jim took pains to downplay his own scholarly abilities. Otherwise the eight months that he spent in Indian Head, completing grade eleven and living independently from his mother, was the most stimulating and socially satisfying stretch of school time that he would experience.

The Indian Head News from January to June of 1924 outlines a new kind of life for the boy who turned sixteen that January. At the bi-weekly meetings of the high-school literary society, Jimmy Ross was made an officer in charge of current events. February activities included a skating party and a society debate on the subject: 'Is a nurse more valued in a foreign district than a teacher?' Arguing in the affirmative were Jimmy Thompson, Beth Crawford, and Jimmy Ross, although judges decided in favour of the negative side.[16] Jim Ross was also a member that winter of the Presbyterian Boys Club. In March the club had contests in 'story telling' and 'public speaking,' although Jim did not place as one of the winners in either category.

Indeed, when he entered the Indian Head high school in the late fall of 1923, he may have thought he was bound for failure that year. The school report for November lists James Ross as twenty-ninth in a class of thirty-two, with a failing grade of 41 per cent. But that soon changed, for the December report lists James Ross at the top with 94 per cent, displacing Belvah Howatt, the daughter of the local hardware merchant, who had always enjoyed being first in the class.[17] 'He was the competition,' Miss Howatt would remember years later; 'but you couldn't feel angry or jealous if he won the top prizes because he was very smart and he never boasted.' Jim and Belvah were friendly rivals: 'We both had the same philosophy of school; we liked to study and to work, and we didn't give much thought to the social life.'[18] Grace Campkin had similar tastes and, according to the author, there is a glimpse of these three school friends in *Sawbones Memorial* when Sarah Gillespie is thinking about her friendship with the 'good girls,' Fern and Beulah. Throughout the winter and spring months, James Ross placed first in the class, Belvah Howatt second, but at the end of the school year, when awards were given, Belvah Howatt received the governor general's medal for the best all-round student and James Ross was given the less lustrous academic proficiency award. He was also awarded a special prize for top marks in third-year history, an award made by the Great War Veterans Association. He would have to wait nearly seventy years before he was honoured by Canada's governor general. Although James Ross did not leave Indian Head as the collegiate's top student, the town had given him the experience of a world with greater scope than the one-room schoolhouses of his childhood, or even the high-school classes of eight and ten pupils in Stoughton. The larger world, however, of which he was beginning to dream, would continue for a few more years to exist chiefly inside the cover of books.

three

Bank Clerk
1924–1929

In the summer of 1924, Jim was back at Sid Ketcheson's farm with his mother, and life was much as before. He had the same bedroom in the large house and the same chores to perform. Sid chose his hired hands carefully, and the same men returned each year. Lady was there to ride about the farm and occasionally into town, and she could still 'strike sparks' from the imagination. The crops were good that summer – the rains came regularly and gently – and there was a general feeling of prosperity in the area. This was the third time that Jim had come to live in Abbey, and in a benign way it was like returning home.

But an unresolved question hung in the air that summer: what would Jim do after the harvest was over? Grade twelve was part of the high-school program, but it was taken chiefly by those who were planning on college or a university degree. Jim had been thinking for some time that he would like to teach school, and grade eleven was sufficient to apply for Normal School and a teaching certificate. But Kate viewed the life of a schoolmaster with contempt; she wanted her son to 'go further' and saw the business world as his best chance. To her mind, a place in a bank would be a good start. Both expressed their views and then said no more, one of those tense silences settling over the house that would come to characterize their lives together.

Jim worked again in the fields stooking wheat during the harvest. With extra hands to feed that year, Kate found herself overworked, and Sid reluctantly agreed to hire someone else for the kitchen. But in the end, a parsimonious man, he arranged for his sister Eva to come to the farm and help out on busy days. Eva Ketcheson was herself a schoolteacher, unmarried and still relatively young, and her presence on the farm that summer would also 'strike sparks.' As an attractive woman, she lent a certain glamour to the profession that the sixteen-year-old boy was contemplating. Her relations with the other

farmhands (mostly single men from Swift Current) also had an aura of glamour for the boy. Mac Hayman was a young man with nice manners; he was
quiet, gentle, somewhat boyish, and Kate was very fond of him. But Mac lived
another life, as Kate learned from a newspaper one winter which reported that
Mac had been arrested and put in the Swift Current jail for consorting with a
prostitute. Bill Forbes was a bigger fellow, genial, but not so couth as Mac – in
idle talk, he alluded frankly to the frustrations a young bachelor experienced.
'Scottie,' from the old country, tended to pugnaciousness and was not so popular with the women. Eva, instead of bustling between the stove and table
when the men came in for their meals, would stop and talk, and the seriousness of farm work gave way to laughter and provocative banter. Jim was fascinated by the sexual innuendos in all the talk and humour. Kate, perspiring
over the stove, would lose her temper and shout orders, but at the same time
she rather liked the girl. And so there was a patch of colour that summer in a
season otherwise heavy with work and indecision. Jim would remember the
men when he wrote about cowboys and hired men in his fiction, possibly
when creating Philip in 'Cornet at Night,' certainly when in As for Me and My
House Paul remembers his boyhood on a ranch: 'It was good for me – tough-
ened me up, taught me self-reliance. There were the cowboys, and I was always
trying to hold my own with them. They weren't heroes exactly, but on the
average they were pretty fair men' (93).

   In his room in the evenings, Jim would read. He didn't want to forget the
French he had been learning in three years of high-school study, and so he
read the remaining stories in the French authors text they had been using in
Indian Head. And to extend his vocabulary, he compiled and committed to
memory long lists of words from a French dictionary. He also reread The Mill
on the Floss, by George Eliot, the novel with such strong brother and sister feelings that they had hurried through it in grade eleven, and Shakespeare's As
You Like It, with its delightful confusions of gender. Most farm families had a
bookshelf, but finding good books to read was not easy because, apart from the
Bible and possibly a school 'reader' of Romantic and Victorian verse, shelves
were stocked largely with the popular fiction of the day, authors like Marie
Corelli, Zane Grey, Caine Hall – 'mostly tripe' was Jim's judgment years later,
'though mother thought those authors were pretty deep.'[1] He remembered too
that borrowing books was no simple matter lightly undertaken: a book was
loaned with the understanding that it would be returned in good condition
within an agreed upon period, and the owner would pursue the matter if the
volume was not brought back on time. This was an intimidating proviso for
the reticent son of an itinerant housekeeper.

   Sid Ketcheson's bookshelf contained almost nothing in the way of light reading. It was stocked instead with encyclopedic volumes on a wide range of subjects, most important being a veterinarian's guide to the injuries and diseases of farm animals. But the shelf held a number of music catalogues which the impressionable boy read through without a context for real understanding. There were few chances to hear classical music – occasional gramophone recordings, poorly performed vocal and piano solos at local concerts – but the desire for good music was strong in the boy. He read about Wagnerian operas, about the great divas who sang Wagnerian arias, and he came to believe that Wagneria was an actual country which produced much of the world's great music. Years later, he would write a novel about an uneducated boy's musical yearnings and about the special country of his imagination; he would title it 'Day Coach to Wagneria.'[2]

Kate was growing tired of her life as a domestic; she was nagged always by her sense that the work she was doing was beneath someone from her background, and she spoke of this to her son frequently. Jim found her pride in pedigree ridiculous and maddening, but when he grew older he understood how it helped her through some bad times with her employers. About the time harvest was winding up, Kate heard that there was a teller's position available at the Union Bank in Abbey. She telephoned through to the manager, a man by the name of Miscampbell, spoke of her son's diligence and mathematical abilities, and coaxed him into giving the boy a chance. Though he hesitated inwardly, Jim obediently reported for work at 9 a.m. the following Monday, and so began the forty-three-year career of James Sinclair Ross with what would soon become the Royal Bank of Canada.

In 1924 working for the bank paid twenty dollars a month. Jim earned an additional twenty dollars by doing the janitor's chores. In the winter months, this consisted chiefly of looking after the furnace, which burned a 'dirty' Drumheller coal and produced a lot of clinkers that had to be pried loose and removed every day; in summer, it meant sweeping and keeping the building dusted. The money seemed good (it was more than his mother made), and in that sense Jim regarded himself privileged. There were four on staff in the bank: in addition to the manager and Jim there was an accountant by the name of McAllister and a young woman, Cornelia Schamp, who worked as a stenographer. Although Jim would no longer be working on a farm, his job at the bank kept him in close contact with farmers and the realities of their lives as they prospered or failed according to the markets and the seasons. Banking itself, however, the daily ciphering of large and small sums, held no interest for the sixteen-year-old boy, and as he had foreseen, it quickly became a dull and monotonous routine. But Jim's employer, like those that were to follow, recognized the accuracy and precision of his work and never had misgivings about his honesty.

When Jim started work at the bank in November, he and Kate moved into town, where they rented a small house. Henceforward Kate would no longer hire out as a domestic, but would keep house for herself and for her son, who was now the family breadwinner. It was a pattern of living together they would follow for the next eighteen years – in fact, Jim would support his mother financially for the rest of her life. It was a fairly good life for Kate: she was no longer confined to the company of a widower or bachelor farmer in a remote part of the country; nor was she tied to the routine of housekeeping and providing good meals from a stingy food allowance. She now did a lot of fancy baking and always had the tea kettle ready should anyone drop by. With her evident pleasure in company and her flair for conversation and storytelling, she made friends easily. She was also generous with her handiwork and baking, making gifts for people and donating her work to the church sales. However, the shared life of mother and son in a series of small towns and eventually in Winnipeg was not always cheerful or comfortable. There was a constant strain between the uncertain young man, as he started to wish for a life of his own, and the strong-willed older woman, afraid of losing her only certain purchase on family and social life. Disagreements were followed by long stretches of uncomfortable silence. In 'Just Wind and Horses,' he recalls hearing his mother say to her friends: "'He's getting terrible to live with. Such a glum look, the weight of the world on his shoulders. And never a word out of him unless he's got something to say'" (96). This tension between a man and a woman left an indelible mark on the future author and can be seen to characterize the relation of the sexes in many of his short stories. It is especially unrelenting in As for Me and My House.[3]

Although he didn't think about it at the time of writing, Abbey, according to the author's statements, is the principal model for Horizon in As for Me and My House; indeed, in his imagination, he would often return to this village of his boyhood and youth. Located in south-western Saskatchewan, in one of the driest stretches of the Palliser Triangle, Abbey would be especially devastated by the great drought which began in the summer of 1929. For most of the 1920s, however, Abbey enjoyed a prosperity that was evident in its population of over three hundred, the variety of stores and services it offered, and by the five grain elevators along the railroad track. Its streets were unpaved (and remain so today), and its main street was an architecture of false fronts, but when the Rosses moved into town there was still considerable optimism for the future, bad years so far never lasting more than three years in succession. Most impressive in the village was the large Presbyterian church on the street south of and running parallel to the main thoroughfare. Distinctly less impressive was the adjacent manse, remembered as a cold, evil little dwelling, which eventually was relocated to the main street and became the village toilet and way station.[4]

The Rosses lived on one of the sloping side streets, where the homes were slightly protected from the elements by caragana hedging. Abbey was still very new: homesteading did not begin until 1909, and incorporation as a village took place in 1914.[5] The stark exposure of the village to the sun and wind was not yet mitigated by the newly planted poplars and Manchurian elms. Respectability was a flower border planted with tough-rooted peonies, bleeding heart, and a low-growing, wind-resistant variety of shasta daisy. The Rosses rented their home from Dennis Kennedy, a prosperous homesteader who had named the area for his native village in Ireland and who continued to be important by coming to town with milk and eggs from his farm. The one-storey frame house was small: a kitchen and living room, and one bedroom. Jim slept in the little pantry off the kitchen. There was no electricity and no running water, and it was one of Jim's daily chores to bring two pails of water from a pump, located half a mile from the house on the edge of the prairie.

Despite the lack of space, one of the first things Jim decided on was the purchase of a piano – in fact there were two that winter, the first one being quickly replaced by a much better instrument. Payments were fifteen dollars a month (nearly half of his bank wages) for more than three years, until the full price of the piano had been paid – six hundred dollars. This was not only an extravagance for the Rosses, but a subject of wonder and speculation for the people of Abbey. But immediately the piano became the centre of the boy's life, as if there was another living being in the house. Just as he had once spent hours on Lady, making her do his will, so he now sat at the keyboard for long stretches every evening, learning the intricacies of harmonic form, mastering scales and arpeggios, and coaxing from the instrument that relation between form and skill that allows for self-expression. It was an exhilarating new focus in his life.

There were music teachers who stopped in Abbey. Generally they lived in Swift Current and travelled by train up the Empress line as far as Leader, spending a day in each of the towns, where they would rent a room in someone's home or at the local hotel to give lessons. Jim had lessons from two such teachers – both women who, in his estimate, probably knew very little about music. The first he remembered for her monotonous measure of rhythm: 'a-one, a-two.' Keeping time was all that seemed to matter; she had little more to offer than a metronome in good working condition. Early in the series of lessons, she assigned Haydn's 'Gypsy Rondo,' a difficult piece for a beginner, and it took several months to get the timing right. There is a rather charitable portrait of his second piano teacher in the character of Dorothy Whittle, Sonny McAlpine's music teacher in *Whir of Gold*. Although she is physically not very attractive ('a dreary piece of teeth and leather' is the cruel estimate of one of the locals), the narrator tells us that 'there was a spark, an urgency, an area of rapture. She couldn't play Beethoven but she knew how he should be played' (91). Jim would recall these teachers working the line again in *Sawbones Memorial*: Phyllis Devine, with a red wig, and Mrs Gracey – 'very good, no wig' (98). Lessons cost fifty cents for half an hour. By the time he was seventeen, Jim was giving lessons himself to the children of Abbey, and because he played so well, he was able to charge seventy-five cents a lesson without any protests from parents.

At approximately the same time, Jim found an easier and more direct form of self-expression in painting – both watercolours and oils. He had always been able to catch a likeness; Miss Pooley had encouraged him to draw, and a picture he made of a dog won a school fair competition in Riverhurst. His mother, in the meantime, had been impressed by a Scottish farmer she had known at Indian Head, who did tolerable watercolours during the winter months and sold them to the locals for what she considered a handsome price. Jim's sketches of animals and flowers won not only his mother's approval but the respect and interest of the acquaintances she invited to the house for tea and gossip. Wilfred Bowen, the new manager when the Union Bank became the Royal Bank in 1925, was also interested in his young employee's sketches and bought him his first set of oil paints. What the local people wanted were the conventional subjects of calendar art – animals, mountain scenes, world-famous buildings – and Jim, in return for the paints, gave Bowen a painting of the Grand Canal in Venice, which the latter admired extravagantly and for a while showed to others at the bank. Eventually it was hung in a prominent place in the Bowens' home, which did much to boost Jim's worth in the eyes of the villagers, for the Bowens represented 'society' in Abbey.

Wilfred Bowen was born in Scotland, and like many westerners with a British accent, he was accorded social prominence. Moreover, his wife, Cecily, who had previously been a widow, had money of her own and drove a car. Their endorsement of the young teller was not unnoticed. Indeed, Jim quickly acquired a reputation in Abbey as a talented young painter, and his mother, acting as his agent, displayed and took orders for his work. When he came to write in *As for Me and My House* about Philip Bentley's desire to paint rather than preach, he wrote from the border of a life that had beckoned to him for a time. But he felt early that his talent was not genuine; unlike Philip Bentley, he could not paint the Prairie landscape, nor its work-roughened inhabitants. One cold Saturday morning, when they were visiting Effie in Indian Head, he tried to make a pen and ink sketch of the landscape near the Experimental Farm, but he failed to transfer the elemental geometry of sky and earth to paper. He never tried again. But he continued to paint conventional subjects, because he was enjoying his sense of an audience – people who liked what he was doing praised him for it, and were eager to see his new pieces. This would not be the case when he started to write.

It was in Abbey in the spring of 1925, when Jim was seventeen, that he made his first serious attempt to become a writer. He had composed stories from an early age, but he had shown them to no one, not even teachers like Miss Pooley and Miss Edmonds, or later Mr Pickel, who had fostered his interest in the English language and in good writing. But already the two strong motives to write were beginning to assert themselves: the need to com-municate to others what he was seeing and feeling, and the wish to leave the bank and make his living in the arts. The first story he tried was titled 'The Call of the Canvas,' and as he remembered it years later, it told about the life and death of an artist, someone a little like the Ontario painter Tom Thom-son. There was no plot, 'just something about the desire to paint, written in earnest.'[6] Jim didn't own a typewriter yet, though he wanted one badly 'the way a child wants a toy,' and so he used the typewriter at the bank after hours, slowly teaching himself how to work the keys. When he had prepared a good copy of the story, he sent it to *Liberty* magazine in the United States: 'a daring gesture, and of course foolish, but I wanted to start at the top.' He knew that the American markets could make a writer rich. There was the spectacular instance of Martha Ostenso from Manitoba, who had just published her sometimes realistic Prairie story *Wild Geese*, which in addition to best-seller royalties had garnered the Dodd, Mead Prize, worth $13,500. Jim and his mother were reading the story that year while it was being serialized under the title 'The Passionate Flight' in the *Pictorial Review*. In the 1920s, *Liberty* and other popular American magazines paid no less than one hundred dollars for a story. When the American magazine returned Jim's piece, he made some changes and sent it off, more soberly, to *Maclean's* in Canada, knowing that forty dollars was the standard fee; nonetheless, that represented a month's sal-ary in the bank.

One of the author's most vivid memories of that summer was of going to the station in the evenings to be there when the train came in bringing the mail. As he would one day relate in *As for Me and My House*, for anyone growing up feeling the cramp and pettiness of a little Main Street town, the train was a link to the larger world; the young Philip Bentley 'watched it, hungered, went on dreaming' (39). Although there were postboxes in Abbey, it was part of the social life of the village – especially in summer – to gather in the evenings at the station, to greet people who had gone for a day's shopping in Swift Current, and to pick up the mail directly from the postmaster. The manuscript was finally returned from *Maclean's* with a curt statement that the story was 'not suitable'; however, the story editor did take pains, for which the young writer was later grateful, to instruct him on submission protocol – the stamped, self-addressed envelope. The advice seemed to have a faintly positive aspect, as if the editor felt there was reason for future submissions. *Saturday Night* returned the story quickly, but with a letter of encouragement, saying that the story was too good for the magazine. Twice revised, the story had failed to find a publisher, and at that point Jim could think of no more likely markets for his story without a plot.

He usually went quickly to the train station by himself, but it became a custom for Jim and his mother, in good weather, to go for a walk in the evening together. Kate was growing heavier, and she felt the walking did her good. Seventy years later, elderly citizens of the Abbey area recalled the regularity of this ritual, enhanced on Saturday evenings by a five-cent ice cream cone.[7] Much of Jim's social life while he was still in his teens involved his mother. They continued to see Sid Ketcheson: the latter would take them out to the farm in his car, and Kate would cook him one of her good Sunday dinners. When a neighbour in Abbey acquired the first radio, Jim and his mother would go to listen to a program, usually in the company of several others. Reception was uncertain and sometimes nothing could be heard during the whole evening, but it was an excuse to socialize, to talk business and gossip. What Kate loved above all were the two or three days of Chautauqua each summer, when she could combine her gregarious instincts with her exuberant love of ideas and interest in the arts. Jim and his mother attended together all the events – the lectures, concerts, and plays – that were presented in Abbey, usually in the basement of the United Church, and they would take the train to nearby Cabri to see additional entertainments. The most lasting memory of Chautauqua for the author was not a lecture or a play but a concert given by what Jim believed to be a Russian Orthodox Church choir. It was a unique and haunting sound to the young man so sensitive to music, and it was a link to a larger world that beckoned.[8]

But the immediate social and cultural centre for life on the Canadian Prairies was the church, in a small town almost invariably the United Church of Canada. After church union in 1925 (the joining of Presbyterians, Methodists, and Congregationalists), Jim and Kate for a time went separate ways, Kate remaining with a small band of 'staunch' (that is, continuing) Presbyterians. This gave Jim a little more freedom to develop socially, although for the first two years in Abbey he seldom ventured outside the perimeter of church activities – teaching Sunday school and providing music when the church organist was absent or had resigned. Jim was always immaculate and well dressed, as was expected of a bank clerk, but the people of the town came to realize that his quiet, introverted appearance did not tell the whole story. Pupils in his Sunday school class still remembered, nearly seventy years later, their surprise when the apparently painfully shy young man would start the lesson and begin speaking clearly and easily on ideas that stretched far beyond anything they had known or experienced. He made them think about the stories of the Bible in the context of their own lives. He also believed in the value of memorizing passages of scripture, correctly, and for this he was known as a 'perfectionist.'[9]

The church, and the behaviour of its members, would supply the future author with some of the characters in his most famous book, As for Me and My House. As prototypes for fiction, they are worth considering for a moment, for their lives give us a glimpse of the larger social and historical context from which the novel emerged. Gossip and backbiting gave the long cold winters considerable excitement, and Mrs Frank Millard, wife of the local hardware man, was one of the liveliest gossips in Abbey – a veritable 'Greek chorus in one.'[10] She assumed Abbey to be the centre of the world and convinced others there was no reason to think differently. Mrs Fred Worth, wife of the dry goods merchant, was especially keen to investigate and report on the failings of her fellow villagers, and she did so with a particularly harsh, judgmental air. Her husband, more guarded in his opinions, sang in the church choir. The Worths, in fact, inspired the portrait of the Finleys in As for Me and My House. More than once, this couple included Jim and his mother at the table for Christmas dinner, and so Jim could learn for himself at close hand something of the complexities of Christian charity. And he enjoyed its ironies. Frank Viney, the butcher, sang in the choir and was praised for his renderings of both 'The Holy City' and 'Sheep May Safely Graze.'

But the one individual in the church remembered most vividly by the author and by the surviving townspeople so many years later was a woman named Lettie Macdonald, the wife of the municipal secretary. Fred Macdonald was a quiet man and a hard worker; his tall, red-haired wife was flamboyant, arrogant, and quarrelled with everyone. Her temperamental nature focused on music: for a time, she played the piano and led the church choir. She made her uncertain health a central issue in her quarrels with others and at the peak of one of her battles would rush off to Swift Current for an 'operation,' holding the town hostage for sympathy until she reappeared at the next community dance. She is especially remembered for trying to lead the choir during a practice when she was not sober; she was sent home and immediately became ill. Although her presence in Abbey was a catalyst for much of the gossip and ill will that characterizes the world of 'matrons and respectability' in the Horizon of As for Me and My House, Lettie Macdonald was not a prototype for any specific character in that book. However, according to the author, the deadly feuds in which she was engaged inspired the warring caricatures of Mrs Jack and Mrs Billy in Sawbones Memorial, and perhaps as a red-haired singing teacher (there was speculation that she wore a wig) she lives on in the brief glimpse of Benny Fox's first piano instructor in that same book. The surnames of Abbey residents Harp and Gillespie also survive in Sawbones Memorial.

As for Me and My House, in fact, had its genesis in Abbey in a talk Jim had with one of the ministers serving the church there. Jim was approximately eighteen at the time. Recognizing the young man's intelligence and his interest in spiritual and artistic matters, the minister said that a college education could likely be arranged if he would agree to study for the ministry. Although Jim always asserted that he was not tempted, the offer of a university education was no small bribe.[11] As he grew older, the idea of university more and more acquired the aura of something 'magical' from which he had been excluded. But a deep and resolute vein of honesty would never permit him to accept assistance or rewards if he did not believe he merited them. He had no certain convictions or faith in the church's teachings and could only foresee a life like Philip Bentley's if he were to become a minister.

Another experience that would make its way into As for Me and My House was holiday time spent on the Yeast ranch, located approximately twenty-five miles west of town. The Yeasts were farmers as well as ranchers and brought produce to town for sale. Kate became one of their regular customers, and when Mr and Mrs Yeast learned about Jim, they arranged that he should give their two older children, Frank and Nancy, piano lessons in exchange for eggs and milk and vegetables in season. Jim grew to be very fond of the boy and girl, and eventually he was invited from time to time to spend a few days at the ranch. Those were good times: Jim went on his own and spent most of the days there on horseback, exploring the area and enjoying the company of the Yeast children.

In this part of the country, he also met a spirited woman by the name of Madge Radcliffe, a careless housekeeper but an excellent horsewoman with a dashing, handsome husband in tow. Kate Ross did not like the woman, felt she was probably immoral, but the shy bank clerk and Madge Radcliffe were instantly compatible and sought out each other's company. They both loved horses, and Madge had an appreciation of beauty that was not common among farm people. When they were out riding, they could both be stopped by the light in the sky at sunset, and could share the richness of that moment without having to reach for words. With her husband, Walter, and his brother Tex, Madge used to take part in the rodeos held at the Braaten brothers' farm, known as Dipping Vat Ranch. In a local history of the area, Madge is remembered by the author, Lars Larson, as 'the only bucking horse lady rider I knew.'[12] In spite of her duties as wife and mother, Madge preserved large areas of freedom in her life, and what was then regarded as her 'mannish' verve and her love of horses are distilled fictionally in the character of Laura Kirby in As for Me and My House.

The character of Steve, the boy taken in to live with the Bentleys, may have been suggested to the future author by a boy of east European background known as Johnny 'Cross the Tracks.' Johnny lived with his father, Carl Kozak, who ran the coal dock, and when Kozak left town, the boy, then about twelve, stayed on for the best part of a year with another Abbey family.[13] There were very few middle or east Europeans in the immediate vicinity of Abbey; Germans, Poles, and Ukrainians settled in communities further north in the Lancer area, where there was a Catholic church. However, one Ukrainian family did settle in Abbey and would inspire an important chapter in Jim's fiction.

A Ukrainian, Frank Hunchiak (variously spelled Hunceac, Hunchaik), came to western Canada from Austria, settling in the Abbey area around 1913. He was a cobbler by trade, but he made his living by working on the CP section. When he had saved enough money (ten years had passed), he returned to Austria to fetch his wife, Anna, and their son, Nick. (In his absence, Anna had also given birth to a daughter, Lena.) The Hunchiaks lived in a small house on the edge of town, where Anna worked a large kitchen garden, raised chickens and pigeons to sell, and kept a milch cow. When Nick Hunchiak arrived in Abbey and started school, he was ten years old and could not speak English; the other boys in the town teased him mercilessly, called him 'Hunky,' and played mean tricks on him to his uncomprehending dismay. Jim observed the tormenting of this immigrant boy in the streets of Abbey, and it recalled the hostilities endured by the Myketiak brothers, also Ukrainians, in the Rolling Prairie school. They would merge in his imagination to form the character of Nick, the young doctor who is off-stage in Sawbones Memorial. Frank Hunchiak worked hard to adapt himself and his family to life in Canada: he insisted they speak English at home as well as in public, and they joined the United Church to be part of the community. Like the fictional Nick Miller, Nick Hunchiak would eventually enjoy success and the esteem of his fellows, not as a doctor, but as an airman during the Second World War, and later as a policeman in Edmonton. In the meantime, his parents remained marginal though vivid figures in the largely Anglo-Saxon community. Anna was a strong woman of peasant stock who would pitch hay and oat sheaves with the men; her dressed squab and poultry were prized by connoisseurs because she used a slow, dry pluck method leaving the flesh more tender. Frank's health gradually deteriorated, first from a lung condition exacerbated by the coal dust where he worked, and later by mental instability. He was eventually incarcerated in the mental hospital in Weyburn, Saskatchewan, where he died in 1948.[14] Jim would adapt these figures to his imaginative needs in *Sawbones Memorial*, creating the strong peasant mother whose chastity is compromised for practical ends, and the little cobbler husband who spends much of his life in a sanatorium.

In town, Jim's social interests remained centred in the church, and, like Mrs Bentley in *As for Me and My House*, he viewed the church chiefly as a venue for his music. He occasionally went to community dances and to parties in individual homes, but his greatest pleasure and the focus of his imaginative and social life at that point was in performing at concerts and 'socials' that took place either in the church or the community hall. By the time he was nearly twenty, he had taught himself to play some of the large works of the classical composers. Especially popular was his rendering of Rachmaninoff's difficult and showy Prelude in C-sharp Minor. It invariably brought sustained applause calling for an encore, and Percy Grainger's light-hearted, popular 'Country Gardens' exactly suited that demand. Jim was more than willing to accommodate an audience that responded so warmly to his performances.

The one irritation was the terrible condition of the Abbey church piano. There was a much finer instrument at the Odd Fellows Hall, and for very special occasions it was sent out on loan. Occasionally, Jim would be asked to play piano selections to round out a program for a guest lecturer. One such evening, the speaker was Nellie McClung, popular novelist and suffragist, and he asked that the better piano be brought over. But the request was ignored. With time he forgot the specific subject of McClung's talk, but he would remember that he played 'To the Skylark' that evening, one of the popular *morceaux de salon* by the nineteenth-century Polish composer Theodor Leschetizky, and how badly it sounded on the old piano. The next time he was asked to perform and the piano was still not tuned, he stopped after playing a few bars and explained to the audience that he would not continue, because 'it was not right to execute such fine compositions on such a miserable instrument.' It was a 'Romance' by Chopin, and he felt the beauty and delicacy of the piece were being strangled by the sour notes. The forthright words from the modest little bank clerk would still be recalled seventy years later by Bessie Cottingham, one of the startled young members of the audience.[15]

One of the families most interested in the cultural life of the village was the Levines, the owners of a general store on the main street. They were the only Jewish family in Abbey, and concerts and lectures were the one contact they had socially with others in the community. There was more than one general store in Abbey (Worth's also carried a wide variety of goods, from groceries to clothing to hardware), and the rivalry inevitably evoked racial prejudice, some Abbey citizens preferring to give custom to people of 'their own kind.' Mr Levine had a brother who was Jim's age, and the two young men became friends. One winter evening, they walked together out to Sid Ketcheson's for dinner – at dusk, through four miles of snow – and the talk never stopped. Jim's dream of the perfect friend that he had experienced with Hughie Adams, the short-lived son of the minister in Stoughton, was for a time rekindled in his friendship with Maurice Levine, but it was a relationship on the periphery of society, which boded further loneliness, not the link to community that he also craved, and he gradually let the friendship lapse.

Kate's attitude was very different. She too liked the Levines, and though she seldom shopped except by Eaton's catalogue, she would flaunt Mrs Levine as a special friend in the face of Abbey society. The continuing Presbyterians had disbanded, and Kate now belonged to the mainstream United Church, where she was an active member of the women's groups. One day when it was her turn to host the Ladies Aid meeting, she included Mrs Levine in the gathering of church women. The unvoiced but strongly felt criticism of this gesture prompted Kate to exclaim to her son later: 'And they call themselves Christians!' Kate liked to make a show of her Christian charity. To the neighbours in the next house, a widower and his three daughters, she took her baking, and because the father was lame, she made sure that Jim carried water for them from the town pump every day.

There was an emotional jolt in the fall of 1927: Kate received word that, at age sixty, her husband had died of cancer on October 14 in Edmonds, Washington State, where he had been living for five years near one of his sisters. The specific cause of death was cancer of the lip, which had metastasized to the jaw.[16] Peter Ross was remembered, certainly, as a man seldom without a pipe in his mouth. Kate reacted with strong feeling to the news of Pete's death. She broke down and cried when she read the letter, and never having said a good word about him before, she now told her son, 'Peter Ross was the best man that ever lived.'[17] She instructed Jim to ask Bowen for three days off from the bank and arranged that they spend a time of family grieving at Effie's in

Indian Head. On the train journey, Kate created for her son a Ross family history – a mentally unstable mother, a father's defection, grinding poverty. 'The poor boy never had a chance' was her tearful summary to what she saw as a family tragedy that continued to spread its dark influence. Effie Price's sorrow was less complicated; she and her father had always gotten along well and she would miss him. Her life was in many ways akin to his; she worked hard to maintain a home and help support her three children, but her husband was chronically ill, unable to work, and they lived in mean circumstances. (Two years later, Matt Price would die, and for a time Effie would place her children in foster homes while she worked as a domestic in Regina and Moose Jaw.) Jim was only nineteen when his father died, and because he had not seen him since he was seven, his father's physical death was something remote and abstract. He resented what he felt was his mother's melodramatic and hypocritical show of grief, the loss of three days wages, and the thirty dollars spent for travel to Indian Head and back.

Abbey and its people were the centre of Jim's world. While he was in his late teens and living with his mother in the village, Jimmy Ross was very much part of the social mainstream, indeed very much 'babied and petted' by the townspeople for his gifts at the piano and easel. By 1928, when Jim turned twenty, several of his paintings were hanging on the walls in Abbey homes, and a number of children were taking piano lessons at the Ross house. One of these was Kathleen Milne, the daughter of a prominent Scottish couple who lived adjacent to the Rosses. Kate was very fond of the girl and treated her like a favourite grandchild. At his mother's insistence, Jim gave the girl music lessons; she memorized and thumped out her pieces cheerfully, but with no interest in music whatsoever. Kate taught her to dance the Highland fling and would call her in to perform when she had ladies for tea. (Kathleen would remain very fond of the Rosses and would continue to visit Kate until the latter's death.) At the bank, D.E. McAllister, who was on the church board, followed the bank manager's lead and bought one of Jim's paintings; McAllister and his wife were socially ambitious and took the young man under their wing, promoting his talents in their own search for social status. Similarly, Jim and his mother were always welcome at the home of the Dowsleys, the new young doctor and his wife who came to Abbey with considerable experience of the larger world. Years later, Theodora Dowsley, living in West Vancouver, would recall Kate Ross as a smart, well-dressed, and well-spoken woman who gave the town a bit of class, and remembered Jim playing the piano while the young couple had a late evening dinner.[18] In Abbey, then, Jim had an 'audience,' with everything associated with that word for an artist – purpose, appreciation, well-being. The good opinion of the local people and the relatively comfortable life in Abbey made it difficult accordingly when Jim was informed at the bank in April of 1928 that he would be transferred to another town.

Lancer is located approximately twelve miles north-west of Abbey on the Leader line. It was and is a smaller village – about 150 people in the late 1920s, less than half the size of Abbey. Lancer is closer to the Great Sand Hills region where arable land gives way to stretches of heavy sand that shift in high winds. Bank policy was to move its employees around the different branches – to extend their knowledge and skills, and to avoid power becoming entrenched locally with certain individuals. In one respect, life was more comfortable for the Rosses in Lancer; they lived in the United Church manse (the incumbent bachelor minister was boarded elsewhere), and in this relatively spacious home Jim had his own bedroom. And there was gossip to savour: it was rumoured that the bachelor minister had gotten the schoolteacher pregnant. But for both Kate and Jim the move meant a diminished social life; although Lancer and Abbey are very close by present-day standards, means of travel in the 1920s meant a greater distance, and it was often a month or six weeks between trips to Abbey. Both mother and son felt they had moved out to a margin.

Jim spent much more time alone now. The piano had been trucked to Lancer, and he devoted more hours than before in trying to master the instrument. He took lessons with a Mrs Stringer, the wife of an accountant in the town, feeling however that his own skills were commensurate with hers. He only occasionally played in public, when a substitute was needed for the church pianist on Sunday, or when a silent film on a biblical theme was shown in the church hall and an accompanist was needed to create a 'soundtrack.' Growing more reclusive, he was becoming intensely aware of the observation he gives to Paul Kirby in As for Me and My House – that 'the worst penalty inflicted by education [is] the way it separates you from people who are really closest to you, among whom you would otherwise belong ... a ranch boy with a little schooling, he fits in nowhere' (28). At the same time, he was equally oppressed by his realization that he lacked a comprehensive, formal education, and, determined to continue learning, he undertook to read books like Gibbon's six-volume Decline and Fall of the Roman Empire and H.G. Wells's The Outline of History. Those books, which he found so laborious to read in places, seemed nonetheless to promise the encyclopedic overview of world history and culture that he craved. But what he especially remembered years later was the melancholy pleasure he experienced that year reading Edward Fitzgerald's Rubaiyat of Omar Khayyam. The poem's hedonism, its carpe diem advocacy of the sensual life, rooted in a philosophical certainty of the vanity of all things, had a direct appeal to the young man, who was asking questions about life's purpose and about his own acute feelings of loneliness. He was also beginning to feel strongly an unfocused nature to his own sexuality.

One of his tasks as a clerk in Lancer was to deliver bank drafts to customers, collect promissory notes, etc. This brought him in contact with the few businessmen of the area, including a harness-maker who lived and worked in a two-room shack on the edge of town. The man was a bachelor in his forties, an Irish immigrant by the name of McLeod, who drank excessively and whose unkempt, ill-lit quarters were strewn with sections of leather, broken machine parts, items of taxidermy. At times, younger men would live in ambiguous relationships with the harness-maker in his shack. One of these young men was a good-looking Irish youth in his twenties, supported by a veterinarian father in Ireland. He would invite Jim inside for a drink when the latter stopped there on business for the bank. Jim did not accept the liquor, but he liked the young man's lively, self-assured friendliness, and he began stopping at the shack when he was not on business. One day the Irish youth suggested they go for a walk together; he led the way. It was snowing large wet flakes, and when they came to the railroad, he directed Jim to step inside one of the boxcars. In the dark, Jim felt a surge of fear as the man took hold of him and pulled back his clothing; he was being sodomized, but he didn't struggle. This would be his strongest memory of being initiated into gay sex. He would later picture that moment in his life as crossing a boundary; he would see himself stepping back out into the familiar world of snowy fields, grain elevator, and sleepy village, but now an outsider. In the years ahead, when he was a writer and a respected public figure, he knew that he was also a transgressor, and that his work depended on his being both of these things.

four

_____

Musician
1929–1933

I believed then, naively, that when I became a successful artist, I would own a
home, drive a car, and have a wife. – JSR in conversation

In June of 1929, the piano teacher, Frank Woodbury, answered a knock at the
door to find a shy, vaguely familiar-looking young man standing on the
threshold of his parents' home in Arcola.[1] Jimmy Ross identified himself and,
in a little speech he had prepared in advance, carefully explained his visit. He
was twenty-one years old and working for the Royal Bank of Canada in
Lancer, but he was discouraged by the prospect of a life-long career in the
bank and dreamed of making his living as a musician. There was a transfer
position open at the Arcola branch of the Royal Bank, and he would apply for
it if Frank would accept him as a pupil at the piano. Jim remembered Frank's
sensitivity as a teacher and was aware of his reputation as a musician in the
province. A shiver of pleasure ran through the older man, whose vanity was
being stroked. He was indeed working hard to establish himself as a presence
in the province's music world: that April he had started a music festival in
Arcola, he was actively involved in the southern Saskatchewan festival program, and several of his students were placing with high marks in the compe-
titions. The fact that he was being sought out by a young man of artistic
sensibility and taste was not lost on him. He welcomed his former pupil.

When Jim spoke to Frank Woodbury, he had in fact already been transferred
to Arcola (the bank at that time moved its young single employees about
according to its own plan). Until his mother arrived with the furniture a few
weeks later, Jim stayed at a boarding house run by Ellie Kerr, a wizened, hard-
working little woman known, not without respect, as 'Aunty' Kerr. In her
rough-and-ready manner, she quickly filled Jim in on the town, telling him

about the new doctor by the name of Stone, whose smart American wife was of Bohemian descent, recommending for lunches the Club Cafe run by Wong Dong and his brother Happy Dong, and confiding with a wink that the wife of the blind tobacconist was a woman who entertained young men generously.

Jim felt good about the move. Arcola is located in the more prosperous farming region of south-eastern Saskatchewan, on the eastern periphery of the Palliser Triangle, where the weather is more favourable and crops are more certain. It is an older and more substantial town than Abbey or Lancer, dating back to a post office with that name established in 1889.[2] CPR track reached the area in 1901. The town grew to include a brick factory, a flour mill, and six grain elevators, and by the 1920s it had several buildings made from hand-hewn stone and from the tan-coloured Arcola brick made at the local brick-yard. Especially handsome was the town hall with tower and bell, a multi-pur-pose building that housed council chambers, cells for the confinement of prisoners, and on the second floor an auditorium with proscenium stage, foot-lights, and balcony, referred to locally as the opera house. To Jim's amaze-ment, the manager's office at the Royal Bank had a working fireplace. Moreover, the town had trees, for in the first decade of the century a bonus was paid to citizens who planted and tended trees in front of their homes. Arcola is the name of an Italian village made known through a battle in the Napoleonic wars, but why it was given to a location in Saskatchewan remains undetermined.[3] For Jim, however, it gave the town an air of history and sub-stance; he felt too that Arcola in 1929, with nearly seven hundred people, had a solid sense of society.

For the first year and a half, Jim and Kate lived on Carlyle Street in a house next to the St Andrew's United Church manse. Theirs was a large house, but it was built on raised beams with no basement, and so the floor was very cold in winter. It was the first house in which they had running water, but during periods of deep freezing temperatures, Jim more than once had to crawl under the house to thaw the water pipes. Jim would remember it as old and run down, 'with heaving floors and a leaky roof,'[4] but it was all that was available when he arrived in the town and the rent was only fifteen dollars a month. Their closest neighbours were an elderly couple named Whitman. Kate took pity on them because they were reaching a point of not being able to care for themselves, and their son, who lived in Regina, was also in poor health. She cleaned their house and cooked for them, and because they were poor, she took no money for her services. Instead she liked to tell her son, and others, that she enjoyed 'doing the Lord's work.' In Arcola there were sharp eyes and ears to measure such activ-ities. Mrs Matilda Hanna, a devout Roman Catholic, lived on the same street and was Kate's rival in charity. The two women went back and forth to each other's homes for tea, but neither refrained from identifying the other as a meddlesome gossip. Among the citizens of Arcola there were names that one day would be familiar to Sinclair Ross's readers, names like Bird and Finlay, and nearby a town named Kisbey, echoed in Kirby and Kelby.

Frank Woodbury, thirty-one, unmarried, still lived with his parents, two houses down the street from where the Rosses were renting. He advertised himself in the local newspaper as 'teacher of piano and theory' and able to prepare students for exams set by the Toronto Conservatory of Music, the McGill Conservatory of Music, the Regina Conservatory of Music, and the National College of Music, London. Every afternoon, on his way home from the bank, Jim could hear Frank teaching piano pupils in his parents' front parlour. (Frank liked to teach by playing pieces while his pupils watched.) And every evening, when the weather was good, Frank would see Jim and his mother pass along the sidewalk on their regular evening walk together. Many years later, Frank would remark, 'In those days it was hard to imagine Jimmy without his mother.' But, in fact, Jim spent most of his time in the evenings at the piano, often to his mother's annoyance, pushing himself, sometimes as much as three hours an evening, to master pianoforte technique. Frank Woodbury was a source of inspiration, as he had been earlier to the fifteen-year-old boy living in Stoughton; his talent, energy, self-confidence, and physical attractiveness drew many of the young people of Arcola to the arts. Jim took both painting and music lessons from Frank and was drawn inside the intense and exciting sphere of activities that he generated in the town.

A brief scan of the *Moose Mountain Star-Standard* (the area newspaper) reveals quickly how the townspeople followed with great interest Frank Woodbury's activities and how he set the agenda for the social and cultural life of Arcola. He is described taking part in a variety of church activities, including the men's club; and in 1930 he was appointed a Chautauqua officer for the Moose Mountain area. He was a member of the Arcola Tennis Club, serving on the social committee, and a member of the town's curling club as well. His comings and goings as a musician, particularly his activities in Regina, are followed with special interest. After graduating as an Associate of the Toronto Conservatory of Music (ATCM), Frank continued to travel to Regina to study piano with Cyril Hampshire, director of the Regina Conservatory, and with George Coutts, his former piano teacher at the conservatory. With violinist James Fenton, he gave concerts that were broadcast on radio station CKCK from Regina. But especially prominent in the Arcola paper are accounts of those musical events he directed and sometimes hosted in the town. In the late winter and spring of 1930, he arranged for no less than three recitals to be given by his pupils.

A small recital was given by advanced students at Frank's 'studio' in his parents' home on 11 February 1930, providing, according to the *Star-Standard*, 'intense delight [for] those present, forming ... an oasis in the desert of the sometimes dreary winter evenings.'[5] The recital opened with a duet by James Ross and Carol Patterson, which was followed by a piano solo by Dorothy Cornell. Carol Patterson, with whom Jim would perform jointly on a number of occasions, was a young man who, for a whole winter, had been ill with rheumatic fever when he was a boy and was left an invalid. The talented Dorothy Cornell, still in her teens, was already an associate of the Toronto Conservatory of Music and was the newly appointed organist of the United Church. That evening Jim played two solos, praised by the reporter for their mastery of technique. Higher praise, however, was bestowed on Patterson, and especially on Frank Woodbury for his rendering of a piece by Leschetizky 'entirely with the left hand.' The reporter writes that 'with closed eyes it was impossible to believe it, and with open eyes one could not but help envy his command of his instrument.' Frank and Dorothy concluded the recital with a Beethoven duet on two pianos, and Frank's mother served a 'dainty lunch' at the evening's close.[6]

Frank Woodbury's flair for showmanship is further in evidence in the newspaper's account of a recital on March 28 of the same year:

> Mr Frank Woodbury, A.T.C.M., held his annual piano recital in the Town Hall, Arcola, last Friday evening, before a fair sized audience, some thirty pupils taking part, presenting a very creditable programme.
>
> The stage was tastefully decorated with numerous coloured streamers which formed the background of the setting, with coloured polka dots on front. In front of the footlights coloured stands were placed and when the fairy princess waved her magic wand, flowers came down from the ceiling sufficient to fill the twelve stands.
>
> The Armilla grocery store did a roaring business, and holders of the lucky numbers, duplicates of which were drawn from a box by the fairy princess, each received some useful article in the grocery line. Unfortunately, soon after the intermission the electric lights went out and stayed out and other lighting had to be quickly arranged, though very much to the disadvantage of the players. Dancing followed till two in the morning with music by the Footwarmers.[7]

In this town, the winter months provided lively entertainments, and spring brought music festivals. In Arcola, Jim was not quite a central figure in the arts, as he had been in Abbey, but he enjoyed the more competitive spirit of this place.

In the late spring of 1930, Jim was appointed associate music director of Arcola's St Andrew's United Church under Dorothy Cornell, the gifted young woman who had completed her ATCM and was considered second only to Frank Woodbury in Arcola's musical society. Jim's chief duty was to play the organ for services when Dorothy was out of town or sick. Services at St. Andrew's were in the evening (as they are in *As for Me and My House*), the circuit preacher serving at Willmar in the morning and at the South Arcola United Church in the afternoon. Jim and Dorothy had a happy relationship together as church organists and, among their activities, were conspirators in attempting to modify the heavy seriousness of the church's official music director, W.F. Youngblud. It was the latter's duty to lead the choir and to attend to the 'business' of the church music, managing a small amount of money to pay the organist, buy hymnals, see to organ repairs, etc.; but he also had a voice in the choosing of hymns to be sung, and heard requests and complaints from the congregation regarding musical matters. His portly wife was the principal soloist in the choir and frequently gave her much applauded rendering of 'The Holy City.' Youngblud, in his late fifties, operated a successful men's furnishings store in Arcola, was a member of the Masonic Lodge, a former mayor of the town, and an organizer of the Arcola Agricultural Society. The Youngbluds had no children and put all their energies into town activities. Many years later, the author would remember them as good people, generous with their invitations for turkey dinner, but he would also remember them as solemn and humourless in their religiosity and philanthropic enterprises, and he would write accordingly in his first published novel that there were such people in every Prairie town – 'austere, beyond reproach, a little grim with the responsibilities of self-assumed leadership – inevitable as broken sidewalks and rickety false fronts' (8).

Something of the relation between the minister of the Arcola United Church and the townspeople would emerge specifically in *As for Me and My House*. The Reverend Bert Howard and his wife came to call on the Rosses shortly after they took up their pastoral charge in Arcola in the summer of 1929. Kate took an immediate dislike to what she called an 'unctuous' manner in this couple and felt herself ungenerously withdrawing from their invitation to be actively involved in the work of the church. The Rosses found that this pair were not well liked by the congregation at large. Moreover, scandal clouded the air. Mrs Howard, who was a skilled violinist and entertained at public concerts, had serious health problems (it would prove to be cancer), and the couple hired a girl, Mabel Twigg, to do domestic chores at the parsonage. When the girl left Arcola for a time, it was whispered that she was pregnant.

When he arrived in Arcola, Jim had what he calls in *As for Me and My House* 'the typical countryman's feeling of disadvantage before town people who wear smarter clothes and write a better hand' (92). But, like Paul Kirby, whom he was describing in that passage, he soon came to know the people of Arcola 'for what they really [were]' and recognized most of his own values to be sounder. At this time, active in the church life of the town, Jim, like some of his fictional characters, was especially pressed to think about religion and the question of belief. Paul Kirby, again functioning as the author's surrogate, explains to Mrs Bentley that he is a rationalist (111), that he cannot believe in the efficacy of prayers for rain. This does not mean, however, that he will stop attending Sunday services; 'quite the contrary,' he says, making it clear that he attends church for social reasons. But Jim's most probing reflections on religion were given to Philip Bentley: '"Religion and art ... are almost the same,"' he says; they are just different ways that humankind has of turning away for a time from the material, common-sense world for one that is 'illusory, yet somehow more important' (148). Philip states that it is when an individual looks into a void that he begins to create, to give the void life and form, whether that be a religious belief to explain humanity's origins and significance, or art to provide emotional release that is sometimes called 'ecstasy or rapture.' These important ideas were beginning to take shape for Jim as he took part in the religious and artistic life of yet another small Prairie town, while attempting to reconcile his own independent thinking with social practice.

Arcola would furnish the future author with other materials for his fiction. His closest experience of the drought and Depression took place in this town. The first year he spent in Arcola, 1929, was the driest so far on record, and the harvests were a third of their normal yield. In south-eastern Saskatchewan, 1930 brought more rain and the promise of a better harvest, but a devastating hailstorm on July 26 destroyed between 75 and 100 per cent of the crops in the Arcola area. The storm struck on Saturday at the supper hour and lasted less than half an hour. Arcola only received a heavy downpour, but south of the town the hailstones lay upon the fields to the depth of two and three feet in some places. In hundreds of buildings, windows were smashed, although nobody was seriously injured.[8]

Money became so scarce that year that on the notice for the Chautauqua in October, the people in Arcola were told they could bring farm produce in lieu of money for the seventy-five cents admission. Each year thereafter was drier than the one before, the most barren year being 1934. Two local histories[9] describe the severity of those years: drought, grasshoppers, and wind were turning the plain into a desert. High winds and summer temperatures, regularly above 100 degrees Fahrenheit, shrivelled the crops and eroded the

soil; and what little survived was destroyed by grasshoppers in plagues of biblical proportions. Some years there was not even enough crop for seed. The
dust storms, which began in 1931, were the hardest trial to contend with:
'dust sifted through windows and cracks of houses, forming drifts on the furniture, beds, and even getting into the food.'[10] Familes would take their prepared meals and eat with a neighbour if the latter had a 'tighter' house. The
skies were blackened with the drifting soil, and outdoor community events,
baseball games and fairs, had to be cancelled. With the deflation of money,
many farmers had no means with which to continue and left the area, hauling
their family and possessions, usually northward, in a caravan of wagons and
emaciated livestock. Of those who remained, about 90 per cent were forced to
seek government assistance; these included many townspeople, for their livelihood was directly dependent on the prosperity of the farmers.

Jim's recollections of the drought and Depression would turn especially to
the farmers he knew who did business at the bank. W.J. Boynton-Coffey
became manager of the Royal Bank in Arcola in 1930. Jim would remember
him as an authoritarian, often drunk, upper-class Irishman who adhered
strictly to bank policy. When Boynton-Coffey left town on business or on
holiday, Jim was appointed acting manager, and Boynton-Coffey left him a
list of those to whom he was not to lend money. But as the Depression deepened, the list grew long and included some of the better farmers and tradesmen in the area. Jim made some small loans while the manager was away the
first time – in one case, seventy-five dollars to enable a farmer to repair equipment in order to harvest what crops he had. On his return, Boynton-Coffey
was unrelenting in chastising his young accountant. The plight of the farmer
was deeply imprinted on Jim's sympathies and imagination, as were the more
heartening scenes of people helping each other out in times of sore need.
Government assistance was not always enough: homemakers' clubs gathered
clothing, food, and seed to help people 'on relief.' In spite of hardships, the
crisis drew people together in a shared plight and there was surprising cheer-
fulness and neighbourliness when things were at their worst.

In this setting, friendships were becoming increasingly important to Jim. At
age twenty-two, in fact, they were a pressing need. His days were rigidly
divided between working hours at the bank and a stringent regimen of piano
practice at home, and when he went out, except for piano lessons, his mother
invariably accompanied him – on walks in the evening, to church on Sunday,
to meetings or concerts during the week. But when Kate would take the train
to Indian Head, to spend a few days with Effie, he invited the friends he was
making to the house for the evening. To them he seemed shy and painfully

reserved, unable to mix easily in company, but they knew he wanted to 'mix,' because on those evenings he played modern dance tunes and popular songs at the piano, not classics. Among the half dozen men and women Jim knew, he was particularly fond of Margaret Watt, who worked as a stenographer at the Royal Bank. In his eyes, she was a wholesome, straightforward girl, who was a good office mate and genial companion. To others she seemed a very sophisticated young woman, but Jim, who was easily intimidated, felt none-theless relaxed and easy in her company. There was also a young man his age, Cal Ingram, for whom he felt a special attraction. Cal lived on a farm with his parents nine miles outside of Arcola and only came to town on weekends. But by the time Jim arrived in Arcola, this energetic and humorous youth already had a reputation as a ladies' man, a local Lothario. When he came to Jim's for the evening, he would invariably bring a couple of girls, and by pouring a few drinks and starting the dancing, he tried to initiate his inexperienced friend.[11] Jim's awkwardness, however, was only partly inexperience; it was also a confusion of feelings and roles, for he was finding that his stronger desire was for Cal's company, not for the young women Cal had in tow.

At the same time, he found himself increasingly attracted to Dorothy Cor-nell, with whom he shared his intense interest in music. To Jim, Dorothy was sexually exciting while being at the same time very refined: 'she was the kind of girl that aroused you physically,' he explained, 'but you did everything pos-sible to hide it.'[12] The Cornells had a nicely appointed home, and even dur-ing the worst years of the Depression they appeared to have sufficient money on which to live comfortably. Dorothy's father was a land agent and one of the few men in Arcola with a steady salary from the federal government. Jim felt welcome at the Cornell home, especially by Mrs Cornell, who liked his gentle manners and who, perhaps, thought he had a better background socially than most of the other young men in town. Like Kate, Mrs Cornell always had a cup of tea and a piece of cake ready for a visitor, or on a hot sum-mer day a jug of lemonade on the verandah. Dorothy's father was polite, but to the diffident young accountant from the bank he appeared an austere and intimidating figure. Dorothy gave piano lessons in the evening, but during the day she helped her mother with the upkeep of the house. Courting a girl like Dorothy was conducted within narrow confines in Arcola: the Cornell home was a place of formalities; moreover, Dorothy had a younger cousin, Ada, living at the house, who seemed to be present whenever Jim was there. Church meetings and concerts, of course, were very public, so that practising the piano together at the church and walking back to Dorothy's house was the extent of their time alone together. And there was Kate's watchful eye. Although she conceded that Dorothy came from a good family (they had money and social standing), Kate was anxious that she might lose her control over Jim, and so she pronounced the girl insipid and inconsequential.

Kate much preferred to see her son with Keith Clarke, a young man whom Jim would remember as 'an innocent boy with a large sense of fun.'[13] To many, who remembered Keith's early death overseas at the beginning of the war, he was one of the finest boys the town had produced, good-humoured, gentle, and a fine sport. He was also remembered for having one brown eye and one blue. Keith's father ran a grocery store, and in the summers the boy delivered groceries around the town. During the school months, he attended Wesley College at the University of Manitoba, where he worked towards a bachelor of arts degree. Jim and Keith became good friends in the summer of 1930, drawn together by a shared love of music and art, although Keith also had a passion for tennis. Mr Clarke, Sr, an amateur ornithologist, led a community choir, and Jim served as his accompanist, the circumstance which initially brought the young men together. That summer, Jim and Keith went on double dates, a form of chaperoning that satisfied Kate but which did not inhibit the boys from seeing 'how far they could go,' for as they said to each other and warned their dates 'we're no angels!'[14] Jim's date was usually Margaret Watt from the bank (he didn't have the courage yet to ask Dorothy). She and Jim would sit in the back seat of Keith's car with their arms around each other, cheering as Keith would hold up, one by one, items of clothing he was removing from his protesting girlfriend.

Keith Clarke enjoyed vivacious girls willing to have fun, but, like Jim, the girl he admired and had a special feeling for in Arcola was Dorothy Cornell. It seemed that Dorothy excelled in everything she did. She had been an exemplary student in school, winning the IODE medal when she passed into high school, and a silver medal in high school on completing grade ten. She spent her grade eleven year in the city at Regina College, where she studied music under George Coutts and obtained her ATCM with first-class honours at the age of sixteen. On completing high school, she won the governor general's medal for highest marks in grade twelve, and almost every year she captured medals at the Southern Saskatchewan Music Festival. As well, she was accomplished athletically, and in the summer of 1930 she and Keith were winners of a cup in the mixed doubles at the Cannington tennis tournament.[15] Jim would long remember Dorothy on the court, with what he called her arrow-like stance, mistress of the situation; and he would remember Keith's frolicking energy and skill. Jim was in awe of these gifted friends.

Occasionally, Jim and Dorothy and Keith would spend a Saturday afternoon in each other's company (the bank closed at 1:00 p.m.), or go to a movie together in the evening. Years later, he would recognize in his friendship with

Dorothy and Keith a pattern for the most intense and satisfying friendships he would experience during his lifetime. They would involve the simultaneous enjoyment of a man's and a woman's company, where he was a welcome third party and where he felt attracted to the man and woman equally. When he was older, it was usually in the company of a married couple, a man he might know at work whose wife he also found interesting and attractive. Years later, when he eagerly read Alfred Kinsey's *Sexual Behavior in the Human Male* (1948), he would come to understand better for himself those sexual feelings for both a man and woman that society regarded as incompatible. Kinsey's famous 'report' described a scale from 0 to 6 for measuring degrees of heterosexuality and homosexuality. Jim came to see himself on this continuum as 'predominantly homosexual, but more than incidentally heterosexual,' although he would feel situation and circumstance were more important than any numbering system could account for. Bisexuality became a comfortable way for Jim to think about his nature, and triangular emotional relationships would emerge significantly, though covertly, in much of the fiction he wrote.

In the meantime, in the curiously idyllic summer of 1930, after the tennis tourney at Carlyle Lake had concluded, Jim and Keith went for a few days together to the Clarke family cottage, which was located at Fish Lake Resort in the nearby Moose Mountains. (Fish Lake was also known as Lake Kenosee, and like nearby Carlyle Lake, it was a shallow body of water formed by glacial action that deposited the terminal moraine known as the Moose Mountains, a geographical formation typical of 'mountains' on the prairie.) Jim and Keith swam at the lake, hiked the trails, and picked wild berries for a pie. As a little moisture had fallen in that area and it had been spared hail there were some edibles in the garden and hay in the little pastures in the mountains, a con-trast to the increasingly barren environs of Arcola. In September, Keith went back to Winnipeg to continue working on his degree.

For fall, Jim set himself a rigorous timetable at the piano. He got up at half past six every morning and practised for an hour before it was time to go to work. He slipped home from the bank during his lunch hour and, after a quick bite, had time for a half hour at the piano, working at those musical phrases on which he had stumbled in the early morning. In the evenings, he spent an hour working through all the technical exercises – scales, chords, arpeggios – before starting to work at the pieces for future examination. Most days, to his mother's despair, he spent six hours practising. On weekends, that regimen was expanded to include music theory and history. In winter the house was cold and dark when he started in the morning, and his fingers were barely limber when it was time to stop, but the future he envisioned – release from the bank, a career as a musician – was built on sacrifice.

That year, Jim took his vacation in December (those at the bank who passed up the summer months were rewarded with an extra week), and he boarded a train for Winnipeg on the 3rd to join Keith, who was finishing classes for the fall term. It was the first time he had been to the city – to any big city – and Keith showed his friend inside the imposing public buildings, the city hall, the Manitoba legislature. What they also enjoyed was looking through the furniture stores together, critically eyeing the paintings for sale, examining the rugs. In Eaton's they found a copy of a popular painting depicting an angel in a white robe, on the back of which was an image of the devil. That painting seemed to amuse Keith immensely. 'That is pretty much us,' he suggested to Jim, 'our reputation as "good boys!"'[16] They walked the snowy, windy streets of the city, entering a store every second block to keep warm. But a great adventure for Jim that week was to attend, for the first time in his life, a full symphony concert. The Minneapolis Symphony was playing concerts for three nights in Winnipeg, and the friends from Arcola went on two consecutive evenings.

And there was another adventure. Keith lived at a rooming house near the college, and Jim was staying at the YMCA, but one night, after talking about girls and joking about their sexual frustrations, they masturbated each other and Jim stayed the night in Keith's bed. Although it would happen again more than once during their friendship, Keith would not speak openly of it to Jim, treating it as if it was 'something that hadn't happened.'[17] But it was important to Jim, for this was the first time he had experienced physical intimacy with a friend.

During the long winter of 1931 in Arcola, Jim turned with concentration to the piano. As well as working at the keyboard, he was preparing himself to write the theory paper in music history, taking the textbook to the bank to memorize during his noon hour break. But as the exams prescribed by the Regina College Conservatory of Music approached, Jim grew uneasy about the kind of preparation he was receiving from Frank Woodbury. His method of showily playing a passage, sometimes the whole piece, for his student to imitate, became increasingly a questionable pedagogy. Moreover, Frank wandered from the curriculum set down by the conservatory – he had Jim playing Cécile Chaminade's 'Autumn,' an audience favourite, rather than working at the required list of examination pieces. Frank's students did better than average at festivals and exams, perhaps because they were temporarily energized by his great zest for performance, but Jim had misgivings about the accuracy and finish of these performances. Moreover, as a teacher, Frank always seemed a little distracted, as if during the lesson he had other, more pressing and important, things to attend to.

Indeed, Frank had more than teaching on his mind. In February 1931 there was the second annual recital by the Orpheus Musical Club held at his studio; in April the music festivals in Stoughton, Whitewood, and Redvers to adjudicate; and in May a series of four piano recitals at the studio which drew audiences totalling 150, roughly a quarter of the people in town. For two nights in the latter series, Jim played Moritz Moszkowski's 'Spanish Caprice' as a solo and then joined Dorothy Campbell, Dorothy Cornell, and Frank in a two-piano rendering of Schubert's 'Military March.' In Jim's opinion, Dorothy's talent as a musician equalled or bettered Frank Woodbury's, but her demure nature made her less popular with the public at large. The concerts at Frank's studio were, according to the local newspaper, well received by a capacity audience; in the still Victorian sounding language of the day, the paper reported that 'formal words of appreciation were tendered the artists by the Rev. Bert Howard,' and both evenings 'concluded with refreshments' served by Frank's mother, assisted by Mrs W.L. Cornell.[18]

On a hot and dust-stormy day in June, Jim wrote the history of music exam at the studio, invigilated by a member of the Regina Conservatory. Here Jim felt keenly the lack of preparation and instruction from Frank. One of the five questions focused on Palestrina, and he could not recall enough from reading the music history text to formulate an answer. When they were reviewing together, Frank had skipped over the pages on sixteenth-century Italian music and given his pupil no indication that it was an important and examinable subject. Jim couldn't let himself worry over it because he was scheduled to take the pianoforte examination for his ARCM (Associate of the Regina Conservatory of Music) in July, and every waking moment when he wasn't at the bank had to be given to practising. Keith had graduated with his B.A. from the University of Manitoba and was home working with his father again, but there was no time for his company until the exam was over.

Frank became even less helpful now because suddenly he was preparing to be married. He had bought a house to occupy as of August, and he was anxious to pack up the things in his studio in preparation for the move. But he was more than usually distracted that June because there were rumours circulating about his interest in some of his male pupils. Before Jim wrote the music history exam, Frank had arranged that they take a picnic up to Arcola Bay and go over the textbook and notes together. When he returned home, Kate forbade Jim to ride in Frank's car again because she had heard the gossip. Although Jim felt no physical attraction to Frank, he was profoundly affected by the rumours, and unhappy that Frank's attentions would be further diluted. Frank was married to Gladys Waters at a small church ceremony in Regina at the end of June, and he and his wife spent an extended honeymoon in Banff. They stayed away from Arcola until school and music lessons resumed in September.

In the meantime, before Frank left, the director from the Regina Conservatory of Music came to Arcola and examined the senior candidates. The examiner was Cyril Hampshire, a dignified and pleasant man with a strong English accent. Jim had met him once before at Frank's studio when he had come to Arcola to adjudicate a festival. His reserve gave the occasion a formality and importance it might not have had under someone else's direction. Frank assured Jim his preparation was meticulous and that he would score top marks. Jim himself felt that he executed the technical part of the program well, but that some of the pieces, particularly the Bach, could be justly criticized. Indeed he felt *The Well-Tempered Clavier* would take a lifetime to prepare. Nonetheless, he came away hopeful that he had made a strong impression on Hampshire, who was the leading figure in musical education in southern Saskatchewan. And, accordingly, he was disappointed not to receive first-class honours. The pieces were criticized, especially the Bach, and his total score was only in the 'honours' or second-class range. Similarly the music history exam, where he had not been able to answer one of the questions, also scored in the 'honours' category. Of the two, he had done slightly better at the pianoforte exam.

The results, announced early July,[19] made a significant difference to Jim as he thought about his future. He could only have a career in music if he had top marks. Both Dorothy and Frank had earned their degrees from the Toronto Conservatory with first-class honours. If he couldn't at least match their achievement with the Regina Conservatory, there was little room for him as a musician in towns like Arcola, much less in cities like Regina or Winnipeg. That summer, so dry and full of dust storms, was a disheartening one, for he could no longer see his future direction. He was only twenty-three, but the seven years at the bank already felt like an eternity, and as the Depression deepened there was no way out visible. He continued to practise the piano that summer, partly out of habit and partly with the notion of taking the exam again under the auspices of the Royal Toronto Conservatory, and he and Keith resumed their close friendship, but he was now without a rudder and a sure sense of where he was going. He recognized, moreover, that his strong feelings for Dorothy Cornell likely had no future.

Many in Arcola were experiencing displacement, but for specifically economic reasons. The crops in 1931 were so meagre that farmers could not pay their bills. They were forced to feed their livestock Russian thistle. Businesses in Arcola closed, unemployment rose steadily, and many went on relief, administered first by the local town council and after August by the provincial government. When school started, teachers were asked to wait for their wages. Kate reminded Jim every day, or so it seemed, how fortunate he was to have his secure post at the bank. They were in fact now able to afford a better home. The little house on Carlyle was not snug, and dust from the storms sifted into the house through every crack in its porous frame. Like so many other housekeepers, Kate placed dampened rags and newspapers along the window sills and baseboards, and stored the dishes in her cupboards upside down, but still everything was covered with dust. When they moved to a better-built home on Main Street, a cottage covered with Virginia creeper and with the whimsical name 'Sans Souci' (without a care), they did feel privileged.

That fall, Jim turned to writing fiction again, to that more solitary and secretive craft. As he would eventually write of Philip Bentley in *As for Me and My House*, 'The important thing was to fulfill himself ...' (24). He set himself exercises such as describing in words a character's appearance, the way an artist would work at a portrait sketch; or sometimes he would attempt to render the mood of a farm scene or landscape in words. In an extended piece, he tried to describe the excitement and the apprehension felt by a young woman the night before her marriage. He gradually filled a notebook with sketches as he tried, in this methodical fashion, to teach himself to write. At the same time, he mapped out in his mind plans for a long narrative, a novel if he could manage it. It would tell of a young man in a small Prairie town who falls in love with a singer, a circuit performer of questionable moral reputation. He hid his notebooks as best he could from his mother's prying eyes.

When Frank Woodbury returned to Arcola in September, Jim learned how fragile and uncertain a music career could be. Several families felt they were no longer able to pay the seventy-five cents that Frank charged for a half-hour lesson at the piano. Facing this reduction in income and with a new house to pay for, Frank offered lessons at sixty cents, the same fee that Dorothy Cornell was charging. He also offered to drive out and give lessons at homes in the country; and when the family was absolutely strapped, he would take eggs and butter in lieu of cash payment. In town he visited former pupils individually, trying to bring them back to his studio for lessons. He urged Jim to take the Toronto examination, to give himself a second chance, but by September, Jim had lost his strong sense of motivation and told Frank he could no longer afford the fee for lessons. To boost morale and enhance his studio, Frank also decided to present what he called 'Gold Awards' to the students with the highest standing in their grade on the exams. The award seemed specious to Jim, however, since he would be the only candidate that year in the associate category. Frank's desperation was mirrored in a quieter way by the plight of

Carol Patterson, the disabled youth who had earned his ATCM but, to eke out a living, was forced to take the train to Stoughton, Creelman, and Heward to give lessons. That fall, Jim continued to work at the piano sporadically and get advice from Dorothy. She practised at the church on Saturday afternoons; Jim would join her there, and they would work together on duets. Keith, also puzzled about the future, decided to return to Wesley College and take the actuarial course.

The love of music and the dream of a musical career did not die easily. Lingering in Jim's mind was a courteous invitation from Cyril Hampshire to come to Regina for a talk in his studio. Even though he had failed to win high marks from Hampshire on the exam, he felt there was sincerity in the invitation and accordingly did not feel presumptuous writing to him in November to ask for an interview. Hampshire responded positively and offered to arrange lodgings for him at the Regina College residence. So, on December 1st, Jim left by train for Regina, where he would stay for three weeks at the college residence, exploring the province's capital city but, more importantly, exploring what possibilities there might still be for a career in music. In his increasingly methodical way, Jim had arranged in advance not only his lodging and meals, but for a series of lessons with Cyril Hampshire for two weeks, using the best part of his year's savings to pay for them. They were held in Hampshire's studio at the college, which housed an impressive grand piano, and focused on *The Well-Tempered Clavier*, which the examiner felt earlier had been insufficiently prepared.

In his reserved but cordial way, Hampshire was hospitable to the young bank clerk. He invited him to his home to meet his wife and family and to have a meal with them. He also helped him to get tickets to concerts in the city. It was bitterly cold in Saskatchewan that December, the thermometer going down as low as minus 45 degrees Fahrenheit, and some days Jim simply stayed at the residence, where he practised several hours a day at a piano in the common room. By the second week of December, most of the college students had gone home for the holidays, and Jim had the piano to himself. On what was possibly the coldest day, however, he braved the weather for a Sunday afternoon concert at the main college auditorium. It was part of a popular public concert series which Cyril Hampshire both organized and performed in. The audience was small but appreciative, and it was the first time Jim heard a xylophone played or saw an accordion featured on a concert stage of any kind.

As the days in Regina drew to an end, Hampshire gently gave his opinion that Jim had probably started at the piano too late to become a truly accomplished musician. He felt that with the world in a deep economic depression, he could not, in all good conscience, advise Jim to give up his employment at the bank. The risks in trying to make a living at music were too great. A young man living alone in a rented room might be able to subsist by playing a church organ and teaching piano lessons, but in the present conditions he would not likely make enough money to rent a house and support his mother, much less a wife and family of his own some day. They talked about taking the examinations with the more prestigious Royal Toronto Conservatory, but again Hampshire could see no appreciable value in this. The Englishman's tact and sincere goodwill helped soften his bleak estimate of Jim's future in music. Perhaps it was his sympathetic concern for the young bank clerk that motivated him to take the same train to Arcola on December 22. On that journey, they continued to talk about music and about a life dedicated to the arts.

Jim arrived for Christmas, which he and Kate shared that year with an unmarried schoolteacher from Ontario, but he found it hard to be interested in the table conversation. Keith was home for the holidays, and though money was scarce the young men went out with their dates from the summer – to a movie one night at the Princess Theatre (to see *The Hot Heiress* starring Ona Munson and Walter Pidgeon) and to a New Year's Eve party at the church. And Jim watched Keith play hockey for the local team and score three goals one night against the team from Carlyle. After Keith went back to Winnipeg, the winter of 1932 stretched ahead, and Jim again took up the long story he had been planning in the fall, the story of the young man from a small Prairie town who becomes involved with a travelling singer. The story was titled 'The Wife of Peter Guy,' and some of the exercises Jim had worked up, particularly the landscape descriptions and the seasonal mood pieces, were fitting nicely into the narrative. And some of the secondary characters, based loosely on Arcola locals, seemed to him to have an authentic ring. As Peter Guy is discreetly ostracized for marrying a 'strumpet,' he turns to some of the marginal characters of the town for sympathy and advice – women based loosely on Marie Sturgess at the Arcola House Hotel and Dr Stone's aristocratic wife of foreign descent. The writing went slowly, usually only one or two paragraphs in an evening, but the paragraphs were accumulating into a novel-length fiction. Writing, however, was terribly lonely – his mother complained that he was sulky and secretive – and so when Dorothy Cornell suggested that they work on some duets for the music festival, Jim decided to return to the piano.

He was happy for an excuse to spend time with Dorothy. It wasn't just music they shared, but an ironic view of life and specifically of their fellow townsfolk. Mr Youngblud, they observed, was growing more rigid in his opinion about the hymns that were chosen and about the way they should be played; the church ladies, they agreed, spent as much time at their meetings discussing the minister's private life as they did the state of their missions abroad. And they were both eager to learn: Dorothy was continuing her education by taking correspondence courses in English and French from the University of Saskatchewan. But what especially made Jim and Dorothy accomplices that winter were the chilly relations with Frank Woodbury. Dorothy was becoming the competition in Arcola; some of Frank's former students were now taking lessons from her, and Jim had resisted all Frank's attempts to enlist him as a pupil again. In spite of effusive greetings on the street, they knew Frank resented their defections by the infrequent invitations that winter to the Orpheus Club. But Jim and Dorothy had decided to enter the music festival in April and so worked on a duet together for several months.

Dorothy still represented for Jim all that was desirable in a young woman: she was intelligent, sensitive, and suave, and her ironic sense of humour, so guarded, had a quality of intimacy. But her virginal demeanour and her parents' position in the town made her unattainable in the eyes of the young bank clerk with no background and few prospects. Jim was painfully conscious too of his diminutive physique: at five feet, seven inches, and 123 pounds he was as 'big' as he would ever be. Dorothy's powerful father, former hockey player and deputy sheriff for the judicial district, towered over him. Marriage, moreover, was not permitted for someone at his salary level at the Royal Bank; it was a question of security, for a married man under financial stress was viewed as more likely to steal. The longings, however, that Dorothy engendered in the nascent writer are experienced by those boys and young men in his fiction who want to be worthy in female eyes – characters like Sonny McAlpine in 'The Outlaw' and Whir of Gold, young Tom in 'Saturday Night,' or Paul Kirby in As for Me and My House. Dorothy and Jim played a Beethoven sonata in the music festival held again in Arcola in April; they only tied for second place, but there was a curious thrill for Jim in seeing their names reported in the newspaper as 'Dorothy and James Ross.'[20]

That winter Jim had a series of heavy colds, and Dr Stone ordered him to take up a sport to build up his physical stamina. Thinking of Keith, he considered tennis, but he was ashamed at how badly he played. So, instead, early in the spring of 1932, he rented a horse from William Gill, the town's burly blacksmith, and began riding in the country on Saturday afternoons, as he had done as a boy. It brought him close to the land again, which each year was growing drier and more depleted. The winter had been bitterly cold, but there had been little snow to put moisture back into the earth in the spring. As Jim rode about the country, he noticed that many of the houses and barns were falling into disrepair and left unpainted, and he imagined the kind of lives that people led, especially the women, in such lonely and hard-pressed environs. A vivid encounter he would never forget took place one day when he was temporarily lost. It was only April, but the sun was already hot and the fields dusty. He rode up to a farmhouse to ask for directions and found a woman on the back porch trying to nurse her baby. Before she could finish giving the young man directions, she started to cry and explained that there was almost no food in the house, that her husband had gone away. The pathos of this woman's situation, the desolation of the countryside, and his inability to help her would always be part of what the Great Depression meant for Sinclair Ross.

He would have more opportunities that year to see first-hand the effect of the Depression and the dry years on the country. In the fall of 1931, a young missionary pastor named Forbes Murray had come to Arcola to take over Knox Presbyterian Church and its charges. Although the Presbyterian congregation had been greatly reduced by union in 1925, the church still conducted a vital ministry in the farm country, where services in good weather were usually held every second Sunday in the local schoolhouse. Murray needed someone to travel with him and play the piano (or organ if one was available), and Jim, accordingly, would go with him on Sunday afternoons – north to Fine View school, near the Moose Mountains, or west to the Gap View school. A warm friendship developed between the two young men. Forbes Murray was regarded as handsome and was certainly outgoing by nature, and he immediately became a favourite in Arcola. Within a month of his arrival in late October 1931 he gave the Remembrance Day service address at the memorial and took part in the town's St George's Dramatic Society presentation of *Tea Toper Tavern*.[21] Murray had none of the reserve or studiousness associated with many ministers at that time and is remembered instead, during his brief stay in Arcola, as a young man who liked to enjoy himself. Kate and other women in the town liked to hear him preach, and the Presbyterian church, which held services Sunday morning in the Vrooman law office on Main Street, showed signs of reviving.

To Jim, the schoolhouses where he and Murray conducted the services were lonely and remote places, but they were not unfriendly in his eyes. He knew such places from his childhood, and from the makeshift services he had attended himself at Wild Rose and at the Rolling Prairie school. The great difference was the diminishment in numbers and spirits in the congregations. At the most ten or twelve would be present, the stalwart remains of communities being devastated by the drought. But the farm people dressed formally in their suits and best dresses, clothing that had been worn for several seasons, and their quiet determination to continue on the land would one day inspire the best of Jim's fiction. The services at Partridge Hill schoolhouse in *As for Me and My House* are a fairly direct rendering of Jim's experiences with Forbes Murray that summer. In one of his paintings, Philip Bentley renders the country '[a]lmost a lunar landscape' (105), but that barren landscape, says Mrs Bentley, heightens the significance of the human presence that persists: 'Five years in succession now they've been blown out, dried out, hailed out ... [yet] in the face of so blind and uncaring a universe they were trying to assert themselves, to insist upon their own meaning and importance' (26). Murray, too, was awed by the resolve of these country people; he wanted to help them as individuals and friends, and he felt that praying for rain from the pulpit was almost an insult to their dignity and intelligence. Instead, he spoke somewhat sheepishly of God's will and humanity's limited understanding.

During the summer of 1932, Jim found himself falling in love with Forbes Murray. It was the first time he had become emotionally committed to another man, a feeling very different from his friendship for Keith Clarke. All week he would anticipate the long drive to the schoolhouse on Sunday afternoon when he and Forbes would be alone together, and then dinner with Kate when they got back to 'Sans Souci.' For three weeks of that summer, Forbes was in Flin Flon, Manitoba, visiting his parents, and Jim experienced the agony of being physically apart from someone he loved. 'It was hell,'[22] he vividly remembered more than sixty years later. When he played hymns at the school and other pieces at home, he tried to show Forbes through his music how he cared about him, and finally one day summoned up the courage to tell him of his feelings. But Forbes could not respond. It was not in his nature, he said; however, he did not push Jim aside in disgust, and they talked openly and easily about their friendship. In fact, Forbes was also falling in love – with Isabel Gill, the eighteen-year-old daughter of the blacksmith. So when Jim picked up his horse on Saturday afternoons, he would often see his rival. Jim liked Isabel too – for her energetic brashness, her spirited good nature – and he found that being with Isabel and Forbes replicated something of that curious pleasure he felt with Dorothy and Keith.

The sexual confusion that Jim was experiencing that summer would lie at the heart of his best fiction. Calvinist assumptions about character and destiny were still strong in the religious atmosphere of small Prairie towns, but their messages of guilt and innate depravity were a legacy which the young man could not accept.[23] His reading and his observations of behaviour around him (that of his male friends like Keith Clarke, Forbes Murray, and especially Frank Woodbury) made him think that not just character but circumstances also made you what you were – that the rigid, codified expressions of gender in the little farm towns of his growing up were an aspect of survival in a harsh country. He had known for a long time that he had feelings that were regarded as both 'normal' and 'queer,' and, from reading Freud, he wondered if his strong feelings for Forbes Murray, a self-confident leader, involved the absence of a father when he was growing up.[24] Emotionally, his life was a 'tough, deep-rooted tangle,'[25] but he would eventually come to think that his failure to achieve a firm sense of self and his resistance to those models of identity provided by little rural towns would be the wellsprings of his art.

Hot dry winds blew all that summer of 1932, and the skies again were dark with moving topsoil. The number of unemployed mounted and there was no work for young people who were finishing school. Keith Clarke was home again helping his father at the grocery store. (This promising young man's future seemed to lose momentum as the Depression worsened, and except for a position with a life insurance office in Arcola, he made no career for himself. He joined the RCAF in 1938 and was the first Second World War casualty from Arcola.)[26] The townspeople increased their efforts to assist those in need. At the United Church, Rev. Bert Howard had organized a men's club to help with the relief work, an activity which served to distract people from some of the bleak realities of everyday life. For Howard there was not only the grinding burden of the drought and Depression, but at home he was forced to watch the cruel advance of his wife's illness. She spent several weeks that summer at a hospital in Winnipeg and seemed to improve, but when she was brought home to Arcola, she grew worse again. The Men's Association held suppers, concerts, and dramatic events, raising money for relief projects and bringing a little fun into the lives of the participants. Some events drew as many as three hundred people. Forbes Murray joined in these activities, engaged more in the social life of Arcola than in ministering to its spiritual needs.

The only distraction for Jim and Kate that summer was a visit from Stuart and his new wife. Stuart had eventually left Wild Rose and gone to the United States, where he found work at General Motors in Detroit. He wanted his mother and brother to meet his second wife. The latter practised Christian Science, a relatively new American religion and a system of therapy for which Kate had only contempt. The visit wasn't very comfortable, for Stuart remained one of his mother's 'monsters,' a designation that had once included Pete Ross and his sister in Seattle, but Kate managed to control herself and the visit was at least civil. Stuart's wife seemed very religious indeed, although she did have a passion for playing golf. On the weekend, they all took the train to visit Effie and family at Indian Head, and Jim had an afternoon by himself at nearby Lake Katepwa in the Qu'Appelle River Valley, where he could watch young people enjoying themselves at the little beach.

Jim spent more time on his novel manuscript and found life with his mother increasingly difficult. Her domineering manner and her possessiveness were growing harder to bear. She made fun of his attempts to be an author: 'So the little fool thinks he can write,' she sneered on one occasion, when she was particularly irritated by her son's sullen mood.[27] He would never forget his vulnerability and the seemingly unwarranted cruelty in that taunt. Having failed to make any mark as a painter or musician, he kept his manuscript pages hidden as best he could and often took them with him to work, to preserve their secrecy. Yet the need to show them to someone, to get an opinion, was strong, and late that summer he mailed a story and some poems to his widely published uncle in England. He wanted his uncle's firm judgment and also asked him if he thought he should enrol by correspondence in a writing school. He enclosed a watercolour for his Aunt Constance. Perhaps if his uncle approved of his efforts, his mother would be more reasonable.

While Kate chided her son at home, sometimes mercilessly, in public she boasted of his attempts to be a writer. That year she had befriended the postmaster, Ernest Thompson, and his wife, and in response to their curiosity about her son's writing, she forced Jim to show the Thompsons a story he had written. Thompson was polite but confessed he didn't think the story had much chance of being published. Because it was a farm story, possibly an early version of 'September Snow,' Jim decided to send it to a newspaper in Winnipeg. Thompson knew the story had gone out and watched with interest to see if it was accepted. When Jim received the rejected manuscript, the envelope had already been opened by the postmaster, who next day said he was sorry about the disappointing news. Apparently there was no privacy anywhere.

At the same time, Jim craved an audience, and he decided to show his writing to an interested contemporary. Tom McLellan was a rancher skilful with words (a local journalist and wit, he was also the district licensed auctioneer), and Jim showed him the rejected farm story, some sketches, and anecdotal bits. Tom's enthusiasm prompted Jim to show him the novel he was working on, and he asked if Tom recognized any of the local people in fictional dress, particularly Dr Stone's wife, whom he did not know personally but whose unlikely presence in Arcola stirred his imagination. He also showed Tom the unusual sketch he had done of a woman's thoughts the night before she was to be married. Many years later, Tom McLellan wrote down his recollections of Jim in Arcola, which give us a glimpse of how he was viewed by other young people in the town:

> Jim was a strange acting young man who took no part in any sport or social event. He was a loner and had few if any close friends. I often ran into him sitting on

some hillside, in my pasture, writing script for what he intended to have published in book form some day. I read much of his writings and, to me, they were often mixed up and confused. His Mother was a friend of my Mothers [sic] ... To me she seemed to be a very determined person and was very proud of her son Jimmie. It is my opinion that it was she who urged Jim to become an author ... Jim was brought up in some town near P[rince] A[lbert] Sask. and knew little about nature or wild life that he saw in my pasture. He looked upon the Moose Hills as a desert and often wondered why I pastured my cattle on such barren land. He was hard to converse with but always insisted on me reading his script. I do not know where he went after leaving Arcola but was much surprised when 'In This My House' was published. To me it seemed impossible for Jim Ross to publish such a book. There was certainly nothing brilliant about him. Early in the mornings he would take a lunch with him and walk five miles to the Moose Hills and spend the entire day sitting on some hillside day dreaming and trying to put his dreams on paper. At dusk you would see Jim wending his way slowly homeward. To me, he was a strange young man at a stranger job. I must have been mistaken because he has become a noted author of novels. In spite of the facts I still believe that Jim Ross's books were more edited by his Mother than he.[28]

McLellan's insensitive commentary reveals how misfit and lonely Jim was in small towns, and how completely misunderstood as a young artist. There were others in the town who, sixty years later, would not remember Jimmy Ross at all, though his mother's presence remained vividly etched in local memory.

The tension that had been building between mother and son was relieved at the end of 1932 when Kate decided to make a trip to England to see her brother, now Sir John Foster Fraser. Kate had come to Canada in approximately 1892, so that it had been about forty years since she had seen her brother, and for most of that time they had not been in communication with each other. But after Kate had seen his picture in the newspaper when living at Nels Forfang's, she had sent him a letter to acknowledge his accomplishments, and he, in turn, remembered his sister every year with a birthday cheque for £25 (worth about $125 Canadian at that time) and another £25 at Christmas. Kate and Jim began to count on those cheques as part of their annual income and budgeted accordingly. Kate had decided she would go to Edinburgh first, stay at an inexpensive hotel for a time, and then visit her brother and his wife in Buckinghamshire before leaving. But when she wrote to him of her plans, he sent a peremptory message and a cheque saying he would meet her ship at Southampton and she should count on spending Christmas and at least the month of January at his place, and see Edinburgh later. Jim encouraged his mother to make the trip by giving her the $200 he had been able to save in the last two years. But many years later, Jim would still remember how anxious she was before leaving. In 'Just Wind and Horses,' he described her as frightened of the prospect of appearing in English society: "'I haven't the right clothes – Yes, but I don't know what to buy ... And how to behave with people like that – it's easy for you to talk, you don't understand'" (88).

But eventually she rose to the occasion and made the most of it before her departure. The people of small Saskatchewan towns were always somewhat in awe of Kate because of her titled brother and in Arcola there was considerable excitement as the time of her leaving approached. The November 23 issue of the *Moose Mountain Star-Standard* describes an evening entertainment 'honouring Mrs Kate Ross, prior to her departure for England ... [where] she will be the guest of her brother and sister-in-law, Sir John and Lady Foster Fraser.' Kate was entertained by Arcola society, not just the ladies of the United Church. The hostess for the evening was (in the formal reporting of the time that omitted women's first names) Mrs John Hopper, whose husband owned the town's hardware and furniture store. Mrs Hopper was active in the affairs of the Anglican Church and regent of the IODE. Mrs J. Murison, the wife of the local veterinarian, presented Kate with a Jaeger travelling rug.[29] Mrs Murison saw herself as the town's intellectual woman; she had recently become a Christian Scientist and expounded her exorbitant beliefs with no small amount of pride and superiority. (Kate felt herself superior to this high-strung woman, and when Mrs Murison, seeing Kate one day with a cold, had said she would pray for her recovery, Kate reported to Jim, 'What insolence!') But at the farewell gathering, Kate indeed felt honoured and well treated and enjoyed herself immensely. She left Arcola on November 28, staying for a few days with Effie at Indian Head, then heading on to Montreal, from where she sailed to England December 8th on the SS *Duchess of Richmond*. She would be gone until March.

Jim was living on his own for the first time in his life, and it did open up the world a little. At first, he revelled in the prospect of the unstructured days ahead, the freedom to come and go at will, and so he was surprised to find that he was as much keeping to a routine as if his mother were still at home – the working day at the bank, an hour or more at the piano in the evening, and a couple of hours at the novel. Occasionally he would have a dinner at the Chinese cafe; otherwise, he fixed himself a spartan meal, a pork chop and a potato, or a box of macaroni and cheese. His mother had left the cold pantry well stocked with desserts. On the weekends, he tried to take advantage of his mother's absence and invited friends to the house. One Saturday after a dance, he persuaded Cal Ingram to stay the night; but Ingram remembered from that visit how very awkward Jim remained socially, how he seemed unable to relax and mix easily with the young people of the town.

Emotionally, Jim was feeling bereft by the surprise departure of Forbes Murray. With neither strong spiritual convictions nor a gift of oratory, Forbes resigned when the season of country services came to a close that fall, ending his ministry after just one year. In November he joined the RCMP and moved to Regina. On his frequent trips back to Arcola, he came, not to see Jim, but to continue his courtship of Isabel Gill, whom he would eventually marry in 1939. Jim fell back on his friendship with Keith Clarke, who was working at the family store that winter, but who was otherwise at loose ends, coaching a softball team and on one occasion driving the CGIT (Canadian Girls in Training), led by Frank Woodbury's wife, to a wiener roast and picnic in the Moose Mountains. And Tom McLellan would come to town and stay over with Jim. In Jim's eyes, Tom had 'a cowboy's rough manners,'[30] but he was interested in writing, had little regard for social conventions, and, like Jim, had a dry sense of humour. Jim continued to share with him the progress of his novel.

After Christmas (spent with the Pattersons), Jim began receiving lengthy letters from his mother, written almost daily, giving the details of her adventures abroad and admonishing him to remember the chores and rituals to be performed around the house. But the letter he received that winter that he would always keep was one from his fabled uncle in England, containing praise, advice, and a cautious but fatherly offer of assistance. It also contains a delightful portrait of his mother abroad:[31]

Jan 8th, 1933

My dear Jimmie
You will have heard from your mother how she is getting on in the old country. My wife and I were very glad to have her and so far she has been with us just over three weeks. Soon she is going to London to stay at some small comfortable hotel and toddle round on her own, before going to Edinburgh to revisit places she knew as a child and I think her plans are to sail from Glasgow for Canada on March 4th. Unfortunately before Christmas I was bowled over with influenza and a touch of bronchitis so I have not been able to give her as much attention as I would have liked – we've been down here alone for a few days getting some sunshine and sea air. Forty-five years is a long time since I saw your mother. I didn't expect to recognize her and yet when we met I knew her by her eyes. She has certainly led a brave life and she is so frank and cheerful that I am filled with admiration. Of course her life and outlook has been circumscribed by her long

years in Saskatchewan. It could not be otherwise. Everything, even in London, is judged by the ways of Arcola, the size of the hotel at Regina and the thickness of the carpet in the Hudson's Bay stores at Winnipeg! She is terribly loyal, amusingly so at times. This is all a new world to her, but everybody she meets she has to tell about the way things are done in Arcola and about 'my Jimmie.' I've chaffingly told her that the folk she talks to don't really care a damn about Arcola and that other mothers have sons of their own of whom they think a heap – and this she thinks is criticism. To me she is a very loveable and interesting study, but mentally there is a great and impenetrable space between us – for my life has been spent in the world and hers has been spent in Saskatchewan. I'm afraid she must have bored the people in Arcola – Arcola has a bigger bank than we have in the village of Princes Risborough – with talk about her brother Jack. I chaffingly tell her she is a real snob, pestering people about her titled relatives. When she gets home and she starts talking about this country you must restrain her wearying people. My experience of untravelled western Canadians is that they really do not want to know that there is anything better on earth than they have. Years ago when your uncle Theodore was here he did an intelligent round of both England and Scotland. Before he returned to Prince Albert I casually observed he would have a lot to tell his pals about London. He replied 'No, I've got to live with them and I don't want to make myself unpopular and be told I'm a liar because I say London is more interesting than Winnipeg. They won't and can't believe it.' And I can't stop your mother talking – as she threatens to talk – about Constance and myself. Personally I hate that kind of adulation and I want my sister to be extremely happy with the good and genial souls of Arcola.

I ought to have written you long ago acknowledging some manuscript of a story and some short poems. First let me say have nothing to do with any institute which in return for dollars will teach you to become a novelist or poet. These concerns are mostly fraudulent, tickling the vanity of people with qualified praise in order to get their money. There is only one school, natural aptitude, the careful study of other people's work and keeping at it. Quite freely let me say – and I'm not given to gush – you have not only the artistic temperament but have something near genius. I gathered from your mother about your music and heard that your favorite composer was Chopin. Good! The landscape you sent your aunt Constance is an amazing piece of work for one who has, I suppose, never been in touch with the great artists. The story you sent me has real power– a little sombre in treatment, but that is your present nature. I'm told the *Atlantic Monthly* – certainly the best story magazine in the English-speaking world – is holding a story of yours. Splendid. Well Jimmie you've got it in you – and I'm an old and experienced bird in the game of writing for the public. Something must be done to get you away from the cramp of Arcola – notwithstanding I've been told I'll meet my intellectual superiors there!! Nothing however must be done rashly, because I know your financial situation and what a good son you have been to your mother. What a great and delightful and amusing story there is to be written about Arcola – as I've gathered from asides in conversation – but you have got your face so slap up against the picture you can't see it. If you could live for a year in Montreal, Toronto, or Ottawa you'd get perspective then see it. I could now map you out a real seller about the city of Arcola; but I don't know the background. Tell me what is in your mind that you have ambition to do – and we will see if some ropes can be pulled. I've not a shilling in the world I have not earned, but I think I could help you a bit if you need funds. And keep on reading and be 'a sedulous ape' as R.L. Stevenson was when he taught himself writing. Read some artistic writers – Henry [Harland] (now forgotten); read his 'Cardinal's Snuff Box'; Maurice [Heroletts's] 'Little Novels of Italy' and give yourself a good dose of Leonard Merrick's novels – all artists in writing as well as story tellers. All luck to you.

John Foster Fraser

As Jim came to view things, brother and sister were a match for each other when it came to boasting of their adventures. John had made considerable capital from his three-year trip around the world on a bicycle, with stories 'about being rotten-egged in China and fording rivers with his bicycle on his back.'[32] Kate, in turn, had regaled, and apparently sometimes wearied, her English listeners with stories of homesteading the northern prairie – temperatures sixty below zero, horses bleeding from the nose, tying a rope around her waist to get back from the barn during a blizzard, delivering a baby that came three months ahead of time. Kate must have 'rattled on,' Jim decided, but in spite of her brother's criticisms, she had a wonderful time and came back to Arcola full of her adventures abroad, full of 'titled bigwigs' who had never heard of Saskatchewan but who were eager to hear her stories once she got started. Jim knew there was much exaggeration involved, but Kate had brought back a photograph that attested to the substance of some of her stories – a picture taken at a New Year's Eve ball in London in which she appears at the head table, 'vivid but unperturbed in the glare of the flashes. Looking genial and pleased with herself, completely at ease, as if she had just finished a stint on the early days and was ready for another as soon as Constance gave her the nod.'[33]

Before Kate returned at the end of February, Jim had completed a first draft of 'The Wife of Peter Guy.' Tom McLellan would recognize more than the doctor's wife among the local dramatis personae, although the eponymous Peter and his wife were largely imagined characters. Jim was also busy in January and February preparing pieces for the third annual recital of the Orpheus Club held at Frank Woodbury's studio, Monday, February 20. Once again, among the participants were Dorothy Cornell, Carol Patterson, Dorothy Campbell, Frank, and his wife. And on Friday evening, February 24, Jim went to the United Church Men's Club supper and concert, where a short play by the Rev. Bert Howard was performed. It was titled 'An Irregular Meeting of the Depression Club,' featuring Keith Clarke, both Frank and his father, and W.F. Youngblud among its players, and the newspaper reported that it had been a long time since so much laughter had been created this way in Arcola. Some of the townspeople, however, questioned the propriety of this 'merriment.' The minister's wife had died four days before Christmas, not yet two months ago, and her husband was entertaining the town with a comedy he had written during her last days. Moreover, he was now openly courting the woman who had been their housekeeper during his wife's long sickness. It seemed that many things had happened while Kate was away: Keith got a position in town representing Manufacturer's Life Insurance; Boynton-Coffey was being transferred to a branch of the bank in Winnipeg, and there was a farewell social for him at the town hall with community singing, speeches, and card games. February saw one of the heaviest blizzards in living memory, with thirty-mile-an-hour winds and temperatures minus forty, and 'Aunty' Kerr had her hand mangled in an electric clothes wringer.[34] Kate was not the only one with news on her return; Jimmy too had stories to tell.

five

Winnipeg
1933–1938

Kate had only been back in Arcola for a week when Jim was informed by the bank that he was being transferred to Winnipeg. As he read the notice, Jim felt misgivings and simultaneously a sense of injury at being moved about against his will. He still liked Arcola. It was a substantial and safe little community, its citizens no better or worse than most, and he had come to play an agreeable if minor part in its daily affairs. Moreover, his emotional life was still bound up with his Arcola friends – Dorothy Cornell, Keith Clarke, Forbes Murray, Isabel Gill, even Frank Woodbury. Kate, by contrast, was ready to move on. Her individual friendships tended to follow a pattern of initial intense enthusiasm, an involvement leading to a crisis, and then disappointment or indifference. Her friendships had pretty much run their course in Arcola; she had reached the zenith of her popularity and social pre-eminence at the farewell party before her trip to Britain. She welcomed the opportunity now to live in a city.

Jim knew that his mother was ready to leave and that she was ambitious for him to advance himself in the bank. He also knew that she had discussed the situation with her brother. What he didn't know, then, was that his uncle had been in communication with Sir Herbert Holt, the head of the Royal Bank in Montreal, and arranged for Jim to be sent to the Portage Avenue branch in Winnipeg. Perhaps Fraser felt his nephew's artistic talents would never take root if he had no wider experience of life than small Prairie towns; perhaps he was simply placating his importunate sister. It was when a cheque arrived from Britain to help with moving costs that Jim was apprised of his uncle's part in the transfer.

The cost of moving, not subsidized by the bank, was an expense to be reckoned with, as was finding living quarters in the city. But stung by his mother's interference, he sent the money back to his uncle and turned instead to Joe

Ayles, the elderly caretaker at the bank, for assistance. Joe lived in a room that had been fixed up in the basement of the bank building. Illiterate, miserly, making his living from an assortment of menial jobs in the town, Joe had managed over the years to deposit something in the order of ten thousand dollars in his savings account, and his greatest pleasure during the week was to make another entry, however small, taking account of the interest, and discussing his slowly accumulating riches with the young teller. There was something of a bond between the two; Jim, who had read *Silas Marner* with sympathetic interest, understood how for this lonely old man money had become a substitute for human contacts. He was not a little surprised, however, when Joe was willing to loan him three hundred dollars to defray moving costs to Winnipeg, a debt he repaid with a bonus as soon as he had established himself in the city. He was spurred on to repay the loan by the visit of an unfriendly woman who claimed to be one of Joe's relations and who announced herself suspicious of the young man's intentions. Despite this unpleasantness, there was no small satisfaction for Jim in returning his uncle's money untouched and listening to his mother rage on in her inconsistent way about his foolish independence.

Jim and Kate made the move to Winnipeg in April 1933, Jim going ahead to find a place to live before he had to report for work on April 11th. Fortunately, Keith Clarke was in the city for two weeks, writing the actuarial exams he had been studying for during the winter months, and they stayed together at the YMCA. It made the break from Arcola a little easier. Jim was also fortunate to find a house at 347 Arnold Street, which was within walking distance of downtown; it accommodated their furnishings nicely, including the piano, which had been shipped by boxcar from Saskatchewan. In fine weather, Jim could make the walk to the bank and save bus fare. But the break with Dorothy was harder. For a while they wrote to each other, and Jim played with the idea of going back to Arcola for a visit, but by the time he did return, at some point in the late 1930s, Dorothy had married an older man, a widower with two children. Eventually she moved to Edmonton; she had no children of her own but was a much loved stepmother.[1]

In the 1930s, Winnipeg, with its population of more than a quarter million and its strong sense of being an imperial city, gateway to the West, was the dominant urban centre of the Prairies; railway lines converged here, and most western agricultural products flowed through the city. Winnipeg was also a manufacturing centre, with perhaps the country's most multi-ethnic labour force, particularly with workers from eastern Europe. A notoriously harsh physical climate – extremes of temperature, steady winds, and insect life – has always challenged its inhabitants, but for Jim it would be more than compensated for by the city's cultural life, particularly its love of music.

The Rosses knew no one in Winnipeg, and so the city was socially unmediated territory to explore. The only friend Jim made during the first months in the city was a young man named Roy Reynolds, who was a teller at Portage Avenue and broke him into the routine at the bank. Jim brought him home for dinner more than once, which proved pleasant because Kate liked to entertain young men and serve them her favourite desserts. Although Reynolds did not have literary or artistic interests, he was a good-natured and reliable companion, and he frequently took the Rosses for drives in his automobile. (His sudden and untimely death a few years later from uraemic poisoning shocked his co-workers at the bank.) Jim also made friends with another young man at the bank, an accountant by the name of Leroy MacPherson. ' Mac' was also genial, unmarried, and enjoyed home-cooked meals when he was invited to the Rosses. Like Reynolds, MacPherson had no particular interest in the arts, and the friendship consisted chiefly of bank gossip and the occasional movie. But such friendships were, and would always remain, important to Jim, who respected, and felt just as comfortable with, working people as with those of stellar ambition and talent. His personal sense of integrity and worth was grounded as much in everyday jobs well done as in extraordinary achievements.

New in Winnipeg, Jim spent most of his time on writing when not at the bank. He set aside the 'Peter Guy' manuscript and turned his attention to short stories, polishing a little sketch, titled 'Circus in Town,' which he had drafted in Arcola and which drew on childhood memories stretching back to Wild Rose. 'Circus in Town' tells of an eleven-year-old girl whose quarrelling parents make it impossible for her to attend the circus, and of her subsequent fantasy in the barn loft of being there nonetheless, resplendent in purple tights and riding a rejuvenated and bedizened farm horse. It is a poignant and exquisitely crafted vignette of youthful longing and the transforming power of the imagination, but trying to find a buyer for the story was for the author a repetition of his experience with 'The Call of the Canvas.' That first summer in Winnipeg, he sent the story to *Liberty* magazine in the United States, and when it was returned, he again tried *Maclean's* and *Saturday Night* in Canada. All the editors deemed it too slight, too negligible in terms of plot, to interest their readers.

Seeing Jim at his desk every evening, Kate reported to her new acquaintances that her son was learning to be a writer. Although Jim always cringed to hear his mother's boasting, her talk this time led to an important connection. One of his mother's friends arranged that he should meet Will Conyers, a young man who also had aspirations to be a writer. Will was married and had two small children, and he invited the shy bank teller to have dinner and meet his family in a house in the suburbs of the city. Jim found the Conyers family living communally in a large house with four other young families, where they practised nudism, yogic exercises, a vegetarian diet, and other avant-garde ideas that had become fashionable in North America in the 1920s. Jim went several times to the house that autumn: the talk was always good, the young couples were attractive, and there was an atmosphere of daring and sexual excitement in the air. At their informal gatherings with guests, the communards were always clothed, but little boys would brag about the size of their fathers' penises (for they had 'seen'), and adults told comic anecdotes about the shocking effect their behaviour and presence had in the neighbourhood.

But more important to Jim's future as a writer were Will Conyers's literary connections. He belonged to an informal study group of amateur philosophers and would-be writers who met downtown every other Friday evening and called themselves the Phoenix Club. Originally a men's group that first met in 1932 at the Grange Hotel and that identified itself as 'The Round Table Club of Philosophers,' the Phoenix Club gradually admitted women, and as membership and subject interests grew, the meeting place was shifted to private club rooms off a restaurant on the third floor of the Montgomery Building at 215 Portage Avenue near Main.[2] The founder of the club was Ernest Court, a middle-aged Englishman who ran a small private hospital, and who had a reasonably wide knowledge of the literary world. Court wrote fiction but had little success in placing his work. His chief role was to encourage others in whatever way he could.[3] The members of the writers' group, mostly prose writers, would read stories, essays, or excerpts of longer works aloud, and the others would offer praise or suggest improvements. The atmosphere was low-key and friendly – there were no really accomplished authors in the club – and Jim, though by nature not a joiner, fell easily into the Friday night routine. The only published writer in the group when Jim started attending was Nellie Anderson, a stout, self-assured woman, who had placed a piece on dieting in *Chatelaine*. Later Tora Talgoy, whose father, Magnus, was editor of the Norwegian newspaper *Norrona*, would place some of her sketches with the *Winnipeg Tribune*. Harriet Duff-Smith was a presence at these gatherings. She had little talent herself but was the daughter of a wealthy Winnipeg couple and would give lavish Christmas parties for the club at her parents' home.[4] As Jim did not like the high, thin sound of his own voice, Harriet would read his stories to the group for discussion.

In the winter of 1933–4, Jim revised a story he had written about the struggles of a farm woman, Hatty Glenn, and brought it to one of the Friday night meetings. When Ernest Court heard the story read, he recognized its peculiar power, the intensity of its language, and something unique in its vision. Here was a piece of writing drawn resolutely and unadorned from the harsh, mundane experiences of Prairie life. Perhaps, he thought, it was both exotic and authentic enough to attract the notice of a non–North American readership. He offered to send it, on Jim's behalf, to *Nash's–Pall Mall Magazine* in England, a journal he subscribed to himself, which at that time was running a short-story contest for previously unpublished writers. Many years later, the author would reflect gratefully on the older man's enthusiasm and generosity, for Court sent the manuscript off at his own expense. But the mentor's gesture was repaid handsomely: 'No Other Way' won third prize in the competition, and the twenty-six-year-old author received a bank draft for twenty pounds, the equivalent in 1934 of approximately one hundred Canadian dollars, more than a month's wages. For the rest of his life, Sinclair Ross would credit Ernest Court as his first (and only) mentor and benefactor.

The story appeared in the October 1934 issue of *Nash's–Pall Mall Magazine*,[5] and one of the Winnipeg newspapers ran a photograph of the young author, with a caption stating that there had been over eight thousand entries in the competition. The encouragement was enormous, especially given the fact that the stories had been judged by three prominent literary figures: Somerset Maugham, Desmond MacCarthy, and Rebecca West.[6] In a biographical notice accompanying the story, the author wrote that he had given up on two novels that were not published, and that now he was working on short stories 'hoping gradually to build up a better technique without the cramping grind that writing a novel after office hours demands.' For the first time, with Ernest Court's approval, Jim had used the name 'Sinclair' to identify himself as an author, a name from his father's side of the family. Plain 'James Ross' had brought him no success with earlier submissions. 'Sinclair' was more fashionably literary perhaps, even in North America, where Sinclair Lewis was the best-selling American author in the 1920s and 1930s, and Upton Sinclair was long established as one of the most radical voices in American fiction. In 1934, after the success of 'No Other Way,' it seemed that the commercial possibilities for a fledgling writer were more likely in short fiction than in novels, and for the next five years Jim spent his writing time learning and perfecting the art of the short story. But the success of his first published story would prove an anomaly – it would be the only piece he wrote during his life that would win a significant prize and the only piece for which he was paid so high a price as one hundred dollars.

'No Other Way'[7] evinces the struggle for craft. It opens with an elaborate periodic sentence that is awkward to read and, with alliteration and personification, announces literariness. Stock phrases appear throughout the text: 'her eyes narrowed shrewdly'; she cut turnips 'with feverish haste'; 'the still, frosty air.' However, more striking than convention is the frequent freshness and originality of expression that emerges from the author's close engagement with the western setting and the psychology of the central character. There is the description of Hatty Glenn's hands, 'wrinkled and red, like forked carrots grown in lumpy soil'; her panic as she enters a party in 'a smother of faces and dresses'; and her self-conscious embarrassment at an untidy wisp of hair that 'lay like a hot bristle on her neck.' In this first published story, the reader can already recognize certain stylistic features that will become trademarks of Sinclair Ross's writing. The language of the story is heavily accented by short, monosyllabic words – words such as 'wince,' 'cringe,' 'glare,' and 'steel,' drawn from the Anglo-Saxon part of the English lexicon and evoking the harsh and repressive austerity of the subject matter. Similarly there is a syntactic matrix of simple sentences, sentence fragments, and elliptical dashes, whose brevity are the stylistic measure of the high-strung subjects. Significantly these short structures use non-finite verbs, verbs whose action is ongoing or incomplete ('There was snow in the wind'; '... she could never go through with it'; 'Greedy old brutes – pulling out the sheaves and trampling them –') extending the action to an unchanging, often unrelenting, condition. And in 'No Other Way,' we are introduced with sympathy to the psychology of the unattractive and unloved woman, the subject of much of Ross's strongest work.

There is another pattern in this story of a more general kind that repeats itself in much of Ross's fiction. As Karen Bishop has observed, Ross's writing focuses intently on the interplay of destructive and creative elements, where frequently in a character's experience of either happiness or suffering there is a sudden reversal or insight that brings a one-sided experience of life to an end.[8] In 'No Other Way,' Hatty Glenn feels so beaten down in her relationship to her husband that she decides to commit suicide by throwing herself down a well. (Perhaps in this detail Jim was remembering the grisly and often told story of Mrs Soles in Wild Rose, who fell into the well on her own property, broke her neck, and drowned.)[9] But at the last moment, the cows get out of their yard and start eating the turnips, and with a sudden upsurge, Hatty's creative instinct to save the crop takes hold and she chases after the cows with her broom. The story seems to say that the downward course of Hatty's life will be similarly reversed in the future by such gestures of defiance and by practical necessities, and neither happiness nor misery will wholly prevail, neither tragedy nor comedy, but a domesticated blending of the two. With a few exceptions, most notably 'The Painted Door' and 'Jug and Bottle,' this pattern dominates in Ross's short fiction.

Buoyed by the international success of 'No Other Way' and by the praise of his peers in the Winnipeg writing circle, Jim began to dream again of a life outside of the bank, this time of a career as a writer, and he resumed his efforts to be published in the high-paying magazines in the United States. In the spring of 1934, he started mailing out a story he first drafted after arriving in Winnipeg; it told the all too familiar tale of a family's hopes for the future pinned on a wheat crop and the annihilation of those hopes by a brief but devastating hailstorm. It was titled simply 'A Field of Wheat' and was set somewhere on the Great Plains, without geographical or political references. In all of his western fiction until *The Well* (1958), Jim would omit specific local markers with the hope of appealing to as wide an audience as possible. He sent the story first to the *Atlantic Monthly*, receiving a handwritten note from an editor who said he liked the story, but that they only used one or two stories a month and sometimes a thousand were submitted. It was a discouraging reply,[10] although years later Jim would single out that note as the most encouraging one he ever received from an American magazine. He then sent the story to the *New Yorker*. It came back quickly with that familiar American verdict – that the story was too short on plot – and after three more rejections, he decided to put it aside. Harriet, however, had read the story out to the writers' group, and when Jim admitted his disappointed ambitions, Ernest Court, again excited by the vividness of the style, suggested that he try the Canadian academic journal *Queen's Quarterly*, which published fiction and verse of high quality. The story was accepted, and for the next seventeen years, all but three of the stories published by Sinclair Ross would appear first in the pages of *Queen's Quarterly*.

Unfortunately, almost nothing of the author's correspondence with the editors of the journal in the 1930s has survived. The chairman of the editorial board in the mid-1930s was Alexander Macphail, but Jim wrote chiefly to his brother, Sir Andrew Macphail, whose letters (two of which are extant) he would later describe as genial but seldom instructive. Sir Andrew Macphail (1864–1938), a native of Prince Edward Island, taught medicine at McGill, but he was also a man of letters, a fiction writer and an essayist of some distinction, perhaps best known for his posthumous *The Master's Wife* (1939), a family narrative which was reprinted for a time in the New Canadian Library. His writings, especially his biographical studies in *Essays in Puritanism* (1905), are characterized by a lively appreciation of the Puritan spirit – the rugged individualism, self-reliance, and vision of progress he saw inherent in men of consequence – and also by a compressed, at times epigrammatic, prose style. One expects that this man of letters, with his rural background, warmed to something of the same mood and manner in the stories by Sinclair Ross. Certainly, after reading some of his work, he urged Jim to send more stories to *Queen's Quarterly*.[11] In a letter of 10 February 1935, he said he was eager to read the novel Jim was working on. He also recommended that Jim read an article on the short story in the *Quarterly Review* (London), and he praised a piece of short fiction in the most recent number of *Queen's Quarterly* titled 'As the Tree Falls,' by Hal B. Kirkland, 'written by a farm labourer' and 'precisely like yours.'[12] In the meantime, according to the author, Alexander Macphail only once insisted on an editorial revision, urging a name change for a character in a story, otherwise commending his work.

Certainly, there was much to commend in 'A Field of Wheat.'[13] This story had its germ, as many would, in a momentary experience that etched itself indelibly on the author's imagination. While walking in River Park in Winnipeg after a brief rainstorm, he saw in the sky a magnificent formation of clouds, the mirage of a mountain landscape, all pinks and golds, suspended in the heavens. He was filled with the longing to share this experience with someone else, someone like Dorothy Cornell or Keith Clarke. In changing winds and light, the arrangement quickly broke up, but the intense urge to describe such beauty remained. It was later that he learned that the farms to the north of the city had been hailed out, recalling in turn the effects of the devastating hailstorm he had witnessed first-hand in Arcola. The language of the story is charged with the mystery of such deadly loveliness. One of the plainest of Ross's stories in terms of plot – a straightforward description of a summer hailstorm that destroys a fine crop of wheat and postpones a family's hopes for another year – 'A Field of Wheat' contains writing of exquisite power, documenting with exactness the often brutal struggles of farm life, but conveying simultaneously a rich drama of the imagination. There is the vivid description of the hail:

> ... a sharp, crunching blow on the roof, its sound abruptly dead, sickening, like a weapon that has sunk deep into flesh ... Again the blow came; then swiftly a stuttered dozen of them.

These are images and sounds of battle, and bring into focus the language of struggle and physical violence that saturates the whole text and defines the lives of its subjects – words like 'blade,' 'sheath,' 'choke,' 'gash,' 'split,' 'whip,' 'pommel,' 'pinioned,' 'bitten,' 'crushed,' 'clawed,' 'beaten.'

But 'A Field of Wheat' is at the same time a story about beauty, as the opening sentence announces in a lush description of the wheat field: '... a still, heat-hushed mile of it, undulating into a shimmer of summer-colts and crushed horizon blue.' The phrase 'summer-colts' is used, like 'sun-dogs' in winter, to describe a certain effect of sunlight over a prairie field; and 'crushed' collocates with velvet to evoke something infinitely tender in the early summer landscape. Another magnificent moment in the story is the surreal image of the landscape 'slipping down the neck of a funnel' as the light disappears with the approaching storm. For it is beauty finally which restores and sustains the quarrelling, beaten family. The wife's rage at her plight is curtailed and chastened by the sight of her husband weeping against the neck of his horse, but her ability to start over again comes at that mysterious, pentecostal moment when the sun illumines the storm clouds on the horizon, transforming them into a vision of unearthly splendour that fuses together the 'allure' of the wheat field with the husband who 'breasted the sun.' She hurries into the house to make a 'good supper,' to take up the struggle once again, and as Ken Mitchell has observed, a story drenched with pathos becomes a parable of existential hope.[14]

'A Field of Wheat' was published in the spring 1935 issue of *Queen's Quarterly*. The fledgling author was keeping good literary company: in that issue there was a poem by E.J. Pratt and a humorous essay on Mark Twain's Canadian connections written by Stephen Leacock. Just before 'A Field of Wheat' appeared in print, it was awarded ten dollars as second prize in a writing contest sponsored by the Winnipeg branch of the IODE, and later that same year it was selected for inclusion in the Clark, Irwin anthology *A Miscellany of Tales and Essays*. So began the frequent reprinting and anthologizing of Sinclair Ross stories. Although Jim only received twenty-three dollars from *Queen's Quarterly* for 'A Field of Wheat,' the journal's prestige and the editor's laudatory letter of acceptance meant a great deal to the young writer. Kate, however, was less easily impressed. Reading over Macphail's letter, she said to her son, 'It was nice of him to write that – even if he didn't mean it.'[15]

Macphail's suggestion to send more stories prompted Jim to look again at some of the pieces he had written earlier, and he decided to revise one he had first drafted in Abbey and that stretched back in time to his boyhood in the Rolling Prairie District. It was titled 'September Snow' and drew on memories of the hilly landscape around Forfang's farm and a specific instance of hurrying to finish the stooking before the onset of a blizzard. Unlike in 'A Field of Wheat,' beauty here overtly plays no annealing role. 'September Snow'[16] is the kind of story that forty years later Margaret Atwood would designate as typically Canadian – a story of hardship, striving, and bare survival. In fact, the story of the young farm couple, Will and Eleanor, includes the woman's death as she is giving birth, alone, during a blizzard. She is alone because her husband has spent the night trying to bring the cattle in out of the storm. The story ends in a series of positive strokes – the new day is warm and spring-like, the cattle file home on their own, and the baby is born alive – but alongside Eleanor's death these are mordant ironies. Again there is beauty in the language used initially to describe the farm scene – the 'smoky sheets' of rain that swept down from the hills, 'the thick swift flakes [of snow that] made a lace' in the light from the doorway – but this descriptive language does not cohere into a salvific pattern. At the story's close, Will is immobilized, not energized, by the sun-spangled snow, by an eerie absence of sound in the landscape, and, in the baby's crying, by 'the same plaintiveness and protest that had been in Eleanor's voice.' It would be much harder to describe this story as a parable of hope.

When published in the winter 1935–6 issue of *Queen's Quarterly*, 'September Snow' drew a curious response from Andrew Macphail: while praising the story by exclaiming that 'Kipling could not have done better,' he also wrote that the woman giving birth should be 'entitled to a certain secrecy. Those lines lack beauty.'[17] Jim did not know if he meant the story was prurient, or whether it would be more artistically effective if less was said about the fact of childbirth at the end.

There occurred an unforgettable event for Jim in the summer of 1935 – a visit from his uncle, Sir John Foster Fraser, and his wife, Lady Constance. From the time Jim was a small boy, Uncle John's career and person had a mythical dimension. Although Kate placed her brother's achievements in the context of a titled family stretching back for many generations, in fact John Fraser's story is more accurately characterized as an American-style tale of rags to riches. When he was still a boy, his father died, leaving the family with little means, and when he was in his early teens, his mother remarried and left for Canada with his younger siblings. He apprenticed first as a printer, and then trained as a journalist in Sheffield and Manchester. By 1892, at age twenty-four, he was working in London as a parliamentary reporter. But his big opportunity came in 1896 when he was offered the chance by a newspaper to make a trip around the world on a bicycle, accompanied by a photographer. The trip took 774 days, and the two men travelled across Europe, through Siberia and Manchuria (then closed to foreigners), and across the United States, sending articles and pictures back to England. According to Kate, there were thousands waiting in the rain to cheer the young traveller when he arrived back at St Pancras Church after covering more than nineteen thousand miles. The articles became a book, *Round the World on a Wheel* (1899), and Fraser, a celebrated lecturer, charged, according to his sister, a fifty-guinea fee per lecture. '"Ambitious," she would say ... "trust our Johnny – once he had his mind made up about what he wanted he let nothing stand in his way, absolutely nothing."'[18] He continued to travel and write, publishing more than twenty frequently reprinted volumes, mostly travel books about places as distant as the Balkans, Russia, the Middle East, and Argentina, but also highly popular books about contemporary politics. He had crossed Canada in 1904 for a book he titled *Canada As It Is* (1905), but there is no record of his having visited any members of his family at that time.

In 1935 Fraser was on a business tour in the United States, and from Minneapolis he and his wife made a side trip north to spend a long weekend in Winnipeg. They stayed two nights at the Royal Alexandra Hotel, at that time the best accommodation in the city. Kate had known some time in advance of her brother's forthcoming visit and occupied herself for several weeks house-cleaning, planning meals, polishing the silver. But the big day from the beginning was a strain and a disappointment for everyone. When Sir John and his wife stepped out of the taxi in their expensive and tasteful clothing, both Jim and his mother were overawed. And when the Frasers entered their home, mother and son felt how small and shabby the Arnold Street bungalow was. The Frasers were tired from their travels, and despite Kate's most ebullient efforts – recounting again her homesteading adventures – the conversation over lunch was formal and dispirited. Lady Constance, Sir John's second wife, was an attractive, pale blonde woman, very poised, and in her nephew's eyes 'very English.' She was, in fact, twenty-seven years younger than Sir John, who was by then sixty-seven, but to Jim she seemed more than her forty years in the summer of 1935.[19] She was cordial and without pretensions, but it was clear that she was not very impressed with Canada. There was no literary talk between uncle and nephew; in fact, no reference to their both being writers was made, as if one letter of advice was all that was appropriate on the subject. The issue of *Queen's Quarterly* in which 'A Field of Wheat' was handsomely printed remained on the shelf, unreferred to. For a few minutes, Jim was alone with his uncle, but the latter was very guarded with respect to the future. He felt that there was a war on the way and probably a long one, and one would have to wait and see how things fell out before making long-term plans. And on a more practical level, if Jimmy were to live in England, what would he do about his mother?[20] As the hot afternoon wore on and the Frasers grew visibly more weary and disinterested, a dream died for the young author – the dream of at last meeting the famed uncle-father, the professional writer who could free the nephew-son from his mother and the bank.

When the Frasers announced they would be going back to their hotel, Kate was noisily upset for she had planned her best company dinner, had held the silver in reserve for the evening meal. Not to disappoint his sister too greatly, Sir John invited Kate and Jim, in a compromise gesture, to join him and his wife for dinner at their hotel. After some protests from Kate, the invitation was finally accepted. But when it became clear to Kate that she could not rival or impress her brother and sister-in-law, she began to adopt a free and breezy manner (the very opposite of the fine English lady she played in small Prairie towns) and seemed to take fun in exhibiting a plain-spoken, democratic side to her character. Before they left for downtown, she went into the garden and cut a bouquet of weedy-looking flowers – sun-bleached phlox and wilted dahlias – for Lady Constance to carry back with her to the hotel. Something of a row ensued over their mode of transportation: 'We always take the tram,' Kate insisted, but the Frasers apparently did not want to be seen getting off a bus near their hotel and so ordered a taxi for the return trip. As they were about to enter the hotel, Jim overheard Sir John hiss to his wife carrying the flowers, 'Get rid of those damn things.'[21]

In the hotel dining room, Kate had problems reading much of the menu, as it was in French, and so she asserted in a loud voice, with little trace of a British accent, 'I'll just have some well-cooked beef.' For the most part, Sir John presented himself as an equable, polite, good-humoured man, but Jim glimpsed another side to his nature when he berated a waiter over the bar service. Sir John ordered his favourite brand of scotch with soda, and when the waiter replied meekly that it couldn't be had, he thundered, 'Why the hell not? I want to speak to the manager.'

Next morning, Kate and Jim went to the train station to see the Frasers off on their return trip to Minneapolis, and they found Sir John upbraiding the stewards and baggage handlers for their inefficient service. The Frasers were travelling in the best car on the train and expected their luggage to be loaded first. The handlers paid little attention to the Englishman, who, in a rage, turned to his nephew and demanded that he do something. There was a half-hearted invitation for Jim to visit London and then Sir John and his wife left, obviously with a poor opinion of their Canadian nephew, who in turn felt both disillusioned and deeply disappointed. Sir John had turned out to be a caricature of an English aristocrat, and not knowing the protocol for deluxe train travel, Jim felt himself more than ever a poor country hick. He would only hear from his uncle once again. Before the Frasers left, he gave Sir John a copy of the *Queen's Quarterly* in which 'A Field of Wheat' appeared. The Englishman wrote to his nephew saying that the story, in his opinion, 'appeared to be touched with genius,' although he added that he had no way of measuring literary talent himself.

After the Frasers' visit, Jim and his mother drew closer together for a while. They were agreed that while Lady Constance had been a pleasant visitor, Sir John was arrogant and overbearing, that his modesty and manners were false. For Kate, especially, it was an illustration of something anachronistic and unhealthy in the English class system. Yet, that 'something' still worked its poison, for mother and son both felt unsatisfied now with their little bungalow on Arnold Street, and that fall they moved to more modern, slightly larger quarters on Nassau. They only stayed there, however, for a year because of an antagonism that developed between Kate and the landlord. Oddly, they quarrelled over religion: the landlord belonged to the Salvation Army, for which Kate had little patience. The Rosses moved again the next spring – into a building at 272 Cockburn Street, where over the next two years they occupied three different apartments.

Jim's failure to interest American magazines in his work did not in any way diminish his curiosity about that vital nation to the south. In October of 1935 he made his first trip to the United States, taking the bus and stopping first in Minneapolis for a couple of nights, then proceeding on further east to Chicago. Minneapolis was a little disappointing; it seemed only slightly larger than Winnipeg and no more interesting. He went to a symphony concert on the second night and decided to continue east the following day. His bus arrived at the Chicago station at 5 p.m., and feelings of excitement and apprehension gripped him as he looked out the window. The station seemed enormous – one could easily get lost – and there were crowds of people, many of them Black, milling about the terminal. There had been Blacks on the bus, and it was the first time he had heard them talking to each other, and in the tenor of their voices, their speech and laughter, he glimpsed a world he had never known before in Abbey, Arcola, or even Winnipeg. His sense of danger would at first increase, then gradually abate as he grew accustomed to this very different, vibrant world.

When he stepped off the bus and stood for a moment to get his bearings, a hawkish-looking youth approached and asked if he were looking for a hotel. He shook his head and moved forward to find the station exit. But out on the street, he realized that he was being trailed. Again the sharp-featured youth came forward and offered to show him a hotel, explaining that he was trying to find customers for the family business. So Jim let himself be guided to a hotel on State Street, not very far from the bus station, where the proprietor's son insisted they have a glass of beer before Jim was shown a room. 'What the hell are you doing here, boy?'[22] the waiter in the pub asked, which made Jim feel more than ever a vulnerable country hick. He hadn't taken his coat off, and he kept his leg pressed against his valise while he sat there. But after a second beer, he let himself be registered for the night, and because the hotel was clean and not very expensive, he remained there for the eight days he was in the city. In fact, he came to know the proprietor as well as the son and even showed them his copy of Queen's Quarterly with 'A Field of Wheat.' For in a mean-spirited moment he had packed his only copy of the journal with him, so that his mother would not be able to show it around to her friends while he was away. The hotel manager and his son proved affable and trustworthy people. Americans really were, he felt, somehow different.

And Jim's initiation into the criminal aspect of big-city American life also proved relatively benign. On a walk along the lakeshore, he encountered a group of four young men ('street corner types familiar in the Depression') who wouldn't let him pass without conversation. They offered to show him around the city, and to 'protect' him, in return for beer and meals. Two of them would meet him at the hotel every morning, or on the street corner, and for part of the day would accompany him on his walks in the city. It was less exploitative than it first seemed, because they took him to places and into buildings he would never have thought to investigate. Most memorable was the lobby of a private club where the curtains were thick with plush linings and the Persian carpets of a richness and design he had never seen before. There was always the troubling thought that these street boys would eventually beat him up and rob him, but that didn't happen; on the contrary, the five wound up having good sex together along the lakeshore,[23] and then one morning they simply did not appear again. Jim returned to the pleasant company of the hotel-keeper and his son, who seemed genuinely to like to talk about books and plays.

Before leaving the city, Jim went to see a road-company production of Erskine Caldwell's *Tobacco Road* that had Chicago in turmoil. With its daring representation of sex scenes on stage, it was at the centre of a censorship storm; a court-order injunction had halted the opening performance, and church groups continued to pressure politicians to defend the city's honour. But the production went forward, and the controversy only enhanced the play's scandalous appeal. Jim had never witnessed in public anything so exciting. On a Sunday afternoon, his fascination with the Black people of Chicago, who made the city so different from Winnipeg, lured him to buy tickets to what was billed as a 'Negro Musical,' but that proved to be nothing more than a minstrel show, not so very different from the likes of 'Arkola's Koloured Komedians.'

The exhilaration of that first trip to a big American city hung over the young writer for several weeks. He wrote to the hotel-keeper and his son, thanking them for their friendly service and good wishes, and promising to send them a copy of his next story when it was published. Eventually he received a short, perfunctory reply, but by the time it arrived he had come to feel that American hospitality was something very different from its Canadian counterpart. He answered the letter but knew he would not hear from his Chicago friends again.

Jim continued his association with Ernest Court and the Phoenix Club. The latter had expanded to include study groups in a variety of subjects, including philosophy, science, economics, and foreign languages, and Jim attended the French conversation classes as well as the meetings for story writers. As a centre for adult education, the Phoenix Club in its aims and objectives was shaped by the conditions of the Depression. It was more than simply a social club for like-minded men and women interested in ideas and culture; its stated objective was to create a learning environment and nourish a community spirit which would promote the good of society as a whole rather than the advantages and accomplishments of individuals. In a brochure citing Scandinavian study circles as a model, the club organizers describe the socialist spirit of their club as an antidote to the conditions that were fostering the emergence of dictators and demagogues in parts of Europe:

> In the past individuals have been able to win economic security by application of their own initiative. But now, in a world dominated by the machine, these traits are of little value. The individual can no longer improve his position at the expense of others, or flee across the frontier to build a haven beyond their reach. Today, instead of competing against his fellows, he must learn to co-operate with them in procuring a common security for all ... To prepare the way, the Phoenix Club nourishes a community spirit where social distinctions, racial prejudices, as well as differences in religious, political beliefs and family ties give way to wider and more wholesome friendships.[24]

In this atmosphere, Jim was exposed to some of the radical strains in Prairie politics and to religion as a social gospel. The Phoenix Club sponsored Saturday noon-hour lectures in the Montgomery Building, where for thirty-five cents one could have a substantial lunch and listen to a speaker of interest. Lectures ranged from analysis of current unemployment to thoughts on evolution to a study of Ibsen's *Peer Gynt*. A speaker from the Young Men's Section of the League of Nations spoke on the subject 'Should Canada support Britain in a European war?' and J.S. Woodsworth spoke on 'the present political situation.' Ernest Court had been active in the Labour Party in England, and his socialist views had a strong influence on the Phoenix Club and its program of lectures. Jim would remember Court's unsuccessful attempt to get him to attend the Woodsworth lecture. He was mildly curious to see the man who headed the Co-operative Commonwealth Federation party, but in the end aesthetics, not politics or economics, was his first and compelling interest.

Jim's friends in the Phoenix Club were anxious to see him find more illustrious and profitable markets for his fiction. Nellie Anderson, who wrote so persuasively on dieting (though she never lost a pound herself), said one day to Jim about his novel: 'Let me have that manuscript for half an hour and it will soon be on the best-seller list.'[25] Nellie made large claims and was often the humorous butt of her own stories. Lost in a snowstorm in Minnesota, she explained to the police officer that she was from Canada. He nodded his head and said it was easy to see that she was an Eskimo. More serious and successful as a literary adviser was the retired journalist Lillian Beynon Thomas, a former suffragist and a moderately successful short-story writer and playwright. Mrs Thomas was well known as a creative-writing teacher in Winnipeg (one of her private pupils at that time was Gabrielle Roy), and she too offered to revise Jim's manuscripts for the larger commercial markets. But he knew that expanding the plots and creating romantic interests would destroy what he wanted to do in his stories. At this point in his life, Jim was not unlike Philip Bentley in *As for Me and My House*. His wife writes about his apprenticeship years that '[t]he only artistic life he could make contact with was genteel and amateurish. It wasn't what he expected or needed; he went on studying alone' (44). Jim found himself going to the Phoenix Club less frequently and decided to join the Men's Musical Club of Winnipeg.

For the first time in their lives, Jim and his mother were not associated with a church. An aggressive minister with a broad Scots accent had called on the Rosses shortly after their move to Winnipeg and pressed them to join the local Presbyterian congregation, but Kate took such a strong dislike to the man that she refused to go. Arcola would be the last place in which mother and son attended church regularly. What Jim missed were the musical opportunities; now the only time he played the piano in public was at the occasional bank party, though he continued to play at home. There was music sometimes when he visited the Conyerses and their friends. He would always remember one evening when Will's sister-in-law sang Puccini's 'One Fine Day' from *Madama Butterfly*; she sang exceptionally well and was accompanied at the piano by a handsome blonde youth who was also talented. On one occasion, that same young man, after a party at the Conyerses', invited Jim to his bachelor apartment, and they both played the piano for each other. Later, after the young man had left Winnipeg, Jim learned that he was homosexual, but that evening neither had approached the other. Physical intimacy for Jim during the early years in Winnipeg was confined to 'blind' encounters in River Park, where in good weather circumspect men would meet. Some were married but, anxious to avoid scandal, sought anonymous and uninvolved contacts. Their brief meetings dispelled lust but not loneliness; and so Jim joined Winnipeg's established musical association, which for the next seven years would be at the centre of his social life.

The Men's Musical Club of Winnipeg was an umbrella organization for a number of musical activities in the city and the province. The club was formed in 1915 and in the years that followed sponsored the formation of the Winnipeg Male Voice Choir, the Winnipeg Orchestra, the Manitoba Music Festival, and the Winnipeg Boys Choir; eventually, it also took over the financial operations of the city's Philharmonic Choir. One of the club's chief objectives was to bring distinguished artists to Winnipeg, and the Men's Musical Club did indeed put Winnipeg on the circuit for many of the world's top musicians and performers. More than fifty years later, Jim would remember concerts given at the Civic Auditorium by Sergei Rachmaninoff, Yehudi Menuhin, Marian Anderson, Fritz Kreisler, Ezio Pinza, and Lily Pons. Jim approached this august club with some diffidence, because many of the members were socially prominent men who wore evening suits, while others were professional musicians and formed something of a clique. But that fall the younger men in the club started meeting separately in a less formal atmosphere. The Young Men's Section met every second week in the Music and Arts Company Building at the corner of Broadway and Hargrave Streets, where members most often listened to soloists perform, both vocal and instrumental, but on occasion were entertained with chamber music as well. Discussion and refreshments would follow the performances.

The Young Men's Musical Club was quickly the source of new friends for Jim. Chief among these was Chester Duncan, an aspiring musician and writer and later an English instructor at the University of Manitoba. Chester was a stimulating presence among the younger members of the club; a small man, full of enthusiasm for the arts, he was particularly excited by all aspects of 'modernism' and contemporary aesthetic theory. He had the kind of self-assured and dynamic nature that Jim lacked but warmed to in others. Duncan was also something of a rebel and viewed many of the older, more professional members of the club with contempt. In the winter of 1936–7, some of Duncan's closest friends, including Jim, started meeting separately from the club, to play for each other and to discuss aspects of 'modernist' styles that were of little interest to other members.[26] Chester wrote music for the piano and performed his own compositions at these informal gatherings. Frank Thorolfson, the first president of the Young Men's Musical Club, later to become a professor of music, was already an accomplished pianist, and with his first wife, Irene, who was a violinist, would entertain the group with duets. Chester Duncan also wrote verse, and the group broadened its focus to include poetry readings and discussions of novels, plays, and painting. Unlike the Musical Club, Duncan's group, which eventually became known as the Contemporary Club, included women at its gatherings. Frequently they met at the home of Helen Aubert, a young woman from an affluent Winnipeg family whose life was circumscribed by her having had polio as a child. Another vital member of the group was Ada Elwick, whom Chester Duncan would marry in 1943.

Jim continued at the same time to be involved in the Men's Musical Club, which resulted in one particularly memorable exposure to artists and the artistic personality. During the 1930s, the internationally celebrated musician Arthur Benjamin (1893–1960) spent several weeks each year in Winnipeg, as guest conductor of the Winnipeg Symphony and as an adjudicator of the Manitoba Music Festival. With his urbane but dynamic personality, and his artistic commitment to filling the gap between serious and popular music, the Australian-born Benjamin was immensely popular with both the city's musicians and the concert-going public. His own compositions, which would include comic operas such as *The Devil Take Her* and *Prima Donna*, and the immensely popular 'Jamaican Rhumba,' were being performed in theatres and concert halls around the world. He was a shining hour in the Manitoba musical year. At one of the meetings of the Young Men's Musical Club, the shy young author caught the older musician's interest, and a friendship began which lasted until 1941, by which time Benjamin had become principal conductor of the CBC Vancouver Orchestra and no longer adjudicated the Manitoba Festival. Benjamin, like Chester Duncan, had a self-assured and extroverted manner, and in 'taking up' the young writer, he invited himself one day to the Ross home. For Jim, an important aspect of both the Phoenix Club and the Young Men's Musical Club was that they gave him some independence from his mother. Concert tickets were expensive, and Kate reluctantly agreed that they couldn't both afford to attend. So when Jim started bringing Arthur Benjamin home, she was delighted to entertain the famous musician and took great pleasure in serving her best company dinners and telling stories of her illustrious forebears and famous brother in England. Jim was delighted to see how well his mother could hold her own with this polished musician, engaging in spirited debate. One evening, she was hostess for a small party at the apartment which included Frank and Irene Thorolfson and Helen Aubert, as well as Arthur Benjamin.

In an obituary article on Arthur Benjamin in a Winnipeg newspaper, the musician's involvement in Manitoba musical culture is attributed to a long interest in amateur music-making and the festival movement. He is reported to have said that among the most memorable musical experiences he ever had was his hearing, for the first time, the Winnipeg high-school choirs in the Manitoba Festival.[27] But there was a deeply personal aspect to this interest as well. When he adjudicated the music festival in 1934, he was thrilled by the talent and poise of a ten-year-old cellist, a boy named Lorne Munroe. Drawn back each year to observe the development of this gifted boy, Benjamin in

1937 arranged with the Munroes, a musical family from Russia, to sponsor Lorne's education at the Royal Conservatory of Music in London, England, where Benjamin himself at that time had his permanent residence. He wrote music for the boy to perform, and in April 1939 (Munroe was only fifteen) they gave a joint recital at the Young Men's Musical Club, where, together, they played a 'sonatina' Benjamin had written the previous year for violoncello and pianoforte.[28] The flavour of this life, with its clandestine intimacies and assumptions of artistic privilege, was brought home to Jim one night when Benjamin took him to his hotel room after a concert. Jim, who kept his sexual life private, rejected the older man's advances and was angered by his presumption; the friendship between writer and musician thereafter cooled.

In the summer of 1936, Kate and Jim received word from England that Sir John had died on June 7th in a London nursing home from a combination of ailments including phlebitis, gallstones, and emphysema. Despite his illustrious career as a widely read newspaperman and travel writer, Sir John had not always lived happily; his divorce from his first wife, Helen Mary Lawrence, an American woman from Seattle, seems to have remained something of a personal tragedy. In his will, probated in London on August 14 and valued at £34,109 after debts had been paid, he made provision that Helen be paid an annuity of £500 until her death or remarriage. Helen had petitioned for and been granted a divorce in 1923, but no co-respondent had been named. In his will, Sir John left £1,000 to a Josephine Currie of the Christian Student Movement House in London 'for her sisterly regard and understanding patience during the dark years of my life.' Perhaps most bitter to Sir John was the defection of his two daughters, neither of whom is named in his will, although one attended his funeral. Sir John left the bulk of his estate to Constance, his second wife, but in addition to small legacies to such bodies as the Cheyne Hospital for Children in Chelsea and St Mark's Unitarian Church in Edinburgh, he left £1,000 to his sister in Winnipeg.[29] When Kate received the money, she bought a sealskin coat and other items of clothing that caught her fancy; she was never guilty of frugality. Jim upgraded his piano through Eaton's second-hand piano department and acquired a baby grand which filled much of the living-room space. The apartment was further gentrified with a portrait of Sir John painted in England and sent on by his widow, although Jim never cared for it and moved it several times to find a wall space that would diminish its oppressiveness.

In October of 1936, lured again south of the border, Jim spent his holidays on a first trip to New York City, which would remain in his memory one of the most important experiences of his life. He travelled there two days by bus, sitting up at night and getting his first glimpse of the Manhattan skyline on a sunny fall afternoon. When he arrived in the city, he went to a hotel recommended by a friend at the bank, but it was so disreputable-looking – dirty and seemingly unsafe – that he only stayed one night and moved to the YMCA the next day. On his first full day in the city, he simply walked the streets of central and lower Manhattan, in amazement at the wide but high, crowded streets that stretched on for miles and miles; in the evening, he discharged a duty that he promised his mother he would perform.

One of Kate's younger brothers, Stuart, had moved to New York as a young man and had made his living there; Jim had never met his uncle, but his mother made him promise to pay a visit. Stuart and Clara Fraser lived out in the Bronx, and Jim took a commuter train there to have dinner with them. They lived on the fifth floor of an apartment block without an elevator, and Jim felt winded as well as anxious by the time he reached their flat. But they gave him a warm welcome, serving him a company-style turkey dinner, and after the ice was broken, the threesome had a pleasant evening together. At first they talked about family, and although this uncle had a slight Scottish accent, it was hard to conceive that this ordinary, working man was a brother to Sir John Foster Fraser. Stuart worked as a clerk for a steamship company, and to judge by the apartment, he was a man of modest means; his wife was a plain-spoken New York woman. More interesting to Jim that evening was listening to his aunt and uncle talk about New York and all the things he could see during his visit to the city.

The following day, he joined a tour group which took him to see famous landmarks like the Statue of Liberty, Grant's Tomb, Chinatown, and the Empire State Building, the latter giving him a sharp experience of vertigo. Late that same day, he walked around lower Manhattan, beginning to learn the signs of recognition between gay men. One of the reasons Jim had come to New York was because, in the early part of the century, it was known as the gay capital of North America.[30] In New York there was both a flamboyant gay culture (drag queens and 'fairies') and an extensive underground for gay men who lived anonymous, straight lives during the day (many of them married) but who cruised certain streets, parks, and bathhouses at night. Jim came to recognize codes of dress and speech as signalling availability, but was surprised that evening when a very ordinary-looking, middle-aged man in a bar ('no signals') suggested he follow him to the back of the building. Beyond the washrooms there was a series of small rooms where men met for sex. What amazed Jim about New York was that he could meet so easily men like himself, who did not identify as 'fairies' or 'queers,' but who nonetheless craved sexual experience with other men. The special nature of that encounter in

New York was the other man's age – he was possibly fifteen years older, Jim guessed – and it made him reflect later that his need for physical intimacy with another man was surely tied to his lack of a father.[31]

The other great attraction of New York for Jim was the opportunity to go to theatre and concerts. He saw Helen Hayes in her award-winning performance in *Victoria Regina*, and a play about juvenile delinquency called *Deep End Boys*. The musical highlight of that week in New York was hearing Melchior and Flagstad in a concert of arias from Wagnerian opera. He also acquired tickets for a couple of concerts at Carnegie Hall. To save money, he stood in line for tickets that went on sale for half price or better on the day of the concert. It was at the theatre, at the performance of *Victoria Regina*, that he made contact with a young New York couple of some distinction. Before the play began, he overheard a man and woman in the next seats discussing the books being published that fall in New York. Jim's interest in the subject overcame his deep-seated shyness, and for once he introduced himself and joined in the conversation, which continued during the intermission. Jim presented himself as a writer from Winnipeg (the *Nash* prize and its judges still gave him the confidence to think of himself as a writer), and the other man introduced himself as Kenneth McCormick, an editor at the Doubleday Publishing Company, accompanied by his wife, Elizabeth. When the play was over, the McCormicks suggested that Jim join them for something to drink at a nearby cafe, where they discussed some of the fine points of Hayes' memorable performance as Queen Victoria and continued their talk of books and book people. Before saying good night, the McCormicks invited Jim to have dinner with them in their apartment in Greenwich Village.

That experience made Jim feel he had entered a sophisticated world he had only read about before. Although Ken and Elizabeth McCormick were just a couple of years older than Jim, they seemed to the raw Saskatchewan youth many years older in the ways of the world. (Indeed, Ken McCormick was already launched on a career with Doubleday that would span sixty-three years and would make him one of the most powerful and best-known editors in the business.) Their little apartment in the village was tastefully decorated with prints and drawings and exotic-looking plants, and it was crowded with books in a way Jim had never seen before. The apartment seemed much larger than it was because it was on the ground floor and looked out directly on a walled garden, where the McCormicks took their meals in good weather. Ken and Elizabeth (who preferred her nickname Tibby) took a genuine interest in Jim, recommended plays for him to see and books to read, and made him promise to send copies of the stories he had written. It was the beginning of a special friendship, special because it gave Jim a contact in the great publishing world of New York, and because it gave him friends to contact on those otherwise lonely visits to the vast city.

Before leaving New York, he accepted another invitation to have dinner with his aunt and uncle out in the Bronx, and further agreed to meet his uncle in Manhattan the afternoon before his departure. To Jim's surprise and amusement, his uncle took him to a 'girlie' show. He had to hurry to catch his bus back to Winnipeg. It had been a thrilling experience to visit New York City, and though he had made contact with his aunt and uncle and made the acquaintance of the McCormicks, Jim still felt lonely much of the time he was in the city. He returned to New York in the fall, two years later, and wrote a postcard to Harriet Duff-Smith which said: 'Hello Smithy: Enjoying myself tremendously here, but wishing now and then for some of my friends to share things with.'[32] Feelings of loneliness would always do battle with Jim's desire for independence and his instincts to remain, in his own phrase, a loner.

In May of 1937, Jim entered Winnipeg General Hospital to have his appendix removed. For several months, he had repeatedly suffered with upset stomach and constipation; his doctor concluded that it was caused by a chronically infected appendix. He was kept for more than two weeks after the surgery. Kate visited the hospital every day, and one afternoon Roy Reynolds and Leroy MacPherson from the bank came to his room, each carrying a large armful of lilacs that they had picked in gardens en route. 'We've come to lay you out, Jimmy,' they said.[33] There was a good laugh that afternoon, and the stay in hospital made Jim aware that he counted for something at the bank, that ordinary working people were the bedrock of his friendships. For literary history, the stay in hospital was significant in this way: it was another dry, windy spring on the Prairies, and lying in bed all day the young writer could hear the steady strum of the wind on the corner of the hospital building. His imagination was stirred by that unrelenting sound, and 'The Lamp at Noon' began to take shape in his mind. Although the city sheltered people from some of the harshest realities of the drought, Jim had not lost sight of what was happening in the West, for he and his mother still made trips to Saskatchewan to stay with Effie during the holidays, and they still received letters from friends in Abbey, located in one of the driest and dustiest regions of the province. According to the author's account, the first draft of the story wrote itself quickly, for there was no tinkering possible with the story's simple and unswerving plot.

If there is a quintessential Sinclair Ross story, it is this tragic account of a young farmer and his wife who have been 'blown out' during five rainless years. All the elements that have become trademarks of Ross's work come into play in 'The Lamp at Noon':[34] the quarrelling husband and wife, the remote farm burdened by crop failure and debt, and the sense of doom that engulfs not only the couple and the farm but their small child. The story is deeply rooted in the author's personal experience of family, his parents' unhappy marriage and to some extent his sister's. There is almost no communication between husband and wife. The wife has come from town and has taught school; she has some education and chides her husband repeatedly for not following scientific methods of farming, rotating crops and planting alfalfa. Inarticulate but resolved, he struggles on against the land and the weather, sinking further into debt every year. The man's angry stoicism leads to his wife's emotional breakdown and to the death of their child. 'The Lamp at Noon' is especially powerful because it resonates with the unique historical conditions of the 1930s, when dust storms scourged the West, hard-working farm families lost their land, and some people went mad.

'The Lamp at Noon' appeared in the spring issue of *Queen's Quarterly* in 1938 and would become one of the most frequently reprinted stories in the Ross canon, including a translation into German. From Head Office in Montreal, this time from the advertising department, Jim received another one of those letters that he would treasure for a lifetime. This letter was from J.C. Nelson, who wrote that he did not wish to seem fulsome, but that he couldn't help saying in all sincerity that 'The Lamp at Noon' was one of the finest things of its kind that he had ever read. 'Others with whom I have talked feel the same way,' he said, and he was sure Jim must have received many letters of congratulations by that time. Nelson went on to suggest that Jim send his stories to magazines like the *Atlantic Monthly*, for he felt it was in that magazine's style and it would pay him very well, adding in bankerly fashion, 'there is no question whatever that you have exceptional gifts as a writer and it seems a shame not to capitalize on them.' He also asked Jim if he would be willing to write the occasional story for the bank magazine.[35] Words of praise for his fiction were few and far between – from Ernest Court when he dropped by the Phoenix Club, and occasional compliments on being published from his fellow workers at the bank, though there was seldom any indication that they had actually read his stories – and so a letter of congratulations from Montreal from someone he had never met was truly exciting. For what he craved most now were readers, an audience.

six

Days with Pegasus
1938–1941

The period from 1938 to 1942 is at the centre of Sinclair Ross's creativity; it was his high tide. Between the age of thirty and thirty-four, he wrote several of his best stories, including 'The Painted Door,' 'Cornet at Night,' and 'One's a Heifer'; he also wrote two novels, most importantly *As for Me and My House*, upon which his reputation as a major Canadian writer squarely rests, and he planned a third in some detail. It was a time of creativity unaided by public interest or support, and it came to a premature close with the author's enlistment in the army to serve in the Second World War. Nonetheless, those were the artist's best years, and they gave Canada some of its most valuable and enduring works of literature.

A story Jim published in 1938 shows him poised at the threshold of this intensely creative period: it was titled 'A Day with Pegasus.'[1] In conception and style, it differed from his previous fictions. Its provenance was in no specific scene or incident other than the author's recollected boyhood excitement when animals, particularly horses, were born on the farm. Otherwise it was a wholly imagined sketch of farm life in which he tried to convey the antithesis between a boy with intense imagination and his prosaic country surroundings. The story has more dialogue than most; but to render the mundane, a laconic narrative voice frequently employs dashes and sentence fragments as the equivalent of thoughts scarcely articulated. Only in the third paragraph from the end, where the boy dreams of some day riding a newborn colt across the prairie, does the spare prose become lyrical and release the pent-up feelings of the boy, who wants to escape and fly over the roof of the world to 'see its vault and spaciousness' (48). It is one of the most powerful passages in Jim's writing, the horse a synthesis of passion and imagination. Years later, he was disappointed when the editors at McClelland and Stewart decided not to include 'A Day with Pegasus' in *The Lamp at Noon and Other*

Stories, for he felt strongly that it had as much quality as the others collected from the pages of *Queen's Quarterly*. Writing 'A Day with Pegasus' had been an exhilarating experience for the young author, for he had proven to himself in that near final paragraph that as a writer he could fly, that he could execute intricate feats of the imagination and soar, like the winged horse of Greek mythology. His fiction in the next four years bore that out.

What particularly marks the writing in this period is the author's first tentative exploration of illicit sex. 'The Painted Door'[2] is not unlike 'September Snow' in documenting the hardships endured by a young couple on an isolated Prairie farm, but in 'The Painted Door' the temporarily abandoned wife takes a lover for the night and the story expands with the theme of sexual excitement and guilt. The author was never able to recall any details surrounding the genesis of the story, except that the opening paragraphs, which establish setting and distances that are crucial for the plot, were for some reason difficult to write, and he rewrote them what seemed like dozens of times. Otherwise the writing was straightforward because, unlike the previous stories he had written, 'The Painted Door' had a strong, sure sense of plot. During a heavy blizzard, Ann, the wife, stays alone in the house while her husband, John, treks through the snow to help his father. She paints the kitchen woodwork to pass the time. Their bachelor neighbour, Steven, comes by to help with the chores, but, as the evening wears on and it seems clear John will not return that night, Steven seduces Ann into spending the night in bed with him. In the morning, Ann discovers to her horror the consequences of her infidelity – John's body is found frozen in the pasture, but on his hand is a streak of fresh paint.

Like 'The Lamp at Noon,' this story features those thematic elements considered the bedrock of Canadian writing: a landscape so bleak in winter that it 'seemed a region alien to life' (94), but a house standing nonetheless against that wilderness, 'a refuge of feeble walls wherein persisted the elements of human meaning and survival' (110). The farm couple are familiar from other Ross stories: a woman who wants fine things and a social life, but a slow, taciturn, country-bound husband who only aspires to paying off the mortgage. The conversation is about crops and cattle, the weather and the neighbours. Some of the women in these stories go mad or die, but in 'The Painted Door' the woman is temporarily released from the frightening boredom of her existence by a night of love-making with her neighbour. But then the story's strongest theme emerges, that of Puritan guilt. The spirit of labour (or the work ethic) is part of that guilt: 'Sometimes they did sleep late, sometimes they did play cards, but always uneasily, always reproached by the thought of more important things that might be done' (98). But this theme's fullest expression is when Ann wakes up during the night and sees hellish flames from the fire in the stove, leaping and sinking fantastically, whips of light like snakes (108–9). The torment of knowing she caused her husband's death makes Ann's fate no more desirable perhaps than that of the other women in Ross's fiction. Jim always felt 'The Painted Door' had the most successful ending of any of his stories, perhaps because it came closest to the O. Henry style surprise ending that American magazines prized so highly. The smothering of the baby in 'The Lamp at Noon' has that same effect of suddenly putting everything in a new light at the end of the story, but the little detail of the fresh paint on John's hand, revealing without any doubt that he had witnessed his wife's adultery, is a classic example of a revelation that is not a trick but a fulfilment of the story's thematic designs.

When Alexander Macphail read the story, he asked for one small change – that the husband's name be John rather than Elmer. In Macphail's opinion, 'Elmer' seemed to mark the dull-witted husband too clearly as a loser. It was the only editorial suggestion made by Macphail that Jim agreed to. The story appeared in the summer 1939 issue of *Queen's Quarterly*. 'The Painted Door' has proven to be Sinclair Ross's most popular story, with several reprintings in mainstream anthologies and translations into German, Chinese, and Serbo-Croatian. Also it has three times been made into short films: by CBC Television in 1968; by the Simon Fraser University Film Workshop in 1975, where it was retitled 'Blizzard'; and by Atlantis Films in 1984. The latter project was directed by Bruce Pittman, featuring Linda Goranson, Eric Peterson, and August Schellenberg, and was nominated for an Academy Award in the short feature category.

'Cornet at Night,'[3] written in 1938, is also one of Ross's most popular and frequently studied stories. Here he explores something approaching a boy's homoerotic feelings for a young man. Jim was drawing on memories of his teenage years and his relations with young farmhands, men like Mac Hayman, who came to work at Sid Ketcheson's during the harvest. Mac only played a mouth organ, not a cornet, but he had a gentleness and dreamy side to his nature that were appealing and suggestive to the boy. There is a first glimpse of the fictional rendering of this figure in the cowboy nicknamed Slim in 'A Day with Pegasus,' a 'big, handsome fellow,' who is a hero and mentor to the boy. In 'Cornet at Night,' Jim was also recreating something of his parents' lives as he remembered them quarrelling incessantly over the children, the running of the farm, their religious and social obligations.

'Cornet at Night' is a story about a boy making choices that will determine the kind of man he is going to be. In the initial scene, the parents are in conflict because the father is going to cut wheat on Sunday, breaking the community's religious taboo against working on the Lord's day. The boy becomes entangled in the quarrelling because the father wants him to miss school on Monday and ride into town to find a man to stook wheat. The mother is opposed, not wanting her son to miss a day of school or his music lesson. She wants to civilize him, which, in terms of a Prairie farm, is to feminize him. Beneath the rather bleak details of the opening scene there is the question of which parent the boy will side with and obey, with whom will he form an identification. His mother's argument – that she wants her son 'to be different' from his father – has some appeal because the boy is sensitive, likes music, and wants to fit into the social life of the community. At one point, he thinks to himself: '... a sudden welling-up of social and religious conscience made me ask myself whether one in the family like my father wasn't bad enough' (30). When dinner is served, the father is made to eat alone; after he has gone back to work, mother and son sit down to a cold, unappetizing meal. The boy spends the day under his mother's vigilant eye, dressed up in his 'knicker corduroys,' reading the Bible, and practising hymns on the piano. Yet, his compliance is in part a strategy to gain his mother's permission to go to town with the horse next day, to go about his father's business, for 'I was inordinately proud that my father had suggested it' (31).

Tommy Dickson does go to town, but he is burdened again by his parents' conflicting instructions: his father wants him to hire 'somebody big and husky' (33), while his mother insists it be someone who is clean. At the diner, he is 'courted' by two men looking for work. A brawny, unshaven man aggressively offers himself as a harvester, displaying for the boy his muscles. The other man, slim, well-dressed, nonchalant, says nothing until the husky one has left, but he has already caught the boy's eye and attention: not because he promises to be a strong worker; rather, his attraction is almost feminine: 'His hands were slender, almost a girl's hands, yet vaguely with their shapely quietness they troubled me, because, however slender and smooth, they were yet hands to be reckoned with, strong with a strength that was different from the rugged labour-strength I knew' (36). In choosing Philip Coleman, Tommy appears to act again according to his mother's wishes, but Philip is an androgynous figure, with both masculine and feminine qualities that reconcile the claims of identification made on the boy by his parents. More importantly, his musicianship transcends the limits of gender. That night at the Dicksons' farm, he plays his cornet, and the notes 'floated up against the night ... clear and visible. Sometimes they mounted poignant and sheer.' Both the mother and father are visibly moved by the young man's skill at the cornet: they are left 'wondering,' 'half-incredulous,' 'helpless' (44). Philip leaves the following day after failing miserably in the fields, for as the boy narrator observes, 'You always have to put the harvest first' (45). But his presence and his music have stirred the boy's imagination ('intimately and enduringly now they were my possessions' [41]), and he is left with a new measure: 'A harvest, however lean, is certain every year; but a cornet at night is golden only once' (45). The admiration the boy feels towards the older man is one of those complicated erotic velleities that gives depth and complexity to the fiction of Sinclair Ross. The story also reveals the author's recovery of his own complicated feelings as he struggled with sexual identity as a boy.

When asked to name his favourite story, Jim would almost invariably answer 'Cornet at Night.' Like 'Circus in Town' and 'A Day with Pegasus,' it describes a child's imaginative escape from the hard labour and scant resources of a small Prairie farm. As in the other two stories, a horse is the vehicle for that release and self-realization: 'Alone with himself and his horse [a farm boy] cuts a fine figure. He is the measure of the universe ... fearless, resourceful' (34). But another important dimension to that release is suggested in this story – transcending the mundane through falling in love, and through art. In 'The Painted Door,' Ann temporarily escapes the bleakness of her cabined existence on a remote farm by spending a guilt-wracked night with her husband's friend, but in 'Cornet at Night' there is no guilt associated with the homoerotic infatuation that Tommy Dickson feels for Philip. 'The Painted Door' is a drama of adultery played out within the legal and religious strictures of a Puritan farm community; 'Cornet at Night' is a story of the imagination and a new dispensation in gender and art.

'Cornet at Night' has been dramatized four times: on CBC Radio in 1958; as a National Film Board short in 1963; on CBC Television in 1973; and as an Atlantis Film directed by Bruce Pittman in 1983. In 1993, on the occasion of the one-hundredth anniversary of Queen's Quarterly, 'Cornet at Night' was reprinted in a special commemorative issue titled 'Sounds That Echo Still.'[4] Almost certainly it will have a long future. But when it was accepted in 1938 for publication, and appeared in the winter issue of the quarterly for 1939, there was no public indication that he had written so well. Macphail had sent his usual letter of acceptance with no editorial suggestions. (Actually it would be his last letter.) A few friends in Winnipeg said they liked the new story. Otherwise it seemed to pass unnoticed.

By the time 'Cornet at Night' was published, Jim was well advanced on his second novel manuscript – the story of a preacher and his wife, two artists who attempt to escape the little Prairie town where they are confined. The germ for the novel was the incident in Abbey when the minister said that a college education could likely be arranged if Jim would agree to study for the ministry. In a taped interview in 1970 the author recalled the matter this way:

I was living in a small town, and a United Church minister, he thought that I might make a better minister than I would a banker. So he made the suggestion which was made to Philip: 'Would you like to go into the church?' And of course I said 'no.' It didn't tempt me at all, but, and probably this is what they mean by having a writer's mind, I started thinking, well, supposing somebody did accept that offer and then he finds himself trapped ... That was the idea. The United Church minister was a kind fellow and meant well, but he was not a very good judge of human nature, of human character.[5]

Philip Bentley was to be the central character, and initially the story was to be told from his point of view. The success Jim experienced in writing 'Cornet at Night' encouraged him to try first-person narration again. But having Philip narrate his own story was too limited and too full of bitterness, and so to give the novel greater scope, he decided to use Philip's wife as the narrator and her diary as the form for the story. 'Keeping Philip off-stage,' he later wrote, 'gives him a power, makes him a presence looming in the background more impressive for the reader.'[6] There was a popular precedent for the diary form in western Canadian fiction. Arthur Stringer's trilogy of novels, *The Prairie Wife* (1915), *The Prairie Mother* (1920), and *The Prairie Child* (1922), described the struggles of a young homesteading couple and enjoyed a large readership in both Canada and the United States. The stories are narrated through the medium of the sophisticated wife's letters and diary, and the strongest impression they leave is of an intelligent, courageous woman betrayed by her humourless husband. Kate and Jim had both read the novels and rather liked them. But for Jim the diary was an ideal vehicle, not only for developing the intensely personal nature of his story, but for facilitating the writing itself. Employed steadily at the bank weekdays from nine to five and on Saturday mornings, he had only evenings and part of the weekend in which to write. It was difficult, as he had experienced with 'Peter Guy,' to sustain the momentum needed for a long piece. The diary entries more exactly suited his working schedule of two or three hours, and occasionally he was able to write an entry in one sitting.

But the other thing that happened in the writing was that the narrator began to take over the story. In a 1972 interview with Myrna Kostash, the author said that he intended the novel to be a study of Philip Bentley's hypocrisy, but that Mrs Bentley ran away with the story: '[The fact that] her flaring life-exuberance overwhelm[s] the account of Philip's tight-lipped retreat away from her and into the arid core of his self – this ... was accidental.' He had not meant to write the book that way; 'it "wrote itself" in the process of story-telling.'[7] This would frequently be the author's experience: a story, no matter how carefully planned, 'would invariably change during the writing.'[8] This would especially be true during the writing of a long work of fiction, and he eventually approached writing novels without trying to plan how they would end. The setting and the characters, as they developed, would determine the shape of the story.

As Jim was writing *As for Me and My House*, a third point of view became important – that of Paul, the 'slightly ridiculous' schoolteacher who is nonetheless 'a useful chorus – a bit of a nut, who could say things for me, quoted by Mrs Bentley in her diary, which she couldn't say.'[9] Gradually he realized that Paul was the character in the novel he was closest to – an observer of the Bentleys' marriage, emotionally involved, but an outsider. A triangular relationship formed around Paul, who projected the author's point of view and experiences – the country boy with a little education who fits in nowhere. Paul attaches himself to the Bentleys, with strong feelings for the wife and a keen but muted interest in the plight of the husband. As he reworked various parts of the manuscript, Jim took pains to keep all three points of view in the story viable. Later he would describe it as 'something like cross-writing':[10] the diary was written from Mrs Bentley's point of view, but reading over and revising, he would make adjustments to accommodate Philip's point of view and in some places Paul's – 'to be fair to them all.'[11] This gives the novel an enormous degree of complexity and depth, and makes it a text that readers continue to construct and reconstruct for themselves.

The best part of a first draft was completed by the time Jim was ready to take a vacation in the summer of 1939. He had arranged to rent a cottage for two weeks on Lake Winnipeg with a new friend by the name of Bill Thorne. He met Bill through a Miss Preston, who managed the bookstore at Eaton's. The latter had an avid interest not only in sales but in books and especially in the authors who wrote them. It was Jim's habit, almost weekly, to stop at Eaton's and browse in the bookshelves, and he gradually got to know Miss Preston. When he told her that he had published some stories in *Queen's Quarterly*, she took a strong interest in Jim and, in his words, 'cultivated him.' One day she introduced him to another young man who was idling away an hour in the store. This was William Thorne, a garrulous, energetic young student who was completing an arts degree at United College and who wanted to be a painter. Thorne was tall, well-dressed, and to Jim his self-confidence bespoke good family connections and a degree of affluence. Although Thorne was still in his early twenties and by now Jim was thirty, the two men enjoyed each other's company and a common interest in the arts. They took meals in each other's homes, and Jim came to like Bill's parents, who were devoted to their only child.

Although Bill wanted to paint, he knew teaching and journalism were more practical ambitions to pursue. He had written a few articles for the college paper, including a review of a painting exhibition in the city, and when his last year was finished he started writing pieces for publication on a wide variety of subjects. He also took a job that summer on the railroad with the 'extra gang,' near Regina, doing hard manual labour. When one of his articles was rejected, he wrote to Jim from Regina asking for advice, and, in a letter that has survived, Jim gave him some practical suggestions on matters of style. Above all, he urged simplification, avoiding as much as possible subordinate clauses and participial constructions in favour of short, simple sentences that don't make the reader work too hard. American magazines, he reminded Bill, demand a simple, deft style, and so one should avoid not only complex sentence structures but long, learned words as well. Most readers, he adds, don't grasp the 'heavy stuff.' Some of these ideas may have originated in a book he had received from his uncle titled *Some Secrets of Style*.[12] Jim underlined passages in the book and made notes to himself. He underscored, for example: '... words from Latin have a more rigid and stately character ... they are sonorous.' In a few paragraphs to Bill Thorne, we find a writer setting out the practical guidelines of his craft. Sinclair Ross would remain steadfast in their application.

When Bill returned in mid-August from Regina, he and Jim decided that a couple of weeks together at Lake Winnipeg could be pleasant. This holiday with Bill Thorne would have repercussions for Canadian literature. Thorne was greatly preoccupied with aesthetic theory and discussed at length the ideas surrounding modernism, particularly the debate between Romantic subjectivity and modernist detachment. Thorne had been caught up as a student by the essays of the Bloomsbury theoreticians, Clive Bell and Roger Fry, and allied himself vigorously with the high modernists. Jim, however, couldn't help ask whether emotion didn't play a significant part in the aesthetic experience and whether background knowledge and associations weren't also important. In his essay 'The Aesthetic Hypothesis,' in *Art* (1914), Clive Bell writes that aesthetic emotion is a matter of significant form – 'lines and colours ... forms and relations of forms.'[13] To appreciate a work of art, he writes, 'we need to bring with us nothing from life, no knowledge of its ideas and affairs, no familiarity with its emotions. Art transports us from the world of man's activity to a world of aesthetic exaltation.'[14] Bill gave Jim some of the Bloomsbury essays to read, and as Jim continued to rework the manuscript of *As for Me and My House*, something of the Romantic-modernist debate entered the novel. Mrs Bentley's romanticism is challenged by her husband's diametrically opposed views:

According to Philip it's form that's important in a picture, not the subject or the associations that the subject calls to mind; the pattern you see, not the literary emotion you feel; and it follows, therefore, that my enthusiasm for his little schoolhouse doesn't mean much from an artist's point of view. (105–6)

And later in the narrative, Philip again tries to instruct his wife that form and design are what count, not the associations she brings to the pictures he has painted:

'These things all mean something to you because you've lived in these little Main Streets – with me while I was doing them. You're looking at them, but you're not really seeing them. You're only remembering something that happened to you there. But in art, memories and associations don't count. A good way to test a picture is to turn it upside down. That knocks all the sentiment out of it, leaves you with just the design and form.' (202)

Years later, the author would remember how the debate with his young friend had been so stimulating that, when he returned home, he inserted its gist into the novel, and he felt 'very lucky' about its success because he had done so on instinct rather than on the basis of a careful study of art theory and history.[15] Sinclair Ross has been credited with writing one of the few self-consciously modernist fictions in Canadian literature, but one should remember that the actual form of As for Me and My House predated the discussion of modernist aesthetics with Bill Thorne.

What Jim remembered specifically from that holiday on Lake Winnipeg was waking up at dawn the first three days, reading through the manuscript, and feeling confident, for the first time, that it was good. The writing had been slow and painstaking, but it had been steady, and that regimen seemed to have worked. The storyline cohered, the characters, including Philip, were solidly executed, and the austere lyricism of the setting seemed fully realized without sentimentality, always balanced by the realistic documenting of life in a little Prairie town. He hadn't waited for inspiration, but rather made himself sit down routinely at the desk and sharpen his pencil. Once under way, the project had acquired the solid, practical values of craftsmanship: 'so many pages written by the end of the month, certain passages nicely polished, others needing more work.'[16] The diary form had made that way of working possible.

But Jim had another vivid memory from that holiday at Lake Winnipeg. The manuscript he had brought to tinker with was the only complete version of the novel he had, and while at the lake he nearly lost it. Walking along the beach, Bill and Jim became acquainted with two young men sharing another one of the cottages at the lake. One of these men was Parisian French (later, when he enrolled for teacher training, Bill discovered that he was teaching at the University of Manitoba);[17] the other was from Winnipeg. They both referred to themselves as novelists. The eager and extroverted Thorne invited the two men to their cottage, and Jim cooked a dinner of steaks, mashed potatoes, and fresh peas. There was talk of the new fashions in European fiction, and when Bill told their guests that Jim had just finished writing a novel, the French teacher asked Jim if he could read his manuscript. Jim agreed, but somewhat reluctantly parted with the manuscript since it was the only typed and revised draft he possessed. The days passed – Jim and Bill explored the area, went swimming at Silver Falls, where Bill did some pen-and-ink drawings – but Jim's manuscript did not come back, and then it appeared that the two men had left the lake: their cottage was closed down. Jim felt sick at the thought of trying to write out again some of the passages that had been added to the most recent version of the manuscript, the one he had taken pleasure in reading over when the holiday began. He reflected bitterly on what he suspected were contemptuous attitudes in the men who had taken the manuscript away; his farm-boy upbringing made him feel a twinge of disgust for these men: 'probably homosexuals' – while his relation with Bill Thorne was 'innocent.'[18] But on departure day, the French teacher miraculously appeared again, and As for Me and My House was returned to its author, although that wouldn't be the only time the manuscript would survive a close brush with oblivion. Jim would always remember the day in 1939 when he and Thorne left the lake; at the train station that morning there was an announcement over the loudspeaker saying that Canada was now at war.

The exhilaration at completing a manuscript was eroded by the nagging awareness that it would probably not be easy to find a publisher. Jim's experiences so far had been discouraging. At some point after moving to Winnipeg, he had submitted the completed manuscript of 'The Wife of Peter Guy' to the Atlantic Monthly Press contest held every other year. It came back; the rejection note made him view it as deeply flawed, and he set the manuscript aside. But when As for Me and My House came close to completion he had to think again where to send a novel-length work. By this time, he had come to know a vibrant little English woman by the name of Kathleen Strange, a published author whose immigration narrative, With the West in Her Eyes (1937), was enjoying a wide success. They first met at one of Harriet Duff-Smith's parties in 1938 at which Kathleen was being fêted for her book; Jim would also see her at parties hosted by Nellie Anderson, and occasionally at meetings of the Phoenix Club, where more than once she was a guest speaker. He would remember her as being a 'highly animated little woman, bursting with energy and always thinking of the future.'[19] They developed a warm friendship, and Kathleen gave Jim invaluable professional advice on becoming a more widely published author.

In the late 1930s, Kathleen Strange was enjoying her position as Winnipeg's top-selling writer. Her book, winner of the McLeod-Dodge Prize and published by Dodge in New York, had appeal to easterners and westerners alike, and enjoyed substantial sales in Britain. *With the West in Her Eyes* is an autobiographical account of how the author met her husband, a widower with three half-grown sons, and how for health reasons they decided to emigrate from England after the First World War to farm in central Alberta. Harry Strange, an engineer by profession and a commissioned officer with the Corps of Royal Engineers during the war, had no experience in farming, and Kathleen had not the slightest idea of how to run a kitchen; but not only did they learn to survive for ten years on a Prairie homestead, they also managed to establish a prosperous seed farm that became renowned across Canada. Much of the interest in the book derives from the greenhorn English couple learning to master the essential tasks – baking bread, digging a well, threshing – and dealing with the local inhabitants and farmhands. One is reminded a little of Susanna Moodie's pioneer experiences nearly a century before, except that Strange's narrative is suffused with optimism and light-hearted humour and has none of the sombre depths or personal complexity of the Ontario story. Kathleen Strange was buoyed up with success when Jim knew her. She had become a personal friend of Martha Ostenso, another successful writer connected to Manitoba, and liked to tell how Martha was so excited the day she was awarded the Dodd, Mead Prize for *Wild Geese* that she forgot to put on her stockings. Kathleen was much sought after to speak to writers' groups, and in 1940 she ran the Winnipeg branch of the Canadian Authors Association, an organization Jim would never join.

In spite of her high public profile and popularity at the time, Kathleen and Jim became what he called 'soulmates.' The basis for the friendship is suggested from time to time in her pioneer narrative: beneath the exterior surface of high energy and success was a small woman from Britain who, like Kate Ross and by extension Jim, remained an outsider in North America. The reasons were personal and intricate. Her awkwardness at practical domestic tasks such as milking cows, but particularly at cooking and housework, was seen as a failure to fulfil her role as a woman. Gender expectations were further complicated by her refusal to dress according to the clothing codes of central Alberta: for wearing riding breeches, when decent women only wore skirts, she was for a time ostracized from the community. Her failure to fully integrate is also reflected in the number of times she was cheated by those around her.

Jim understood all too well the many ways, subtle and not so subtle, that a small farm community can exclude someone who is different. So Jim and Kathleen enjoyed each other's company; she read his stories, and he took genuine pleasure in her success. Jim never introduced Kathleen to his mother, however, because Kate had read *With the West in Her Eyes* and seemed to be affronted by it; she felt that she knew the West much better than this latecomer, that it was *her* West, and that Mrs Strange had sometimes gotten it wrong. When Jim showed the manuscript of *As for Me and My House* to Kathleen, she said very positively that it was time he had an agent, who could place his work with a major publishing firm, and she suggested the man who worked on her behalf in New York.

His name was Maximilian Becker, and with his partner, Ann Elmo, he ran the AFG (American-French-German) Agency in mid-Manhattan.[20] Max Becker was born in Cairo, Egypt, in 1903 and, as an accomplished musician, immigrated to the United States in 1929. He intended to pursue a career as a concert pianist (he had played for the King of Siam as a youth), but a skating accident at Rockefeller Center, in which he broke both of his wrists, changed the course of his career. He established instead a literary agency and occasionally produced plays on Broadway. The agency with its international flavour, was moderately successful, representing among other notables Georges Simenon and Saint-Exupéry. Max was exceptionally good-humoured and well liked by his business associates – he is described by Stacey Schiff in her autobiography of Saint-Exupéry as 'an impish man of courtly demeanor and quiet humor'[21] – but he was also a perfectionist and fastidiously slow with clients. Kathleen told Jim of her experience, but she recommended Max nonetheless because he had acquired considerable knowledge as a literary agent and was shrewd at matching manuscripts with publishers. Sometime early in 1940, he accepted Jim as a client on Kathleen's recommendation and set out to sell the manuscript of *As for Me and My House*.

Kathleen's enthusiasm had inspired Jim to make contact with Max Becker, but before he could send the manuscript off he had to have a clean copy typed, because on every reading he kept making extensive changes. As typing the manuscript in the evenings would take several weeks, Jim decided to employ the services of Tora Talgoy, the young woman he had met through Ernest Court. Tora inherited an interest in writing from her father, Magnus Talgoy, editor of the Norwegian newspaper *Norrona*, and decided to join the Phoenix Club sometime in the late 1930s, enrolling in the creative writing classes. Sufficiently impressed with her talent for landscape description, Ernest Court suggested that the diffident young woman take a sample of her writing to Jimmy Ross (as he continued to be known to his friends and acquaintances) and ask for his advice. By this point, Jim was considered the outstanding talent in Mr Court's writing group. Jim remembered their first meeting this way: a young woman came into the bank one winter morning and, with little introduction, brusquely handed him a folder of writing, saying she would call back shortly for his opinion. Tora, for her part, remembered being pressed by Ernest Court and finally, gathering her courage, shyly offering samples of her writing to the bank clerk, of whom she was in awe. Most of the writings in the folder were impressionistic sketches – nature walks, the change of the seasons, a Winnipeg street, a friend's home being torn down. Jim advised cuts, sometimes expansions, but particularly he advised deleting passages that had become 'too imaginative' or ornamented. Tora recalled describing a red buoy on the lake as bobbing on the water like a red apple. Jim said the simile was a little trivial, and when she substituted 'like a red radish,' he advised against a simile altogether.[22] Tora's articles and sketches, however, had a particular appeal, and she was successful in placing several of them with the *Winnipeg Tribune*. Jim couldn't help envy her success, for she was paid ten dollars for sketches of only five hundred words, sketches sometimes produced in an evening.

But Tora was not otherwise employed, and after they had come to know each other (Kate was especially fond of the young woman), Jim asked her if she would be willing to type out a clean copy of his novel. She agreed to the proposal and used the 'good' typewriter in her father's office after the newspaper quarters were closed for the day. It was slow work because the typescript she worked from had so many deletions and additions, but she was enthusiastic nonetheless for she felt instructed by all the markings on the typescript. The writing already impressed her, but she was fascinated to see how a good sentence became even better by the steady process of revision. Tora was in awe of Jim, and when she came to his apartment she paid attention to and remembered all his observations. He told her books should never be jammed on shelves – there should always be a little looseness so that they slip in and out easily. He also told her that pictures should be changed regularly on the walls – otherwise you stop seeing them. Jim was very different from the other young men she knew, and she felt he took her wish to be a writer seriously.[23] Jim, in turn, was pleased with the work she did in typing up the manuscript for *As for Me and My House*, and he paid her fifty dollars, subsequently asking her to type up a story he was sending to the *Atlantic Monthly*.

In New York, Max Becker sent the manuscript to Duell, Sloan and Pierce. The readers there were sufficiently impressed to say they would consider it as a second novel. Did the author have another novel manuscript with more straightforward, popular appeal? Following Max's direction, Jim sent him 'The Wife of Peter Guy,' although with misgivings because it did not have a strong plot-line either. At the end of the story, Peter and his wife leave the town that has ostracized them, but their future together is anything but certain. After what seemed like a long wait, Duell, Sloan and Pierce turned down both manuscripts. But then occurred an extraordinary bit of good luck for Canadian literature: Max Becker sent the manuscript of As for Me and My House to Reynal and Hitchcock, and within two days it was accepted for publication.

Canadian literature owes a great debt to the shrewd judgment of Max Becker and to the discriminating taste and generous offices of the New York publisher Eugene Reynal. Expensively educated at Harvard and Oxford, independently wealthy, Reynal chose for publication the manuscripts he personally liked with little concern for their commercial possibilities. In partnership with Curtice N. Hitchcock, he published a series of distinguished art books, which were in fact commercially viable, as well as books of more general interest. When Becker sent him the manuscript for As for Me and My House, he read it when it arrived. He did not have to solicit readers reports or take his selection to an editorial board, and so he contacted Max with an acceptance in what must be a record length of time, just two days. Other publishers might have questioned the book's commercial possibilities, and Jim would likely have destroyed the manuscript for As for Me and My House, as he would eventually do for at least three other novels.

Reynal wrote to Jim in November of 1940: 'We are extremely enthusiastic about your present novel, AS FOR ME AND MY HOUSE, and particularly impressed with the fluency of your style. It seems to all of us here that you have great promise as a writer, and that if you do not try to push yourself too fast, you have a real future ahead of you.' But Reynal was also shrewd in matters of business, and although he does not hazard a guess as to the novel's commercial potential, he cautions Jim that writers' reputations are made slowly: 'Your agent, Mr Becker, tells us that you are anxious to give up your job and devote your entire time to writing. This does not seem to us a wise decision at the moment ... Building up a reputation as a novelist is a slow, laborious job unless you happen to get the very special breaks that come perhaps once in a thousand times. You have a whole lifetime ahead of you and a promising writing career. Because it is so promising, it is all the more important to take it slowly and let it develop as you yourself develop.'[24] Reynal encouraged Jim to show them any other manuscripts he had and to write more books for Reynal and Hitchcock to publish. Jim, however, instructed Max not to send Reynal the manuscript of 'Peter Guy,' because he had lost faith in its worth. Looking back, Jim would feel that the letters from Eugene Reynal were the most encouraging and helpful he ever received from a publisher during his career as a writer.

Preparing the manuscript for publication went fairly smoothly with only a couple of minor problems. Reynal, like Alexander Macphail, did not ask for any editorial changes, and so the book went into production shortly after it was accepted for publication. Jim in the meantime had a photograph taken for the dust jacket, and near publication date it appeared in a Winnipeg newspaper along with a short announcement of the forthcoming book. When the proofs arrived, Jim noticed at once that the running head on each page read 'As for Me and My Home'; it was decided to omit the running head altogether. Otherwise the compositor's work had been accurate, and the formatting of the text impressed the first-time author: the type and leading made for easy reading, the margins were generous. The dust jacket for the book, however, was another matter. When Jim saw the blueline proof, he was upset by the copy an advertiser had put together for the back of the jacket; it included disparaging remarks about the Canadian setting, stating that the characters in the novel were trapped by the backward nature of society in Canada. Since he had taken pains, in order to find an American publisher, not to identify the setting as Canadian, Jim felt he must object to this statement on the cover.[25] The jacket designer replaced the blurb about the novel on the back with some advertising for other Reynal and Hitchcock books. The dust jacket that resulted is not attractive: a small cartoon-like drawing of a church and manse is situated between the title and the author's name; the colour of the jacket is chocolate brown. There is no picture of the author, and one reviewer (Rose Feld in the New York Herald Tribune) assumed it was a woman who had written the book.[26] The mistake was not unreasonable. The blurb inside the front leaf of the jacket reads: 'How a woman who was deeply in love with her husband won him back from himself and his despair over his own failure – that is the story of As for Me and My House.' There is no reference to, or account of, the author anywhere in the book or on the jacket, just that '[the] story is told by the woman whose strength, devotion and sacrifice heal the wounds of the man who is her life.' From the outset, then, ambiguities of gender would mark this text as confusing and unsettling in terms of both characters and authorship.

seven
_____

As for Me and My House
1941

Why don't you write something more cheerful that people will read? – Kate
Ross

The genesis and the writing of As for Me and My House, described in the previous chapter, culminated in the novel's publication in New York on Valen-
tine's Day of 1941. The timing can only be viewed as ironic, since this novel
hardly celebrates romantic love, but the timing was unfortunate in a larger
sense. The novel's realism reflected back an era that had just closed and there
was little public interest in reading about the Depression and dust storms.
The world, now plunged into war, still wanted escapist entertainment. American reviewers hardly knew what to say about a book which seemed to them
so drab and was such a vivid reminder of what was, for most people, the bleakest period in living memory.

The novel's setting is a small Prairie town, appropriately but ironically
called Horizon,[1] and its time span is roughly a year in the life of the Bentleys,
a clergyman and his wife who have already served the church in a series of
small towns. The story is told in the form of a diary kept by Mrs Bentley (she
has no other name), and from the first page the reader is aware of the cheerless, frustrated existence these two people lead. In twelve years of marriage,
neither Philip Bentley nor his wife have found any lasting source of happiness. Philip is miserable in his vocation: he had wanted to paint, to be an artist, but he could not afford an education. Moreover, he is filled with guilt
because he does not believe what he preaches. Mrs Bentley, who has not been
able to bear children, lives only to make her husband happy, but her attentions are met with indifference: 'To have him notice, speak to me as if I really
mattered in his life, after twelve years with him that's all I want or need' (23).

The novel, like most Ross stories, has little plot. Mrs Bentley schemes to save enough money so that Philip can leave the ministry and open a small city bookstore. She comes to believe that he has had an affair with Judith West, who sings in the church choir and becomes pregnant. Otherwise the novel records life's smaller passages: planting a garden in the spring, looking after an orphaned youth, a summer holiday, a concert, friendships, but, above all else, the weather – the spring rain leaking into the parsonage, the heat and dust of summer, and the wind that never stops blowing. After a year, the Bentleys leave Horizon for an uncertain future in the city, taking Judith's baby with them, but the reader feels little has changed in their lives.

The reviews that appeared over the next few weeks in the United States were not exactly hostile, but they did not give the book-buying public any reason to purchase As for Me and My House. They were chiefly plot summaries with only brief critical assessments. Most of them acknowledged the book to be well written: Rose Feld, for example, writing for the New York Herald Tribune, observed that the book 'shows a real ability to depict a mood and to catch a character,'[2] and the reviewer for a Dayton, Ohio, newspaper, in what was Ross's favourite notice, described the style as 'appealing ... easy to read.'[3] Marianne Hauser, herself a novelist, stated in the New York Times Review of Books that it was 'written with remarkable honesty, and often with strength.'[4] Only the anonymous reviewer for the Springfield Republican complained that the 'style ... is liable to become tedious when the narrative runs a bit thin.'[5] Some of the American reviewers did feel the plot was thin, but more particularly they were puzzled that a novel should be, in their opinion, so dreary and cheerless. Hauser pointed out that Ross had an 'almost uncanny feeling for the drab and depressing,' and observed of the Bentleys that 'their life [was] nothing but defeat.' In an optimistic American way, she draws attention to 'a bright last scene ... interpreting if not justifying all previous desperation.'[6] The Dayton reviewer called the book 'an interesting study' but not 'happy or cheerful.'[7] Clifton Fadiman's short review in the New Yorker concluded that there were 'some good things here, but the book is very gloomy.'[8] That succinct judgment probably explains better than any other why Reynal had to report to Jim at the end of the month that so far there had been almost no U.S. sales.

McClelland and Stewart imported some copies of the book for the Canadian market which were distributed at the end of March that year, along with a promotion notice identifying the author as a bank clerk originally from Saskatchewan. The book was greeted more enthusiastically in Canada; it was judged by the country's most important reviewers as an excellent novel, and Sinclair Ross was hailed as a young writer of great promise. There was a feeling expressed in several of the Canadian reviews that this was the kind of artistic novel that the country had long been waiting for, that *As for Me and My House* would be read for many years to come. Unfortunately there was no clipping service for the Canadian reviews, and many of them Jim did not see. In retro-spect, it was particularly regrettable that he did not read the review written that April by Robertson Davies in the *Peterborough Examiner*, for it was the most exuberant and far-seeing. Davies, then a twenty-eight-year-old journalist writing for a small newspaper, welcomed the novel as 'a remarkable addition to our small stock of Canadian books of first-rate importance,'[9] a book written with great sensitivity and skill. He predicted that it would also be read outside the country and one day be put on university reading lists, foreseeing the clas-sic status it would eventually be accorded. His one misfire in the review was to predict that Canada would soon gain a professional author of first-rate impor-tance and that the Royal Bank of Canada would lose a clerk.

W.A. Deacon's review in the *Globe and Mail*, which Jim did see, was more realistic when it observed that Ross's faithfulness to the 'dreary monotony of the once-hopeful West almost kills any chance of popularity.'[10] But Deacon also welcomed *As for Me and My House* as a 'promising first novel' and, ever the fervent nationalist, said Ross was a novelist who should be encouraged because he was performing the most useful function of a writer, namely the interpreting of Canadian life. Similarly, the reviewer for the *Winnipeg Free Press* praised Ross as a 'mature and thoughtful artist,'[11] drawing attention to his sensitive rendering of Prairie moods and atmosphere. Jim was glad that the local review was supportive. He felt strongly that he was exposing himself to public ridicule in presuming to publish a novel and had cringed at the thought of a negative notice in the home paper. Some of the other large-cir-culation dailies, however, such as the *Vancouver Sun* and the *Daily Province*, were not so kind. Without a sophisticated tradition of book reviewing, they both dismissed the novel in brief notices as a 'very gloomy picture of the prai-ries,' 'depressing,' and 'remarkably unfair' in its presentation of little Prairie towns.[12] In spite of some good notices, the book sold very few copies in Can-ada, and it soon dropped from sight, earning Jim no more than $270, which was paid in advance royalties.

It would be seventeen years before the reading public would hear of the novel again. It had left a positive impression on a handful of academics, among them E.K. Brown, Roy Daniells, Edward McCourt, and Desmond Pacey,[13] and when Malcolm Ross established the New Canadian Library for McClelland and Stewart in 1957, *As for Me and My House* was chosen as one of the first titles in the new paperback series, with the cover labelling it a 'classic.' This might have seemed a facile designation when the book was still so new, but almost at once critics began writing about this text as a significant landmark in Canadian culture, and in years to follow it would become the subject of more critical discussion and debate than any other single work of Canadian fiction. Some early critics such as McCourt, impressed by the book's historical authenticity, valued it above all for its portrayal of the Depression era in the drought-stricken West, and that value remains strong. Part of that historical authenticity is the book's rendering of Canada's Puritan past, some critics viewing it as life-strangling, the church as social panopticon, others seeing the Prairie church and its social gospel as the bedrock of the country's social and spiritual life.[14] There would be several readings of the novel as primarily an artist's story.[15] But the most vigorous debates that surrounded the novel for several years focused on the reliability of its narrator, Mrs Bentley. Was she to be seen as 'pure gold,' as Roy Daniells urged in his introduction to the original paperback,[16] or was she to be viewed as a dissembler, a self-centred, at times mean-spirited woman, unwittingly but systematically destroying her marriage?[17] Feminist reasoning has tried to balance these views by situating the character's fallibility in her textual origin – that is, in a man writing about a woman who is writing about a man.[18]

An early essay by W.H. New, titled 'Sinclair Ross's Ambivalent World,' identified some of the conditions of the text that have made it readable from so many different points of view. New argues that blurred images – for example, 'dust clouds lapping at the sky,' 'planks of sunlight' – and competing perspectives – Philip's, his wife's, their friend Paul's – undermine the notions of 'reality' or 'truth' in the novel, leaving in their place a complex study of human responses. Probably the best example of this ambivalence, he suggests, is the final line in the text, in which Mrs Bentley says about naming the baby Philip: 'That's right, Philip. I want it so.' Her closing statement can be read as revealing the new-found humility that she has experienced, or the stranglehold of a manipulating woman forcing decisions on her husband.

Beyond New's study of imagery and point of view, one can situate this ambiguity in the actual linguistic materials of the text, the unknowable as an effect of a style in which the author has used grammatical structures that produce indecipherability. Two such features stand out. Near the close of her diary, Mrs Bentley describes a final meeting with Paul Kirby. They have been walking in the country and Paul has been speaking in riddles until Mrs Bentley, noting the time, says she must go home to prepare Philip's supper. Paul at first seems not to hear her, then agrees that they had better return. Four simple sentences conclude the scene:

> *It* was a kind of avowal. *It* asked nothing of me. *It* didn't try to explain or defend *itself*. We came home leaving *it* there. (208–9, emphasis added)

Striking in these plain sentences is the repetition of the indefinite pronoun; the reader is left wondering what 'it' refers to. There is nothing in the preceding text, nor in what follows, that explains what has transpired between the two characters; grammatically 'it' remains empty of reference, a mystery. On the basis of this ambiguity, critics have constructed Paul and Mrs Bentley as potential lovers, Paul as Judith West's lover and father of her child,[19] and recently, in queer readings of the novel, Paul and Philip conjoined within a homosexual fantasy, with Mrs Bentley averting her eyes.[20] A similar effect is produced by the use of transitive verbs that lack an object. In a passage after she believes she has discovered Philip and Judith making love, Mrs Bentley is rehearsing in her mind how impossible it is to know her husband, and she says to herself four times, 'I must remember' (177–8). But she does not tell us exactly what must be remembered; from surrounding text, the reader can supply many answers.[21]

The answer, to Jim's way of thinking about the book, was centred in Paul Kirby, whom he would describe in conversation as a self-portrait, a common little man from a farm background with an interest in ideas and an eccentric fascination with the genealogy of words. As a schoolteacher, Paul is something of a loner, with just enough education that he no longer quite fits in with his country origins. Jim started writing the novel in Philip Bentley's voice and then shifted to his wife's, in what Peter Dickinson has described as 'a Canadian example of "narrative transvestism"' (18), revealing the instability of gender categories. But Jim pointed out several times that Paul's point of view is equally important to the others, that he is attracted to both Philip and his wife and, with this expanded range of emotional capacity, can identify with them both.[22] Another way of reading the text, then, evoking a bisexual projective fantasy, is to identify, in spite of the gaps and silences of the text, a homosocial/sexual connection between Paul and Philip, both lovers of horses, that is made possible through Paul's 'courtship' of Philip's wife.[23] Written in the modernist style, *As for Me and My House* fosters these speculations, its author intuiting that human personality, especially sexuality, is so complicated as to be finally unknowable. Yet, however the book is read, at its heart is the solid matter of its 'unique, lapidary' style,[24] its indelible rendering of the harshness of the Prairie landscape and the lives of its beleaguered inhabitants, and its creation of Mrs Bentley, an archetypal Canadian figure compounded of so many personal and cultural forces.

In 1941, of course, Jim could not know how well he had written, because overall the reception of the book proved to be discouraging. Nonetheless, he did enjoy for a while the attentions he received as the author of a novel published in the United States. He heard again from J.C. Nelson, manager of the advertising department at the bank's head office in Montreal, who wrote to congratulate him and promised a mention of the novel in a future issue of the *Royal Bank Magazine*.[25] His friends in Winnipeg showed their interest too, although they found it difficult to discuss the book itself. For example, although Harriet Duff-Smith had been part of the Phoenix Club and had tried her hand at writing fiction, her questions for Jim centred on prototypes for the characters, not on the novel's ideas or craft. It was easy enough to explain to her that *As for Me and My House* emerged from his experience of the Prairie towns in which he had worked as a banker, particularly Abbey and Arcola, where the Depression and drought were an inseparable part of that setting, as was the atmosphere of petty social ambition and religious hypocrisy. But it was hard for her to understand that the characters of the novel were wholly imagined, or else amalgams of various individuals and situations, and that actual prototypes did not exist. In his mind, the character of Philip Bentley, for example, had at least three sources the author could point to: in Abbey the author imagined *himself* in the situation of someone who accepted a position in the church in return for an education; but he also observed the life of the Reverend Bert Howard in Arcola, an amateur dramatist and a type of man who professed piety but was dogged by rumours. There was also Forbes Murray, whose spiritual well had run dry and who left the ministry. Mrs Bentley's feelings for Philip (his stature as someone unattainable) owed something to the author's strong feelings for Murray, whom he accompanied to services in the country. Similarly, the town of Horizon was a composite of Abbey and Arcola, but as its name was meant to suggest, it is at once everywhere and nowhere. But how to explain this skill in weaving together essential elements of human nature and landscape against a vivid historical backdrop when the polite interrogator has a more literal understanding of how fictional characters are created.

Here perhaps is an appropriate place to mention a further insight into the creation of *As for Me and My House*. An early manuscript version of Ross's memoir, 'Just Wind and Horses,' suggests yet another source for the character of Philip in the story of his maternal grandfather, John Foster Fraser, the Unitarian minister who was said to have died in the pulpit in his early thirties. In this longer version of the memoir, his grandfather gets a girl pregnant when he is a twenty-year-old student in Edinburgh. His mother, an austere widow, says she will never accept an adventuress in the family and sends him a hundred pounds in a letter saying, 'use this to get her out of the way.' But instead he marries the girl (Jessie Patterson), his financial support is cut off, and he ekes out a living as a tutor while continuing with his studies. The young couple live in two shabby rooms; before long there are two babies to look after

and there are quarrels. After a period of study in the United States and con-
version to Unitarianism under Theodore Parker, Fraser returns with his family to Scotland, where he preaches in three different congregations. They are
small churches, and like the congregations in *As for Me and My House*, they
grow disapproving and are impatient to be rid of their minister. Why? asks the
narrator of the memoir, and his mother explains the situation this way:

> A strange laddie. He loves his fellow man but has no illusions about him, and
> perhaps when he preached, some of it came through. Perhaps in the pews his lis-
> teners felt confusion hovering over them – confusion, uncertainty and lack of
> faith – felt it as a warning, an accusation of fault, directed against them, and they
> in turn – subconscious retaliation – were mistrustful.[26]

As narrator, Jim speculates that his young grandfather was in a muddle and
went off-track. Was he just a vagabond and idler, or did Unitarianism fail to
fire him with a spiritual purpose and goal? Did he lose his beliefs? As the type
of fatherless young intellectual whose faith has grown cold, his grandfather
seems to lie closer to the heart of the novel than either Bert Howard or Forbes
Murray. Perhaps, in his evasive way, Jim cut this part of his family's history
from the final version of 'Just Wind and Horses' because it exposed too openly
both family history and his own creative process in the writing of his famous
novel.

Publication of *As for Me and My House* roused some curiosity about the
author among members of the English Department at the University of Manitoba. Especially prominent in his attentions was Professor Roy Daniells, a
Milton scholar and a poet, who also had a keen eye for contemporary Canadian writing. His interest in Jim predated the publication of the novel: he had
read his stories in *Queen's Quarterly*, recognized their worth, and, according
to the diary he kept, invited Jim to his place for dinner in late October of
1940.[27] Over the years, Daniells would prove to be one of Jim's most ardent
admirers and boosters. Although their friendship was always a courteous and
formal one, there were unspoken bonds of sympathy between the two men.
Roy Daniells, English born, had been raised on Vancouver Island in a strict
religious community known as the Plymouth Brethren. Although he went
through a severe religious crisis and broke away from this millennial sect,
Daniells remained strongly attached to his parents, particularly his mother.
While at the University of Manitoba, he was deeply in love with a young student, Ruth Schlass, but he spent his summers on Vancouver Island, taking his
mother shopping and going for regular walks with her. Jim sensed in Daniells

a kindred spirit, someone who had once been imprisoned in a series of failures and burdened with similar family obligations.[28]

While still reading *As for Me and My House*, Daniells wrote to Jim in an excited mood that the book was "fine ... really excellent" and urged him to start work on another right away: 'You should be able to produce that phenomenon we've been waiting for since Confederation: the great Canadian novel. *As for Me and My House* is very close to it. Brodersen and Miss Saunders, two staff whose judgment is excellent, are both wild about it, and "wild" is no exaggeration.'[29] As Jim remembered, he and Daniells would frequently meet for lunch, and occasionally he would attend the afternoon teas the latter gave at his apartment for gifted students and close colleagues. There Jim met such men as Dr Meredith Thompson, who also taught in the English Department, and students like Douglas Tunstell and William Ross, who had impressed their professors as having considerable promise. Daniells was imitating the practice of his Victoria high-school mentor, Ira Dilworth, whom Jim met more than once at Daniells's afternoons. To Jim, these gatherings represented the magic circle of university life from which he had been excluded by fate and circumstance.

But invitations were now coming to him to be part of that circle. One Saturday morning in early April, he answered the door at the apartment to find two women who had read *As for Me and My House* and wanted to meet him. They were Dr Doris Saunders of the English Department, to whom Daniells had referred in his letter, and her friend, Edna Riley, the daughter of a Winnipeg judge.[30] The two women, in their early forties, stayed for half an hour, and Dr Saunders declared her intention of assigning *As for Me and My House* as the Canadian novel on the introductory English course in the fall. She hoped there would be a paperback edition for students to buy. Further, she hoped Jim could be persuaded to speak to her class and answer questions. She was deeply impressed by the book, particularly the style and the rendering of Prairie life, but she felt the book was not without flaws. She suggested to Jim that he had given Mrs Bentley music that was too difficult to play for someone with her background, and Jim agreed that was probably the case.

Kate had been ironing when the two women arrived, but from her bedroom she listened to the conversation and soon joined the group in the parlour. She was favourably impressed by Doris's intelligent and sober demeanour and by Miss Riley's social graces, and after the women had left she said to Jim that in her opinion 'they were real ladies.' It wasn't just education that impressed Kate; personal comeliness, self-confidence, and a dignified manner were necessary too. She liked Roy Daniells for his reserve, but was not impressed by Ira Dilworth, who was fair and rather stout and flamboyantly sported a sharp little beard. Nor was she persuaded of excellence in the young and eager Desmond Pacey. After he had called at the apartment, she pronounced in broad Scots, 'Hae nae mooch.'[31]

For some time Jim had planned a trip to New York for April – he hadn't been back since 1938. When he described his plans to Roy Daniells, the latter insisted that Jim also make some time for a few days in Toronto; he wanted him to meet Ned Pratt, who had been his mentor at the University of Toronto, and also E.K. Brown, his former colleague and head of English at the University of Manitoba. He felt these contacts would be good for Jim. Roy wrote to his friends in Toronto and told them about the young novelist who, in his opinion, had written one of the best books ever produced by a Canadian.

In New York for a week, Jim indulged himself as usual with theatre and concert performances, and again made contacts with gay men at nightclubs and hotel bars. Years later, he would say that those experiences were appealing because they were so easy; young men especially were eager for quick sexual gratification and made no other demands. But a powerful element in those anonymous encounters was the admiration he received from other men for being, in common parlance, 'well hung.' He could never get enough of it. It gave him a feeling of power in those encounters and allowed him his preference for being the passive partner in oral sex: 'I liked to have it done,' he said; 'I never liked to do it.'[32] He had no interest in anal sex, perhaps because of his fastidious nature, or more likely because it involved an intimacy that he could never quite enter into. Similarly in his relations with women, his preference was for oral sex, to be fondled and admired.

Jim visited the McCormicks, who made a lively fuss over the publication of his novel, and for the first time he met his agent, Max Becker, and Max's partner, Ann Elmo. Jim went out for dinner with Max and Ann, and he assumed they were married; he was very surprised to learn much later from Kathleen Strange that Max was a confirmed bachelor. Max was funny, very knowledgeable, full of 'moxie,'[33] and Jim recognized his good luck in being recommended to him by Kathleen; but at the same time, Jim felt more comfortable with Ann, whom he would remember as a small, attractive Jewish woman, with dark hair and eyes and a gentle manner. As Max did not wish to discuss business at dinner, a couple of days later Jim met with him again over a beer to talk about a new novel manuscript he was working on. Max was sorry that *As for Me and My House* was not selling but reassured Jim that he wanted to continue as his agent. One thing did not happen during the week in New York – he did not meet his publishers. Jim had written to Gene Reynal, giving his travel dates and address, but there was no invitation or message in reply. He thought about phoning to the publishing company but in the end did not find the courage to do so. He could not help feel that Reynal's silence was a form of rebuff reflecting the dismal sales of the novel. In that regard, he left New York feeling disappointed.

The stopover in Toronto began badly. When English professor E.K. Brown heard that the young novelist was coming to Toronto, he left a message at the YMCA asking Jim to meet him for lunch. But Jim went to the office of the wrong Professor Brown, a theologian; neither was the wiser, and the two had lunch together, making polite but desultory conversation. Another message from E.K. Brown alerted Jim to his error, and the following day E.K. hosted a luncheon at Hart House and Jim found himself, in addition to Brown, in the company of E.J. Pratt, Earle Birney, John D. Robins, Robertson Davies, and Northrop Frye. But for Jim the previous day's error only seemed compounded, for he found himself out of his depth surrounded by these literary men, who (or so it seemed to the shy author) not only ignored him but probably looked down on him. The table hummed with conversation, but Jim was seldom asked to give an opinion. This was the Canadian literary establishment – eastern, educated, and exclusively male – whereas Jim was a farm boy from the West, with only grade eleven schooling, and more at ease in mixed company.

As lunch progressed, Jim felt John Robins was actively hostile towards him. When the conversation turned to the late Sir Andrew Macphail, Jim joined in and, uncharacteristically, boasted that Macphail once wrote to him that he had written three of Canada's best short stories. Robins expressed his scorn by dismissing Macphail as someone who had grown out of touch with the literary scene and become an insignificant hack. (The following year, Robins edited an anthology of Canadian writing titled A *Pocketful of Canada*, and Jim was not surprised to see that his work was not included.) For Jim, this introduction to Canada's foremost authors and educators seemed largely abortive, although, in fact, Robertson Davies would go away and write a glowing review of *As for Me and My House* and Earle Birney the following year would solicit a story from Jim when he was planning a collection of Canadian writings for the American magazine *Story*. But Jim came away, not excited by meeting these men of letters, rather, disappointed by the conviction that his shyness and lack of education would never permit him to be one of their illustrious company.

But, on further reflection, perhaps this company was not so illustrious. An afternoon listening to Sir Charles G.D. Roberts (by then eighty-one) talk continuously about himself was a disheartening affair. Jim had long admired Roberts's animal stories and was keenly disappointed to find the author such an eccentric and bore. An evening with Northrop Frye was no more reassuring. Frye, who had said almost nothing at the Hart House lunch, suggested dinner in a small French restaurant near the university, but again conversation lagged, even though the two young men (Frye was only twenty-eight) had things in common. Frye, in fact, had spent the summer of 1934 in rural Saskatchewan as a student minister for the United Church – he had ridden a pony to conduct services in a country school and lived in a small drought-ridden town like Horizon; accordingly, his appreciation of As for Me and My House was genuine and would be lasting. But Jim would only remember one part of that evening's conversation. Frye allowed that he knew something of the homosexual life when he had been abroad as a student – on trips he had made to Paris – and he alluded to knowing of gay men at the university. 'Of course, you know what I'm talking about,' Jim quoted Frye as saying. But, as Keath Fraser has observed, Jim always spoke disparagingly of Frye, and whether this was because of assumptions he made about Jim's sexual life, or whether it was because he felt a deep-seated inferiority in relation to this distinguished intellectual, it would be difficult to say.[34]

More stimulating than the academics were the newspaper and magazine reviewers, and the opportunity to look around Toronto, which, to him, had 'an old and strangely "peaceful" atmosphere.'[35] By chance, the young Ottawa-based historian Stuart C. Easton, who in March had written a very positive review of As for Me and My House for Saturday Night, was also staying at the YMCA in Toronto for a week, and he and Jim had a lively discussion of the novel and the conditions of Prairie life that had led to its writing. Similarly W.A. Deacon, who was preparing a review for that Saturday's Globe and Mail, interrogated the author in a vigorous and professional way. Accordingly, it seemed to Jim by the end of his stay in Toronto that the literati, the writers and academics, were too self-preoccupied to pay genuine heed to an author or his work, and that the real work of disseminating knowledge about writing was done by more 'ordinary' men and women.

Roy Daniells remained the exception. When Jim returned to Winnipeg on Sunday, April 27, there was a letter from Daniells filled with praise for As for Me and My House. Jim sent Daniells a reply that same day saying, 'There's no use pretending that a word of praise isn't sweet. I find my appetite for it enormous.'[36] Shortly after his return from the trip east, Jim made a brief appearance in one of Doris Saunders's classes at the university, and shortly thereafter Roy Daniells and Doris Saunders arranged a party for the author, which was held in Doris Saunders's apartment. Some of the students Jim met at Roy's teas were there, and also some members of the musical association, including Chester Duncan and his fiancée, Ada Elwick. The surprise of the evening was the appearance of Arthur Benjamin, who heartily joined in praising Jim and his book. He was there largely because he was a good friend of Edna Riley, who helped Doris with the preparations for the party. Jim would remember that evening with great pleasure, the only irritating aspect being the presence of Ira Dilworth from Victoria. Dilworth behaved as if he were the guest of honour, dominating the conversation.

In 1941, Winnipeg's *literati* were few in number and played a fairly insignificant part in the country's cultural life, but Jim was flattered nonetheless to receive an invitation to meet the city's grande dame of letters, Mrs Laura Goodman Salverson. She asked him to come by for tea and biscuits on a Sunday evening, and Chester Duncan agreed to go along. Chester viewed Mrs Salverson with some suspicion: 'she expects people to bow down' was his estimate, and he warned Jim that she was 'a bit of an old crone.'[37] Mrs Salverson had enjoyed best-seller status with her first novel, *The Viking Heart* (1923), a romantic account of Icelandic settlement in Canada, and her recently published memoir, *Confessions of an Immigrant's Daughter*, had won the Governor General's Award for 1939. When Jim and Chester had tea with Mrs Salverson and her husband, she did indeed refer frequently to her award and to the wide sales of her writings, and praise for her work was not lost in making the evening a pleasant occasion. Although Mrs Salverson was only fifty-one at the time, she seemed older and more authoritarian than her years. She told Jim that she thought *As for Me and My House* was a credible first novel, but that there were grammatical flaws that seriously distracted from the pleasure in the writing. He should have had someone from the university with a strong background in English read carefully through his work. Chester felt vindicated for his harsh remarks by these comments. Although Jim was puzzled by her counsel and could see she took great pride in her own work, he felt that she was nonetheless a simple country woman underneath.

Jim was subjected to a similar criticism at the Winnipeg Library. He was invited to appear there one Saturday afternoon to sign copies of his book provided by Miss Preston, who managed Eaton's bookstore. Only a few copies were sold – to the women who attended the library club meetings – and afterwards the librarian in charge suggested to Jim that poor sales were perhaps caused by the stylistic flaws in his writing: his failure, as she put it, 'to turn a phrase.'[38] There was criticism at home, too. Kate had read the novel and was not impressed. The problem with the book, as far as she was concerned, was that the characters had been married too long for their relationship to be believable. 'Mrs Bentley's devotion would not have stood up to Philip's aloofness and lack of response for so many years. Two or three, at the most, and then she would have lost patience and told him off.'[39] Perhaps Kate was thinking about life with her own dour and taciturn husband, with whom she had quarrelled so violently, and from whom she had finally parted. At any rate, though she had a healthy Scottish respect for books and 'things of the mind,' she also valued success, and on every ground she deemed *As for Me and My House* a failure.

An earlier verdict of his writing, which rankled, was Kate's dismissal of his short stories as 'just wind and horses.'[40] She deeply regretted that he was unable to write plots and sell his stories to high-paying magazines, and she didn't hide her disappointment. In the spring of 1941, *Queen's Quarterly* published one of Jim's least developed stories in terms of plot, but one of his most vivid depictions of the drought and the hardships endured by Prairie farmers during the Depression. 'Not by Rain Alone,'[41] a sketch more than a story, portrays the squalid farm conditions a young man endures while trying to earn enough money in order to marry. Most memorable is the glimpse inside a bachelor's two-room 'shack,' its unmade bed, smelling of sweat and heat, its kitchen with unwashed plates covered in grease or in flies strangled in syrup. At the same time, this sketch has descriptions of great power. As young Will anxiously waits for rain, we are told that in the evenings 'thunder clouds banked steep along the west, but always they glimmered with summer lightning for a while, then drifted south and disappeared. The days were still, brassy, pitiless. Swift little whirlwinds scoured across the fields' (46). As he sets out to visit the girl he hopes to marry, we are told the sun 'struck [him] like a drill, as if all its power were focused on him in a single ray,' until 'a shadow like a wing swept across the field, stately and cool ... as if a curtain were being drawn' (52). Will feels he cannot ask Eleanor to marry him – her family are prosperous farmers with a seven-room house and a motor car (an echo here perhaps of the way Jim felt in his relationship to Dorothy Cornell and her family) – but when they meet, she indicates that she too is tired of waiting and will marry him in November. The few words they exchange constitutes the action of the story. For later publication in the New Canadian Library, Jim would join this story to 'September Snow,' creating a two-part story with 'Not by Rain Alone' (retitled 'Summer Thunder') as a prelude to the tragic account of the young wife who dies in childbirth during a September blizzard. Both stories were revised slightly, and 'Not by Rain Alone' was the title chosen for the amalgamated whole.

At the end of May, Jim received a disappointing memo from the members of the university's English Department. After 'careful consideration,' it read, the English Committee decided that *As for Me and My House* would not be suitable as a first-year text, that it would be 'better to have a text in which the traditional approaches to character, plot, setting, and theme are more easily made and in the teaching of which a greater variety of cross-references can be made to other novels.'[42] The memo was reluctantly penned by Roy Daniells just before his annual departure for Victoria. It dashed the author's hopes for a paperback version of his novel. Perhaps Mrs Salverson was right, Jim thought; perhaps the novel just didn't measure up technically or grammatically.

Jim was no stranger to disappointments, and they left their scars. But he was beginning to find that disappointments were often balanced by encouragements from unexpected quarters. One Monday morning in June, Jim was approached at the bank by an energetic young lawyer who had just read *As for Me and My House*. He insisted that they have lunch together. Miss Preston had sold him a copy at Eaton's on Saturday, and he had hardly slept until he finished reading it. He wanted to talk to the author of this amazing book he had just read. The young lawyer's name was Roy St George Stubbs; he was just a year older than Jim, and, like Roy Daniells, he was to become one of Jim's most enthusiastic admirers and long-time public supporters. Stubbs was from a legal family with United Empire Loyalist roots in the Turks and Caicos Islands, but he was also a Prairie socialist and used his position in the courts to fight for greater social justice. In addition to being a lawyer (and eventually a judge), Roy St George Stubbs was eager to be a writer and by 1941 was already a published author with *Lawyers and Laymen of Western Canada* published by Ryerson in 1939 and *Men in Khaki: Four Regiments of Manitoba* forthcoming. Stubbs's books to date were legal and military histories of the West. He wanted now to write fiction set in western Canada, and *As for Me and My House* was proof that it could be done with considerable artistry. After meeting with Jim again for lunch on the following Saturday, Stubbs wrote a piece titled 'Presenting Sinclair Ross' that appeared in *Saturday Night* on August 9th.

   This article was the first introduction of the author to the public at large. Stubbs describes Sinclair Ross as someone 'who does not fulfill the popular conception of an author,' a shy, unassuming bachelor who does not smoke or drink, and does not like crowds. He identifies Jim as a modest bank employee and sketches in the Ross family background, devoting two paragraphs to Sir John Foster Fraser, whom he describes as 'the first and greatest literary influence in [Ross's] life.' Much of the article focuses on Jim's apprenticeship – writing poetry and short stories as a boy, the first magazine rejection, the uncle's advice that the life of a writer is a hard one, and the 'two' novels written and torn up before *As for Me and My House* was published. But the most interesting part of the article, its gist, is Stubbs's interest in the author's work methods: 'Mr Ross composes slowly, some of his sentences being torn up by their roots from his brain. But he holds himself to schedule. He is a warrior of the pen, who trains as rigorously as a prizefighter. Nothing will persuade him to fall short of his weekly stint of work.' He goes on to say that Jim has not touched life at many points, lives largely within himself, because writing is his consuming interest – 'the pleasantest thing he knows.' This is an important interview article because it gives a clear portrait of Jim in 1941, a picture which changes significantly with time. For example, Jim presented himself to Stubbs as no great reader because his urge, he said, was always to rewrite a book, whereas in later years Jim was an avid reader of all kinds of serious and popular literature. In 1941 he cites Hemingway and Richard Hughes among his favourite authors, but these would not be lasting interests.

Meeting for lunch and especially for a beer in the evenings became a regular habit for Jim and Roy, and they were frequently joined by Dyson Carter, author of a recently published novel titled *Night of Flame* (1940) and subtitled 'Behind the Scenes in a Great Hospital.' All three men were in their early thirties and they had each published one book, but otherwise they came from very different backgrounds and held very different views. Carter, who was crippled with polio and used crutches, came from an affluent family and was staunchly conservative in his views. He lived with his parents in one of Winnipeg's most imposing homes, with dark-panelled rooms and rich furnishings that intimidated the boy from Wild Rose. Stubbs, by contrast, had turned away from privileged circumstances to take up the cause of social justice and contented himself with a minimum of material goods. What the three had in common was the desire to be writers, and their talk consisted of little else. But that was more than enough, and they would spend hours at a favourite pub talking about the new books, about getting published (by a strange twist, Dyson Carter's agent in New York was Ann Elmo, Max Becker's partner, and *Night of Flame* had been published by Reynal and Hitchcock), and about the different techniques available to writers to tell their stories well. More than fifty years later, Roy Stubbs would recall that 'Jimmy seemed the least likely of the three of us to succeed and amount to something in public opinion. We were all going to write the great Canadian novel, but now I realize Jimmy had already done it.'[43] Those evenings the talk would go on until Jim would suddenly jump up and leave because, as Stubbs recalled, 'there was his mother's curfew.' To Stubbs and Dyson, this seemed extraordinary behaviour for a single man of thirty-three. Moreover, Jim usually limited his drinking to half a glass of beer, because his mother was a staunch prohibitionist.

Jim felt more acutely than ever the constraints of living with his mother. It seemed to him that they argued incessantly, that one or the other was loudly silent in anger or hurt. At times Kate fought with Jim as if he were an unfaithful husband, accusing him of deceitful behaviour and demanding a detailed account of his whereabouts and all his activities: Who were these men he went drinking with? She wasn't fooled. Why didn't he take her to meet Mrs Salverson or to the party at Doris Saunders's apartment? She liked Dr Saunders and planned to invite her to their apartment for dinner with her nice friend, Miss Riley. And she wanted to know more about these women at the bank – someone named Alice, and a Miss Heaslip. Jim, in turn, became increasingly secretive, less and less forthcoming about his activities. He used the bank address for all his mail and instructed his friends to reach him there by telephone. After an evening out with friends, he would ask them to drop him off a block or two from home so that his mother, watching from her bedroom, could not see whom he had been with. She always let him know on his return that she was still awake, couldn't sleep while he was out. Sometimes she said she hadn't been feeling well that evening.

What Kate enjoyed was entertaining the young men whom Jim befriended, but he was becoming more and more reluctant to bring them home. He decided not to introduce Roy St George Stubbs or Dyson Carter to her, nor the young men whom he had met at Roy Daniells's teas. Lovell Clark, a young man who worked for the city and frequently came into the bank, was another matter. One day, Clark came by the apartment unannounced, and he and Kate instantly hit it off; he became a regular visitor thereafter. Clark was energetic and garrulous, and Kate was always in good spirits when he dropped by for one of her home-cooked dinners. On those evenings, Kate invariably 'took over.' Clark encouraged her, and as they told stories, laughing and urging each other on, Jim saw himself as extraneous, feeling in fact a little bored by all the merriment. Clark was genuinely fond of Kate, as something of a surrogate mother, but there was a vein of mockery in his appeal to her appetite for telling stories; on her side, she found him very entertaining, though she sometimes complained to Jim of his overly dramatic behaviour. Although she enjoyed his company immensely, Kate was probably forced by Clark to face the fact, for the first time, that her son was not celibate, that he had a sex life that was judged by the laws of the land as criminal.

An intimate relationship had developed between Jim and Lovell Clark, though neither entertained the idea that they had 'fallen in love.'[44] When Clark was moving that summer, Kate invited him to stay at their apartment for a few days until his new lodgings were ready; he slept on the sofa in the parlour. But one hot, humid night, Kate agreed with the suggestion that Lovell and Jim would be more comfortable if they slept together on a bed made up on the narrow porch. At dawn, they were enjoying sex before they realized Kate was up, sewing in the next room, which looked out on the porch. Nothing was said, but Jim always felt thereafter that his mother must have known of his relationships with men. At that point, however, he didn't really care if she knew.

By fall it was clear that *As for Me and My House* was not going to sell. Max Becker and Gene Reynal had both been optimistic and said it sometimes took a few months for a book to catch on, that sales might pick up as word of mouth got around. But it hadn't yet sold three hundred copies, in spite of the good reviews in Canada, and there was little reason now to believe that would change. Indeed Jim would not receive any further payment from Reynal and Hitchcock beyond his three-hundred-dollar advance, minus the agent's fee. Jim expressed his disappointment to Roy Daniells, and the latter arranged to review the book on CBC radio, November 25th. The typescript of the broadcast shows he first described the action of the novel and the characters, and then went on to 'sell' the novel by praising its western authenticity, the 'powerful' concentration in the diary's single point of view, and the book's satiric humour, 'as fresh as Mark Twain's.'[45] In his diary that night, Daniells judged his 'broadcast on Sinclair Ross: middling, no better.'[46] The following week, he described for the radio audience the short stories of Sinclair Ross, giving special attention to 'A Field of Wheat.' Although Daniells didn't feel overpleased with the broadcasts, Jim greatly appreciated his friend's efforts and began taking the position that the failure of *As for Me and My House* was not the fault of the public, that he should have made his story more interesting. The radio broadcasts made little difference; Jim was told by his publishers that just under three hundred copies were sold.

Feeling let down, Jim stopped attending meetings of the Phoenix Club in the fall of 1941. Part of the reason for this was that most of the energy for creative writing had been channelled into a newly organized women's group called 'The Penhandlers.' Lillian Beynon Thomas and Nellie Anderson were now the dominating presences, and Jim felt he had learned everything he could from knowing these two women over the years. Nellie Anderson kept saying to Jim, '"If only you had let me see the manuscript [of *As for Me and My House*] – half an hour and I could have turned it into a best-seller."'[47] He occasionally paid a visit to Ernest Court, however, for the latter remained proud of Jim's work and was gratified to think that one of his group had sold a novel to a major New York publishing house. Jim also kept up his friendship with Harriet Duff-Smith and her husband, and when he attended their New Year's Eve party that year, Harriet made him the guest of honour, praising his novel and stories extravagantly. These words of encouragement helped him to press on with another project. This would be the ill-fated novel titled 'Day Coach to Wagneria.'

eight

War Years
1942–1946

The friendship that Jim had established with Roy Daniells and Doris Saunders at the university brought a request for a story for the winter 1941–2 issue of the *Manitoba Arts Review*. Jim appreciated their enthusiasm for his work but was reluctant to break from the novel-length project to write something new. With the New York publication of *As for Me and My House*, however unimpressive the response, he was determined to move away from small academic magazines and break into the mass markets for fiction. His dream of having a large audience for his work and of tending his resignation at the bank was still a powerful motive to keep writing. To comply with his friends' request, he revised a story that had been rejected by *Queen's Quarterly*. The story was 'Nell,'[1] a straightforward sketch of a hard-working farm woman, not unlike Hatty Glenn in 'No Other Way,' who is largely ignored by her still youthful, handsome husband. Jim would never feel the story was wholly successful, perhaps because it was taken too directly from life, for he was retelling in 'Nell' a story often told around Sid Ketcheson's table about Sid's handsome brother and the Saturday night that he went home, forgetting his wife and son in town. Farm drudgery and the pathos of the wife's situation perhaps overburden this story, although in his radio talk Daniells spoke favourably of its poignant ending. As with the Bentleys, Jim created sympathy for the neglected woman, but also an interest in the physically attractive man.

The novel manuscript Jim was working at in 1942 also took its inspiration from days spent on Sid Ketcheson's farm. 'Day Coach to Wagneria' (alternatively 'The Bus to Wagneria') was his story of a sensitive farm boy who grows up to be an artist. Jim put his own experiences into this novel in a straightforward way, following the classic pattern of the *Bildungsroman*. The title came from his mistake, when he was a boy, of thinking that a 'Wagnerian' singer was a reference to nationality. The title was meant to reflect both youthful naïveté and aspiration, but above all the desire to escape the mundane life of the farm for a world of art and music, a magical place called Wagneria. But the youthful hero is also 'tethered' to the reality of the community where he lives. Reflecting both his romantic innocence and a desire to please his unsophisticated audience, the boy sings Victor Herbert's popular 'O Sweet Mystery of Life,' as Jim himself had so often played Grainger's 'Country Gardens.'

Jim's letters in the spring of 1942 are marked by the pressure of trying to finish the new novel by May. In a brief letter to Doris Saunders in March, he says that he is in the process of revision 'and hating every damned word of it.'[2] To Ralph Gustafson, who had written requesting a story for a Penguin edition of Canadian writing, Jim replied in mid-April that he was extremely busy finishing a novel and could not submit anything for the proposed anthology. He had sent the only story he had, a piece titled 'One's a Heifer,' to Earle Birney for the Canadian issue of Story. But a few weeks later, apparently clearing this with Birney, he sent Gustafson a copy of 'One's a Heifer' for the Penguin volume. By May 22 he was able to write in a letter to Gustafson that the new novel manuscript was now in Reynal and Hitchcock's hands and he was waiting for their report.[3]

The correspondence with Earle Birney and Ralph Gustafson marked a new phase in Jim's development as a writer; for the first time, he was in touch with young contemporary writers who were at the forefront of the literary scene in Canada. Jim met Birney at the Hart House lunch in Toronto but appears to have initiated a correspondence when David and Other Poems was published. In January 1942 he wrote to Birney saying he had read and reread 'David' and wanted to let him know what a deep impression it made on him: 'I thought it a moving, sensitively handled piece of work. Some of your lines, particularly "into valleys the moon could be rolled in," and "the last of my youth, in the last of our mountains," made me really envious.'[4] Birney replied, warmly thanking Jim for his letter of praise and asking him if he would contribute something to the American magazine Story, which was planning an issue on Canadian writing.[5] Jim sent him 'One's a Heifer,' and Birney thanked him for what he thought was an excellent story.[6]

Ralph Gustafson appears to have initiated the other correspondence, requesting a story for his Penguin volume. When Birney's plans fell through for Story, Gustafson had the manuscript for 'One's a Heifer,' but the Penguin collection was extremely slow in taking shape and by the summer of 1943 Jim was asking that the story be returned, since he had received no further word about its publication.[7] In these first letters with contemporary Canadian writers, Jim showed himself to be generous in his praise of others' work and, by turns, both self-deprecating and defensive about his own writings. He could also be businesslike and curt on occasions. This would characterize much of his correspondence over the years.

While he waited for word from Max Becker about 'Day Coach,' he had time to reflect further on a project he had formulated in 1941 – a historical novel on the life and times of Louis Riel. First mention of this project is made by Roy Daniells in his CBC broadcast on the Sinclair Ross short stories. The author would recall the project having its germ in a talk with Curtice Hitchcock, who came to Winnipeg sometime in 1941 after the publication of *As for Me and My House*, although a letter Jim received from Eugene Reynal advising him on his career makes the same suggestion. Reynal writes that 'what we have in the back of our minds is the possibility that your real field might be in the historical background of the Canadian northwest. So far as we know, nobody has done in that area what Walter Edmonds and Kenneth Roberts have done in northeastern America, and it seems to us there is a very wide field of endeavor for someone with talent such as yours.'[8] This deduction seems curious, given the body of Jim's work thus far, but the meeting with Hitchcock seemed to propel him forward with the idea of something on Riel. Jim enjoyed meeting Hitchcock; he was a forceful personality and, in Jim's eyes, an exceptionally handsome man. He was in Winnipeg to visit with his friend John Dafoe at the *Winnipeg Free Press*, and Jim and Kathleen Strange were able to spend an hour with him as well.

In the fall of 1941, Jim put together an application for a Guggenheim fellowship that, if successful, would temporarily release him from the bank. Roy Daniells was asked to serve as a referee, and a copy of Jim's proposal has survived with Daniells's papers. In it he states that he would write a biography of Riel in fictional form – 'not ... an historical study, but simply an attempt to tell the story of Louis Riel, to think with and reveal the man.' He states frankly that his interest in the man is more psychological than political and adds, tentatively, that he does not see him as he is usually depicted in history textbooks: 'I may not be able to agree with certain groups of his admirers who look upon him as a patriot-martyr; on the other hand I feel there is a strong case to be made in his defence. Misguided, undisciplined, "psychotic" perhaps, but no mere renegade or adventurer.'[9] What fascinated Jim, although he doesn't mention it in the application, was the idea that Riel may have been bisexual. And, too, Riel had been a significant player in an episode of Saskatchewan history, and this was important in a region where there was so little recorded history. Even Kate, in the excitement of storytelling, liked to stretch the truth and say she had been involved in the Saskatchewan Rebellion.

The summer of 1942 was a disappointing and troubled one. The application for a Guggenheim was not successful, and shortly afterwards Jim received word from Max Becker that Reynal and Hitchcock had decided against 'Day Coach to Wagneria.' He describes the rejection in a letter to Ralph Gustafson dated 2 August 1942:

> The second novel that I mentioned in a previous letter has been turned down by Reynal and Hitchcock – 'too thin in plot' – and the agent is trying it on some other people[.] I am not very hopeful. It's about a farm boy from the age of 14 to 18, and there's not much action or drive to it. I feel there is some good writing in it – but it's better in spots than as a whole. Perhaps after an interval I may see it in clear perspective, and succeed in shaking it into firm form. A disappointment – yes – but [...] this is a very bad time for a novel, and perhaps I may ultimately gain by the delay.

Becker continued to send the manuscript out to American publishing houses but had no luck in placing it. Jim set it aside for a later reworking, though he would remember that in its original version the novel ended in a way that gave him a great deal of artistic satisfaction. The eighteen-year-old boy arrives in New York to study music, and he is last seen by the reader standing in front of a gigantic clock. Only time would tell.

Characteristically, Jim turned from this disappointment to spending less time at his desk and more time pursuing his sexual compulsions. His relationship with Lovell Clark had cooled, although the latter still spent a lot of time around the Ross apartment. In the meantime, Jim became involved with William Ross, one of the students from the university he had met at Roy Daniells's afternoon gatherings. Kate met him once, did not like what she called his cool, arrogant manner, and began an active campaign to quash the friendship. This led to the first real estrangement between mother and son. Jim reacted to Kate's ferocious meddling by spending nights away from the apartment – at Bill Ross's home, where the latter's mother was very friendly to Jim. After a particularly bitter quarrel with Kate, Jim took some of his things over to Bill's house and they spent a few days together at a rented cabin on Lake Winnipeg.

Kate was suddenly desperate. She seemed to realize now that in spite of her efforts to keep Jim from marrying, she might lose him anyway. The idea of his living with another man, certainly someone like Bill Ross, seemed more odious to her than she had ever imagined, and so when Jim returned, she began inviting young women to the apartment, hoping to change her son's behaviour. Kate had looked around. She was frequently visited by Tora Talgoy, who enjoyed spending an afternoon with the older woman, but she knew that Jim would never be interested in this pale, diffident girl. Mary Johnson, however, the daughter of one of Jim's co-workers at the bank, was a more cheerful, out-going woman in her early twenties, and they had known the Johnsons socially for several years. Kate accordingly invited the family for Sunday dinner. It was a strained afternoon for Jim, who was not feeling well. His mother insisted he play the piano for the Johnsons while she finished preparations for the meal, and when he played Bach she interrupted with 'Play something nice and light, Jimmy, not one of your old classics.'[10] She told her guests that Jimmy was so serious as a boy that she had to pay him *not* to practise, that she herself always preferred a good laugh. Retaining his dignity, Jim played 'Country Gardens.' After dinner, they all went for a drive (Kate liked to 'get out'), and Jim was sick in the back seat of the car. Kate nonetheless was set on her course, and she arranged that Jim and Mary go to the movies together during the week.

That summer Kate also encouraged Jim's long-standing friendship with Kathleen Scroggie, who worked with him at the bank. In addition to the workplace, Kathleen and Jim had one thing in common – they were both liv-ing with aging, domineering parents, Kathleen with her father, who kept as strict a watch over her life as Kate did over Jim's.[11] Jim felt nothing romantic for Kathleen, but they did occasionally go out together in the evenings, once to a pie social (where guests who did not bring a pie paid twenty-five cents instead), but more often to a movie. But Kate's anxiety that summer is best measured by a scene recalled by Audrey O'Kelly, who lived with her mother and sister in the same apartment building. Kate and the O'Kellys had devel-oped a warm friendship since the Rosses had moved into the building, and Jim enjoyed talking to Audrey, who wanted to be a writer. One afternoon, Kate approached Mrs O'Kelly and said she would give her fur coat to the girl in the family who would marry her Jimmy.[12] Kate seemed to feel her son was just shy around women, and that with the right prompting he would be will-ing to marry any girl who was interested. But Jim had quite a different response to his mother's increasing complaint that he should behave more like other young men. One day, she announced dramatically that a friend's son had made his mother proud by joining the army, and so, in late July 1942, Jim called her bluff and signed up for basic training – to escape her unhappy domestic world and, for the first time in his life, to have an adventure in the world of men.

Basic training took place at the Fort Osborne Barracks, where Jim had his first introduction to parade drills, learning to 'slope arms' without putting any-body's eye out, and enduring the terrors of kit inspection – 'folding blankets into precise squares, labels all lined up.'[13] There were long physical fitness sessions, and one had to accept, calmly, orders and sarcasms from the non-commissioned officers. But the camaraderie of the 'boys' in the bunkhouse – practical joking, 'girlie' magazines, poker games until 'lights out' – more than compensated; always living at home with his mother, these were things Jim had never experienced before. To Ralph Gustafson he wrote: 'The lads seem a decent sort. Farmers, mechanics, tradesmen, clerks – all nationalities – but there is a curious blending, paring down to masculine essentials. We get along. I begin to like it.'[14]

He realized, of course, that some of the country boys were disillusioned – they had simply traded the drudgery of farm labour for parades and fatigues. He would preserve something of those reactions in a little story titled 'Barrack Room Fiddle Tune,' inspired by the month of training in the Winnipeg camp. Training was not easy for someone like Jim, who had been physically inactive and underweight most of his life and who was now thirty-four; but when the draft was to be made, he still hoped to make the cut. The first doctor who examined him reported that, at 117 pounds, he was 'too thin and prone to illness to be suitable for military service,'[15] but a second doctor, whom he and his mother both knew in the city, intervened and recommended him for the Ordnance Corps. It was a tense and embarrassing episode, and he returned to it in a slightly fictionalized memoir forty-seven years later:

> The day they called me for my medical was the worst moment. I can still see the red-faced captain, irritated, perspiring, who burst out of his office waving my files as if he were being attacked by a swarm of hornets, advancing on a sergeant and shouting ... 'A hundred and twenty pounds and that cough – overseas, not on your life!' And then my own voice, a tinny bleat of protest. 'I want to cancel my enlistment then. I'm not going to spend three or four years sweeping out an orderly room and cleaning cigarette trays.' That was the bad moment, when it seemed I had lost it all. But then old Dr Collins stepped in. Not in uniform, but working three or four afternoons a week as a volunteer in the recruiting office ... He leaned forward and with a swift wink said 'skinny, but tough. I've known the family for years. Couldn't kill them with arsenic. He's got to eat a little more, that's all.'[16]

And so Jim, in uniform and heavy boots, weighted down with a greatcoat and two cylindrical duffel bags in the late summer heat, and filled with 'a vague dread of not standing up to what the future held,'[17] left with nine others on a train for Ottawa on 27 August 1942.

In the capital, Jim found himself with two thousand other men barracked at the Lansdowne Park exhibition grounds, taking meals in the horse show arena, and sleeping in the horticultural building. In letters to Audrey O'Kelly and Doris Saunders, he reported that morale was high, with discipline more relaxed than in Winnipeg and the officers friendlier.[18] Wake-up was at 6:00 a.m. and physical training was more rigorous, but there is no real complaining about this in the letters, just wry self-deprecation. To Doris he wrote: 'Not being very "hefty," I've found it hard in places, but have managed to grunt and grumble through. Mechanically I'm the most useless person alive, so you can imagine the fun I've had learning to take a Bren gun apart and put it together again.'[19] Routine marches, an easy commando course, and lectures on VD and athlete's foot filled the days. As in Winnipeg, what he continued to enjoy was the experience of living with other men, which is conveyed by the amused tone with which he describes his surroundings while writing to Audrey O'Kelly:

> If you saw – or even better, heard – the writing room! A juke-box with a cowboy yodelling – some of the boys tap-dancing, some of them playing ping-pong – everyone drinking coca-cola and eating raisin pie – my neighbour at the table determined to tell me about the car and girl he gave up to join the Army.

In the letter to Doris, he reflects on how much the army can teach him about life and people. He thought that knowing farmers and white-collar workers at the bank had exposed him to the range of humanity, but he was wrong. Ordinary working men, 'indifferent to "us" with our books and theories,' can be infuriating one day and opposite the next, but they embody nonetheless a vision of humanity grounded in 'good ideals and noble resolves.' What is usually lacking is the strength and will necessary to carry them out.

This attitude to his situation and the men around him is reflected in the description of Jim by one of his fellow soldiers. Robert Savory, with the draft from Winnipeg, got to know Jim on the train travelling to Ottawa. Jim, he remembered, was not an 'outgoing' fellow, but he was in no way a loner or snobbish. He was quiet, certainly, and physically small, but he liked being with the group, was good-humoured in a shy sort of way, and was never baited or harassed by others. One day Bob glimpsed a copy of As for Me and My House in Jim's kit and that way learned he was an author; but otherwise Jim didn't talk about his writing, nor about his mother or his past. He seemed to Bob quite young and inexperienced, and he was surprised to learn eventually that Jim was ten years older than he was.[20]

Although Jim believed books and theories were insignificant to working men, he knew they were still the greatest pleasure in his life. But what distressed him was the vanity that tainted so much writing, including his own.

To Doris he explained:

> In writing, vanity is the most difficult thing to overcome – and there are a hundred forms that vanity can take. It seems if I could only be genuinely humble, that then I could turn out worthwhile work. Between the conception and the execution there is always this self-seeking 'me' pushing forward. You say you have been reading Dostoyevsky, so you will know what I mean. I have just finished *The Brothers Karamazov* for the second time, and I have the feeling that the writer has almost completely effaced himself.[21]

He had also brought along Virginia Woolf's *To the Lighthouse*, although it wasn't always easy to read in the barracks – 'frequently the boys throw a pillow or magazine at me to bring me back.'[22]

He made only one small contact with the literary world while he was in Ottawa. Charles Clay, an acquaintance from Winnipeg who had worked at the *Free Press* and had published a successful juvenile adventure story, *Young Voyageur* (1938), was now freelancing in Ottawa, and he and Jim met a couple of times. Clay introduced Jim to Eric Gaskell, national secretary of the Canadian Authors Association, and the latter took Jim for dinner to the home of Madge Macbeth, an elderly woman who had published in a variety of genres – short stories, novels, dramas, and an autobiography. Her most critically acclaimed work was an early feminist novel titled *Shackles* (1926), but her best-known works were two satirical novels about Ottawa and parliament, *The Land of Afternoon* (1924) and *The Kinder Bees* (1935). Jim had not heard of her before, possibly because these political novels were published under the pseudonym of 'Gilbert Knox,' and he reported to Doris that he 'had a tough time of trying to conceal [his] ignorance of who she was and what she had done.'[23] Perhaps his observations on the vanity of most writers were inspired by this visit – Macbeth seemed to assume her 'reputation [was] taken for granted.' At any rate, he admitted he was not doing any writing himself, although later correspondence reveals that he brought with him the 'Day Coach' manuscript. For now, he felt, 'an enforced fallow period' would be good.

In the meantime, he was enjoying the city itself and described for Audrey some of the visual pleasures he had experienced; one morning, his company went on a march with a pipe band along the Rideau Canal: 'Trees and grounds so beautiful it was almost like a stage setting – weeping willows, Balm of Gilead, rowan and evergreens – ornamental shrubs that I had never see before.' On another occasion, he went for a walk after dinner, with Charles Clay pointing out the best views: 'Hull across the river, with the "flèche" of its cathedral silhouetted against the sunset, and the Parliament Buildings from behind, on a cliff that rises almost sheer out of the river.'[24] But when departure for Britain was announced, he wrote again to say he was looking forward to leaving, and he thanked Audrey and her family for all the attentions they were giving his mother.[25] This would be a repeated refrain in his letters to Audrey, and he concludes his October letter to Doris Saunders by reminding her that his mother would be 'awfully pleased' to see her.[26] He was exulting in his freedom, but it was not without a measure of guilt.

In late October the company entrained for Halifax. In the unpublished war memoir, Jim wrote: 'From Ottawa to Halifax ... a blur of heat, sweat, fatigue near breaking point and a vague fear of not standing up to it. [And on arrival] a shower, a meal and a night's sleep and the dread still hovered.'[27] One good thing transpired: each man was responsible for two duffel bags, but army transport decided to ship one of these separately, so that he was able to stuff that bag with heavy things. Jim lists three pounds of coffee, some canned meat and fish, and a tin of candy, but most importantly he was able to pack some books, including Hemingway's For Whom the Bell Tolls, which Kate had sent him while he was still in Ottawa, John Gunther's Inside Europe, and some books he found in a French bookstore in Ottawa – Madame Bovary, Le Rouge et le noir, and a heavy French dictionary.

On October 28 they boarded the new passenger liner Queen Elizabeth, which was still being fitted out and was not yet in commercial service. 'Embarking was like entering a deep tunnel.'[28] Twenty-two thousand troops were loaded into the ship. In a room built to accommodate one or two persons, twelve men slept in six tiers of double hammocks that went up to the ceiling. Jim was in the ship's library, where there were no books but dozens of canvas hammocks and metal bunks. He was on the top row. 'Sardines in a can,' was Robert Savory's memory of it.[29] After being loaded, there was a four-day wait that was never fully explained to the men, although anxiety about German torpedo submarines in the Atlantic helped to prevent unrest on the ship. In a war story titled 'Jug and Bottle,' Jim described the trip over as 'a bleak, rough crossing ... [with] choppy seas and gusts of rain, [and] an icy wind ... that on deck every morning made us huddle together on the sheltered side like shivering cattle' (76). In his war memoir, he describes the suffocating closeness of the men's quarters with the sour smell of seasickness and sweat, and 'bladders beginning to bite' in the long line-ups for the washroom.[30] The men could not undress or bathe, and they had to wash and shave in cold salt water. And to that discomfort there was always the anxiety about what lay ahead. The only excitement was the sighting of two whales and a German broadcast picked up by the boat claiming the Queen Elizabeth had been sunk![31]

On November 5th, after five days on the ocean, they disembarked in Scotland on the Clyde, cold and hungry. It was the middle of the night with a war-time 'blackout.' After walking for a mile, carrying their equipment through the dark and rain, they were put in barracks that had no real heat. They were wakened at 7:00 a.m. for cold sausage and bread, then drilled in a mock battle for the rest of the day – 'a grim start.'[32] Jim's company, the following day, took a train south to Camp Borden in Hampshire to complete three more weeks of basic training – 'rifles, Bren guns, grenades.'[33] Shortly thereafter Jim took an examination which qualified him for work as an Ordnance clerk and the chance to live in London, which at that point he realized had always been the goal of this adventure.

For a young North American with artistic or intellectual yearnings, a trip to England or Europe in the last century was a rite of passage and cultural apprenticeship. No one felt they could really claim to be a serious artist with-out having crossed the Atlantic and discovered the 'Old World' with its great stores of music, theatre, and art. For Jim, whose best work was already mostly behind him at age thirty-four, this initiation was a curiously belated one, but it was no less exhilarating. During his first winter in London, he revelled in the amount of theatre he could see and listed for Audrey O'Kelly some of the plays he enjoyed, including Turgenev's A Month in the Country, Ibsen's Hedda Gabler, Shaw's Heartbreak House, and Noel Coward's Blithe Spirit. Only a pro-duction of The Merchant of Venice had disappointed and bored him. He recog-nized that pretty much everything being staged was revival theatre – few new plays in wartime – but as it was his first chance to see these plays on stage, that hardly mattered. England instead was turning out new films, as part of the war effort, and he recommended that Audrey and her family see the Noel Coward and David Lean production, In Which We Serve.[34] On Sunday after-noons, he went regularly to a symphony concert.

While in Ottawa, he had written to Doris Saunders that he wasn't going to write fiction for a while, but in December that same year he was reporting to Audrey that he had just finished a new story and was rather pleased with it: "I have a lot of things planned – I really think the change has stimulated my mind and imagination – [though] an Army hut is no place for writing.'[35] What Jim appears to have worked at from 1943 forward was a complete revision of the 'Day Coach' manuscript, changing the second half to incorporate his army experiences. The sensitive farm boy no longer goes off to New York to find himself as an artist, but is swept up in the war and discovers the larger world of art and culture by serving overseas.

Jim's renewed self-confidence in his writing was partly stimulated by the request from Earle Birney for a submission to the American magazine Story. Although Birney eventually wrote to say the Canadian issue of the magazine was being called off and that he was going into the army, they exchanged letters for a while and Birney recommended Jim to the British poet and editor John Lehmann. The latter, who was Jim's age, was already regarded as one of England's most distinguished men of letters; he worked as general manager of the Hogarth Press and as an advisory editor for the *Geographical Magazine*, but he was especially well known for founding and editing the influential New Writing series. Jim met Lehmann sometime during 1943 and in a letter tells Birney that Lehmann has asked him for a story, but since he feels it was only out of politeness he has sent the one story in his desk off to his agent in New York. The latter, he says, has warned him against the English markets as likely drawing him away from his 'natural bent,' that is, Prairie fiction. He admits, nonetheless, that he would like to get into a publication like *New Writing*.[36]

The correspondence between Earle Birney and Jim flourished that summer, perhaps because, according to a note he sent Harriet Duff-Smith,[37] he was back at Camp Borden and feeling cut off from his literary and artistic contacts. When he received a negative report about the story he had sent to Max Becker, he confided to Birney that he just didn't have the right stuff for the 'slick' magazines, that he could not plot a story to suit *Saturday Evening Post* and was probably '"doomed" to write what no one wants to read.'[38] In August 1943 they agreed to meet the next time Jim was in London, but it was a disappointment on both sides. Jim, perhaps intimidated by Birney's height and officer rank, felt that he was being looked down on. Birney, for his part, found Jim too quiet and withdrawn to be interesting company. The admiration and respect they felt for each other's work did not translate into a friendship, and their correspondence tapered off.[39]

Jim's preferred way of connecting to the art scene in London was to attend theatres and concerts. He would especially remember a lecture series at the Churchill Club, where he heard de Gaulle speak and T.S. Eliot read and talk about poetry. It was there that he met and enjoyed a friendship with American editor and poet Oscar Williams, who was enjoying the early success of his New Poems anthologies, published throughout the war. They both knew Ken McCormick but had other things in common: Williams, though born in New York, had spent the Depression years in the West, where he had worked in advertising. Like Jim, he had never finished high school, but despite this deficiency he would eventually become one of America's leading literary anthologists, his New Poems series being followed by the Little Treasury of Modern Poetry volumes. Jim would give Williams, in fact, most of his books when it came time for him to leave London at the end of the war.

For a time, Jim also belonged to what he would later describe as 'a little art group' that met at the National Gallery. His strongest memory from those gatherings was a concert given by pianist Dame Myra Hess, during one of the darkest periods of the war, and how some members of the audience burst into tears. At one of those concerts, he met relatives of economist and journalist Maynard Keynes, who invited him to their home. Jim also made some connections to the art world through the city's homosexual underground, eventually meeting John Lehmann at a pub frequented by gay men. As Keath Fraser has observed, Jim would consider London the great event of his life, and he never wanted it to end.[40]

After returning to London from the country in the fall of 1943, Jim remained in the city for the duration of the war, working as a clerk for the Ordnance Corps at Fairfax House. Since army personnel were spread around the city in case of a bomb hit, he did not live in barracks but instead, more agreeably, was on his own in a small bed and breakfast hotel near Russell Square. He was free to move about London when off duty, and often he just walked the streets, in all weathers, enjoying the crowds of people and the chimes of Big Ben solemnly marking every quarter hour. There was still danger, not on the scale of the air raids during the Battle of Britain in late 1940, when civilian casualties in a six-month period numbered more than twenty-three thousand, but there were rocket attacks and explosions without warning. In a letter to Audrey O'Kelly in 1944, Jim describes a 'close call' when he had just walked away from his desk and a rocket explosion shattered the windows, injuring some of his co-workers with flying glass. 'It wasn't a pretty sight, but everyone behaved splendidly – no panic or hysteria, and over and over you heard "Mine's not serious – I'll wait till the doctor gets around to the others."'[41] There were still regular rehearsals for evacuating Fairfax House, with much shouting and blowing of whistles, and fire drills with gas masks. Although these had become routine, and one had become as used to them as seeing the bombed-out areas of the city, there was always a renewed urgency after a rocket attack. But Jim came closest to seeing the human cost of war when he spent a few days in hospital having surgery on a salivary gland. He was surrounded by men with severe injuries and deforming amputations, and he could only marvel at their spirits: 'You begin to see what war really is. The men are fine – always cheerful, never a word of bitterness or complaint, and some of them now haven't a great deal left to live for.'[42]

The devastations of war also made Jim think about religion. When he wrote to Audrey O'Kelly, who was a strong Roman Catholic, he avoided the subject and simply commented on the literary merits of some of the Catholic authors she recommended or sent to him, but he felt he could express his atheism openly to Doris Saunders. He paused in one of his letters to her to reflect on what he perceived as humanity's collective helplessness: 'If ever poor humanity needed a religion she needs it now, and the religions left us, I'm afraid, are not of much avail. We have absolutely nothing but ourselves, and when we stop and take an honest look at ourselves the picture is not too encouraging. To me it seems that the world's tragedy is poor timing: the crutch [of religion] has grown rotten before we are strong enough to do without it.'[43] In *As for Me and My House*, Philip Bentley says to his wife that religion and art are the same thing, but in a more philosophical mood in his letter to Doris Saunders, Jim seems to suggest that art can only 'stimulate,' not nourish. He lists some of the performances that have recently thrilled him – 'a magnificent *Lear*,' Olivier's *King Richard III*, Gielgud's *Hamlet*.

Because she belonged to the Penhandlers in Winnipeg and was attempting to write short stories, Jim freely shared with Audrey his experiences of writing while in London. He tells her that he has written a number of short stories that year, but doesn't feel they are any good. He is trying to use some of his European wartime experiences and finds himself 'approaching the material self-consciously, almost gingerly – as if [he] had gloves on.'[44] He was also plodding along with the novel. In fact, only one story was published during the nearly four years that Jim was overseas, and that was 'One's a Heifer,' a story written sometime in the late 1930s. It was a story Jim had confidence in, but actually getting it published was a frustrating affair. Max Becker had tried to place the story with American magazines, because he felt it had just the right mix of mystery and suspense to meet the demands of the popular market. But eventually he returned it to Jim, who was then able to send it to Birney for the more academic magazine *Story*. When that project was shelved, he had the request from Ralph Gustafson, who was editing an edition of Canadian stories for Penguin. But the project was delayed and postponed repeatedly. He wrote to Gustafson in June 1943, inquiring politely about the Penguin volume and the status of his story, but having no reply by September, he wrote again, this time instructing Gustafson to return the manuscript.[45] Gustafson wrote mid-November assuring him the project was going forward and that he would be published in company with the country's major writers, and he provided a list to plead his case.[46] A year later, November 1944, Jim wrote to Gustafson once again; this time it was one curt, exasperated sentence: 'Will you please return at once to the above address my ms "One's a Heifer" which has been in your possession since the spring of 1942.'[47] But the Penguin volume, titled *Canadian Accent*, was now published, and in a few weeks Jim would have a copy in hand and a cheque for a disappointing seventeen dollars and eighty-five cents, the lowest fee he would ever be paid for a story.

'One's a Heifer'[48] is the story of a thirteen-year-old boy sent out on his horse to find two calves that have strayed from his uncle's farm during a blizzard. In his search, the boy comes upon a strange farmer living alone on the edge of the sand hills in a decrepit dwelling that seems to the boy more like a small barn, with a table littered with tools, a grindstone, animal skins drying, and an owl with a broken wing squatting in the corner. The man is repairing harnesses. The boy is convinced that Arthur Vickers has hidden his uncle's calves in his stable, but even though he stays overnight he is unable to locate them. The man remains a mystery. Why did Jim think so highly of this story, such that he would become uncharacteristically rude in trying to see it published? Partly, he probably felt this story came closer to those illusive magazine markets than anything else he had written: the characterization of Vickers creates suspense, and the story has something like an O. Henry ending which suddenly puts everything narrated in a new light. But though its meaning is hidden, this story of a boy's initiation into the complex and mysterious world of adult behaviour was associated in Jim's mind with the troubling initiation he experienced by the grain elevator in Lancer. The character of Arthur Vickers, living in his low-ceilinged, shed-like dwelling, was inspired by the harness-maker, MacLeod, who kept company with young men on the outskirts of the village. Although it was the young Irishman who had initiated Jim into the world of gay sex in a boxcar, it was the image of a sinister father figure in MacLeod that was embedded in his imagination and worked its way out in the story of a boy and a mysterious stall.

Along with 'The Painted Door,' 'The Lamp at Noon,' and 'Cornet at Night,' 'One's a Heifer' is a story that has been anthologized dozens of times. Its mysterious core makes it especially valuable in a classroom. Explaining Vickers can take the reader down several paths: is he 'crazy' as the boy's uncle said of a man who lived alone? He has 'queer eyes all right,' thinks the boy. Or is he a thief? Why won't he let the boy look inside one of the stalls? Or, more darkly, is he a murderer? His misogynist talk of a neighbour girl who has worked for him and is now pressing for marriage leaves the reader suspicious beyond the end of the story. The second last paragraph explains that the calves came home shortly after the boy set out, and that revelation turns the reader's attention to the psychology of the boy narrator. The unstable nature of Vickers also has to be viewed as the construction of an overly imaginative boy, one who cannot clearly distinguish, at one point in the story, dreaming from being awake. Why this title? Jim was sometimes asked, and he would invariably reply that it was something he once overhead: 'Two calves are missing. They are the same except one's a heifer and the other isn't.'[49] His reply is as ambiguous as the story – is it meant as a form of Prairie humour, poking fun at the innocent boy, or is there something latently sinister in the title that connects the heifer to the absent girl on Vickers's squalid property?[50]

Jim was right to believe in this story, for not only would it be anthologized repeatedly but in 1984 it would also be made into a short for Atlantis Films by

Anne Wheeler, who would prove to be one of Canada's most successful directors. And under the title 'Lodging for a Night,' what was likely a pirated version of the story was reprinted in *Argosy* magazine in 1948 in company with some famous writers of the time, including C.S. Forester, James Thurber, Ogden Nash, and T.F. Powys.[51] But in wartime London Jim heard nothing about the story after its publication, even though Gustafson's anthology sold fairly well. It slipped out of sight like *As for Me and My House*. He wrote to Doris Saunders that 'over here, [one's writing] doesn't seem to make any difference. London in wartime tends to diminish your belief in the importance of humanity.'[52]

By the fall of 1944, the war seemed to be dragging on interminably. In a late November letter to Audrey O'Kelly, he wrote: 'It doesn't seem like Christmas over here. So many had hoped that the lights would be on and the war wound up this year and, as another dark wet winter sets in, people find themselves apathetic and despondent.'[53] Jim could share these feelings certainly, but nonetheless he didn't like to think of that time when he would have to return to Canada and resume life with his mother. He knew, guiltily, that Kate had not been faring so well. She had stayed on in the Boyce apartment building, and friends like the O'Kellys and Tora Talgoy were attentive to her needs, but she had to undergo cataract surgery, still a complicated procedure in the 1940s, and her confidence was shaken. She was nearing her seventieth year, and in letters to friends and relatives she wrote how much she missed her Jimmy. Visiting with Effie and family in Indian Head was not the same as having Jim to look after; she enjoyed being 'Granny,' for a time, but invariably there would be a quarrel between mother and daughter and she would take the train back to Winnipeg. Every month fifty dollars would arrive from Jim to pay for her food and rent. Jim's pay in the army had increased slightly: in 1944 he received a promotion from private to corporal, and then in 1945 he was made a staff sergeant.

But in May 1945 the war in Europe did come to a close and Jim had to ponder his future. He remembered the 8th of May, VE Day, and how they were turned loose from the office at noon to celebrate. He felt strangely disoriented and, after an ordinary meal at a pub, wandered around Leicester Square with a group from the office, having very mixed feelings. Many got drunk that afternoon in Leicester Square and Picadilly, and he tried to feel exuberant and join in the celebration, but he knew this spelled the end of what had probably been the best period of his life. However, because he was in the Ordnance Corps, with equipment to dispose of and records to file, Jim would have his duties in London extended for another eight months. He intended to savour these last days of his freedom.

nine

Montreal
1946–1952

I have found childhood lasts a lifetime. – JSR in conversation

Jim's overseas service came to an end on 28 January 1946, and he was demobilized March 22,[1] at which point he was faced with an array of options for the future. Forms completed for the Department of Veterans Affairs, as he was about to leave the army, reveal that Jim had hoped first to complete the novel he was working on, and then to be employed at the University of Manitoba teaching in the English Department for two years. He would subsequently complete an arts degree, he reported, with the hope of being taken back on staff. Jim had in fact discussed this possibility in a letter with Doris Saunders, and she had written back encouraging Jim to apply for a teaching position. The Veterans Affairs counsellor also recommended that, since Jim had been assured by the Royal Bank that there would be an opening there for him with increased salary once he has been discharged, 'he [would] be well re-established if he decide[d] to return to this job.' The counsellor also suggested that Jim 'could fall back on his army office training and look for work as a stenographer or office clerk,' but in his final recommendation he agreed that Jim should work on the novel and pursue a career at the university.[2]

Back in Winnipeg in the spring of 1946, Jim had a phone call from Doris, who had arranged a job interview for him with Roy Daniells, the Head of the English Department, with another member of the university administration present. They were now teaching *As for Me and My House* in a senior English class, and Doris said the interview would just be a formality, but from Jim's point of view it portended a serious and rigorous period of questioning. At the interview, they talked specifically about the western Canadian novel, and Jim, who had read nothing of Frederick Philip Grove's work except a few nature sketches and a couple of short stories, felt he gave wrong answers and too frequently had to admit his ignorance on the subject. He felt more secure when they talked about books like Ostenso's *Wild Geese* and Salverson's *The Viking Heart*, and he had recently read *Grain* by R.J.C. Stead. But the questions kept coming back to Grove, and Jim knew the administrator present was not impressed by his diffident answers. He was not surprised, accordingly, to learn from an apologetic Doris that he had not gotten the job.

The only realistic alternative was to return to the bank. No letters have survived from this period after the war, but Jim's strong memory was of a deep despondency that settled over him after the possibility of university employment had fallen through. Other men he had known in the forces were now getting the opportunity for a university education that had always eluded him. Lovell Cark had joined the air force in 1942 and served overseas, and as a returned veteran he was studying history at the University of Manitoba. While Jim enjoyed the company of his friends at the bank, the work was painstakingly tedious and unrewarding. But hardest of all was living with his mother once again. Kate was ecstatically happy to have him back, but after nearly four years of living on his own, free to come and go as he chose, Jim found her prying and busy ways more than he could tolerate. He was becoming sullen and irritable again and finally decided to apply for a transfer to a post in the East. When he broke the news to Kate, that he had written to head office, she said confidently that she would be happy to move too, although she told him not to think about taking a job where they spoke French. Kate had strong views on the subject of Quebec and felt all Canadians, as British subjects, should make English their first language. Jim, in fact, was offered a position at head office in Montreal, and when her bluff was thus called, Kate, holding on to her pride, said she would not move to a French-speaking province on principle; moreover, she could not move so far away from her daughter, grandchildren, and great-grandchildren. She was deeply discouraged to be left alone again but decided to stay on in Winnipeg because she still had a few friends there. When Jim and his mother were packing up to leave their apartment at the end of summer – Jim preparing to leave for Montreal, his mother taking a smaller apartment in the same building – Tora Talgoy came by for a visit, and she remembered all the unspoken things that seemed to hover in the air that day. Before she left, Jim offered her his twelve volumes of *Harmsworth's Universal Encyclopedia*, and Tora kept them for the rest of her life, in a series of moves that would eventually take her to Vancouver and New Westminster, British Columbia.

When Jim arrived in Montreal in late 1946, he knew no one, but to be in Montreal, a 'wide-open town,' notoriously hospitable to gambling and prostitution and famous for its jazz clubs and night life,[3] was as exciting as first being in London. After the war there were fifteen nightclubs in Montreal, with floor shows and international performers, and there were dozens of smaller lounges around the city, creating a worldly sophistication in Montreal second only to New York in North America. For Jim it was an excitement enhanced by French language and culture, and he found himself deliberately patronizing French restaurants and shops so that he could accustom himself to Quebec French.[4] But Montreal was also exciting for many English Canadians like Jim because its permissiveness extended to forbidden forms of sexuality. As Robert K. Martin has written, after the war 'Quebec became the favourite place for the homosexual fantasies of the proper English Canadian'; a weekend in Montreal was viewed as a possible interlude of licentiousness, a sojourn in Sodom.[5]

Yet the stimulation of arriving in a cosmopolitan and largely French-speaking city, of finding an apartment, and learning the ropes at head office was offset by a persistent melancholy feeling, rooted in the recognition that he would probably live the rest of his life alone. He would soon be in his fortieth year; he had not found a partner, nor was he likely to, for the two or three men and women with whom he had fallen in love had never expressed similar feelings in return. Invariably, friendships cooled when exposed to the mordant pessimism of Jim's deepest nature, and accordingly he was becoming increasingly reclusive, reluctant to make new friends and often hesitant to contact old ones. An incident that occurred shortly after he arrived consolidated that instinct.

'If you are ever in Montreal, be sure to look me up' was Ira Dilworth's solicitous behest the last time he and Jim had met at a party in Winnipeg. Jim kept that invitation in reserve for a few weeks. Ira Dilworth, born in Manitoba, had grown up in Victoria, British Columbia, where he taught high school for several years, and where he made a lasting impression on pupils such as the painter Max Maynard and scholar Roy Daniells. He became Emily Carr's close friend towards the end of her life and helped her edit her writings for publication. In the 1930s, he began working for the CBC and became regional director in Vancouver, where he also conducted the Vancouver Bach Choir. In his 1962 obituary, he is described by a Vancouver columnist as an 'intense and creative' man with a 'somewhat prissy manner,' conservative tastes, and diverse cultural interests.[6] A bachelor like Jim, yet with a wide circle of acquaintances, Dilworth was a man who could perhaps connect Jim to the English-speaking arts community. But when Jim eventually telephoned, Dilworth brushed him off quickly, thanking him for the call and wishing him well in Montreal, making no suggestion that they meet. This apparent rebuff was more than a passing incident in Jim's life; it remained in his mind as deep and wounding evidence that he had made no impression on Canada's art world, either as a man or as the author of a novel and a handful of short stories. It made him feel more strongly than ever before that he never would belong.

For the first couple of years, life in Montreal was very narrow, partly because he had so little money to spare. He was the sole support of his mother, who continued to live for a time in the apartment in Winnipeg, and so he was obliged to take cheap lodgings in a house on Durocher Street, near the corner of Sherbrooke in the university area. It was an old house that had been turned into small one-room apartments, with a hotplate for cooking and washroom down the hall, a building that was airless and heavy with cooking smells in the summer and never warm enough during the winter. This would be the Montreal setting for *Whir of Gold*, a novel that would not be completed and published until more than twenty years later. The apartment house was managed by an attractive blonde woman in her late thirties, originally from Newfoundland. Her first name was Madeline (which Jim would shorten to Mad when he transformed her into a fictional character), and she was living with a 'husband' in what Jim eventually learned was a common-law relationship. Madeline's 'husband,' in Jim's view, was a 'seedy little shrimp, sneaky and cowardly by nature,' and when he had been drinking he became abusive.[7] Jim grew fond of Madeline (she was tender-hearted and cheerful in spite of her unhappy circumstances), and Jim said to her one day, 'You don't have to take it from him.'

Eventually Madeline's lover was gone, and she and Jim became close friends. She would come up to his room in the evenings, and she would talk to him about growing up in Newfoundland and he would tell her about Saskatchewan. Occasionally they would share a meal together, usually something Madeline had cooked in her apartment downstairs. Then she began staying the night, initiating a relationship that Jim found both exhilarating and frightening. Madeline was physically attractive to him, with a 'full-blown and blowsy' sensuality that was enhanced by her openness and good spirits. What was especially appealing to Jim, however, was her physical delight in his body, especially his penis, which she said no other man's could compare with in her experience. He relished her praise and attentions and for several months in 1947 and 1948 found himself looking forward to her visits in his room. But at the same time he was afraid of committing himself in a relationship with a woman; he had spent a lifetime trying to escape his mother's possessiveness and was not willing to be trapped in another binding relationship of that kind.

He was wary of other possible limits to his hard-won freedom. One of these came when the bank offered him a management post in a small northern Ontario city – 'Dryden was mentioned.'[8] But the increase in status and salary held no attraction for Jim when weighed against the cost to his personal life. Indeed the prospect was a frightening one, for he felt that in such a highly visible position he would again be under the watchful gaze of a prying and judg-mental citizenry, living like the Bentleys in *As for Me and My House*. Further, Jim had no desire for a position of power over others beyond what he might achieve through his writing, and he stayed true to that instinct all his life.

For Christmas 1947, Jim took the train to Winnipeg, where he stayed for a few days at his mother's apartment. He made contact with the Men's Musical Club and some other friends, one of whom had arranged for Jim to meet the pianist Neil Chotem, but at the last minute Jim withdrew from the meeting, feeling shy and awkward about meeting a man of distinction in the arts com-munity. He and Kate took the train to Indian Head to spend Christmas Day with Effie and her family. Effie, now herself a grandmother, was newly married to Charlie Swinn. Kate was always critical of her daughter's affairs and never seemed to enjoy herself on these festive occasions where she wasn't in charge, but she insisted nonetheless that the family be together for the holidays.

The winter of 1948 in Montreal, he spent much of his time with Madeline, but one evening he became aware that Madeline was seeing other men; he heard her fighting with a lodger who said he wasn't going to start paying for what had once been free. Jim inwardly recoiled, and the next time she came to his room he became angry and sent her away. He was aware now that she was sleeping with other men in the building, that she was probably a prosti-tute, something he had suspected but kept putting out of his mind. When his sense of betrayal subsided, he was disheartened, not just because he felt cheated, but because he felt sorry for her and could only see a sad life for her down the road. Although he was in some ways glad to be free from Madeline, it was a relationship that left him with regrets, one he would write about as a way of coming to terms with it. He knew he had not entered into the rela-tionship wholeheartedly because of his anxiety about possessive women, and he was forced again to realize that he would always live on the sidelines. He returned to reading in the evenings and listening to CBC radio, and looking for sex on the weekends.

In 1947 Jim had returned to 'Day Coach to Wagneria,' which he now thought of as the war novel manuscript, working at it sporadically throughout the year. Keath Fraser has astutely observed that to write about 'Sinclair Ross' is 'to discuss a shadow author of discarded novels that each help to under-stand his continuing inability to relocate his true voice.'[9] There are at least half a dozen novels, some with fine titles, which Jim composed in full, revised several times, and eventually discarded. The farm boy's growing-up story that centred first on music, then was rewritten to focus on the war, is a particularly striking example of the struggle for voice, if we consider some of the frag-ments of that project that have survived.

One of these fragments, titled 'Barrack Room Fiddle Tune,' Jim published in 1947 in the *Manitoba Arts Review*. It is a slight sketch of an awkward farm boy, newly enlisted in the army, who unknowingly torments his room-mates by playing an old violin badly. What seems to have fascinated Jim in this story is the solidarity of feeling amongst the soldiers – their impatience with the boy's naïveté and the noise he makes and, simultaneously, their sympathy for him when he fails to attract a girl working in the canteen and when finally his violin is smashed. To consolidate that feeling of camaraderie that is so much the subject of the story, Jim experimented with a first-person *plural* narrator, a speaker who refuses to identify himself individually. On the surface it creates a bland point of view, the obligatory voice of community and conformity in an army camp, but it speaks perhaps secretively of an individual narrator who refuses to separate himself from the group, who refuses to come forward and defend the naïve recruit from the rough justice of his room-mates – the voice of someone in hiding. The experiment with point of view is also interesting because it constructs an audience that endorses the events that take place. In a second fragment from the army novel, a story titled 'Jug and Bottle,' to be discussed later, the narrator comes out of hiding, and that exposure has disquieting results.

Jim's career as a writer seemed at this point to be going nowhere. The war manuscript stalled and, as before, when he sent out a story to a commercial magazine, a rejection slip invariably came in answer. Then, in the spring of 1948, Jim received a surprise letter from John Gray, editor-in-chief at Macmillan in Toronto. Gray wrote to introduce himself and to inquire whether Jim was working on a new writing project and, if so, whether he was looking for a Canadian publisher. Gray said he admired Jim's fiction and hoped they might work together in the future. Jim was deeply flattered by the letter, and when Gray phoned one day to say he was in Montreal, Jim agreed to meet him at the Ritz Café for lunch. Jim's shyness was not lessened by Gray's bluff, genial manner, and Jim felt woefully inadequate in conversation with this suave, sophisticated businessman; but Gray's enthusiasm for Jim's work was genuine, and the locale for their lunch – the Ritz was then regarded as the poshest hotel in Montreal – gave the meeting an auspicious cast.

John Gray, descended from an affluent and well-educated Ontario family, had started to work at Macmillan before the war. On his return to the company in 1946, he brought a great deal of energy and enthusiasm not only to building up the Canadian branch of the Macmillan publishing company, but to promoting serious literature by Canadian authors. He had taken over the editing and promotion of established writers such as Mazo de la Roche and Morley Callaghan, and was encouraging the talents of first-time novelists such as W.O. Mitchell and Ethel Wilson. Gray's gesture in establishing a connection with Jim was consistent with his vision of fostering a Canadian literary culture.

A project with Macmillan began to take shape subsequent to Jim's meeting the artist Grant Macdonald. The two men were introduced by a mutual friend sometime in the summer of 1948. Typically, Jim was initially intimidated by Macdonald's self-possessed and assured manner; the latter, in Jim's view, was good-looking and somewhat aloof in demeanour and dressed fashionably and expensively. Moreover, he was already well established as an artist and illustrator. His local subjects included Agnes Etherington, wife of the dean of medicine at Queen's University, who would soon bequeath her Georgian-style brick home to become the university's art gallery. But an eight-month friendship and correspondence between Jim and Grant Macdonald followed a letter in which Macdonald proposed to Jim the idea of a collection of stories for which he would do the illustrations. Jim responded with guarded enthusiasm, pointing out that in his own opinion his stories were 'pretty grim.' They abound, he said, 'with horses, wistful small boys and poverty-stricken farmers.'[10] Macdonald nonetheless invited Jim to spend Thanksgiving weekend at his home in Kingston, during which time they would be able to talk over the project at length.

Jim took the Saturday morning train to Kingston, where Grant was more than an hour late meeting him at the station. Although he apologized for being so busy, Jim read it as an unfriendly gesture meant to assert superiority. It was a bright fall weekend with the leaves on the maple trees at their most brilliant. The Macdonalds, father and son, lived in a comfortable brick home that was interesting to a visitor for the number of sculptures on the premises. Grant was having a studio added to one wing of the house. The two men spent much of the afternoon walking around the university grounds, for Jim had never been to Queen's and was curious to see this institution where so many of his stories had come into print. He would remember the gray stone buildings and the afternoon sun filtered through yellow chestnut leaves as they walked along the streets. The two men talked at length about the collection of short stories, discussing which scenes in the stories were most vivid for pictorial representation, and Grant said he would soon begin work on the illustrations. Grant was gay and the two men fell easily into spending the night together. Jim wondered afterwards what kind of understanding Grant had with his father when it came to overnight guests, and how the housekeeper viewed Grant's relations with other gay men. Jim liked the older man very much; he was a widower, still in his sixties, and a good conversationalist on topics of art and literature. The weekend was pleasantly spent in the older man's company, and in most of the letters he would write to Grant, Jim invariably asked after his father's health and wished to be remembered to him. Macdonald senior, in fact, drove Jim back to Montreal on Thanksgiving Monday.

The two men wrote several letters to each other as the illustrated story project continued to take shape. Jim was, in his own words, greatly stimulated by Macdonald's enthusiasm for his stories; it had the effect of 'making [him] feel important, that [he] really amounted to something' after all.[11] He confided to his new friend that 'since my return from England there has been a kind of hopelessness taking possession of me; now I ask myself if there is still time for fresh beginnings.' He continued in the same letter to describe his reaction to a radio version of Robertson Davies' play *Fortune My Foe*, which he enjoyed for the skill and courage of its ideas. He wanted to see such an attack on Canadian society result in indignation, he wrote, but expected the reaction would simply be apathy and a continuing feeling of smug self-satisfaction among the populace at large. They were not likely 'to be ruffled by anything a mere writing-man or intellectual may have to say.'[12]

There were some Canadian novelists, however, who were enjoying success with the book-buying public. One of these was Hugh MacLennan, whose *Two Solitudes* (1945) analyses the uneasy co-existence of English and French Canada. Another was W.O. Mitchell, who created a heart-warming story of growing up on the prairie in *Who Has Seen the Wind* (1947). Living in Montreal, Jim recognized the importance of MacLennan's subject, but he found little to admire in what he regarded as the author's pedestrian, often tedious style. This could not be said of Mitchell; his exquisite descriptions of the prairie – sights, sounds, and smells – were to be envied. *Who Has Seen the Wind* is a sensitive story of a boy and the earth and the sky and the seasons, yet for Jim the book was not something he could either emulate or feel close to. In Mitchell's book there was a golden haze of nostalgia that he could not experience, for he had never been part of a fixed community or family himself. When his father died there was no mourning and simultaneous maturing because he had hardly known his father. Perhaps, he was beginning to think, there was no material available from his own past experience that could be fashioned into a story the public would want to read. However, there was scattered praise for his short stories; perhaps if they were collected for the public under one cover ...

Grant Macdonald was in close contact with John Gray as the idea for the illustrated stories developed, and when Gray informed him he was stopping in Kingston in early December, Macdonald made arrangements to have dinner with John and his wife, Antoinette (known to friends as Tony). He told Gray in a letter that Jimmy Ross would be there too. But Jim, who was experiencing problems with abscessed teeth and was plagued by a series of colds, wrote to say he couldn't come.[13] Grant continued to invite Jim to Kingston – there was an invitation for Christmas – but Jim had no strong impulse to return and used health reasons as his excuse.

Grant kept working on the story project, further kindling John Gray's interest. On 10 January 1949, Gray wrote to Grant to say how much Sir Osbert Sitwell liked the illustration for 'A Field of Wheat,' which was on display in Gray's Toronto office, and he adds: 'We shall look forward to receiving the book containing Jimmy Ross's stories, and later on to further illustrations. I am very intrigued with this whole proposal and, as a matter of personal inclination, I do hope we can see our way clear to doing the book.'[14] Within the next two weeks, Grant sent Gray's office illustrations for 'One's a Heifer' and 'Jug and Bottle.' Jim, in the meantime, despite a sinus infection and continuing dental problems, was putting in all his non-banking time at the typewriter, trying to complete two new stories to his satisfaction. Their titles were 'Old Chippendale' and 'The Diamonds and the Mills of God.' The latter would eventually be published as 'The Runaway,' but 'Old Chippendale,' though completed, would be abandoned and not published. Jim sent Grant a copy of 'The Diamonds' for an opinion, feeling disappointed with it himself after so much work; Grant's enthusiasm, however, made Jim feel good again about his work.

But in a two-page typed letter dated February 16, Jim writes at length about how depressed and irritable he has been, in part because of gums and sinus, but also because of the work on 'Old Chippendale,' a story of a grotesque Prairie family in which the domineering, histrionic mother finally commits suicide.[15] The abyss of family misery that the author himself had known as a child ('yelling and shaking the poker')[16] reasserted itself while he worked, and he blamed his fit of depression on this project: 'A filthy story – and I wrote and rewrote and *rewrote* it – and even now it still clings to me.'[17] 'Old Chippendale' recreates the conditions of Jim's childhood, while he was still living as a small boy on the farm at Wild Rose. The time and setting are closer to those of *As for Me and My House* – dust storms fill the air and the father in the story is a small-town storekeeper, not a farmer – but the husband and wife and their undersize son replicate the Rosses in every other respect. What makes this unpublished story of particular interest is that the author views the tangle of family misery entirely from the husband's or father's point of view, with no sympathy extended to the woman this time. With her 'aggressive cheekbones,' big hips and breasts, and 'slashing' eyes, she is constructed as a hulking embodiment of frustration and rage, around which husband and son tip-toe furtively. Like Kate Ross vaunting her genteel upbringing – 'that world of means and distinction' represented by an old Chippendale chair passed down in the family – she berates her husband for 'the wretched existence to which his incompetence and lack of ambition have condemned her.' Occasionally her husband strikes back, pleading with her to behave 'like a normal woman' and stop trying to turn their son against him, but in retaliation she points to the rough town in which they live and the plight of the boy:

> 'It's his health and future I'm concerned about. He's not growing as he ought to. Look at his wrists – the breadth of his shoulders – turned out to play with a pack of hoodlums. If you were any kind of man you'd do something. I don't mind for myself – I've given up – but when I see his life being ruined too – when I think of what lies ahead of him –'

In turn, he suggests that they separate, that she take the boy with her and live on her own, to escape the 'quarrels, bitterness and hate,' until they are both ready to make a fresh start together. One wonders when reading this story if in fact it was Peter Ross who proposed the separation that eventually became permanent for Jim's parents.

But this story, with its harrowing and pitiless view of the author's childhood, delves one step deeper into family psychology. Although the story assumes the father's point of view, it creates little sympathy for him; rather, he is exposed as a weak, craven man. What made him give way to his wife? 'Fear – that was it. Not resignation, not forbearance – fear ... When he tried to talk to [the boy] or when he strummed for a few minutes at the piano – always it was fear, shadowing every thought, constraining every movement.' The husband and father believes now that is why she despises him, because he was afraid of her, because she saw him as weak and cringing. The story concludes outside the bounds of the author's biography. The husband resolves to stand up to his wife, and when the boy comes to the store to say his mother has threatened to hang herself, as she has threatened to do before, he does not hurry home to 'save' her. But the old Chippendale chair she uses in her drama gives way (because her husband had broken one of its legs and not repaired it properly), and she actually does succeed in hanging herself. Jim had come to realize that there was no escaping one's childhood; certainly, he held back none of his feelings about his family in this grim tale.

When he wrote to Grant Macdonald on February 16, he referred to hearing from John Gray, who had conveyed his interest in the story collection but had cautiously added that he wasn't sure it could be done. John Gray's caution and his own innate pessimism had pretty much prepared Jim for a letter he received from Gray, written 2 May 1949, in which the latter reported that, 'with reluctance,' Macmillan had decided against the short-story project. The commercial argument against the project was almost crushing from the beginning, he added, but the readers of the manuscript also had reservations from an artistic point of view. They felt there was 'too much similarity of tone through more than half the stories in the manuscript.' Similarly they felt a monotony accrued stylistically from a repetition of 'certain characteristics of language.' Curiously the readers felt the new stories, including 'The Diamonds and the Mills of God' and 'Jug and Bottle', were 'more promising, if not actually better,' than the stories from the 1930s. John Gray expressed this as positively as he could by saying they suggested a new freedom in the writing, a reaching for newer forms and varied themes, and that at Macmillan they looked forward to his future work.[18] A letter from Jim to Grant Macdonald written on May 12 concludes the correspondence and the friendship. Jim writes to let Grant know that if he wants to try another publisher, he has Jim's consent to do so. He tells about a reading of 'One's a Heifer' on CBC (rather displeased by the casting of Vickers in a 'drawling, old-farmer voice which ... left him just a crank and curmudgeon') and about another revision he has made of 'The Diamonds and the Mills of God,' in spite of health problems, which include something like tonsillitis, even though his tonsils had been removed ten years earlier.[19] Grant, however, was buoyantly pursuing other projects: he had been invited to design the sets for a production of Robertson Davies' *Eros at Breakfast* for the 1949 Edinburgh Music and Drama Festival, and was organizing an anthology of stories, essays, and poems by his friends with illustrations inspired by each piece contributed. The collection was to include one of Jim's stories (as well as work by Robertson Davies, Mazo de la Roche, E.J. Pratt, and others), but the project never materialized.[20]

Although he had been in ill health during the winter, Jim had accepted a dinner party invitation for the day after New Year's 1949. From Winnipeg, his bank friend Kathleen Scroggie arranged that he should meet Dorothy and Bill Klyn, old friends of hers from the Prairies who were now living in Montreal. Jim reported to Grant in his letter of January 13 that Dorothy Klyn was 'the lady from the *Standard* who "does" art – and she proved to be a very charming, genuine person. The conversation didn't get round to art, however, so I don't know. Perhaps I warmed to her because she is from a small town in Saskatchewan.'[21] The Klyns instantly warmed to Jim as well, and a strong friendship was established, especially between Jim and Dorothy, which lasted until Jim left Montreal twenty years later.

In a small way, the Klyns provided Jim with the entrance into Anglo-Montreal's social life that he had anticipated through Ira Dilworth. The Klyns gave big parties and were socially fashionable. Bill worked for Canadian

Pacific Railways, and the couple, who had no children, travelled extensively in connection with his work. Better known to the public at large, however, was Dorothy, who in the 1950s became women's editor for *Weekend Magazine* and was the author of a popular weekly column on food, fashions, and entertaining titled 'According to Doyle.' In the 1960s she would have her own CBC television program for dispensing timely advice and interviewing entertainment personalities. Tall, loose-limbed, garrulous, Doyle Klyn possessed a stylishness and quick sense of fun that made her popular with both her country-wide audience and her personal friends. Doyle's generous spirit instinctively embraced the author's gentle nature, but she had, in addition, been born and raised in Oxbow, Saskatchewan, just south of Arcola, and that fact made Jim and Doyle feel, as he once said, like brother and sister.

The Klyns understood Jim in the light of their friendship with Kathleen Scroggie.[22] They saw both Kathleen and Jim as tyrannized by widowed, domineering parents. In Winnipeg the Klyns lived adjacent to the Scroggies, and they knew first-hand that Mr Scroggie demanded his daughter's attention at all times and that, like Kate, he would not go to bed until Kathleen had come home, even though she was by then over thirty years of age. As they saw it, neither Kathleen nor Jim had been able to develop any confidence in themselves as adults. Doyle Klyn would especially remember one snowy evening when they were giving a party for some seventy guests and she happened to look out at one point and saw Jim standing in the street, obviously trying to summon up the courage to mount the porch steps. Jim, for his part, remembered how Doyle would invariably separate herself from her guests when he entered the house, put her arms around him in a flourish, and then walk him upstairs to where the guests put their coats. There was a quick outpouring of the latest gossip he would need to know in order to navigate the social currents below, and then they would go downstairs together to the huge pot of macaroni and cheese Doyle had prepared in the kitchen. She made Jim feel special, and, to her, he was that in many ways; she remembered years later that he seemed like a lost boy and she always wanted to hug him.

It was at one of the Klyns' parties that Jim met Mavis Gallant. The Klyns had known Mavis's husband, Johnny Gallant, when they lived in Winnipeg. The latter, a skilled musician, was now also living in Montreal, where he made his living as a pianist at the Ritz Café supper club, accompanying popular singers like Celeste Holm and Jane Morgan. Through Johnny, the Klyns came to know Mavis and continued to value that friendship after husband and wife separated. In the late 1940s, Mavis was working as a reporter for the *Montreal Standard* and enjoying her first tentative success as a writer of serious short fiction. She and Jim began a friendship – companions in the craft – that would last almost forty years. Their mutual and binding interest was the short story.

In 1949 Jim was in contact with *Queen's Quarterly* again, and over the next three years he would send the journal at least six stories. Poet and critic George Herbert Clarke was the editor, and unlike Alexander Macphail, he had strong opinions on matters of literary language. The first story Jim sent was 'Jug and Bottle,' the other war story, which drew a positive reply from Clarke except for one word: he objected to 'snotty' to describe the army sergeant and suggested 'overbearing' instead.[23] Jim wrote back saying he yielded the word readily, indeed found it unpleasant, but used it 'because it is good "Army."'[24] He listed 'chesty,' 'upstart,' and 'stripe-conscious' as alternatives, although 'cocky' appears to be the word that was finally used in the printed text. Later, when Clarke was editing the story 'Saturday Night,' he objected to the word 'screwy' in the young protagonist's vocabulary, urging literary rather than vernacular language.[25] Jim replied that he would like to keep the word but rewrote the sentence using the phrase 'I've got it bad alright.'[26] Although it was Jim's habit to submit to editors' wishes, in one of his letters to Clarke he defended his use of the vernacular on the grounds of psychological realism: 'I am inclined to be somewhat fastidious and fussy in the choice of words, and I try to remember, when working on a character, that it isn't what is pleasing to me that matters, but what is true to him.'[27] In another letter to Clarke, he asks to be advised of any changes to his story because he has tested the writing carefully 'for sound and rhythm, and I think that, as it stands, there is something like balance between the contrasting parts.'[28] This meticulousness about word choice and phrasing would persist throughout his writing career.

In 'Jug and Bottle,' which appeared in the winter 1949 issue of *Queen's Quarterly*,[29] the first-person narrator is evading the company of a misfit private who keeps attempting suicide. This is a more complex tale than 'Barrack Room Fiddle Tune,' involving the narrator in an intricate web of responsibility and guilt. The story has a double structure: the suicidal private named Coulter tells the narrator about his guilty relationship with a woman named Muriel, while the speaker of the story, in turn, tells the reader about his guilty relationship with Coulter. At the heart of the first story is a man's sympathy and identification with a woman. The eccentric Coulter, physically ungainly and out of step with his peers, takes pity on a young neighbour woman who is an invalid and not expected to live more than six months or a year. He does not love her – she was 'not what a woman means to a man when she's the right one' (78); rather, he sees in her a reflection of his own sufferings: 'Watching her,' he tells the narrator, 'was like ... standing in front of a mirror.' He visits her out of compassion, feeling good with himself that he is bringing her happiness, however temporary, but it transpires that his visits have wrought a miracle, that she will not die after all, and she looks forward to marriage and a family. Coulter, 'all panic,' talks with her about their future together, but she soon recognizes that he is lying and '... the hope and life [go] out of her again' (80). He joins the army, to which he is so ill suited, as an escape and perhaps as a form of self-punishment. The company goes overseas, and eventually Coulter receives a cablegram telling of Muriel's death.

On the surface, the narrator's relationship to Coulter is that of a reluctantly sympathetic listener. But his situation is exactly like Coulter's in relation to Muriel, and we might deduce that he too is standing in front of a mirror. He believes he has prevented Coulter more than once from committing suicide, and he feels the heavy burden of Coulter's dependency on him. By listening to Coulter tell his story, the way Coulter listened to Muriel, he revives in him a wish to continue living; and when he is no longer there to listen, Coulter, like Muriel, dies. The narrator is telling his story as a way of unburdening his guilt: 'Most people,' he says, 'just shrug and ask if there aren't too many sentimental fools already muddling up the world' (69). But the sympathetic reader of Ross's story is, in turn, charged with its burden.

Part of the burden of the story for the careful reader is its opacity. Ross characteristically uses language to veil the deeper recesses of the story from casual scrutiny. The third paragraph sets up roadblocks for the reader; its equivocations, similar to those of As for Me and My House, turn on the use of the pronoun 'it' without definite reference:

> As for The Jug and Bottle – well, *it* was just one of those things. Let *it* go at that. Don't read into *it* what was never there; don't try to fit *it* into some pattern of destiny or judgement. *It* isn't necessary; there's no blame to be shifted. (69, emphasis added)

At the story's end, of course, the reader is aware that there was a mix-up over the words 'jug and bottle,' which resulted in Coulter's despair and suicide. But reread in that light, this paragraph is not much clearer, for the narrator seems to be disingenuous in his insistence that *it* does not matter, that one should not read into things.

A dilated view of the story, one incorporating previous knowledge of the writer and his work, will indeed set the reader looking for patterns and thinking about guilt. One of the deepest of those patterns in Ross's fiction is that of the sensitive man who experiences profound compassion for the suffering of women. We have seen this in the taut, sympathetic portrayals of lonely farm women in the early stories, and it is perhaps the secret to the great success of the character of Mrs Bentley. The male-female relation, however, is one of identification rather than infatuation, 'like ... standing in front of a mirror,' whereby the man is revealed as being like another woman rather than her lover. Perhaps this is the intuitive knowledge that makes the narrator evade Coulter in the camp, refusing what could only be a homosexual friendship if it were to develop, wincing at the sight of Coulter's self-exposure and vulnerability on the parade square. The narrator's reluctance to publicly befriend Coulter is a strategy of survival in the homophobic environment of the army camp; their one long conversation, in which we learn about Muriel, takes place when they are alone on the deck of the ship bound for England, watching a windy sunset. The narrator remains aloof in his relations with Coulter, refusing the companionship he craves, and after Coulter's death he refuses to unravel for the reader the knowledge that Coulter has brought him: '... It was just one of those things. Let it go at that. Don't read into it what was never there ...' But the story's mirror structure, one narrative of identification and betrayal intercalated within the other, reveals the unspoken drama at the heart of this story.

In a taped interview with Earle Toppings, Jim identifies Thomas Hardy as one of his favourite authors and perhaps the chief influence on his work. 'Jug and Bottle' provides a striking example of this influence. In the third paragraph of the story quoted above, the evasive narrator recommends that the reader not look for some pattern of destiny or judgment in his story, but by the close of the same paragraph he appears to contradict himself when he says that 'sometimes the accidental is the inevitable,' thereby evoking fate as a participant in the story he is about to tell. The influence of Hardy is strongest at the close, when the narrator agrees to meet Coulter at the 'Jug and Bottle.' Neither realizes that this is not the name of a pub but a generic sign over a 'take out' entrance. They are in fact waiting for each other in separate pubs across the way; but Coulter thinks the narrator has stood him up and in despair commits suicide. In the manner of Hardy, accident here is viewed as the vehicle of destiny, the instrument of 'the inevitable.'

'Jug and Bottle,' a fragment surviving from the novel 'about a soldier from Manitoba,'[30] is the only piece of fiction Jim would publish that was set partly outside of Canada. Although the story has never been highly regarded by critics, perhaps because of its evasions and what paradoxically appears to be overwriting, it was always important to the author. When Clarke accepted it for *Queen's Quarterly*, Jim had written that it had 'often seemed an impossible story – the ms. has been lying in my desk in an unfinished state for all of two years – and still I have kept coming back at intervals to worry away at it a little more, never, somehow, able to discard and forget about it.'[31] Ross denied it was a personal tale, yet he remained haunted by it.

The next story to appear in *Queen's Quarterly* (Summer 1950) was 'The Outlaw,'[32] a fictional account of Jim's love for 'Lady,' the horse he rode when he lived on Sid Ketcheson's farm. 'The Outlaw' is on one level a conventional story of a thirteen-year-old boy's initiation into young manhood. In the school yard, the boy has been something of a failure: 'butterfingers' when playing ball, and once, in a fight, a coward who turned tail and ran when the school bully punched him in the nose. But his father has purchased a horse with a reputation as a killer, and the boy proves his daring and prowess with her in the presence of Millie Dickson, the prettiest girl in his class.

Millie Dickson, as female admirer, is a conventional figure in this story of masculine testing and triumph. What makes this an original and remarkable story is the role played by the black horse named Isabel. First, she is described in almost erotic language as having a 'gleaming, queenly' beauty that is soft, mysterious, and burning, and that charges the stable with a fierce, secret passion, 'as if she were the priestess of her kind, in communion with her deity' (19). She stirs the youthful narrator's imagination, and he says: 'I charged with her at Balaklava, Waterloo, scoured the deserts of Africa and the steppes of the Ukraine. Conquest and carnage, trumpets and glory – she understood, and carried me triumphantly' (19). But in addition to this rich, historically evocative description of a horse, the story provides Isabel's point of view as well, a point of view that focuses on beauty, but above all on the desire and need to be free. When, in their jubilant ride together, boy and horse have travelled a couple of miles, Isabel halts for a few minutes and 'breathe[s] in rapturously the loping miles of freedom,' all the while forcing the boy to see for the first time the 'austere, unrelenting beauty' of the prairie – 'the white fields and the blue, metallic sky; the little splashes here and there of yellow haystacks, luminous and clear as drops of gum on fresh pine lumber; the scattered farmsteads brave and wistful in their isolation; the gleam of sun and snow' (24). But the horse's point of view is not simply implied; it shifts from indirect speech in a line like '[Isabel] considered my use of the word "master" insufferably presumptuous' to direct speech, in which Isabel is made to give voice to the most important lines of the story, its gist. Drawing the boy's attention to the landscape, 'Look, she said firmly, while it's here before you, so that to the last detail it will remain clear. For you, too, some day there may be stalls and halters, and it will be a good memory' (24). Seldom has a horse been rendered so vividly or passionately in a work of fiction.

'The Outlaw' had been read that year by John Drainie on CBC Radio's weekday program *Canadian Short Stories*.[33] The show was one of several programs for the arts created by Robert Weaver at CBC headquarters in Toronto. Like John Gray, Bob Weaver not only promoted popular Canadian artists on his shows (which included *CBC Stage* and *CBC Tuesday Night*), but he actively sought out and encouraged lesser-known writers to submit their work for broadcast. He first wrote a letter of inquiry to Jim in February of 1949,[34] wherein he praised *As for Me and My House* and asked if he had stories that would be suitable for reading on the radio; to his request, Jim replied that he had asked John Gray to send some stories to the CBC. Frank Upjohn at Macmillan sent three – 'A Field of Wheat,' 'One's a Heifer,' and the previously unpublished 'The Outlaw.' Weaver liked best 'One's a Heifer' and asked Jim to adapt it for radio.[35] But Jim did not find that an easy assignment, and in April he wrote to Weaver that 'taking out the last 300 words just about took me with them.'[36] To a subsequent request, Jim sent 'The Diamonds and the Mills of God' (later titled 'The Runaway') from the defunct short-story collection he had worked on with Grant Macdonald. The story had been refused by *Maclean's*.[37] He told Weaver that his New York agent wanted a different ending for the story, but when he read it Weaver felt the original ending was fine. However, length was again a problem, and he asked Jim for cuts. In the end, they used 'The Outlaw,' which was read on 21 April 1950.

That same year, Jim had another story ready for the public. It was titled 'Saturday Night'[38] and was a romantic sketch of an adolescent boy's dreams and heartbreak. When he sent the manuscript to G.H. Clarke in July, Jim described the story as 'a featherweight,' but defended the character of Tom as nonetheless 'sincere and credible.' He went on to discuss the particular problem he confronted in writing the story: 'For all its simplicity – or banality – it was a hard story to write, the problem being to blend the graceless vernacular in which Tom would naturally express himself with the poetic extravagance appropriate to his condition so that the one would not make the other ridiculous.'[39] He viewed the story as something of an experiment. He had been reading some short stories by F. Scott Fitzgerald, which he concluded were not very good, marred too frequently in his opinion by a rhapsodic sentimentality. Yet he was moved nonetheless by the plight of Fitzgerald's hapless lovers and set out to write a similar story, but one purged of Fitzgerald's poetic excesses. There is almost no action in the story: Tom returns home from his summer job to find that his girlfriend has gone to the Saturday night dance with another boy. Tom works through the painful disappointment he feels by telling himself that he must exert self-discipline and control his feelings. There is a poignancy to the boy's naïve innocence and his vulnerability, but his studied analysis of what he is feeling and how to behave becomes somewhat tedious. The contrast with Fitzgerald's jilted lovers is striking: in the American stories, the thwarted lover embarks on a fantastic plan to win back the girl of his dreams, whereas Ross's boy disciplines himself 'to grow up and be civilized' (97).

Probably, Tom's disillusionment and his determination to behave in a mature way reflect something of Jim's feelings about himself and his career at this point. In his letters in the 1950s, he describes himself as increasingly unsure of his direction. The failure of As for Me and My House to find an audience remained a crippling blow to his self-esteem as a writer, and he was no longer certain that he had the stuff it takes to be a writer of any consequence. Yet he knew he would probably keep 'scribbling at something,' as the habit now was deeply ingrained. He wondered if his physical distance from Saskatchewan and the Prairie sources of his art was having a bad effect on his writing or whether he should be leaving the Prairies behind and turning his attention to Montreal. In a letter to Robert Weaver of 22 May 1950, he wrote: 'I am somewhat at sixes and sevens in my writing at the present time – trying to shift from farm to urban backgrounds, which is much more difficult than you think. I am such a thorough hick – but I hope to have something to offer in good time for you to give it consideration.' In his reply, Weaver encouraged Jim to broaden the scope of his writing material: 'it did seem to me that your use of western rural background ... had become something of a limiting factor in your work. I'd be very much interested at any time in seeing a story by you with an urban background, though this of course doesn't mean that I no longer find the western stories interesting.'[40]

Late the following year, Jim sent Weaver his first attempt at a fiction with an urban setting. From the letters exchanged between the two men, we know it was titled 'A World of Good' and concerned a husband and wife awaiting a visit from the husband's friend. The woman receives the guest in housedress and curlers, and only later puts on evening apparel. The readers at the CBC thought the story unlikely and Weaver rejected it, singling out the 'piling up [of] sordid realistic details' as a serious artistic flaw, cancelling any sympathy the readers or listeners might have in the story.[41] In a reply to Weaver's rejection, Jim explains the failure of his story not in terms of urban setting or uncongenial material, but in terms of having taken the story too directly from life. 'It is an illustration, I suppose,' he wrote, 'of the difficulty of "lifting" from life. The author is so convinced by the experience ... that he probably takes fewer pains in the presentation than he would if it were something built from his imagination.'[42] It is doubtful, however, that Jim was wholly convinced by his own argument because he had 'lifted from life' in his writing before – in numerous portraits for As for Me and My House and the early stories – and would continue to do so, notoriously and most successfully in Sawbones Memorial. 'A World of Good' drew heavily on his friendship with a man named Brown at the bank. The latter frequently invited Jim home to dinner, where he got to know his wife, a likeable woman who was unhappily weighed down by her responsibilities as wife, homemaker, and mother of five children. She took Jim into her confidence, told him of her dreams, and complained bitterly of the drabness of her life. Similarly, at the bank, Brown confided to Jim that his marriage was not an easy one, that his wife was an untidy housekeeper, that meals were never ready when he returned home at the end of the day, and that he sometimes wondered if his wife was becoming emotionally unstable. Jim saw the marriage from both sides and in his story wanted to be fair to them both, as he had tried to be to the Bentleys in *As for Me and My House*. He had also taken pains to make the story as 'realistic' as possible, getting Doyle Klyn's advice on what clothes such a character would wear and how she was likely to do her hair. The correspondence makes clear that the wife and her frustrations were central to the story. In his reply to Weaver's charge that the story was psychologically inaccurate, he gave the following account:

> The inconsistency in the woman's careless appearance at the beginning and her efforts later on to 'put on the dog' is explained by the fact that the poor soul is [...] simply seizing the opportunity provided by her guest to convince herself, not him, that 'she is still in the running.' Her chief concern is re-assurance. The guest scarcely exists for her. Rigging herself up in the vestiges of her pre-marital finery is a gesture of defiance against approaching middle-age and the 'penalties' of motherhood.[43]

The 'guest' in this account is reminiscent of Paul Kirby engaged in his invisible courtship of Mrs Bentley.

At some point in the early 1950s, Jim and Bob Weaver met for dinner at a hotel in Montreal. It turned out that they had things in common beyond their absorbing interest in fiction. At the outset of his working life, Bob had been employed for two years as a teller at the Toronto Dominion Bank, and so both men knew the clerk's routine. Both men had enlisted in the army during the war. There were personal, family congruencies as well: Bob's father had died when he was barely two years old, and he was raised in a family of women; further, Bob's aunt, Emily P. Weaver, like Sir John Foster Fraser, was a writer of some reputation – a popular Canadian historian – and the idea of being a writer was held in high esteem in the family. Bob, like Jim a physically small man, felt intimidated by strong or overbearing men such as Earle Birney or Jack McClelland and preferred, socially, the company of women. Also, both men knew the value of a dollar and lived somewhat narrow lives according to what they felt was necessity.

But in spite of these many similarities, Bob and Jim were completely different men in a social setting. After the war, Bob had completed a degree in

English and philosophy at the University of Toronto, and in 1948 he joined the CBC, working out of Toronto. Well-educated and self-confident, Bob Weaver was good-humoured and garrulously energetic; he loved gossip, one-on-one relationships, and being involved in people's lives. Travelling to different regions of the country for his CBC short-story anthology, he would visit his contributors and, gathering impressions and anecdotes, would pass them along, creating a sense of community among writers in the far-flung parts of Canada. He liked to describe having afternoon tea with Ethel Wilson and her doctor husband in their graciously appointed apartment in Vancouver's West End, and visiting the domestically beleaguered young Alice Munro in North Vancouver before her first story collection was published; he would tell of buying drinks and dinner at the Ritz Café for Jimmy Ross, the painfully shy banker in Montreal, of an excruciating dinner party with the Woodcocks in Vancouver, and of how G.H. Clarke had scalded himself to death in the shower in Kingston.[44] Jim, however, would hasten to modify the picture of the CBC employee generously regaling one of his writers at the Ritz Café in Montreal. Jim remembered one beer in the bar and then 'an unappetizing meal' in the restaurant, and a stingy tip that he felt it was necessary to supplement.[45] Jim liked listening to Bob's lengthy, digressing stories about Canadian writers, but he wearied of what he felt was a one-way conversation. Bob seemed never to listen to or show any interest in what Jim might have to say. Jim disliked his easy social manners and the curious antithesis of his parsimonious habits, but most of all he disliked what he perceived as Bob's ambitiousness and touches of personal vanity. These common human traits Jim would never tolerate in himself, and he had contempt for them in others. Bob was married with a family, and so there was a whole area of his life that Jim could not share with him. He regretted that, given so many things in common, he could never fully warm to the gestures of friendship from Bob. Yet perhaps more than anyone else in the 1950s, Robert Weaver, as a kind of midwife to Canadian writing, kept Jim's name alive for the public.

In a Christmas note to Doris Saunders for 1952, Jim directed her to look at his latest story in the autumn issue of *Queen's Quarterly*. It was the reworked version of 'The Diamonds and the Mills of God,' which he published with the title 'The Runaway'.[46] He stated to Doris he thought it would be his last farm story, and that prediction proved to be true. While still a rural story, 'The Runaway' was a departure from the realistic farm pieces he had written before. As David Carpenter has observed, this is the only wholly comic short piece Sinclair Ross ever published; moreover, it is a 'tale' rather than a 'story,' with a completely different set of assumptions about how a piece of fiction works. Describing it, as Ken Mitchell had already done, as a fiction in the

Faulknerian mode, Carpenter observes that realistic detail in 'The Runaway' counts for much less than in Ross's earlier writings; instead, this is a morality tale in which the characters are not victims of hard circumstance, but have choices to make that will determine the course of their lives. The characters and their actions are drawn 'larger than life, 'exaggerated in order to drama-tize the moral issue at stake.[47]

The tale is narrated, not by one of Ross's 'wistful boys,' but by a self-confi-dent son who is securely situated in a conventional farm family. He tells of his father's love of horses, particularly his passion for Black Diamonds bred by an unscrupulous neighbour, Luke Taylor, and of how involvement with Taylor precipitates a moral crisis in his father's reckoning of the world. Against the community's better judgment, the boy's father trades four of his fat steers for a pair of Taylor's Black Diamonds, and the horses prove to be 'balky,' some-times refusing to move when they are in harness. Taylor is viewed not as any ordinary farmer but, in what Carpenter refers to as the hyperbolic tradition of the morality tale, as a comic embodiment of the devil who tempts the narra-tor's father with his worldly riches. For Taylor has the best property in the area – two thousand acres, a 'handsome grey-stone house' with hot and cold running water, and a 'big red hip-roofed barn,' with never fewer than twenty-four of the magnificent Black Diamonds in its stalls. The narrator's moralizing mother pronounces Taylor's assets to be 'ill-gotten gains,' and the narrator himself refuses an invitation for lemonade in 'the abode of guile'; but for his father, Luke Taylor's prosperity is a complicated moral question. Taylor has cheated his neighbours, and in return he has accumulated riches that the father sorely envies. The narrator puts his father's dilemma this way:

> For years he had been weakened and confused by a conflict, on the one hand resentment at what Luke had done and got away with, on the other ... he had been sustained by the belief that scores were being kept, and that he would live to see a Day of Reckoning. Now, though, he wasn't sure. You could see in his glance and frown that he was beginning to wonder which he really was: the upright, God-fearing man that he had always believed himself to be, or a simple, credulous dupe. (82)

In succumbing to the temptation of acquiring Taylor's horses, the father tem-porarily abandons his high principles and in turn is made to appear a fool when the horses prove unmanageable.

But the larger moral order to which the community subscribes is restored in the tale's final sequence. Luke Taylor, encountering the boy's father on the road trying in vain to start the horses, suggests that he build a little fire under them. "'Being what [Luke] is,'" observes the father, "'the idea of fire comes natural.'" Eventually he takes up that suggestion and in so doing sets a load of hay on fire; the Diamonds in their panic race home with the burning hay to Taylor's place, where the great barn catches fire and Taylor dies in the blaze. As David Carpenter points out, in any other Sinclair Ross story this event would likely be seen as tragic, another instance of human failure in a blind and uncaring universe, but in the moral scheme of this tale it provides a comic conclusion in which the devil is swallowed up in his traditional element. The narrator's mother, who 'keeps score,' reminds her husband and son: '*Though the mills of God grind slowly, they grind exceeding small.*' (This line – Longfellow's translation of Friedrich von Logau's aphorism on justice – had given Jim his original title 'The Diamonds and the Mills of God.') But in a final ironic twist, the mother, like Eve, suggests to her husband that he perhaps think now of breeding colts from the two Diamonds he still owns, and in her suggestion earthly ambitions and desires are once again reborn.

Interestingly, 'The Runaway' has only been reprinted once and that very recently.[48] It has stood as something of an anomaly in the Ross canon, and critics, with the exception of Carpenter, have either ignored it or treated it as offering a less compelling instance of the high price exacted by working the land. Sinclair Ross's fiction has been so thoroughly identified with the bleak conditions of the dust bowl and Depression that anthologizers have passed by this comic tale. Letters imply that through his agent, Max Becker, he had tried to find an American magazine to publish this piece, that he had been willing to change the ending to suit editorial taste, but even this tale in the Faulknerian mode failed to find an American buyer and he offered it once again to *Queen's Quarterly*.[49] It would be the last of his stories they would publish.

ten

The Well
1954–1960

I always run to meet rejection ... a kind of insurance against disappointment.
– Letter to John Gray

In a Christmas greeting for 1954, Jim wrote to John Gray at Macmillan saying he had been hard at work that year on a new manuscript and hoped to have something to show him in two or three months time.[1] Gray replied in his buoyant fashion that he was delighted to hear Jim was writing again, especially to hear he was writing about the West. The combination, he said, should make a good book, and they would look forward to it eagerly.[2] (Gray had kept in touch with Jim, even though Macmillan turned down the short-story proposal, and when he was in Montreal he would sometimes telephone and arrange they meet for lunch at the Ritz Hotel, on one occasion including Mavis Gallant.) The friendly exchange at Christmas 1954, however, was to usher in one of the most difficult and frustrating periods of the author's life. The manuscript to which Jim referred was to become the ill-fated novel *The Well*, published in 1958. Through a confusing series of failed negotiations, bad advice, and ill-conceived editorial demands, the writing and publication of *The Well* became a nightmare for the author and a commercial fiasco for its publisher. The book's problems, however, point tellingly to some of the debilitating forces at work in Canada during this time that created insurmountable obstacles for serious writers.

Jim wrote to John Gray on 23 June 1955 to report that the manuscript was finished except for a final typing. He hoped to get it in the mail within two or three weeks. However, he could not make Macmillan an unconditional offer of the manuscript because he was submitting it first to Harcourt Brace in New York. Jim was in good spirits as he wrote this letter: in a characteristic demurral, he says that Macmillan might not want the manuscript once they have seen it, but he says he thinks it is 'readable,' an almost brash, boastful statement coming from Jimmy Ross. Further, he says he is feeling 'a little more confident and energetic of late' and thinks he might manage three or more novels during his writing career. With this prospect in mind, he asks Gray for advice regarding New York agents. He explains that Max Becker of the AFG Agency placed As for Me and My House and continued to show interest in his work, 'always [being] friendly and encouraging.' But he admits to Gray that he knows very little about Becker and asks if he would inquire at Macmillan's New York office on his behalf.

Jim's confidence in his new manuscript was connected to his reading and his newly awakened sense of the possibilities of fiction. At some point in the early 1950s, he read an English translation of Albert Camus' The Stranger. He recalled being 'shaken' by it, by the powerful sense of recognition, by secret knowledge laid out for all to see.[3] His own situation bore certain resemblances to Meursault's – he too was a clerk, a middle-class bachelor preparing his evening meal alone in a small flat, frequently going to the movies, searching for sex on the weekends. Would his feelings be so different from Meursault's, he wondered, if he received a telegram from Saskatchewan saying his mother had died. Perhaps he also lacked basic human emotions, viewing life calmly from the outside – with irony, but little pity, preoccupied with sensations and textures. He knew himself in middle age to be much like Meursault in the magistrate's eyes, 'a taciturn, rather self-centered person' with an instinct to make the same reply: 'I rarely have anything much to say. So naturally I keep my mouth shut' (70). And had he not come to a similar point in resigning himself, as Camus wrote at the end of his novel, 'to the benign indifference of the universe' (120)? He felt exposed by this book and at the same time exhilarated by the idea that he too could write about young men who experienced the profound alienation he himself frequently felt, and who acted without moral restraint. No longer would he have to hide some of his strong feelings – or, better, his lack of certain feelings – in the guise of moral dramas, as he had done in the convolutions of a story like 'Jug and Bottle.' The Canadian West, moreover, was as likely a decentred locale for such fiction as Algeria. Jim felt empowered by the example of The Stranger, and in his new manuscript, which reached back for inspiration to his early youth on Nels Forfang's farm,[4] but at the same time to recent literary models, he was certain that he was writing abreast a wave of fiction that would situate him in the mainstream.

In the meantime, John Gray did write to Macmillan in New York to inquire about Becker, asking 'how reliable he [was], how imaginative or energetic.'[5] When it was reported that little was known about him, Gray wrote to Jim and recommended that he try Willis Kingsley Wing, whom he knew to be 'a first rate man, genuinely interested in talent.' Wing was agent, he pointed out, for a number of Canadians, including W.O. Mitchell, Ralph Allen, and Pierre Berton.[6] The 1963 listing in *Writer's Market* suggests that W.K. Wing by that time was indeed one of New York's most successful literary agents. He is listed as 'no longer seeking additional clients except in rare instances when the author has already attained professional standing.' Wing is remembered by contemporaries on two accounts: physically, he was badly crippled from a bout of polio in his youth and wore heavy braces to be able to walk; temperamentally, he was an ambitious and irascible character, a shrewd and aggressive businessman who drove a hard bargain. Kenneth McCormick, Jim's New York friend at Doubleday, recalled Wing as 'a testy, complicated individual, a difficult man to work with.'[7] Yet there was no denying his success as an agent: his clientele included such international literary figures as G.K. Chesterton, Alan Sillitoe, J.L. Borges, and John Le Carré; and in addition to those Canadians John Gray had cited in his letter to Jim, he was representing Brian Moore and Robertson Davies in the 1950s, and in the 1960s would add Peter Newman, Adele Wiseman, Margaret Laurence, and Robert Kroetsch to his list. With this strong recommendation from John Gray, Jim mailed off the manuscript for *The Well* to Wing in late July 1955.

Wing proved extremely prompt and efficient, for by August 2nd Jim was able to write John Gray that he had received a report from Wing on the manuscript and that it was highly favourable. He quoted the following passages from Wing's letter to give Gray an idea of how positive the response was from New York:

'Thank you very much for your letter of July 20. I greatly appreciate having had the opportunity of reading your novel The Well, and first off let me say that I am eager to represent you and am greatly impressed with the writing ability shown in this ms.

'Since you say that you wanted to take another look at it to see about re-working certain sections, I would like to hear from you when you have come to your conclusions about what you would like to do to it. At that time, if you would like, I could give you some comments from my readings, which have been very complimentary, on the whole. You will also probably wish to be guided by what you hear from John Gray. I would be willing to send your ms. out now, but I would prefer to have it in the best shape possible in order to make the best impression in the right editorial quarters.

'I see no reason to change your setting from Saskatchewan. You have used this background extremely well ...'[8]

Gray was pleased to hear of Wing's interest and recommended that Jim instruct him to send the manuscript out to New York publishers in its present form. At the same time, he would collect reports on the manuscript from his staff at Macmillan.

The readers reports have survived in the Macmillan files.[9] Two of these, bearing only readers' initials, are in agreement on the manuscript's strengths and weaknesses: the readers praised the author's ability to create plot and suspense and especially his ability to create memorable characters, but they both felt strongly the story was overwritten, that there was considerable repetition that could be eliminated, especially in the early histories of the main characters. The third report was submitted September 30 by Frank Upjohn, who was vice-president of the company and manager of the trade section. His opinion was influential. Upjohn began his report by stating the manuscript disappointed him and went on to detail two major faults. Like the others, he felt the manuscript was far too long; he saw it as a short story blown up to a novel of well over a hundred thousand words and recommended that it be cut by at least a third. But more important are his misgivings about the manuscript's plot, misgivings which would dog the project right through to publication.

In its original version, *The Well* told the story of a young man, Chris Rowe, who has committed a murder in Montreal and, on the run, takes a job as a hired hand during the grain harvest in Saskatchewan. He works for an elderly farmer named Larson, whose second wife, Sylvia, is an attractive, sensual woman of thirty. The arrangement at first goes well: Chris likes his work with the farm animals, especially the horses, and Larson is attracted to Chris because he reminds him of his dead son. But eventually Chris and Sylvia become lovers, and as their involvement deepens they arrange to murder the old farmer and dump his body into the well. Sylvia is intent on having Chris and the old man's wealth as well. But after Chris has killed Larson and disposed of the body, he leaves, and Sylvia, on her own, goes mad. Upjohn's objection was that the murderer 'disappears into thin prairie air, and without even a hint of any sort of justice ever catching up with him.' He argues that Chris is the main character for nine-tenths of the book and is at the centre of the reader's attention and sympathy, and for him to disappear, without facing punishment, is for the author to leave an important part of the story untold. Upjohn's assumptions about character, reader identification, moral order, and closure in fiction were contrary to those of the author, who was then steeped in the works of Camus and Sartre. (The reader was not expected to have sympathy for Chris, just fascination; nor was the reader to expect a moral at the end of the story.) Years later Jim would lament that his editors and publisher 'just didn't get it.'[10] Nonetheless, although Upjohn could not foresee any big sale for *The Well*, he recommended its publication on the condition that it be revised, and accordingly Macmillan became committed to the project and began seeking ways to promote it.

On August 22, Kildare Dobbs, an employee at Macmillan, sent the manuscript to Ralph Allen at *Maclean's* asking that it be considered for the *Maclean's* Fiction Award. The award was worth five thousand dollars and gave *Maclean's* the right to run the book serially, returning all subsequent rights to the author. By September 6th, John Gray was reporting to Jim that the first reader at *Maclean's* was enthusiastic but that the second, while equally positive, was 'doubtful about the theme in a popular magazine.' On September 9, fiction editor Janice Tyrwhitt, later to become Pierre Berton's permanent editorial assistant, sent Jim a letter full of confusing signals. She wrote that she and Ralph Allen thought *The Well* 'an extraordinarily fine book,' but that they saw great difficulties in arriving at a magazine version that would please both author and a pre-paid audience of a million readers. Mass tastes and mass prejudices were not something they could afford to ignore. The manuscript would have to be cut by one-third of its length and 'the tricky sex relationship' would require 'a good deal of condensation for the foregoing reason.' Although they liked the book very much, she reiterated, she thought the odds were three to one that a treatment could be achieved that would suit both the author and *Maclean's*. Her advice was to forget the proposal entirely, but she added, 'Naturally we hope you won't.'[11] Tyrwhitt sent a copy of her letter to John Gray, who in turn wrote to Jim, gently urging him to try the condensation since the award would obviously boost book sales.[12] Jim in the meantime had written to Gray (their letters crossed in the mails) saying he did not see his way to attempting such a major condensation of the book – in August he had already been through the manuscript cutting five thousand words. He said it was 'a very nice letter from McCleans [*sic*]' but 'of course they don't really expect me to do it.'[13] Gray's letter, however, persuaded Jim to give the project second thought. He wrote revealingly to Gray on September 20: 'Yes, I'm afraid I did dismiss MacLean's [*sic*] letter as the rejection courteous, and now, after thinking it over, I realize I was probably quite wrong. Unfortunately it is typical of me. I always run to meet rejection – and not only where manuscripts are concerned. Perhaps it has become a kind of insurance against disappointment.' He was still revising the last one hundred pages of the manuscript – cutting some of Sylvia's talk – and was weary of the project, but said that after an interval he might approach things more positively again.

John Gray continued to encourage Jim to reconsider the condensation for *Maclean's*: 'I still hope that presently it may appeal to you and that you may bring it off.'[14] Jim also received a letter from W.K. Wing, who urged him to submit a cut version to *Maclean's* and pointed out that the same thing was required of W.O. Mitchell, who was awarded the *Maclean's* prize for 'The Alien' (published in a much revised form as *The Vanishing Point* in 1973).[15] Gray's faith in the manuscript seemed to give Jim the encouragement he needed to try the revision for *Maclean's*, and in early October he met with Ralph Allen in Montreal to discuss what would be permissible in a magazine regarding the adulterous relationship between Chris and Sylvia. Janice Tyrwhitt had explained earlier in her letter that there wasn't 'any list of what things are forbidden and what things ... permitted in *Maclean's*. We have to proceed according to an unsure and flexible instinct.' Allen's advice was to imply the sexual relationship between Chris and Sylvia without naming or detailing it. He also suggested that more sympathy be created for Chris and that it be made clear to the reader that Chris will eventually pay for the crime he has committed. Gray continued to send notes of encouragement, and by December 5 Jim was able to write to him that the redacted version – some twenty-five thousand words shorter than the book manuscript – had been mailed to *Maclean's* that morning. Gray suggested he mail that same version to Wing in New York as well, since Wing, who had been turned down by Harcourt Brace, was beginning to express some doubts about the original version from the market point of view.[16] Although the advice Jim was getting was often confused and conflicting, the interest in the manuscript that John Gray was generating in different quarters kept his spirits fairly high. The fall of 1955 was one of the busiest periods Jim had ever spent, and it had included, during his autumn vacation from the bank while he was working at the revisions, an unexpected trip to Saskatchewan to visit his mother. For several months, Kate had been unwell.

In 1955 Kate was in her eightieth year. She was no longer the strong-spirited and determined woman she had once been; she was physically growing old, and her zest for living was greatly diminished. She had not been very happy in the nine years since Jim's departure. She had remained for a time in Winnipeg, but her friendships, never very lasting, had dwindled and she no longer had any interest in making new ones. It was agreed in the family that she should move back to Indian Head, where she would be close to Effie and her grandchildren. In this town, where the family had anchored itself, her spirits for a time revived. She rented a couple of rooms in a private home, and there cultivated the role of 'Granny,' keeping a full cookie jar not only for her own family but for the other children in town who were thus tempted to drop by. She also revived her role of the cheerful, generous English lady who knew the world and could give a shrewd account of its affairs. But by the 1950s, old age had brought its problems – angina, shortness of breath, irregular bowels –

and Kate could no longer manage on her own. A brief stay with Effie made it clear that mother and daughter could never live together, and so, after consultation with Jim, Kate was moved to Moose Jaw's Ina Grafton Gage Home, a residence for elderly women.

She had been unwell during the summer of 1955 with an increasing number of complaints, and a telephone call Jim placed to the matron of the residence was not reassuring. He had postponed a trip to Saskatchewan, hoping to finish work on the manuscript first, but after an unsettling letter from Kate in late October, he felt he had to break from his desk and take the train to Moose Jaw. He found his mother despondent and looking frail. She apparently had no interest in getting to know or impress the other women in the residence; she dismissed them as uninteresting farmer's wives who had never been out of Saskatchewan. Her talk, at first, focused exclusively and graphically on her physical decline. But by the second afternoon of Jim's stay, her spirits began to revive; she introduced him to some of the residents as a famous author and in a few days had resumed her role of overbearing mother and entertaining raconteur. When Jim told her he had toyed with the idea of flying to Saskatchewan to get there more quickly, she told him of seeing two planes crash overhead and body parts and luggage raining down from the sky. Jim had heard of an aviation mishap in Saskatchewan – a small plane leaving from the Regina airport had skidded off the runway – but to his knowledge only one plane was involved and one person slightly injured. He listened to a lengthy account of Effie's failings as a daughter, how she had taken money, then turned her mother out of her home. Effie, moreover, was a feckless housekeeper, by her mother's account, and such a poor manager that it was no surprise the family was always short of money. Jim had started the visit feeling guilty that he had abandoned his mother to a sad and lonely old age, but by the time he came to leave, all the old grievances of being in her presence had returned.

In a 1955 Christmas note to Doris Saunders, Jim reviewed the events of the fall – his work on the manuscript and his mother's poor health. He had shortened the manuscript, he said, from 120,000 to 75,000 words with a view to magazine serialization – 'cutting and expurgating' he adds – with the feeling that the end result was 'rather tight and thin.' He had found it a 'dreary business' and was not really hopeful that the magazine would be satisfied. Now he was faced with revising the manuscript yet again for his agent in New York, who wanted a 'compromise between the original and the cut version,' for there was a feeling that the cuts were an improvement. His own view of the story now was that it was hopeless and ugly, but he asked Doris to keep her fingers crossed for him nonetheless. His mother's ill health, as far as he could tell, was 'nothing more than her years.'

At some point in late winter, Jim heard from *Maclean's* that they had decided against *The Well*. He was not surprised, just discouraged with himself for believing against his better judgment that his story might win a prize and attract a wide readership. W.K. Wing made the same decision, but this time Jim reacted differently. He felt keenly that the latter had acted in bad faith and, in a lengthy letter to John Gray, 8 April 1956, he expressed an uncharacteristic anger towards Wing:

> ... I do think he treated me shabbily. I quoted you at length from his first letter last August – truthfully – so you know that he had many good things to say about the manuscript, none derogatory whatever, and expressed himself as 'eager to represent me.' The revised manuscript I sent him the beginning of March was a great deal better than the original, polished, the repetitions weeded out, and reduced by a hundred pages, but his reply was to suggest that I forget all about it till I mature sufficiently to handle it properly. He also said it was far too long – after the reduction of a hundred pages; no criticism on this score whatever in the first place – that the plot was banal, the characters badly done, the castration theme and the episode of the young girl – 'the little innocent' – both pointless. He concluded that I might show it to John Gray again, but there was no chance for it 'down here.' In other words – 'Canada may handle tripe, down here we're more particular.' All of which was quite unnecessary and gratuitous. A simple 'sorry, we don't see any prospect for it,' would have sufficed. As to his criticisms, I don't quarrel with them. Heaven knows I never made any great claims for the story, or thought I had produced a masterpiece. But he should have made them last August. His job is to appraise manuscripts, and his success as an agent would suggest that he does it well. It is hard to believe that when he wrote his first letter his critical faculties were on holiday. However that is all past now, and it really isn't bothering me as much as what I am writing would suggest. I don't think about him much – perhaps because when I do the irresponsible way he treated me makes me so damned mad, and of course there's no point to it.

In the meantime, he sent the manuscript to Max Becker again, who stirred some interest at Morrow, but the latter wanted radical changes and Jim was left 'up in the air,' although he was already thinking about a new outline for the story.

In a reply dated April 11, John Gray apologized for not writing sooner, but confessed he felt guilty over the *Maclean's* disappointment, having encouraged Jim to undertake the abridged version of *The Well*, which had now come to nothing. In that light, he hesitated to suggest that Jim make further revisions on the chance that Morrow might be interested. Instead he advised Jim to

James Sinclair Ross (Jimmy) with his mother, Catherine (Kate), ca. 1910, in a surviving fragment of a family studio portrait. No picture of the author's father, Peter Ross, has been located.

Skating party in Indian Head, Saskatchewan, 1915. Standing from left: Jimmy, Kate, Matthew Price, and Effie (Ross's sister, who married Matthew in 1916).

Rolling Prairie District schoolhouse, ca. 1921. Jimmy Ross is standing second from left.

The Hunchiak family (Anna and Frank at left, Nick at right), who in part inspired Sinclair Ross's portrait of East European immigrants in *As for Me and My House*, but especially in *Sawbones Memorial*. Photos from the 1920s.

The United Church in Abbey, Saskatchewan, one of the models for the church in *As for Me and My House*.

Arcola, Saskatchewan, 1920s.

Dust storm in southern Saskatchewan, 1934.

Dorothy Cornell, 1930s.

Jim Ross on horseback in Arcola, ca. 1932.

Dies in England

SGT. OBS. W. K. CLARKE of Arcola, whose parents were notified of his death last Saturday. He was killed in a plane accident while on service in England. Born at Arcola 29 years ago, he attended public and high school there, then graduated from Manitoba university in 1934 with a degree of bachelor in science. He joined the R.C.A.F. two years ago as sergeant observer, and went overseas two months ago. Besides his father and mother, he leaves one sister in Ontario. He is the first casualty reported among the enlisted men from Arcola in this war. He was a prominent member of the Arcola band, and one of the best tennis players in the southeast part of the province.

Keith Clarke, ca. 1940.

The 1941 dust-jacket for *As for Me and My House.*

Sinclair Ross publicity photo accompanying 1941 reviews of *As for Me and My House*.

Catherine Fraser Ross, n.d.

3551 Durocher St.
Montreal
Sept 21 - 1948

Dear Grant —
                yes — I think it's
a splendid idea, and I look
forward to an opportunity to discuss
it at length with you. The
first question, of course, is have you
read any of my short stories? They
are pretty grim, and concerned with
horses, wind-fed small boys and
poverty-stricken farmers. Do you
think you could come to terms
with such subjects — I mean
artistically?

        I do hope the Thanksgiving
weekend will work out — I think
there will be no hitch at this end.
I enjoyed our meeting together. To be
frank, you turned out to be much
more approachable than I had
always imagined you to be. More
of this, however, at a later date. In
the mean time thanks and crossed
fingers.
                Sincerely.
                Jim Ross

Jim's Letter to Grant Macdonald responding to Macdonald's proposal for an illustrated
edition of his stories.

Sinclair Ross publicity photo, 1958.

Jim's Montreal friend, broadcaster Doyle Klyn, ca. 1960.

Jim Ross 'en famille' with the Baxters, Dorval, Quebec, ca. 1960.

James Ross working at Royal Bank's head office in Montreal, 1962.

Jim Ross in Málaga, Spain, 1970s.

Sinclair Ross, Vancouver, 1982.

Sinclair Ross and Keath Fraser, 1987.

Sinclair Ross and Mavis Gallant, Vancouver, 1992.

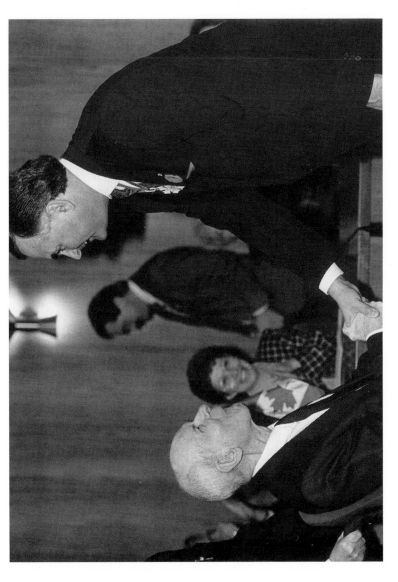

Sinclair Ross receiving the Order of Canada medal from Governor General Ramon Hnatyshyn, October 1992.

Last photograph of Sinclair Ross, 1993.

send him a copy of the revised manuscript, and he would forward it to Ruth May (Mrs A.A. Bendukov), a New York agent who had recently placed two of Ethel Wilson's books with Harper's. In this letter, Gray admits he finds Wing's behaviour shocking and reaffirms his faith in Jim's work, assuring him that Macmillan is willing to do a Canadian edition of *The Well* should the manuscript fail to interest an American publisher.

Jim replied April 23 saying he would not consider Canadian publication alone as a failure, but that he was beginning to lose his bearings with the manuscript after all the chopping and changing. The shorter, revised version he had sent to Wing seemed to him right, and an acquaintance, the poet Phyllis Webb, who had read the manuscript, confirmed his feeling that it was psychologically sound as it stood. But Morrow in New York wanted quite a different story and, if he was going to pursue American publication, he would have to make more changes. Morrow's readers (like Frank Upjohn at Macmillan) felt that more sympathy should be created for Chris as the book's central character, and that in the end he should stand up to Sylvia and not murder Larson, that he should go to town and get drunk, leaving Sylvia to commit the crime on her own. Jim felt wholly negative about these suggested changes to the plot (they were so far from his original conception of the story), and he protested to Max Becker accordingly. Morrow remained interested in the manuscript nonetheless and were willing to let him revise the ending his own way.[17]

Phyllis Webb's positive reading of the manuscript had boosted Jim's confidence. He had met Webb at a party given by F.R. Scott where reticence and mutual regard drew them together during the evening. (Hugh MacLennan was at that same gathering, the only time he and Jim met, and it may have been that same evening that Jim began a short friendship with Naim Kattan.) Webb had published some of her poems in a 1954 collection titled *Trio* shared with Gael Turnbull and Eli Mandel, and in 1956 her first major collection, *Even Your Right Eye*, was forthcoming in the autumn from McClelland and Stewart. Jim thought she was a writer of unusual intelligence and sensitivity, and her reading of his manuscript according to the spirit of its intention was especially gratifying. He still dared hope there was a larger audience for the kind of novel he wanted to write.

But the lure of the American market worked its spell, and by June 9 Jim was writing to John Gray to say he was struggling with an alternative ending – indeed, according to a letter of August 7, an ending on the lines suggested by Morrow. In the meantime, John Gray collected a new set of readers' reports on the revised, shorter version Jim had sent to Wing back in March. All three reports were enthusiastic, praising the characterization, suspense, and the 'tense, brooding evocation of prairie sights and smells and the sound of train sirens in the night.'[18] The one reservation expressed by two of the readers was a 'bookish aroma about some of the more Freudian themes.' From these reports on the second version of The Well manuscript, we learn that Chris still plays a part in Larson's murder by hitting him with a hammer.

Jim's letter of August 7 accompanied what might be called the third sub-mitted version of The Well, one in which Chris takes no physical part in Larson's murder. Between August 10 and November 7 there was no commu-nication between the author and publisher. John Gray broke the silence on November 7 by inquiring of Jim whether he had heard anything yet from New York (the project was still with Morrow). He reported that his readers did not have a clear preference between the second and third versions of the manuscript, but that they were beginning to lose confidence in their judg-ment. In closing, he told Jim he would be in Montreal on the 19th of the month and suggested that they have dinner together at the Windsor Hotel, where they could 'plot the overthrow of the New York publishing colossuses (colossi if you insist).'

During the winter of 1956–7, the manuscript went to Holt and then to Viking. At both publishing houses the decision was negative, but on May 17 Marshall Best at Viking sent Jim an assessment which might still stand today: 'From our point of view, [the book] falls between the audience for serious psy-chological fiction and that for the novel of suspenseful action – it is not quite one nor the other.' Best's evaluation left Jim thoroughly soured on The Well and discouraged about starting another piece of writing. He wrote to John Gray June 24: 'I have two novels pretty well mapped out, but quite frankly I haven't the heart to start. The prospect of a couple of years' drudgery, and at the end of it the dreary business of collecting rejection slips again, makes me falter.' (The one bright note in this letter was the fact that McClelland and Stewart was going to publish As for Me and My House in paperback as part of a series that would be called the 'New Canadian Library.')

Gray's reply was characteristically sympathetic, and he tried to encourage Jim to start another book: 'I know it can't be easy to get on with the new book while this hangs fire but I hope you can find the heart to do so. It is only a question of time until you crack this sound barrier with a resounding roar. So if you have a novel that you are eager to get on with and have in sight, do start.'[19] By the end of August, Jim reported that he had heard nothing further from New York publishers; and so if Macmillan was still willing to publish The Well in the spring, he would send the final revised version which had been circulating via Becker in New York.[20] But on December 10, after Gray had made one more failed attempt to place the novel (this time with Andre Deutsch in London), Jim wrote that if Macmillan wanted to drop the project he would understand: 'I wouldn't want you to feel committed by anything you said a year or 18 months ago ... But if it is to be No, then please let me know as soon as possible so that, within myself, I can write it off and turn the page.' He then restated his misgivings about continuing to write novels:

> Now, after two false starts I have a novel lined up and – I think – satisfactorily under way, but I must confess I hesitate at the prospect of two or three years' hard work and for reward just another long-drawn out failure. I think I shall probably always scribble away at something – it is my nature – but as the years go on one's enthusiasms – even one's compulsions – become tempered by common sense. There's not much point in knocking myself out if I haven't got what it takes. I'm not a youngster any more.

He concludes that he should probably go back to writing short fiction. A deeply sympathetic reply from John Gray was written to reassure Jim that Macmillan still wanted to publish *The Well* and that they would arrange for a fall publication in 1958. 'Send us the revised script,' Gray wrote, 'and we will submit a contract.' He wished Jim renewed zest to carry on with the next novel.[21]

In his letter to Gray of December 10, Jim only wrote one sentence about a significant change in his life: 'Mother became seriously ill last February, and it was a series of rallyings and relapses until her death in October.' When Jim went to Moose Jaw in February, he found his mother bedridden with an undiagnosed ailment. She had lost a lot of weight, and he rather suspected there was a malignancy that the doctor had not yet located. So he arranged for her to be moved to a nursing home in the city, where she would have more medical care and could remain indefinitely. After his return to Montreal, Jim heard from the doctor in Moose Jaw that his mother was suffering from 'congestive heart failure,' and that he could do nothing to reverse the deterioration of her health. At least twice she seemed about to die and Jim arranged to leave work for the trip west, but he would receive word that she was better and so he postponed the trip. Finally, at the beginning of October, the matron at the nursing home phoned to say that Kate had been moved to the hospital in Moose Jaw and that the doctor believed her to be near death, and so he arranged to fly to Saskatchewan, his first time to fly, arriving October 4, the day before his mother died. He was shocked to see how much she had wasted away; she was barely recognizable – a tiny wizened figure under the sheets. She seemed to know he was there, yet he could not be certain. Early the next morning, at the hotel, he received a call from the hospital to say she had died during the night.

That day he busied himself with the funeral arrangements and sending word to the rest of the family. The funeral on October 9 was sparsely attended; none of Kate's old friends like Kath Milne Nordal, Svea Pederson, or Tora Talgoy lived in the area, and Jim decided not to impose on their loyalties by sending telegrams. Instead he later wrote them notes to tell of his mother's passing. Effie, of course, came, and her daughters Irene and Beatrice, and one of the staff from the nursing home. Stuart had been notified, but he did not make the trip. There was a short service conducted by a local Presbyterian minister. According to weather records, it was a warm, sunny day when Kate's body was interred in Moose Jaw's Rosedale Cemetery, but Jim would remember it as cold and windy. Afterwards Jim took his sister and family out to dinner at the hotel where they were all staying.

At the time of her death, Jim did not feel strong emotions; Kate had been unwell and unhappy for several years, and it was in the course of nature that she should depart this life – she was over eighty. But unlike Camus' Meursault, Jim had for a number of years worried about his mother, regretting her physical decline and feeling sorry that she was so far removed from any of her family. Her death was a release for them both: she was released from her depression and physical miseries, and he was freed from the responsibility of her care. He would no longer have to make the dreary, annual, sometimes twice annual, trips back to Saskatchewan, and he would no longer have to write the weekly letter in which he usually had so little to report. And her expenses would also be a burden lifted, for Jim had continued to be Kate's sole support and her last few years in Moose Jaw nursing homes had been costly. For some time after her death, Jim felt no particular emotion that needed to be addressed, but later in his life that relationship would come back to be weighed and reckoned with. The last piece of writing he would publish, 'Just Wind and Horses,' would be about his mother – 'a woman as difficult to describe as she was to live with' (83) – and, hospitalized himself, he would think about her in his own extreme old age. One detail haunted him: after he returned to Montreal, he sent Effie some money to buy a stone for his mother's grave (Stuart did the same), but he learned eventually that Effie had used the money, about eight hundred dollars, to pay some of her debts and that his mother's resting place was unmarked.

The year 1958 began more favourably: in January, Jim received a contract from Macmillan for The Well (and the promise of a two-hundred-dollar advance royalty cheque), and the paperback version of As for Me and My House was under way. The latter, without question, was a great boost to his morale as a writer and would have an enormous impact on his future reputation. The New Canadian Library was initially conceived of by Malcolm Ross, who proposed the idea to Jack McClelland, a former student of his, who was now running the family publishing business. McClelland did not foresee much in the way of profit in this proposal but saw it as 'performing a service to the people of Canada.'[22] In one of the first letters about the series, dated 20 April 1954, Jack McClelland wrote enthusiastically to Malcolm Ross saying that his principal aim would be 'to convince the majority of university English departments in this country that every student studying English at the University level should be familiar ... with Canadian literature.' For, he pointed out, 'we still get graduates from the English language and literature course at Toronto who apply for jobs with us and who have never heard of people like Thomas Chandler Haliburton, etc.'[23] As Malcolm Ross turned to the question of what books to include in such a series, *As for Me and My House* was one of the first titles to come to mind.[24] Although it had attracted no general readership in 1941, it had become something of a classic in the opinion of university teachers and book publishers in the country, and would give the new series high quality. Although Jim was excited by this interest in his book, he typically gave no indication in a letter he wrote to Hugh Kane at McClelland and Stewart: 'For my part, *As for Me and My House* is something that happened a long time ago in which I am now not very interested. I feel that there are a few good things in it – and considerable promise, which unfortunately has not been fulfilled – but none the less *I have written it off as a failure*.'[25] When asked to check over some sentences and phrasing before the book went to press, he claimed in fact to no longer have a copy on his bookshelf.[26]

As for Me and My House, number 4 in the New Canadian Library, was nonetheless ready for distribution by June 1958. Frederick Philip Grove's *Over Prairie Trails* and Morley Callaghan's *Such Is My Beloved* had been issued in the fall of 1957, and Stephen Leacock's *Literary Lapses* was released in June with *As for Me and My House*. The books' covers had a distinctive look – a simple design of torn paper in vertical columns – which appealed to Jim. A predominantly orange-coloured drawing of the author's face appeared on the front cover, which was otherwise mostly blue and white. The back-cover copy was in small orange print but was otherwise unrestrained in its promotion of the book, declaring that it had been 'hailed as one of Canada's greatest novels,' and that it had already become 'a classic in Canadian literature.' In his introduction, Daniells related the book to other Canadian writings and discussed at some length its techniques, but it was here he made a statement which would be challenged repeatedly in the future criticism of the book: taking a wholly positive view of the narrator, Mrs Bentley, he writes, 'She is pure gold and wholly credible.'[27] A subsequent generation of critics would argue at length with this estimate. The book had no great sales at the outset, lagging behind those by Leacock and Callaghan, but reprinting *As for Me and My*

House every second or third year became the pattern, and, unlike with the other titles that launched the series, that has continued ever since.

Publication date for *The Well* was 5 September 1958. Jim received his author's copies in mid-August, and on August 22 he wrote to John Gray to say he was pleased with the book and he hoped it didn't let the company down too badly. *The Well* was in fact handsomely produced, with good quality paper and nicely spaced type. The orange dust jacket bore two simple figures – at the bottom a concentric design suggesting water, and at the top a half necklace like the cribbing for a well. But the high-quality appearance of the book was not enough to guarantee sales, and when the reviews began coming in, it was clear that it would not do well.

The first reviews had negative things to observe. William Hartley in the *Montreal Star* wrote that while Sinclair Ross was a 'good and sensitive technician' he did not have the exceptional abilities necessary to give freshness and credibility to the time-worn plot of his novel – that of the delinquent rehabilitated by rural living.[28] Theodore Honderich in the *Toronto Daily Star* was particularly blunt in his judgments. He began his review by saying that 'it would surely be silly charity to suggest that Mr Ross has made any considerable advance on his other book,' and went on to argue that the novel suffered from its reliance on overworked literary devices, especially blatant forms of symbolism such as the stallion linked to the hero's virility, and that the author spoils his storytelling by diagnosing his characters in the voice of a wordy psychologist: 'This continual butting-in can only have the effect of preventing a reader from being wholly taken up in the story. The mood, which Mr. Ross strives so valiantly to create, dissipates. Finally, one might also censure some rather mechanical flashbacks, and note that the style of the book, so bleak, so harnessed, and so worked-over, saps most of the impact from an essentially dramatic situation.'[29] A review in the *Quebec Chronicle Telegraph* denounced the book as obsessed with morbid sex,[30] while another, written by Dorothy Bishop for the *Ottawa Journal* (September 13), says the story works itself out in clichés and is 'overpitched and unconvincing.' At the close of her review, Bishop concludes that Ross seemed never to decide between writing a murder story or a modern pastoral and his confusion has left the novel muddied.[31]

These were the only reviews to appear before the *Toronto Daily Star* published on September 13 a short piece Jim wrote titled 'Why My 2nd Book Came 17 Years Later – an Answer by Sinclair Ross.'[32] Declining an interview with the paper, Jim put down his thoughts to the central question being asked of him – why had it been so long between books? His answer was that he had been writing all that time, but his efforts had come to nothing, and he described, without using titles, the three novel manuscripts that followed his first published book: 'Day Coach to Wagneria' ('about a farm boy and his struggle to escape'), the war novel ('too long, too ambitious'), and a first novel about delinquency and crime ('as sentimental as it was sombre. Too harrowing, said the publishers. Try it again – later.') Painfully aware of negative reviews of *The Well* coming out, Jim stated that he did not blame the Canadian publishers for his lack of success; rather, his own lack of productivity was the reason. The idea he had for *The Well*, moreover, was, according to the critics, proving to be a flawed one. But always 'a scribbler by nature,' he added, he was working on another story with Saskatchewan material. One of the more interesting statements in this self-belittling article is Jim's claim that by the 1950s he no longer wanted to write about the Prairies – 'I had said enough about wind-whipped towns and courageous, grim-faced farmers' – but was drawn instead to writing 'novels of ideas, of contemporary or social significance.' He winced to read reviews like Dorothy Bishop's which so accurately pointed to confusion of purpose in the novel, confusion arising from all the changes he had made to the manuscript in compliance with editorial wishes. Years later, he would reflect on how he had been pressed hard by agents and editors to revise *The Well* 'according to the popular psychological formula of the day, so that the book was no longer mine in the end.'[33]

Not all the reviews were negative: there were strong ones in the Saskatchewan papers, especially Kathleen Graham's for the *Leader-Post*, which states that while *The Well* on the surface appears a simple story, it is actually 'a subtle and sensitive probing of the values of existence. It explores these against a prairie background profound and compelling.'[34] Graham wrote as if the author's original intent had not been completely erased by all the rewriting. There were short but positive notices in the Vancouver *Province* and *Sun*. With one exception, the negative and positive notices were aligned with East and West, the exception being Isabelle Hughes's review for the *Globe and Mail* (September 20). Titled 'Long Awaited Second Novel,' Hughes's review gives a positive outline of the plot and concludes with high praise for the book as a whole: 'Sinclair Ross's *The Well* is an absorbing, thoughtful, expertly written book. It deserves a high place in the ranks of recent Canadian fiction.'[35] Jim's only regret was that those words had not been penned by W.A. Deacon, the newspaper's chief and highly influential book reviewer, who seventeen years before had written so warmly of *As for Me and My House*. But the number and influence of the negative reviews seemed to reflect the majority opinion. A review by James Scott for the *Toronto Telegram* was titled 'Sinclair Ross Has Forgotten Prairie Smells' as a way of suggesting the new book's inferiority to *As for Me and My House*,[36] and a lengthy review read by Ken Homer on the CBC (November

13) stated bluntly that in spite of obvious craftsmanship *The Well* is not a successful novel.[37] The academic critics were equally harsh: H.V. Weekes in the
Dalhousie Review faulted the author for an unconvincing theory of sociological
predestination and for rigidly selecting details to produce 'a false picture ... of
the frustration and meanness to be found in a small western town' (530).[38]
Claude T. Bissell in the *University of Toronto Quarterly* (July 1959) wrote that,
while it was a superior novel coming from the author of *As for Me and My
House*, its theme of adventure was not adequately projected – the book was not
written 'with sufficient intensity and power to weld together theme and action'
(370).[39]

Earlier in the year, Jim had temporarily felt good about his writing career. At
the office, his impassive manner gave little evidence of his good spirits, but
inwardly he was deeply pleased when his co-workers spoke about the reprint of
As for Me and My House and questioned him about his future writing plans.
During the twelve years he had been at the head office in Montreal, he had gotten to know a man named Bill Baxter in the advertising department especially
well. Jim had gradually become acquainted with Bill and his wife, Molly,
through social events connected with the bank, and he grew especially fond of
Molly, who was an artist, a watercolourist of some skill who had studied in Paris
in the 1930s. The Baxters were well read; they knew about Jim's writing and
collected his stories. Jim talked to them about the forthcoming novel, and
when Macmillan asked for a publicity photo, Bill urged Jim to contact Yousuf
Karsh in Ottawa for a sitting. Karsh's international reputation was intimidating – he was preparing to publish his famous volume *Portraits of Greatness* – and
Jim felt it would be presumptuous to present himself publicly in this light. Bill
nonetheless made some inquiries, and it was only when the price for a session
with Karsh proved to be very steep that he relaxed his pressure on Jim to have
himself famously photographed.

The publishing of a new novel in 1958 prompted Cecil Nelson to ask Jim
for a story for the Christmas issue of the bank's magazine, *The Teller*. Jim
regarded this as an unwelcome chore, but he hated to say no to 'Lefty,' who
had long been one of his boosters. The piece of fiction that resulted, 'The
Unwilling Organist,'[40] slyly incorporates the nuisance request into its storyline, all the while preaching a homily of cooperation and good feelings for
Christmas. A young bank clerk is asked by his manager to play the organ for a
Christmas Eve service; he would prefer instead to play for a dance out in the
country. The story is about religious factions: the town is so small and the
Anglicans are so few – only eight or nine families – that they attend and support the United Church. But relations are strained, with the United Church
supporters always in a superior position, and they come to a head over who

should sing solos – middle-aged Mrs Haley, known as something of a 'screech,' or young, pretty Josie Todd, favoured by Ronnie, the young organist of the story's title. By playing for the special Christmas Eve service sponsored by the Anglicans rather than for the country dance, the initially reluctant Ronnie helps bring about an interlude of harmony and goodwill in the congregation at Christmas. Jim drew on his early working days in towns like Abbey and Arcola for a vignette of bank life and denominational and musical rivalries. There may also be a fleeting glimpse of Jim's feelings for Dorothy Cornell in the presentation of Josie, to whom Ronnie is attracted: 'Her expression was always patient and forbearing, never superior or bored. Then there was her shy smile and her soft contralto ... in fact, there were no angularities whatever about her, vocal or of any other kind' (13). Jim would say years later that the story was 'nothing,' written to oblige, but it has one certain distinction – it is the only story he ever wrote that draws even remotely on his career in the bank.

The compliments and attention attending the reissue of As for Me and My House were not lost on Jim and a small measure of increased self-confidence is reflected in a July letter to John Gray in which he explores the idea of applying for a Canada Council grant and asks John for his advice.[41] He would apply for a year's leave of absence from the bank if his application were successful, and if the bank refused he might take the plunge and accept the grant anyway, now that his mother was gone and he was responsible for no one but himself. John Gray wrote back in August saying he would certainly give Jim his support if it was needed, suggesting a grant for travel abroad might be the most suitable category,[42] and Jim replied to say that he was getting more details and would contact John for support if it seemed worth his while to make an application.[43] But there is no further mention of this idea in their correspondence. The subsequent reviews and sales of The Well comprised a judgment that Jim was not willing to challenge. Looking back many years later, Mavis Gallant reflected ruefully and a little contemptuously: 'Poor Jimmy, he always lacked the courage to put himself forward and press on with his career. He yielded to the slightest criticism.'[44] The public response to The Well seemed to reactivate all his misgivings about his work and his deepest personal insecurities; when John Gray was in Montreal in mid-October and gave a party at his hotel, Jim did not attend, saying he had to work late at the bank that evening.

The curse of The Well had not yet run its full course. In the summer of 1959, Julian Roffman of Meridian Films in Toronto approached John Gray about securing motion picture rights for a film version of the novel. Roffman had won the first Oscar awarded for a documentary film, and his reputation in Canada's fledgling film industry carried some weight at the time. After negotiations, Roffman was prepared to offer Jim $4,000 for the outright purchase of *The Well* for motion picture production, with $800 as an option against the $4,000 purchase price. An eight-page contract was sent to Jim with a copy to Macmillan on 23 September 1959.[45] Jim had hoped for a percentage of film receipts, but Roffman was unwilling to accede to that request. The contract gave Roffman's company all rights to radio, television, and stage adaptations of the novel as well as to the making of a motion picture. Moreover, it gave the purchaser unlimited right to adapt and change the novel to suit himself. The contract was for one year. The lawyer vetting the contract for Macmillan considered it unusual that there were no royalty provisions for the author of the book, and he warned the company that Ross's surrendering of all rights to the novel for Meridian's advertising purposes might encroach on Macmillan's rights of publication. Accordingly a section of the contract was amended to allow the author to retain serial and pocketbook edition rights, thus guaranteeing Macmillan's future interests in the book. Characteristically, Jim had not pressed for his own advantage in the negotiations. He was surprised, after the negative notices and small sales (under a thousand copies sold despite a book-club listing), that there was interest in turning *The Well* into a film, and he had little faith that the project would ever materialize. Moreover, as negotiations were taking place, Jim was preparing to leave for a month's holiday in Mexico, and he wanted the business concluded. Roffman came to see him in Montreal the night before his departure and went over the contract clause by clause.

When he got back from Mexico in November, he heard from his colleagues at the bank that Roffman had been on television discussing with enthusiasm and confidence his plans to film both *The Well* and Colin McDougall's novel *Execution*. The following spring, Jim heard – again from his colleagues because he did not own a television himself – that a production of *The Well* would be shown on television, sponsored by General Motors. He wrote to Frank Upjohn on 6 June 1960 asking for clarification and was told in reply that the CBC production of that title was a play by Mavor Moore, that titles could not be copyrighted.[46] Perhaps it was this duplication that led Roffman to change the title of his film project to 'You Only Live Twice.' In September, Jim wrote at length to Frank Upjohn at Macmillan bringing him up to date on the film project. At the beginning of September, he reported, Roffman had been in Montreal with a New York co-producer and a scriptwriter, and Jim had sat in on three sessions in which they worked on a script. The problem was that a script had been prepared by a 'well-known script writer in Hollywood' – a third version – but it was far from satisfactory. It employed such threadbare western stereotypes as Native 'Indians' and the RCMP, and love scenes between Chris and Sylvia in which they discuss Russian scientists and rabbits on the moon. Another problem was the locale for shooting the film: because the season was getting late, it would no longer be possible to film in western Canada, and they were toying with the idea of Oklahoma. From their meetings, Jim came away feeling Roffman had more ambition than talent. Although he had given his opinions and was listened to, Jim felt that the project had likely stalled and would go no further. If that was the case, he felt he would be relieved – the money was not significant, and the film version would probably be an irritation. He wanted very much to leave the book behind him. His only regret was for all the trouble the book had caused Macmillan: 'I am sorry ... for the trouble you have been put to. *The Well*, I'm afraid, was conceived under an unlucky star. For Macmillans [sic], myself, and now Roffman, it's been headaches all the way.'[47] When Roffman did not renew the option on September 22, both Jim and Frank Upjohn concluded the movie deal was finished.

But it wasn't quite: on September 26, Julian Roffman wrote to say he assumed the renewal date was in January when the contracts were actually signed. To prevent any further confusion, he decided to send a cheque for the remaining $3,200 and finalize his purchase of the film rights. In January 1961, Frank Upjohn received a letter from Roffman reporting on the production – that they finally had a script that felt right (Jim's discussions with the new writer seemed to help) and that filming was scheduled for summer. The film company was now called Taylor-Roffman Productions. But Roffman's chief purpose in writing was to suggest that Macmillan contact a Mr Meyer Hutner of Beaver-Champion Attractions Ltd in New York to explore the possibility of an American paperback version of *The Well*. Hutner handled public relations for Roffman's company and would ideally arrange a paperback publication to tie in with the release of the film.[48] Upjohn accordingly wrote to Hutner on January 30, reiterating Roffman's suggestion, and the latter agreed to take on the task of once again trying to find an American publisher. But the Macmillan file for *The Well* ends with this letter from Hutner dated 20 February 1961. A publisher was never found, and the film project was eventually abandoned.

In the years that followed, *The Well* fared no better. Ross critics have been apologetic for *The Well* in their overviews of his work, describing a 'falling off of quality,'[49] a book with a 'thinner texture,'[50] one lacking in the 'rich external metaphors which ... characterized Ross's earlier work.'[51] Robert D. Chambers's description of the novel's intent best reveals the dilemma created for the reader by the editorial interference in the novel's composition. Ironically, he views it as a novel of moral regeneration by means of traditional rural values, but in his account of the story there are tracings of Ross's original intent:

> The central theme is the retrieval of Chris from alienation as an outsider, from that ruthless pursuit of self which characterizes the loner in twentieth-century society. This theme, while typical of much modern literature, was especially popular in the angry books of the 1950s, and it is likely that Ross saw *The Well* as taking its place within a fashionable literary type. There is here, however, a rejection of the notion that the outsider is an especially attractive figure. Ross makes no attempt to glamourize an anti-hero. From the outset, Chris is sketched as raw and crudely self-centered, and it thus becomes Ross's major task to make us feel and believe that this shrewd opportunist with basically criminal instincts can be slowly, and at last completely, transformed. (43)

Similarly, Ken Mitchell writes that Chris is 'alienated man, but now armed with "country" morality' (57). The author, of course, had not originally intended his anti-hero to be a sympathetic figure, or to acquire any kind of morality. In the first version of the manuscript, Chris killed Larson without remorse and then continued on his journey west. It was at the behest of agents and editors – confident Americans, compliant Canadians – that Jim fashioned Chris into a potentially sympathetic figure, who is redeemed by his feeling for farm animals and by his refusal to kill his fatherly benefactor. But Chambers pronounces an incontestable verdict when he says that, although the conclusion completes Chris's moral development, it is melodramatic and thus fails to have any significant impact on the reader.

In one of his last reflections on the book, Jim wondered if a first-rate novel could ever be made from the insights of another writer. Although the novel was grounded in his own youthful experience on Nels Forfang's and Sid Ketcheson's farms, the impetus for writing *The Well* had come from reading *The Stranger* and from popular renderings of existentialist thought. Perhaps that is what made it so vulnerable to editors and agents. *The Well* is characteristically Ross in its evocation of the Prairie farm and in its erotically charged valuation of masculinity, but even in its handsome paperback reissue by University of Alberta Press, with a laudatory introduction by Kristjana Gunnars, it is likely to remain the least read and least valued of his works.

eleven

Whir of Gold
1961–1971

I have always been tethered to reality ... to prefer a barefaced disappointment to
the luxury of a future I have no just claims on. – 'Cornet at Night'

The failure of *The Well* to find either critical approval or a popular readership
further narrowed Jim's writing life. In the late 1950s and early 1960s, he toyed
with ideas for stories and novels, but felt too discouraged to do much writing.
The Well, he felt, had taken a big chunk out of his life, and he was not prepared to let that happen again. He no longer pushed himself to sit at his typewriter in the evenings. After work he would read in his apartment or go to the
movies, alone; on weekends he sometimes went to the theatre, and he almost
always went looking for sex at the Montreal gay bars. He found himself
declining invitations to occasional literary gatherings, preferring instead the
company of friends like the Klyns or the Baxters. Life was rigidly organized by
punctually kept hours at the bank and a month's vacation in the fall.

In 1959, as mentioned earlier, he spent the first of three vacations in Mexico. He flew to Mexico City and, after two nights in a relatively expensive
hotel, found cheap lodgings in a small but clean European-style *pensión* that
was still located near the centre of the city. His initial motive was simply to
travel somewhere warm and colourful for November, which in his estimate
had become increasingly the bleakest month of the year in Montreal, but he
came quickly to like the Mexican people, their warmth and demonstrativeness
in public places, and found himself drawn back to the culture as well as the climate. To his ear, Spanish was the language closest to music, and he found
himself learning to speak and read it without great effort, studying until he
could read Spanish and Latin American authors in the original. The first holiday was unalloyed pleasure until the last few days when he felt ill with flu like

symptoms. He reported to Frank Upjohn that he came back, wanting to return, but that he had picked up a germ, even though he had not touched the water at all.[1] He wondered to himself if he had contracted something from a female prostitute he had visited, his mother's admonitions ringing 'like a fly in the ear, too deep for match or pin.'[2]

Being in Mexico had made him acutely aware again of his unresolved sexuality. Although he still most frequently had sex with men in anonymous encounters, he could not fully identify himself as a gay man because he was not without sexual interest in women. When he was young, he had read in Freud that the absence of a strong father in childhood favoured the occurrence of inversion in a young man, that homosexuality was arrested development, and he now reluctantly accepted that to be a scientific account of his nature. But the Kinsey report, so much discussed in the 1950s, with its surprising description of a scale for measuring degrees of heterosexuality and homosexuality, gave him an expanded understanding of what, for a long time, had been his intuitive grasp of his sexual nature – that, if categorization was necessary, he was bisexual. He recognized in himself physical attraction to both men and women, with a strong emotional need for men, but a social preference for the company of women. But however sexuality was theorized, he retained a strong conviction that he had never fully grown up.[3]

The trip to Mexico, however, made him increasingly aware that he was not a boy, that in fact he was starting to grow old. In Montreal he had been experiencing neck and upper back pain, which was diagnosed as a ruptured disc, and rest and heat treatments had been recommended; he hoped for some relief while in Mexico, but the condition did not significantly improve. Equally persistent and sometimes as painful was prostate gland trouble. In 1960 he went into hospital briefly for treatment, but his discomfort was only alleviated temporarily, not cured. From the time he entered his fifties, Jim became almost obsessively aware of physical ailments and declining energy, and these preoccupations become a recurring motif in his letters.

His working life at the bank changed in 1959 when, after several years in securities, he was offered a position in the advertising department working under Cecil Nelson. This was the same bank employee who had written letters of strong praise more than twenty years before when Jim was publishing his first works of fiction. Jim's work was still principally that of an accountant, keeping track of advertising costs, handling the billings, but the more creative atmosphere of the advertising offices – the presence of designers doing sketches and layout, the processes of copy-editing and photoengraving – had its appeal. Bill Baxter had been in the department as a designer since 1938, hired shortly after his arrival in Montreal from London, England. Sometimes Jim dealt directly with artists who were employed for occasional assignments, although the department's activities were still curtailed by a bank act which prohibited any major advertising. Cecil Nelson was a good manager to work under; though in Jim's opinion he was somewhat jealous of his position, his efficiency and self-confidence kept things working smoothly in the office, and when he retired in 1963, after twenty-eight years in that post, he was definitely missed.

Jim liked working with Bill Baxter and, along with Bill's wife, enjoyed one of those triangular relationships that fulfilled a deep need in his nature. Jim would accompany Bill home for dinner Friday evenings or take the bus out to the Baxters' home in Dorval for Sunday dinner, and in the evening would enjoy talking with Molly about painters and art schools. Molly had not only studied art in France but had trained in Montreal to be a fashion designer; however, with marriage, she gave up her career to keep a home. Molly's privileged young womanhood gave her a touch of glamour in Jim's eyes, but there was also a bond of deep sadness. Jim had come to know Bill and Molly shortly after a personal tragedy: in 1955 the couple's only child, a nine-year-old boy, was hit by a car on the street outside their home. He died almost instantly. Between them, Bill and Molly could not bear to discuss what had happened, and they distracted themselves from the depths of grief by the adoption of a baby girl, Nora, and by raising a foster daughter, Cecily. It was only with Jim that Molly was able to pour out her feelings and talk of the dead boy. Years later, Bill would observe that he had never before known a man 'who had such a rapport with and sympathy for women.'[4] The death of an only son, of course, was uncannily like a scene from one of Jim's novels – it could have been the Bentleys or Lawsons in *As for Me and My House*, or old Larson in *The Well*, who loses a twelve-year-old son and a seven-year-old nephew. The Baxters' marriage might also have come from one of Jim's fictions: Molly had never realized her potential as an artist, devoting her attention instead to her children and her often incommunicative, stiff-upper-lip husband. Further, there was a social gap between Molly's affluent Montreal family and Bill's working-class London origins. Sometimes there were strains that made it uncomfortable for him to be their guest, yet they remained friends not just for the duration of his employment at the bank but for the rest of their lives.

More likely than with the Baxters would have been a friendship with John Gibbon, who also worked in advertising and who, after Cecil Nelson's retirement, became department manager. John was a middle-aged bachelor who, like Jim, had a lifelong interest in literature and numerous literary connections in the city. His father had been a Scots from Aberdeen who attended Oxford, and when he came to Canada to work for Canadian Pacific Railway in

Montreal, he sent his sons to McGill, where John's oldest brother was selected as a Rhodes scholar. John's father also had literary interests: in company with Stephen Leacock and B.K. Sandwell, the long-serving editor of *Saturday Night*, he founded the Canadian Authors Association, serving as its first president, and in 1938 he won the Governor General's Award for a work of nonfiction titled *Canadian Mosaic*. John himself studied political economics under Leacock at McGill and had good jobs in advertising with Ogilvie Flour and with Seagrams before taking the job at the Royal Bank. John knew many of the same people as Jim, including Mavis and Johnny Gallant and the Klyns. But John's privileged background, his physical stature (he was well over six feet), and what Jim felt was a snobbishness ('he courted the literati, talked endlessly of his family connections')[5] created a barrier to any kind of easy friendship. John also had mental health problems, diagnosed and described then as manic depression, and Jim may have instinctively guarded himself against the emotional fluctuations of John's personality. Jim worked efficiently (his punctuality and perfectionism were a source of office humour) but kept his writing life and his sexuality wholly separate from life at the office. When John Gibbon came to learn that Jim was a writer of some distinction, he could not understand his lack of self-confidence, his willingness to settle for such menial office tasks as mailing flyers and proofing copy. He had a much more glamorous image of the writer in mind, and when over the years he became aware of Jim's importance to Canadian letters, he had increasing difficulty in matching the reputation to the self-effacing man at the bank who, like Gogol's clerk in 'The Overcoat,' seemed to have so little ambition.[6]

Colleagues at head office, however, were made aware of Jim's achievement as a writer when in 1963 the National Film Board made a fifteen-minute version of 'Cornet at Night' and when on 10 April 1964 CBC Radio aired a half-hour dramatization of *As for Me and My House*. The *CBC Times* for that week carried a very flattering critical summary of Jim and his work:

> Few Canadian men of letters have earned such a solid reputation on the strength of a single novel as Sinclair Ross did with his first book ... Ross writes with discipline, forceful simplicity and a deep understanding of the complexities of human nature – in this case the emotional difficulties of a dismally frustrated clergyman and his attractive, talented wife. Ross evokes beauty and wretchedness – sights, sounds, smell – with such vividness that they constantly contribute to the development of the action of his story, set in the Canadian mid-west.

That same year, George Woodcock published a selection of essays from *Canadian Literature* in a book titled *A Choice of Critics*, which brought to wide public attention an essay by Warren Tallman, 'Wolf in the Snow,' which analyses the great power and beauty of *As for Me and My House* and identifies it as a paradigmatic Canadian text. Such testaments to Jim's achievement, however, remained within high art and academic circles and did not filter down to a popular audience for his work.

The Well had dealt a severe blow to Jim's self-esteem certainly and to his ambitions as a writer (seventeen years later he admits in a letter that '*The Well* had left [him] discouraged, a sort of it's-no-use-trying feeling'),[7] yet the compulsion to 'scribble' was still there. For many years, he had been working and reworking the story of a boy named Sonny and his horse, Isabel, which had first appeared in *Queen's Quarterly* (Summer 1950) as 'The Outlaw.' In 1952 he had sent the same journal a story titled 'Sonny and Mad,' but G. H. Clarke returned it as being unsuitable to the journal's needs at that time.[8] In his correspondence with John Gray and others, Jim sometimes referred to other manuscripts he was working on in the 1950s and early 1960s, and clearly the story of Sonny McAlpine was one of them. A completed book-length manuscript about Sonny and Mad (eventually *Whir of Gold*) may have been circulating as early as 1952, for in a December 1954 letter to Roy Daniells, Jim tells of a manuscript on urban crime he had been trying to place in 1952: 'A novel I finished two years ago, concerned with crime and delinquency made the rounds of half a dozen New York houses, receiving good reader's reports from them all and in each case was turned down because of its pessimism and gloom ...' Almost certainly this is the lengthy unpublished manuscript about urban crime that Ross refers to in 'Why My 2nd Book Came 17 Years Later.' One of the repeated criticisms, he says, was that the characters were not worth writing about, but Jim felt very differently: 'Well, as I saw them they were not only worth writing about but also worth *doing* something about, and my failure I suppose was my inability to reveal my intentions. Perhaps, in any case, I am out of my depth in social reform.'[9]

But Jim often said that when he was especially discouraged about his career there would invariably come a word of encouragement – a compliment on a story, a request for a reprint – and he would take up his pen in earnest again. Such a word came in October 1962 when he received a brief note from John Gray that stated simply: 'It is too long since any of us have seen you or heard news of you. Does this mean you have a book on the fire? I certainly hope so.'[10] Jim did not reply for more than a month, but when he did it was with enthusiasm about his writing again. 'I'm working on a novel,' he wrote, 'roughly three-quarters of the way through the first draft. Some fair things I *think*, but how it will hold up as a whole is another matter.'[11] Cautious as usual, but then he adds that he hopes to live to a healthy old age because he has a number of things he wants to write, including at least two more novels, one with a bank setting. He looks forward to retirement in another six years and after that, hopefully, seven or eight productive years. He thanked Gray for his continuing interest and support, which was indeed beyond the conventional practice of most publishers. Gray replied in his concise, urbane fashion that he certainly hoped Jim lived to be a healthy old man, not because he was staking a personal claim on his productivity ('"take good care of yourself, you belong to me"'), but because 'I like the idea of novels by James Sinclair Ross [around] long after I have waived my old age pension.'[12]

But more than three years passed before the correspondence was renewed. In early March 1966, Jim had been in Toronto and present at a Sunday luncheon given by John Gray. In conversation, Jim referred to the manuscript he had recently completed, but as the subject was left dangling, he wrote to Gray after returning to Montreal to give more details. He explained that, after the fiasco of *The Well*, he did not want to burden Macmillan with another Ross novel unless it was coming out in England or the United States. Moreover, he had no certain faith in the manuscript; it was 'an ugly story and probably a very depressing one.' However, he assured Gray that in case something should develop (presumably with the English or American publishers), he did have a copy for Macmillan to look at.[13] John Gray telegrammed Jim at once to say he was eager to see the manuscript,[14] and accordingly Jim sent off sometime before March 21st an untitled copy of what would become *Whir of Gold*. It was the story of Sonny McAlpine from 'The Outlaw,' who is looking for work in Montreal. Sonny enters into an affair with a prostitute named Mad and becomes involved with a petty crook named Charlie. *Whir of Gold* would be another version of the triangulated love story Jim had been telling in his earlier books. He had in the meantime employed Max Becker once again to find him a publisher in New York.

In an irascible mood, Jim wrote to Gray on May 3rd asking for word:

> It is just over six weeks since you acknowledged receipt of the manuscript I sent you: time enough, I think, for you or your staff to have read 250 pages or, at least, to have found them unreadable.
>
> As you haven't written to comment I conclude you think the story very bad and are embarrassed. Well, I am sorry, of course, but not a word is necessary. Just return the manuscript and we'll forget it ever happened. I would be grateful if you would let me have the manuscript by return mail.

In the absence of Gray, who was on holiday, assistant editor Anne Perrie wrote back to assure Jim there was no lack of enthusiasm for his manuscript at the office, but that deadlines for fall publication had prevented a more timely reply.[15] A further letter from editor James Watson Bacque sent apologies mid-June for the long wait, promising some word within the month and assuring Jim of interest at the press.[16]

Anne Perrie and J.W. Bacque, however, were not being entirely honest in their communications. The first reader's report, filed 4 April 1966 by the future novelist Richard B. Wright, then an employee at Macmillan, was wholly negative and advised against publication. The story, in his opinion, was trite and familiar – the 'gawky young farm boy's struggle to distinguish between goodness and evil and his growth from that experience.' But what especially bothered Wright was the old-fashioned quality to the story: 'This has a strong whiff of the urban novel of the thirties about it. Its uncomplicated innocence and serious tone by way of James Farrell; its theatricality most evident in the characters of Charley and Mad by way of the gangster movies; its excessive naturalism (we had pork chops and chocolate pie); and its sentimental ending; all this is reminiscent of another time.' Wright added that it was like 'sitting in a dusty abandoned theatre watching three people perform a play by Clifford Odets.' His negative assessment was not made without some regret, because he states that Sinclair Ross is a fine writer and even in this tedious story he 'manages to charge his prose with a rich and vivid imagery that seldom seems forced or misplaced.' Two further reports were filed on May 12: one concludes that 'apart from the accomplishment of the writing itself, much ado has been made about a slight episode'; the other describes the manuscript's features more positively and concludes that although 'the theme isn't a major one and the canvas is small ... the author knows what he can handle and he does it very well indeed.' This relatively positive assessment prompted the office to solicit one more internal reading. On June 16 a final report was filed, which was mostly negative, describing the novel as predictable and tedious and not likely to win many readers beyond Sinclair Ross's existing audience.[17]

But Jim did not hear from Macmillan again until late September, when John Gray finally wrote on the 20th, apologetically, to say the manuscript had not convinced his readers. He singled out the flashbacks to Sonny's boyhood and the flight from the crime as being well done, but that they were not enough to make the characters come to life. To soften the blow, he suggested that the parts of the book about the boy and his horse were so authentic that perhaps Jim would consider doing a book using that material. In reply, Jim wrote somewhat tersely: 'No – I don't "see" a book about a boy and a horse right now but appreciate your making the suggestion.' In the same letter, he asked Gray if it would be possible to see the readers' reports that had accumulated around the Sonny manuscript, hoping they might guide him in any future revisions.[18] Gray replied that it was not house policy to send out the reports to the authors, but that in Jim's case he would excerpt what he felt were the relevant parts and send them along.[19] Jim was in Mexico when they arrived, acknowledging their receipt on his return November 8. John Gray's anxiety about turning down the manuscript is further evident when he writes on November 10 and suggests that Macmillan might like to consider again the idea of a collection of Jim's short stories. He observes vaguely that 'a good deal has changed' in the eighteen years since they first looked at the idea. Jim was able to reply November 14 that his stories were in fact under consideration elsewhere and that someone had been approached to write an introduction. Except for notices about remaindering *The Well* in 1969 (thirty-five cents a copy) and the mailing of a very small royalty cheque in 1971, this letter concluded Jim's lengthy business dealings with Macmillan. John Gray liked to think of himself nonetheless as Jim's friend and supporter, and Jim continued to appreciate his solicitous regard.

In later years, Jim would look back on his fifties as being one of the bleakest, least meaningful periods of his life. He was still working at the bank, but he was no longer able to tell himself that he would some day write a bestseller and make his living from his fiction. For a biographer there is a dearth of materials from which to construct a life for this period, a pattern that is the opposite for most writers. In fact there are no letters or publications dated 1964 or 1965, and the author could pin no specific memories to those years. Although he now had more money to spend on himself, he continued to live in a couple of small rooms, with a bare minimum of furniture. His social life had narrowed to a few friends in Montreal, chiefly the Baxters and Klyns; his correspondence with old friends had shrunk to Christmas card notes. Montreal, he now admitted, had been a disappointment. In a few paragraphs he contributed to a comprehensive essay by Naim Kattan, he wrote that Montreal was only French in a religious way, that otherwise the way of doing things in Montreal was North American. The city was simply a place where he lived and worked, and he 'knew no artists or intellectual who might have helped [him] see a little further.' He recognized that in the 1960s it was becoming militantly French, but as an Anglo he felt himself as excluded by the new politics as he had been by the Catholic Church.[20] During his youth, he had lived in communities where, many years later, people still remembered Jimmy Ross, but in Montreal he lived alone, like Meursault, his chief pleasure the anonymous sexual encounters he experienced with men and women who were equally lonely. They were often harshly unromantic.

Yet, very slowly, Sinclair Ross's reputation as a significant writer of fiction in Canada was growing. His carefully crafted stories about the dust-bowl days and the Depression were now beginning to attract the attention of readers born well after the events and conditions described, and were beginning to appear in classroom anthologies. The book of short stories Jim referred to when writing to John Gray was *The Lamp at Noon and Other Stories*, published by McClelland and Stewart in the New Canadian Library series in 1968 with an introduction by Margaret Laurence. According to evidence in an internal memo at McClelland and Stewart, Jim himself had proposed to the company a collection of his short stories for publication in a hardbound edition as early as 1964, but the idea had been rejected. A couple of years later, Robert Weaver suggested the collection to Malcolm Ross for inclusion in the New Canadian Library. The earlier rejection, however, left Jim feeling a little prickly on the subject, and when negotiations proceeded without his being kept informed, he let Weaver know of his displeasure.[21] When Jack McClelland became aware that there was some bad feeling, he wrote Jim an apology in September 1967, explaining that with four individuals involved in the short-story project, confusion had resulted. He wrote to say that, as head of the company, he took the blame and sent his apologies, adding that they were anxious to publish the book and were convinced it would be 'an adornment to the New Canadian Library.'[22] A letter from Bob Weaver to Geoffrey Fielding makes clear that it was Bob who suggested the ordering of the stories for the collection, beginning with 'The Lamp at Noon' and concluding with 'One's a Heifer.' (In this letter there is reference to dropping 'A Day with Pegasus,' although no reason is given for this decision.)[23] Another memo identifies Pamela Fry, an editor at McClelland and Stewart, as selecting 'The Lamp at Noon' as the title story for the volume.[24] In a short letter to Bob Weaver of 22 November 1967, Jim complies with the title suggestion – 'I have no strong feelings about it' – but singles out 'The Runaway' and 'One's a Heifer' as other possible titles for the collection.[25]

When Weaver had suggested the story collection to Malcolm Ross, the latter had welcomed the idea and turned to Margaret Laurence, his former student and protégée, to write an introduction. The choice was fortuitous: it gave Laurence the opportunity to express her high esteem for her fellow Prairie writer and to identify him as one of the major influences on her own writing career. She wrote that when she first read Ross's extraordinary and moving novel *As for Me and My House*, at about the age of eighteen, 'it had an enormous impact on me, for it seemed the only completely genuine one I had ever read about my own people, my own place, my own time.'[26] This would be one of the first instances of a Canadian novelist acknowledging publicly the influence of an earlier Canadian novelist, creating a sense of tradition among Canadian writers of prose. Laurence was also pleased to write the introduction because she and Jim had recently become friends.

Margaret and Jim met through their mutual friend, the novelist Adele Wiseman, who was then living in Montreal. Adele had been born and raised in Winnipeg and, like Margaret, had great regard for this older western writer. Jim and Adele met, according to her recollections, when she was asked by CBC Radio in Montreal to interview him over the air for an education program. (Jim remembered the interview differently – as taking place in a high-school gymnasium, not for radio – and he recalled objecting to some of the questions before the interview took place.) Whatever the circumstances, Adele was both impressed and scared at the time, even though it was plain that her interview subject was terribly shy. She remembered asking him technical questions about his craft and his giving only 'romantic' or intuitive answers: 'he did not like to discuss nuts and bolts,' she said, and chase away the magic of writing. As they became friends over time, one thing she admired about Jim was his lack of bitterness about not being more widely recognized; he had experienced a sense of futility with respect to his career, as he explained it to her, but not anger. She also admired his strong Canadian sense of duty, as shown in his lifelong care for his mother.[27] She introduced Margaret to Jim at her home sometime in 1966, when Margaret was visiting from England, and a lively correspondence ensued over the next twelve years.

One of the best letters written by Jim to Laurence is dated 4 December 1966 and opens with strong praise for A Jest of God: 'I finished A Jest of God a few days ago and it is good to be able to write, honestly, without polite hedging, that it is a fine, deeply-felt novel and – most important of all – that it has made me feel and understand a human problem, or predicament, to which I had never before given much thought. That is, it has extended me a little.' He especially liked Laurence's presentation of the small town, 'the feeling of being watched and discussed until, despite yourself, in self defense, you draw in, become pettily careful – it all came back ...' He thanked Laurence for the generous things she was saying about him in interviews (a friend had sent a clipping from the Winnipeg Free Press and there was another tribute in the Montreal Star) and went on to point out the humour in the introduction to Modern Canadian Stories (Ryerson 1966), where the editors identify Ross's trouble as over-devotion to his job at the Royal Bank. 'Well well!' he writes. 'Of all the reasons critics and biographers trot out to account for an artist's failure to mature – drink, drugs, sex, neglect, ill-health – this one is surely unique.' He admits it makes him angry to be called a failure and that he won't be sorry to pack his bags some day and leave Canada. He admits to Margaret that he is angry as well at the way Macmillan turned down his novel manuscript – six months to read 270 pages and John Gray's reason was that he was reluctant to give bad news! The letter concludes on a more positive note, telling of his third trip to Mexico that fall – horseback riding, exploring 'delightful' towns like Oaxaca, San Cristobal, and San Miguel, relaxing and eating well – although once again he picked up a bug which laid him low for ten days. He promised in closing to write again when he had read *The Stone Angel*, but if he did that letter has not survived.[28]

Margaret and Jim met again in May 1967 when Margaret made a return visit to Canada to receive the Governor General's Award for *A Jest of God*. Adele, who had won the award herself ten years earlier for *The Sacrifice*, hosted a party in her apartment where Jim and Margaret spent much of the evening huddled together in the corner talking 'Prairie.' Next day the three friends went out for lunch at a Greek restaurant and talked for several hours together. The talk continued in their letters.

The correspondence with Laurence (though we only have Jim's side) has the special ring of two equals in conversation about their craft, the publishing world, their special interests, and the cultural climates in which they are living and working. They were friends who could take pleasure in genuine mutual admiration, both public and private, based on their significant stature and accomplishments as Prairie writers. On 9 December 1967 Jim wrote to Margaret to say how very pleased he was with her introduction to the NCL *Lamp at Noon* collection, which was due out in the spring. He wrote that her words were not only generous but 'discerning,' especially her summary point that the farm people in the stories come through with dignity, for to him 'they ha[d] always been more than clods.'[29] He expressed wariness about Jack McClelland's enthusiasm for the little book. Jack had been in Montreal in late November and had taken Jim out to lunch, but Jim says he has learned to discount such compliments and optimism: 'I *want* so badly to believe people and even at my age, incredible as it sounds, I *do* – at least till I start thinking things over.' But if the book falls flat, he says, it won't really matter, because by mid-1968 he will be retired and far away from Canada, Greece perhaps. He concludes the letter with praise for *The Stone Angel*, which he loaned to a female friend from Winnipeg on the faculty at McGill (probably Doris Saunders) who was enthusiastic and went out to buy *A Jest of God*. He wishes her every success with the forthcoming movie version of the novel.

In this letter to Laurence, he also makes mention of some of their mutual friends in Montreal – Adele Wiseman, of course, who was recently married, Alvin Goldman, Alec Lucas, on the faculty at McGill, and his wife, Koula. He had met Alec Lucas through Lovell Clark, his ebullient Winnipeg friend whom Kate had found so entertaining. Lovell had not only taken advantage of the veterans' education program, he had flourished in the university environment, completing a B.A. at the University of Manitoba and graduate degrees in history at Queen's and University of Toronto. Married and socially successful (but still active homosexually), he taught history at the University of New Brunswick, where he and Lucas had been colleagues. Lucas remembered vividly the first time he set eyes on Jim in the mid-1960s, of trailing along with Lovell to a gay bar and finding Jimmy Ross, the author of so many of the country's finest stories, a little man sitting in a dark room under a dim light, waiting for the arrival of his Winnipeg friend.[30] In Alec's company, Jim seemed to remain modest and 'buttoned up,' but in the company of his wife, Koula, he was forthcoming and at ease. As Jim thought more about the possibility of moving to Greece on retirement, he sought advice from Koula and took special interest in her cooking and stories from 'home.' Alec was one of the first at McGill to teach full courses in Canadian literature, and he put Jim's work front and centre on his syllabus; his admiration for his writing was unbounded, and Jim could not help but respond to the warmth of this couple's friendly home.

Jim had come to know Alvin Goldman earlier through Doug Tunstell, another Roy Daniells acquaintance from Winnipeg days. Tunstell, who was working for the National Film Board, invited Jim to Ottawa as part of a project at the NFB that involved soliciting literary authors to improve the quality of writing for films. He was also chosen as a western writer to increase regional influence. Little came of the proposal, but Jim did meet Alvin Goldman there and the friendship developed when Goldman moved to Montreal with the NFB in the late 1950s. It was Alvin's wish to adapt some of Jim's work for film, and on 17 January 1968 he did succeed in producing a half-hour version of 'The Painted Door' for *Festival* on CBC television. A few years later, he tried to adapt *The Well* for an NFB feature-length production, but the project failed to materialize in a film.

Jim became increasingly wearied by and suspicious of all the talk of adaptations for radio and film. So many proposals were on the table, and so few ever amounted to anything. But at some point in 1967, Bob Weaver persuaded Jim to accept a commission from the CBC to write a story for radio, and the result was 'Spike,' the tale of a seemingly menacing hitch-hiker whose real goal is to reach his girlfriend's home on an appointed day. It was the only time in his life that Jim accepted payment for a story not yet written, and he was ill at ease until he had fulfilled his contract, although Keath Fraser claims that 'Spike' was taken from the manuscript pages of a larger novel about a cautious, middle-aged family man who is sexually unhappy.[31] Jim felt 'Spike' was forced, and he had little regard for it,[32] but it is not without interest in the body of his work. Its genesis, according to Jim, was not unlike that of *As for Me and My House*; he asked himself, what if he had married and was raising a family, but still felt other sexual urges? In that light, 'Spike' is the story of an older man 'cruising' the street who experiences the danger and excitement involved in picking up an attractive youth who in the first words of the story is 'hunched, threatening, big.' During the course of the story, the hitch-hiker pulls a knife on the older man, forcing him to drive along a different road, but when it seems likely that he will kill and rob him, they reach the young man's destination and the latter then explains how desperate he was to arrive with an engagement ring on his girlfriend's birthday. A patriarchal, heterosexual order is strongly asserted as the boy explains how he must impress his girl-friend's sceptical father with a costly ring on the right day, and the driver recalls his own similar situation twenty years before. The story is a little over-written (there is too much explanation of circumstances towards the end), but the merging of two contending impulses that the author experienced in his life – the physical desire for a young man's company and the social desire to be part of a conventional family as defined in the 1960s – gives it a curi-ously affecting, though slightly melodramatic, power. In "Spike," Jim was exploring the dangerous side of sexual desire, but he was probably also rehearsing once again something of his feelings, as a small man, about Dor-othy Cornell and her powerful father, whose challenge he could never meet. The story was read on the CBC in both English and French as part of a series of Canadian short stories for radio. The original intention was to have the stories published simultaneously in both languages, but only the French ver-sion of 'Spike' appeared, translated by Pierre Villon, in the March-April 1969 number of *Liberté*. It was not published in English until 1981, when Ken Mitchell got Jim's permission to include it in *Sinclair Ross: A Reader's Guide*.

In February 1968, shortly after his sixtieth birthday, Jim retired from the bank. There was a small, late-Friday afternoon office party at which Bill Bax-ter made a speech and proposed a toast. Jim surprised his co-workers with an extended reply in which he wished them well, in turn, and made wry jokes about the things he was going to miss at the office. It seemed to Bill Baxter an unusually happy occasion, but Jim would recall it later as a shabby, ungener-ous farewell to someone who had been in the bank's service for more than forty years. He did not dwell on his disappointment for long, however, for as he told a reporter for the *Montrealer* magazine, he was off to New York for a short stay, then on to Athens, where he would rent a three-room apart-ment.[33] He was looking forward to the move, especially the climate, but also to the European way of life, which would be more akin to the way he had lived in London during the war. He had recently spent a holiday in Europe, which included a visit with Mavis Gallant in Paris, and he was confident that he was going to enjoy this form of retirement – at least for a while. Gallant would remember years later how uncharacteristically optimistic and energetic Jim was when he visited her and discussed his retirement plans.

Because it was a permanent move, he decided once again to dispose of most of his furniture and accumulated library. His desk and some of his books he gave to the Baxters. According to his own account, he threw out most of the writing projects that were not finished, or that had been rejected by publishers. He also disposed of most of the correspondence that had accumulated in his desk. This was a habitual procedure as he moved apartments in Montreal, but preparing to leave for Greece he did a rigorous clean-out of all drawers and shelves. As he had anticipated in his letter to Margaret Laurence, he did not experience any regrets as he prepared to leave Canada; he said good-bye to the Klyns and Baxters and to Alvin Goldman, had breakfast at the Windsor Hotel with Doris Saunders, who was spending the year at McGill, but otherwise he had gathered little moss. He was energized by the prospect of freedom and new experiences abroad.

Before leaving the country, he wrote to Pamela Fry at McClelland and Stewart, with whom he had corresponded concerning *The Lamp at Noon and Other Stories*, and he promised that once settled in Greece he would send her the new novel manuscript he had been working on.[34] The promise had been made earlier in a telephone conversation, but ill health, including a ruptured disc ailment, a severe attack of sciatica, and prostate problems – 'old-man ailments, the less said about which the better' – had prevented him from getting any work done in the last month. The physical miseries left him particularly anxious to be away from the damp and chill of the Montreal climate. Fry had invited him to a party at McClelland and Stewart that coming weekend, but he didn't think it likely, given his circumstances, that he would make the trip to Toronto. Instead he suggested they look forward to meeting the following year when Jim expected to return to Canada, as there was a book set in Saskatchewan that he wanted to write. It involved a murder and a trial, and he would have to learn more about the Canadian justice system if it were to be written. (This was a reference to what would eventually be known as the 'Price above Rubies' manuscript.)

On May 1st, Jim wrote to Pamela Fry, reporting that he was now settled in a penthouse apartment at 20 Spetson Street in Athens and, despite language problems, was revelling in his new setting – 'day after day of clear blue sky and brilliant sunshine' – which meant that he hadn't been thinking much about writing. Indeed it was not until 26 March 1969 that he could report a manuscript ready for a final typing.

In the meantime, he was taking immense pleasure in being retired and living in the Mediterranean. In a December letter to Margaret Laurence, he apologizes for not writing all year and blames it on the beautiful sunny weather: 'Every morning ... I say to myself a day like this is not to be wasted indoors and away I go gallivanting. Result: sea, sun, retsina and no letters ... *Next year* I'll try to be my age.'[35] And on a Christmas card to Alvin Goldman, he wrote similarly of 'a wonderful summer ... and no plans yet to return to Canada.' Much of the summer of 1968 he spent travelling in the islands – Samos, Lesbos, Rhodes, Skiathos – and he planned to go back the next summer to see more of them. The warm weather brought considerable relief to many of his physical maladies. There was only one drawback to Greece – the problem of language. In his letters, he was calling it 'an outrageous language,' 'a beastly language.'[36] While able to make himself understood reasonably well, he could not follow what people were saying in response to his questions. He was taking conversation classes but was not very hopeful at his age about mastering the language sufficiently to feel comfortable staying in the country for a long time.

When Jim wrote to Pamela Fry in March 1969, he did so because he had a revised manuscript of the novel about Sonny McAlpine that he had been working on for several years. Jim gave Fry every opportunity to decline a reading of his new manuscript. He described it for her as technically old-fashioned, with very 'square' sex when compared to novels like Philip Roth's *Portnoy's Complaint*. It has the virtues of brevity and no difficult passages, he says, but doubts if it makes a significant contribution to Canadian literature.[37] He adds that it has already been rejected by another Canadian publishing house. (He wrote to Margaret Laurence about the manuscript in even more disparaging terms: 'It is, I'm afraid, a bad novel, with some good things in it. The worst kind, because you keep fiddling instead of just chucking it out and putting your mind to something else.'[38])

Pamela Fry wrote back April 1st to welcome a submission and so Jim mailed off the manuscript for 'A Whir of Gold' [*sic*], but again he urged that they give it a hard-nosed assessment, for he himself did not have a great deal of confidence in what he had written: 'Spotty, slack, dull, pointless – a big *So What?* on every page.'[39] Although he had a soft spot for the characters he had created, he clearly did not want (after the experience of *The Well*) the embarrassment of another publishing failure:

As we have been corresponding, and as I have two titles in the New Canadian Library, I appreciate that you may feel uncomfortable about saying, 'This is a hell of a novel – why don't you take up photography?' However, I would be grateful if you would be blunt. I am well on in years and used to obscurity – even comfortable in it – and a firm NO will not be a surprise or a big disappointment. I would much rather, in fact, have it firm so that I can forget these unhappy people and – perhaps – put my mind to something else.

But Pamela Fry, who greatly admired Jim's work and had developed an affection for the man in their correspondence, wrote back enthusiastically on June 12 to say that McClelland and Stewart wanted to publish 'A Whir of Gold' (the indefinite article in the title was not dropped until Jim was reading galley proofs in May 1970). She concluded her letter of acceptance with a statement from Jack McClelland: '"The day we can't publish Sinclair Ross is the day we shouldn't be in publishing."' Jim was surprised and, of course, cautiously pleased.

Pamela Fry's enthusiasm in her letter to Jim did not, however, accurately reflect the opinion of the other readers for McClelland and Stewart. Both Hugh Kane and Bob Weaver, who submitted reports, were on the whole disappointed with the manuscript. Kane put it this way: 'It is a simple little story, rather old-fashioned in a way, and really inconsequential. It is hardly the novel which we might have hoped Ross should produce twenty-eight years after his successful first effort As for Me and My House.' Weaver's reaction was much the same: '... reviewers will dismiss [it] as minor and rather old-fashioned, and I can't foresee any large sale for the book.' However, both Kane and Weaver recommended its publication on the basis of Ross's reputation – his early works and their influence on younger writers. In her report Fry says she agrees with the opinion of the other two readers but praises certain aspects of the story – the relationship between Sonny and Mad, and the evocative sketches of Sonny's childhood on the prairies. She concludes her report with both praise and caution:

> The book is a kind of vintage Ross, beautifully written and constructed, all his remembered economy and simplicity of style. It is not likely to become a bestseller, but it is something we could certainly take pride in publishing. I agree wholeheartedly with what Hugh and Bob have to say on the subject, particularly because I am certain that another rejection would kill Ross dead as a writer. But an acceptance might prove a sufficient shot in the arm to ginger him into writing another book.[40]

Fry's personal enthusiasm for Jim and his work is glimpsed in a letter she wrote June 19 to a colleague in England, Joseph Gaute, associate director at Harrap and Company. After Jack McClelland gave his approval to go ahead with Whir of Gold, Fry wrote to Gaute hoping to interest his company in either joint publication or in taking stock for distribution in England. She lists Jim's credentials in her letter, referring to *As for Me and My House* as 'something of a classic in Canada' and detailing its success in the NCL series. She reveals her attraction to Ross when she writes of his shy, gentle nature, his failure to understand his own worth, and her excitement when his manuscript landed on her desk.[41] Something of this personal interest was communicated in her letters, for Jim would always remember Pamela Fry as the one editor he felt close to during his writing career. He welcomed her editorial suggestions – that Mad's dialogue be tightened up, that Charlie be given a little more background to make him less a villain – and when he replied to her, he suggested they start addressing each other by their first names. A series of friendly, constructive letters went back and forth, as Jim tried to sharpen the characterizations of Mad and Charlie and pursued the right details to 'reveal' them.[42]

Since McClelland and Stewart did not need a revised manuscript until the following January or February, Jim continued with his travel plans for the summer. To escape the extreme heat in Athens, he made a trip to the mountainous regions of northern Greece in mid-summer. Margaret Laurence had invited him to England for a visit, but he decided to postpone that trip in favour of more travel in the Mediterranean – two trips to Lesbos and a two-week trip to Istanbul in September. Travelling in Turkey proved a challenge at every turn (hotels were overbooked, taxi drivers overcharged), and Istanbul was in his opinion an ugly, depressing city, dirty and squalid, though with 'many wonderful and beautiful things ... mosques, Byzantine churches ... the skyline and the Bosphorus.'[43]

In October he made a trip to Rome and then to Naples, where he was especially interested to visit a boy named Salvatore, whom he had been sponsoring for some time through the Save-the-Children Fund. He described the meeting in a letter to Doris Saunders – the hospitality of the Neapolitan family, the large number of children, their crowded circumstances.[44] They served Jim a good dinner made from their own produce, and sent him back to his hotel laden with fruit, nuts, and a gallon of their home-made wine. Salvatore was then fifteen, a gangling six-footer, planning to go to trade school the following year to become a machinist; but before Jim left, the boy's father took him aside and asked in Italian if he would like to adopt the boy, take him to Greece to live with him, and continue helping the family by sponsoring another one of the children. In Jim's eyes, Salvatore was effeminate and he did not find him attractive or interesting, but he politely told the father he would give it some thought. (Jim gave Keath Fraser a very different account, which included two visits to the family. On the first visit, he found the family, minus a father, in a shanty suburb of Naples and learned that neither his money nor letters had been getting through, a corrupt international adoption agency keeping most of the cheques. But he kept up a correspondence with the boy directly and found the family doing better on a return visit a couple of years later. This time Salvatore's father was present, and while Jim was having dinner with the family, the father was hounded for a large sum of money by a man who came to the door. Jim felt he was being set up, and when Salvatore followed him back to his hotel, Jim simply turned at the door and offered to shake his hand. It was the last time he saw the boy.[45] There may not be much truth to this version because his other recollections coincided with the account he gave Doris Saunders. What is interesting here is the idea of an 'adopted' son, which would continue to play in his imagination and would merge with his anxieties about crime and human trustworthiness.)

Despite the frequent trips, by October 31st Jim was asking Pamela Fry if she would look over some pages of the *Whir of Gold* manuscript that he had revised in the light of her earlier suggestions. He had worked especially on the character of Charlie to emphasize how twisted and scared he is, giving him a latent homosexual dimension that Sonny is not aware of, but that explains Charlie's attraction to the simple, country boy. He also reports some tightening in the dialogue and asks that Pamela look again at Mad's big speech near the end of the story – where she tells Sonny about going to church – to see if it should be changed at all. The one thing he was resisting in the editorial suggestions was the development of a small-town background for Mad. The 'small town' he argues has become too much of a cliché in North American fiction: '... just say Main Street and the reader's got the picture – and I suspect, doesn't want to hear about it again.'

In her reply, Pamela Fry begins with praise for the new material on Charlie, because she feels it makes Charlie as much of a person as the other principals in the story, that he has not 'just been dragged into the story for the sake of the plot.' She also likes the deft touches that suggest his homosexuality without spelling it out. But Mad's final speech, in her opinion, needed more work: it needed to be broken up by shifts in tempo, so that the reader would more clearly recognize the point when Mad becomes aware that the relationship with Sonny just won't work. Fry's suggestions are detailed (two single-spaced typed pages) and written from the point of view of someone as engaged with the writing as the author himself. She told Jim not to feel pressed – there was plenty of time – and she concluded her letter with news of a 'nibble' of interest from an English publisher.[46] Jim replied November 23 that her letter was just the 'lift' that he needed and that he would go through the manuscript again with her suggestions in mind and send off a newly typed version by first week of January. Jim's gratitude for Pamela Fry's genuine interest in the manuscript is everywhere evident in their correspondence, and in one of his letters he even suggests that she make a trip to Greece to visit him, the only gesture approaching a personal invitation to appear in any of Jim's letters that have survived.[47] He had developed in his mind an image of Pamela Fry as a discriminating, sympathetic woman, an ideal companion.

Fry could not accept the invitation, but Jim did have Canadian visitors in the winter of 1970 who would become important to him for the rest of his life. In the fall of 1969, he received a letter from Keath Fraser, a doctoral student at the University of London, who had written an article based on the stories in *The Lamp at Noon* collection. Keath and his wife, Lorraine, were newly married and were planning a trip to the Mediterranean, and they hoped they could meet with Jim in Greece. Jim replied cheerfully that he would be glad to meet with the Frasers: 'We'll go to the Plaka for dinner and bouziki – much more fun than Can Lit and the stories in *The Lamp at Noon*.'[48] When they turned up in February, Jim did indeed take them to the Plaka (with male dancers breaking dishes on the restaurant floor), and they had two fine evenings of conversation, with promises to keep in touch and to visit again. Jim felt comfortable with this bright young couple and promised he would visit them when he made a trip to London. He had not been back since his days there during the war, and he was eager to see the venerable city once again. From this first visit, Keath Fraser would remember Jim as 'a curious mixture of candour and caution, faintly comical to a pair of admiring travellers in their twenties.'[49] While the Frasers were in Athens, Jim received a contract for a film option on *As for Me and My House*; it was a good reason for celebration.

For Jim 1970 was, on the whole, an enjoyable year: in early spring, he moved from 20 Spetson Street to Omonia Square, and during spring and summer he continued his travels to various parts of Greece, including the southern Peloponnese, Crete, and Methoni, and in the fall he made a month-long trip to Spain. He was continuing to enjoy Greece, especially the sun and dry air, although the language problem was not getting any easier. The year 1970 was also sweetened by the prospect of another novel being published – Pamela Fry's enthusiasm for the story and her attention to details were making it seem less risky – and by the interest in his work that seemed to be growing in Canada. Keath Fraser had sent him a copy of *Canadian Literature* which contained the 1969 article by W.H. New on ambivalence in *As for Me and My House*. Jim said he felt somewhat in awe of what New had discovered and didn't realize his unconscious had been working so well when he was writing the novel.[50] He had the same reaction when he read Keath's article 'Futility at the Pump: The Short Stories of Sinclair Ross,' which was published in the spring issue of *Queen's Quarterly* for 1970. He laughed, he said, about 'Will returning to the womb' in 'Not by Rain Alone,' just as he had once laughed when Roy Daniells said the grain elevators in his fiction were phallic symbols (storehouses for seed); he laughed, he said, because such things never occurred to him, although he liked to think that his unconscious had been on the job.[51] There had been a few enthusiastic notices about *The Lamp at Noon and Other Stories*: in the annual 'Letters in Canada' issue of *University of Toronto Quarterly* (1969), Gordon Roper wrote that Ross's stories had 'the same concentration in form and emotion that [made] his *As for Me and My House* one of the classics of Canadian fiction in English,'[52] and Jim's old Winnipeg friend Audrey O'Kelly (now Peterkin) also praised the stories highly in a magazine published by the Catholic Church.[53]

At the same time, Doris Saunders was pressing Jim to write a piece about the influence of Manitoba on his work for a special issue of *Mosaic* that was celebrating writers with a Manitoba background. Jim declined; he argued that although it was true his short stories and *As for Me and My House* were written while he was living in Winnipeg, they were about Saskatchewan, not Manitoba. He suggested instead that Doris include one of his stories in the anthology with an editorial note that welcomed him as an outsider whose work would likely ring a few bells nonetheless for Manitobans. Only the novel about a young soldier from the Prairies that he worked on in London during the war involved looking back to Winnipeg, but that project, he reminded Doris, was discarded after two hundred pages. Finally, he says he can't write a piece for her because he simply does not understand his creative processes.[54] However, Doris did get Jim's permission to cobble together a few statements from their correspondence which appeared in *Mosaic* 3 (Spring 1970) with the title 'On Looking Back.' Although Jim demurred as far as analysing the motives and influences in his writing, he did hold strong views on some aspects of writing. One of these was that the writer must not talk about his work before it is completed, and in a letter to Laurence in the spring of 1970 he warns her not to release all her creative impulses by talking with students while she is writer-in-residence at University of Toronto: '... keep enough urges and tensions to make it necessary to communicate with more novels.'[55]

Jim needed, however, to be in good spirits because the final stages of publishing *Whir of Gold* did not go smoothly. By May 1970, Pamela Fry was experiencing nervous exhaustion from overwork, and her planned week's vacation turned into a month's absence from the office. Jim wrote to her with deeply felt sympathy:

I'm sorry you haven't been feeling well and I know what you mean about the urge – desperate sometimes, at least it used to be with me – to pack it all up and break free. I was 43 years a bank clerk and it was even worse probably; for you, I imagine, are interested in your work and I, frankly, wasn't. Sometimes I wonder how I stood it – and sometimes I wonder how the Bank stood me. I'm afraid I wasn't exactly what you'd call an asset.[56]

At the same time as Pamela was experiencing personal stress, a method of computerized printing, which was being used for the first time at McClelland and Stewart, resulted in a phenomenal number of errors in the page proofs for *Whir of Gold*. For all his politeness, Jim could not help reflect his concern about the state of the book, and he referred in a letter of May 16 to 'numerous printers' errors, omissions, repetitions, etc.' At times he was not sure whether he was dealing with major errors or textual revisions introduced by a copy editor. He was advised May 29 not to worry about 'typos,' but if there were serious errors or omissions, he was to cable the firm collect. Dealing with the galley proofs also turned into a major headache, for not only was it painstaking and time-consuming work, but anticipating the arrival of proofs was a source of great frustration. Jim had arranged to be out of the Athens heat for most of the summer and to spend the last two weeks of June with an American couple on one of the islands. He had passed up that holiday, and still galleys had not arrived. He expressed his irritation in a letter to Pamela dated June 25, but Pamela was still not in the office and Anna Szigethy (Anna Porter) cabled Jim on July 2 to say that in four days proofs would be in the mail. When she returned to the office July 13, Pamela Fry wrote a fulsome letter of apology: 'I am ... extremely sorry for the incredible MESS regarding your galleys. Some idiotic new method was tried, which was supposed to be cheaper, but which finally resulted in costing us all more, in money and strain, than if it had gone to a *real* printer in the first place. You will be relieved to know that it is now in the hands of a proper printer.' The galleys promised in June were not sent until mid-July. 'I am really furious about this whole business,' added Fry. 'The MS was so clean, and had so few changes that it should have been in press weeks ago – and I hate to think that we have also succeeded in messing up your summer plans.'

Jim had received the galleys by July 22, when he wrote to Pamela Fry, but he hadn't received her letter of apology, for he told her frankly what a deplorable state the galleys were in and how fed up he was with the whole process. Aside from misspelled words, there were omissions of one and two lines, and sometimes whole paragraphs, all of which would throw the page make-up out of kilter. Some phrasings were back in their original form, the revisions having been lost, and none of the chapters had their number headings. 'Sorry to have been so irritable and impatient,' he offered towards the end of the letter; 'it was just that I couldn't understand why, after telling me so promptly and accurately when the first set was coming, you were so vague about the second.' His irritability at not being able to leave Athens during the intense heat of summer was compounded by the din and dust of excavation for a new building directly across the street from his apartment. Nonetheless, in conclusion he told her of plans to visit Toronto in the fall and asked if she would go out for dinner with him while he was in the city. In her reply of August 5, Fry reassured Jim that all the problems with the galleys were being sorted out, and she hoped he would enjoy his travels during the remainder of the summer. On October 20 she wrote again to say the publication date for *Whir of Gold* was set for November 1st and that he should have his copies when he arrived in Toronto sometime that month.

But there were further delays in production, and the book missed being distributed in time for the Christmas trade. Jim did not receive his copies until after Christmas. He couldn't help feeling disappointed with the final product – the unattractive drawing on the cover, the poor grade of paper, and the narrow leading between lines of type. In a letter to Pamela on 3 January 1971, he says that even 'skimming' he spotted a number of typographical errors: 'laying low' for 'lying low,' 'dead path' for 'dead patch,' 'ignominiously' with its third *i* missing, etc. And he felt depressed by the photo of himself on the dust jacket. He was sure the critics would be unkind. He nonetheless sent a copy to Keath and Lorraine Fraser with a puzzling dedication: 'A tearjerker, as I warned you. If you don't use at least one box of Kleenex each I'll know I have failed.'[57] Was he being ironic, sensing the novel was cloying and melodramatic, or was he sincere? Did he really believe the story of Sonny and Mad was genuinely moving? Perhaps it was a way of saying he knew the book was flawed, that it was in fact laughable. Certainly he was wearing his protective cloak of irony.

But in the meantime he had rather enjoyed his trip to Canada in November. It was the result of an invitation from the Ontario Institute for Studies in Education to do an interview for the Canadian Writers on Tape series. Jim had been flattered by the invitation because he recognized that the other subjects – Earle Birney, Al Purdy, Margaret Laurence, Hugh MacLennan, and Mordecai Richler – were being ranked among the country's most important literary figures. He was offered an $850 fee, which paid for his air fare and four nights at the Lord Simcoe Hotel in Toronto. Earle Toppings was the series host and treated Jim with the special respect owing to someone who has been unduly neglected. In the future, this interview would prove invaluable to students of Ross's writing because it was the only extended discussion of his work he ever engaged in for the public record – he did no other recorded interviews and never appeared on radio, television, or film. His one anxiety and regret about the taped interview was that Toppings would not provide him with a series of questions in advance, so that he could 'mull them over' and give a considered opinion on the different aspects of his writing career they were to discuss. In retrospect, he felt disappointed with the tape, too many hesitations and non-committal replies on his part, and he would regularly dismiss it as having no value for students or young writers.[58] His career, after all, he wrote to Pamela Fry, could only 'serve as a good example of how *not* to do it.'[59]

With the unexpected publishing delays, McClelland and Stewart was not ready to launch *Whir of Gold* while Jim was in the city, but he did have a chance to meet Pamela Fry and take her out to dinner. He found her a genteel, educated Englishwoman in her forties, much more reserved in person than her letters had suggested. They went to a nightclub-style restaurant that Fry recommended, but in spite of the liveliness of the setting, she remained tranquil and withdrawn. It was a somewhat disappointing evening. The following afternoon, however, Fry hosted a small gathering at the office, where Jim met a few other of McClelland and Stewart's authors, including Al Purdy, who greeted Jim warmly and gave him an autographed copy of *Love in a Burning Building*, published that year.

Although *Whir of Gold* was not ready yet for distribution, Jim agreed to do an interview in his hotel room with Peter Sypnowich, book editor for the *Toronto Daily Star*. The piece that appeared November 13 was titled 'A Bachelor on the Run Comes Back to Canada,' and the motif running through it is Ross's enigmatic relations with women. Jim had described for the reporter his experience of fending off eligible females in Athens, how one of his Greek friends invited him to his house for dinner and offered him an unmarried female relative for matrimony: 'led her out like a heifer – was I interested or not? I felt embarrassed for her.' Sypnowich then praises Mrs Bentley as a masterpiece of female psychology and describes the author's affection for his new character, Mad, quoting Jim as saying, 'I do like her very much.' In spite of his considerable success with female characters in fiction, Ross is, reports Sypnowich, a lone wolf and the Greek girls are out of luck.[60] This interview also contains Jim's wistful observation that the women he has been interested in have not been interested in him. He had made the same statement in a letter to W.A. Deacon years before, saying he hasn't gotten married – because 'the ones I want don't want me.'[61]

Since Sypnowich had not yet had the opportunity to read the new novel there is very little about *Whir of Gold* in the interview; the article, however, did serve as a reminder to the reading public that the author of *As for Me and My House* was still writing and that a new book would appear shortly. In the interview, Jim also divulged the information that Peter Pearson had taken out an option to make a film of *As for Me and My House*, that the young novelist Graeme Gibson was doing the script, and that Kate Reid was slated to play Mrs Bentley.

Jim had not been wrong in anticipating some harsh assessments of *Whir of Gold* from the reviewers. In the January 2nd *Globe and Mail Magazine*, novelist Hugh Garner argued that there were two major problems with the novel: it should have been twice the length (he deduced it had probably been cut in half by the editors), and it should have retained its original time period – the late 1940s and early '50s, when young men wore crew-cuts.[62] Garner's observation about time period was to the point: in an era of convention-defying hippies, with their optimism, long hair, and guitars, short-haired Sonny from the Prairies with his clarinet and his doleful prospects was certainly out of step as a portrait of a social type in 1970. John W. Dafoe in the *Montreal Star* simply assumed it had been written during the era in which it seemed to be set, postwar Montreal.[63] Certainly in the company of Atwood's *The Edible Woman* (1969), Kroetsch's *The Studhorse Man* (1969), and David Godfrey's *New Ancestors* (1970), the novel seemed dated. Some critics, such as Malcolm Foster in the Montreal *Gazette*, felt that in shifting his setting from the Prairies to Montreal in the present, Ross was 'throwing away his best card.' Sonny in Montreal, Foster argues, does not ring true; only in the Prairie flashbacks is there authenticity.[64] Several reviewers winced at the character of Mad and the 'whore with a heart of gold' stereotype. For others technique was a problem. Pamela Sykes wrote that the writing is 'obviously vacuous. It becomes difficult to find meaning in many of the disjointed phrases.'[65] The reviewer for the *Windsor Star* was especially harsh in this regard: 'Ross has an aversion to writing sentences. His short-clipped phrases usually have a murky effect rather than speeding up action.'[66] In the *Canadian Forum*, Anne Montagnes pronounced *Whir of Gold* 'a terrible book,'[67] and George Woodcock in the *Victoria Times Colonist* said it was a 'sentimental and obvious story,' that Ross had failed to create interest in the characters.[68] In almost every review there were references to the author's achievement in his 'brilliant' first novel. Montagnes suggested rereading *As for Me and My House* instead of buying *Whir of Gold*: 'It was published in 1941 but it begins to look as timeless as Genesis.'

The most thoroughly negative review, titled 'Maybe Sinclair Ross Should Have Stayed in His Small Prairie Town,' was written by western literature specialist Harvard Dahlie for the Calgary *Albertan*. *Whir of Gold*, began Dahlie, confirms the suspicion that Ross may have long ago exhausted his somewhat restricted fictional world. He had nothing good to say for the subjects of the story: 'The author seems unsure of what to do with his characters once he has created them, and they are left to indulge in aimless speculations, desultory conversation and what must be some of the most insipid love-making ever recorded in Canadian fiction.' Dahlie's bias in favour of western fiction is clear throughout the review and underlies his statement that when Ross tries to juxtapose the rural and the urban he fails disastrously because he just cannot write urban fiction. 'It is a slight and sluggish novel,' concludes Dahlie, which never really gets off the ground, and the reader shares the boredom and impatience so frequently reflected by its main characters.'[69] These were all stinging judgments and made the author feel painfully exposed as a failure and a has-been.

Not all the reviews, of course, were negative: at least five were almost entirely positive. Jim's old friend Chester Duncan, writing in the *Winnipeg Free Press*, found much to praise. He read the novel as approaching a religious allegory, with the descent of grace coming in an unlikely angel of mercy, that of Mad, her name being a variant of Magdalene. As a musician, Duncan was especially drawn to the sequence of Sonny and his music teacher, Dorothy Whittle. In sharp contrast to some of the reviewers, he praised the writing style: '... the prose is wonderfully lean, probing and imaginative.'[70] A Winnipeg friend had sent Jim a copy of Chester's review, and he was very pleased with it, although in a January letter to Margaret Laurence, he confided that Mad, as he knew her, was not particularly virtuous; her good acts were those of someone who is in love and devoted to that person.[71] This was more in line with the reaction of Susan Swan, who, writing for the *Toronto Telegram*, found it a profoundly moving love story. The beauty of the book, she wrote, lies in Sonny's 'haunting and touching limitations.' She conceded that it would not go down as a great Canadian classic, but it was 'in the truest sense, a love story which should be read and remembered.'[72] In a perceptive review, Jamie Portman in the *Calgary Herald Magazine* praised the author's ability to create intense environmental claustrophobia, but argued that in the end Sonny's defeat was rooted in personal flaws and weaknesses, not environment;[73] and Douglas Barbour wrote in the *Edmonton Journal* that Ross had created a portrait of everyman as loser in 'a fine and carefully wrought novel.'[74] But perhaps the review Jim liked best was a brief, poetic appreciation in the *London Free Press* by James Etherington, who described the novel as 'a beautiful, moving love story with an overlay of aching loneliness.'[75] He described Mad as the kind of beauty and goodness that unexpectedly come into your life as a gift, then disappear, and if you try to hold on you will find in your hands only the ruin of what you thought it once was. This was the only reviewer who had touched on the essence from which the novel had been fashioned – 'aching loneliness.'

But these positive notices were not enough to erase the sense of failure and bitterness that so many negative judgments gave rise to. One of the latter that rankled for some time was the review for the *Windsor Star* which said Ross had an aversion to writing sentences. This reviewer also noted how many printing errors the publisher had allowed to pass. As a perfectionist, Jim continued to dwell on this. In the January letter to Margaret Laurence, he said he was 'not at all happy' about McClelland and Stewart and listed his grievances: Why did they accept the manuscript if they had so little faith in it as to give him nothing in advance? Why did they hold up the contract until the very last minute? And why, if it was worth publishing, was it not worth proof-reading? With two titles in the New Canadian Library, he felt he deserved at least 'routine courtesy and consideration.' He felt the computer problem was simply an excuse: 'However they set it, computer, steam engine, donkeys, the responsibility is theirs – they have proof-readers ... It raises some unpleasant doubts, and I'm left wondering why, or who ...'[76] He dropped his correspondence with Pamela Fry, only writing her once more, the following January, to thank her for a calendar sent as a gift from McClelland and Stewart for Christmas 1971.

A job done badly, or that had somehow been botched, was something Jim could never forget; it grated on his deepest instinct to do things right. In a letter to Alvin Goldman (12 January 1971), in a particularly black mood because of recurring prostate problems and a heavy cold, he returned to his bitter feelings about a previous failure, *The Well*. Goldman had been working on a screenplay from the novel that would change the ending, but Jim was reluctant to give him the go-ahead. He acknowledges in the letter that he is being petty-minded: '[The novel] was published with a very bad ending, contrived, forced, unconvincing; and if the film is done with the new – and, I think, greatly improved – ending, it will look as if someone had to doctor up the story for me – in other words, that I was too dim-witted to do it myself. I know – only a handful of people read the book in any case so what the hell? who cares? ... Well, I do, and at the moment I can't see around it.' He goes on to say he wants to do the writing himself and try to get the book republished before a film is made.[77] Similar feelings would persist about *Whir of Gold*, which he felt was flawed not only by production problems but by his own stylistic failings in some places. One of the last projects he attempted in extreme old age was to rewrite *Whir of Gold*, which would remain the favourite of his four published novels. But he never found a way to do it.

Perhaps the problem is that *Whir of Gold* tells two different stories which compete uneasily for the reader's attention: one derives from the author's contemporary interest in crime and tells of a young man who has fallen into a relationship with a prostitute and subsequently takes part in a jewelry store hold-up in a seedy part of Montreal; the other, not so apparent, is the story of a boy with musical talent growing up on the prairie, a kind of *Bildungsroman* that is overshadowed by the story that takes place in Montreal. As reviewers and future readers would generally agree, the most interesting part of the book concerns the boy on the prairie; it is a story Jim had been writing in various forms for more than thirty years. The evidence is in a letter of 15 January 1979 he wrote to Lorraine McMullen, in which he says he once 'had *in mind* a group of short stories having to do with the same boy. In "Cornet at Night" he becomes really aware, for the first time, of the wonder of music – I suppose you could call it an aesthetic awakening. "One's a Heifer" is his first contact with evil ... There was to have been one about death – he loses his parents in a fire, which is why in "One's a Heifer" he is living with an aunt and uncle. "A Day with Pegasus," the mystery of life and beginning, etc.'[78] According to the author, these stories were the backbone of the unpublished manuscript from the 1940s titled 'Day Coach to Wagneria,' about a Prairie boy who will some day become a musician. The idea and some parts of the writing from this earlier project were brought forward once more to *Whir of Gold*; perhaps this is why certain sequences in the novel have a timeless authenticity. In light of Ross's oeuvre, the novel also reveals another persistent and authentic pattern – the young man divided between his love for a woman and his need for a man.

Although Jim was never able to completely revise *Whir of Gold*, one feels he would have been immensely pleased by the 2001 paperback edition published by University of Alberta Press. Not only is it handsomely produced, with a dust-jacket-style cover and attractive illustrations, but it opens with an introduction by Nat Hardy, who describes the novel as 'a masterful *tour de force*,' affirming Ross's status as a major figure in Prairie fiction and demanding critical reappraisal in the twenty-first century. He suggests some of the new ways in which it might be examined – in terms of cultural rifts between rural and urban and between anglophone and francophone, but especially in terms of sexuality, the homosocial bond between Sonny and his criminal friend, Charlie, and Mad's homophobic response to their relationship. The Montreal section, Hugh Garner wrote in 1970, seemed dated. But now in the twenty-first century 'datedness' is no longer an issue, when 1970 feels as long past and dated as 1952. Good writing wins the day, and in the tersely apprehensive style of this novel, we hear the voice of the alienated artist doomed by his own pessimism. Sinclair Ross, it turns out, did not need to rewrite this book; a new audience is not distracted by a novel being out of step with its time, but rather, as Hardy's introduction makes clear, is moved by the love story and its overlay of 'aching loneliness.'

twelve

Tourist
1971–1973

In early fall of 1970, Jim had spent a month travelling through much of Spain, and he wrote to Lorraine and Keath Fraser that he liked very much what he saw and was 'tempted.'[1] In mid-March of 1971, he moved from Athens to Barcelona, in letters to friends giving language as the chief reason for the move. To Margaret Laurence he wrote:

> ... it's the old story, I just can't learn the damned language (and am spending too much time trying). They understand me, but I don't understand them. It isolates me, makes it difficult to know people, and moreover makes me feel terribly stupid. There's been so much to see I haven't minded, but now I feel I would like a place where I can settle in and say 'This is it,' and Greece is not the answer. Heaven knows how Spain will work out but at least the language won't be such a problem ...[2]

He felt he had gotten along fairly well when he travelled in Spain, drawing on his working knowledge of Spanish from his holidays in Mexico. The chief burden he faced was selling his furniture and packing his books. He took a boat from Athens to Barcelona on March 14 and lived in a hotel for more than a month until a furnished apartment in the lower, traffic-congested part of the city came free in late April. He had decided not to go through the lengthy procedure of furnishing an apartment again, although it meant living with what he described as 'the cheapest, ugliest furniture you can imagine.'[3]

Most of 1971 was spent getting to know Barcelona and also making short trips to other parts of Spain – two weeks in the Pyrenees, three weeks on the Costa Brava. Travel was not without problems: crowds of tourists in the summer made it difficult in terms of securing hotel rooms, and a pinched nerve in his foot made walking difficult at times and required cortisone shots to relieve the pain. In the fall, he took the train to Madrid, the capital of the country, situated on the high central plain in the middle of the Iberian Peninsula.[4] At a distance from sea or ocean, Madrid is shaped by the extremes of an inland climate: vegetation exhibits the effects of wind, heat, and dryness; and newspapers and candy wrappers blow about the streets and catch in the hedges and corners of buildings. The architecture is grand and massive, befitting a national capital, but the city reminded Jim, nonetheless, of Winnipeg and Chicago.[5] He spent several hours at the Prado, where he went especially to see the Goyas and the El Grecos. There was no painting in the world that appealed to him more than the work of these two artists, especially El Greco, who had been so responsive to the fanatical religious atmosphere of his adopted country. But he loved Goya too and would report that he never grew tired of the Black Paintings, done when the artist was an old recluse, probably mentally unbalanced.[6]

From Madrid he travelled the forty miles southwest to Toledo, where El Greco had lived much of his working life and where the largest collection of his work is located. In a letter to the Frasers, he wrote that the stretch of country en route to Toledo looked exactly like Saskatchewan – 'the gentle roll of the land, almost flat, the color of the stubble fields (a good literary word would be tawny).'[7] At the Toledo Museum, he spent hours looking at the gaunt, extraordinary figures El Greco had painted, with their elongated hands and feet and flame-like forms. To him they were not just mystical or ascetic figures, but psychosexual emblems of both androgyny and suffering. In this same light, the life of El Greco itself interested Jim: his expatriatism, his refusal to paint according to any of the recognized styles, his brief alliance with a woman when he was about thirty-seven, which resulted in a son, and his long relationship with an Italian assistant. When Barbara Godard published an article on As for Me and My House titled 'El Greco in Canada,' Jim said he hadn't thought about the book in that light while he was writing, yet his long-standing fascination for El Greco prompted him to say 'there might be something to it.'[8]

In 1971 Jim received two letters that, in retrospect, seem to indicate the direction his career and reputation were taking. The first was a letter from a young writer and teacher, John Moss, who was starting a new magazine titled Journal of Canadian Fiction. An ardent admirer of Sinclair Ross's writing, Moss wanted to feature a new story by Jim in one of the first issues of his journal. The letter was flattering, and so Jim agreed at least to give it a try; there were ideas for a story that he had been playing with, and one of these he would develop and eventually send to Moss to be published as 'The Flowers That Killed Him.' He and Moss engaged in a lively correspondence for several years, and the latter wrote engagingly about *As for Me and My House* and would one day organize a symposium about Jim's work.

The other letter was an invitation I sent him, on behalf of a visiting speakers committee at Simon Fraser University, to travel to British Columbia and to read and talk about his work to an audience in the English Department. I knew nothing about the man or his whereabouts at that point and was not aware that a public appearance was a 'terrifying' proposition. Declining the invitation (29 October 1971), Jim wrote at length about health problems that prohibited travel and cited his background: 'Saskatchewan farm boy and bank clerk, Grade 11 education; no experience whatever in public speaking and with anything but a good voice. Add it up and you get two evenings likely to be anything but memorable.'[9] He was also 'mildly astonished' that a university with the name Simon Fraser would be so financially reckless as to sponsor his travels from Barcelona to Vancouver. But he was grateful for the invitation, and a correspondence ensued which led to a friendship in later years and to my eventually writing this biography.

An audience was beginning to define itself; Sinclair Ross had failed to create a readership in the general public, but with the emergence of Canadian literature as a legitimate and significant field of study, an academic audience was eager to make contact with this elusive writer. Donald Stephens, W.H. New, and Keath Fraser had by 1971 published serious critical articles on *As for Me and My House* and on the early short stories. Warren Tallman and D.G. Jones had given several pages of analysis to *As for Me and My House* in their extended studies of Canadian literature. Correspondence with a number of teachers and critics began in the early 1970s wherein the author discussed candidly the patterns and the intentions behind his work.

At the end of November 1971, Jim wrote to the Frasers to say that he had moved to another apartment – 'up the mountain towards Tibidabo, less noise.'[10] As one of his visitors wrote, he was now settled 'in a modern flat with a rooftop patio overlooking a noisy, residential area of the city half-way up the hill where the air is better.'[11] There, in a particularly spacious living area, he resumed his routine of reading, writing, and listening to music, and making his way downtown every evening for dinner. The visitor was Myrna Kostash, one of a growing number of younger writers – particularly from the Prairie region – who, like Margaret Laurence, were coming to see Jim as the literary pioneer who had made their own careers possible. Over time, they would include Robert Kroetsch, Ken Mitchell, Rudy Wiebe, Aritha Van Herk, Keath Fraser, and Guy Vanderhaeghe. Myrna Kostash, a writer from Edmonton with a Ukrainian background, was on a freelance assignment for *Saturday Night* magazine and came to Barcelona to interview Jim in May of 1972. He had received a cable from the magazine's editor, Robert Fulford, while on a trip to Andalusia, and because it was two weeks before he read it, he said 'yes' to Fulford's request for an interview, thinking the writer in the area would have gone back to Canada. He was surprised to learn that a writer was being sent all the way from Canada for just that interview – 'the last word in reckless, foolish spending' he wrote to Keath Fraser.[12] His anxiety about meeting new people was growing stronger with time, but the fact that Kostash was a woman from the Canadian West and that she had already travelled in, and knew something of, Spain broke down his resistance, and he agreed to meet her at one of his favourite restaurants. He soon found himself comfortable with the young woman, who had obviously prepared herself well for the interview, and they talked easily about Spain and about the literary culture in Canada. They had dinner together twice, and they met for gin and tonics in Jim's apartment one afternoon; that time, Kostash had some very specific questions to ask, and Jim found himself being evasive and at a loss for interesting answers. This awkward phase in their meeting, however, resulted in one of the most perceptive accounts we have of Jim in his relation to the public:

> Sinclair Ross has no public face. He is not known to the man on the streets, his photograph does not appear in the papers or on television, he is not quoted or referred to in literary debates. Even those who read him do not know his story or associate him with trends, movements and theories around which other writers' names cluster. There are his books and there is the man himself with no intermediating mask. It therefore is impossible to talk with him in the impersonal, careless and sometimes brutal manner of researcher before a well-armed public personality who need only be pried in the right places for all the answers to come tumbling out. Ross told me, over and over, that he had no 'line,' no official history he could reiterate like a personal liturgy, no experience of contributing to public discussions and that, as a result, he did not know what it was he was supposed to say.

Kostash's 'Discovering Sinclair Ross: It's Rather Late,' which appeared in the July 1972 issue of *Saturday Night*, is on every level an excellent piece of journalism. It provides the reader with a sketch of Ross's Prairie background, his limited success as a writer, and with a glimpse of the bank employee enjoying retirement in Europe. But, as Jim observed gratefully in a letter to Kostash (3 June 1972), she had not just written about him, but had used him as a peg on which to hang other things – shrewd observations about the conditions for being a writer in Canada in the 1930s and 1940s, caustic reflections on the attitudes of Canadians at that time towards the arts, etc.[13] Yet perhaps the best part of the article is the passionate assessment from a 1970s perspective of the tragedy of gender roles in Ross's fiction: '... man and wife,' writes Kostash, 'encounter each other at opposite ends of a cruel axis. He in his allegiance to masculine imperatives of tenacity and grimness, she in her determination to accept his authority and not to humiliate him, to swallow her disaffection – they are lost to each other, beyond any means of yielding and comforting except the most miserly. This incapacity for tender relationship, for rejecting the strictures of an impossible virility and unnecessary submission, dooms the Ross people to endless seasons of isolation and waste.' Jim liked the article very much, commending Kostash on her style, and accurately predicted that there would be articles and books from her pen in the future. There followed over the next five years one of the warmest correspondences from Jim's pen that has survived.

Although being interviewed had not been the ordeal he had anticipated, Jim was still reluctant to put on a face for the public. After the article appeared in *Saturday Night*, CBC television contacted him about doing an interview, saying they would bring the film crew to Spain, but he turned them down. To me he wrote: 'I'm just not the right material for it, I would be miserable and unhappy about it – literally in dread – for weeks, and the result would be of little or no practical use to me and would mean just a dull half-hour for the watchers.'[14] He was finding that even the slightest bit of fame came with a price. There were two stories from this period in his life which he repeatedly told. In a polite exchange with a fellow passenger on the plane from Toronto back to Greece in November 1970, he had identified himself using his published name. When the young man confirmed Jim was the author of *As for Me and My House*, he burst into a tirade against Mrs Bentley – what a bitch she was, how much he hated the novel – and about how much he resented having to read the book in college. Jim found it unsettling. The other story, retold by Kostash in her magazine article, was of the hippie travellers from Canada who one day showed up at his apartment in Barcelona saying, 'Oh, wow, we dig your book' and 'Could we stay here for a while?' Jim liked to point out that he hadn't been fooled. They had heard his name in a Canadian literature course somewhere and descended on him like tourists on a souvenir shop. He had turned them away.

By late summer of 1972, Jim had decided to move again. He had found the winter months in Barcelona damp and chilly, which aggravated his back trouble (a ruptured disc in the lower neck), and he was increasingly aware that it was also the most expensive city in Spain. On his trip to Andalusia during the spring, he had pretty much made up his mind to try the Costa del Sol and so at the end of summer decided to look for a furnished apartment in Málaga, which boasted the best year-round climate in the country. By October he was writing to Myrna Kostash to say how happy he was with his new situation: 'I have an apartment right beside the sea – 12th floor, the top – with a view, sea, mountains, port, which I haven't got used to yet, just can't believe. I stare and stare and go on staring.' The apartment itself was smaller than the one in Barcelona – three 'pokey' little rooms 'with a balcony just big enough for a small table and a couple of chairs' – but the perspective over the sea, where on a clear day you could make out the coast of North Africa, gave his living quarters a spaciousness he had never experienced before. On that balcony, he could reflect on North Africa and on Paul Bowles, an expatriate American writer living in Morocco, with whose writing he felt a kinship, especially *The Sheltering Sky*, with its enigmatic, bisexual protagonists and stark, ruthless landscape, not unlike the prairie as rendered in *As for Me and My House*.

Málaga itself seemed a cluttered little city after Barcelona: 'an impressive facade, the park and palm-lined boulevards, and then an endless warren of rather mean streets and small shops.'[15] He did not find the restaurants very good and soon assumed the habit, at least twice a week, of taking the half-hour bus ride west along the coast to Torremolinos where he found the restaurant competition keener and the food better. There was one restaurant in Málaga, however, which sometimes drew his patronage. It was called El Chinitas and boasted on a tile near the entrance the words of the poet Garcia Lorca, who had eaten there and written warmly of the restaurant in a letter. Jim found himself taking guests to El Chinitas because of this romantic literary association. In his life of increasing solitude he found himself thinking about those artists – writers, musicians, painters – who had given him so much pleasure during his life, and sometimes found himself in a silent conversation with them.

In the same letter to Kostash, Jim hints at the turn his sexual life had taken since moving to Spain. In Málaga, he says, he has been befriended by a man who shines shoes on the street – a widower named Raphael, thirty-four, with three children – 'that, at least is his story' – and he says that Raphael can get him anything he wants – 'bueno or malo, just name it.' In a later explanation of this letter, Jim would say that many of the shoe shine boys – and men – were also male prostitutes and could be hired for a reasonable price. He would buy them a drink, and then they would follow him back to his apartment on the Paseo Maritimo. He had become a customer. To Kostash he wrote somewhat disingenuously of the striking difference between European and North American culture in this regard: 'You seldom see on the streets a far-out, fairy type of homosexual, mincing and fluttering – in comparison, say, with Greenwich Village – yet they say there is a great deal of homosexuality, that it is increasing, or at least recognizing itself. But they certainly do have a greater range of gesture and voice – seem so much more alive and exuberant than ourselves.'[16] In the same letter, he tells Kostash she might like to look up the new story he has written for the *Journal of Canadian Fiction*. Its title is 'The Flowers That Killed Him.'[17]

What is unique in this story is the lengthy depiction of a sexual crime. The narrator is a thirteen-year-old boy who tells how his father, the school principal, sexually assaulted and murdered his two best friends. He also reveals how he himself killed his father in order to preserve the family's honour. The ending is in the tradition of detective fiction, the reader kept in suspense trying to figure out 'who done it.' The story develops out of some of the writer's long-standing preoccupations, the dysfunctional family being a central one. Here the boy knows there is no love between his parents, and he knows that they remain together for his sake and out of concern for public respectability. The mother's hatred is only barely concealed; the boy observes her holding herself back, but when she speaks to her husband over dinner, he hears her voice 'hard, sour, snapping the words ... so you could almost hear the teeth' (129). But hypocrisy and the great gap between public and private lives are also foremost in this story, especially at the father's funeral, where the boy listens to the minister's words: '*Devoted husband and father ... outstanding example to the community*' (126). Also important is the vulnerability of the marginal members of society. Both of the boys who are raped and murdered come from families that are not considered respectable: one boy was born a bastard and was being raised by his unmarried mother; the other was from a family where the father is a shiftless drunk and his mother is rumoured to be a prostitute.

As a young man thinking and reading about 'family,' Jim was persuaded by Freud's Oedipal account of child/parent relations. In this story, one can identify an Oedipal drama in which the boy narrator mourns the lack of a phallic father to bequeath manhood and social respectability. The father is an embarrassment to the boy in public because he tells 'corny' jokes, is laughed at in the school yard, and is called 'old Creeper' because he cultivates flowers. At home the boy is aware that his father does not share his mother's bedroom. At the end of the story, the dead father-teacher is completely disfigured; the son has literally killed the father and taken possession of mother and house. But how are we to interpret this story? The father's rape and murder of the boys is the crime of a pedophile, but the narrator has softened that portrait by telling us that his father worked hard to rehabilitate the town's outcasts and that he made concerted efforts to instil a love for nature in his students. Or are we meant to read these gestures more cynically? Is the father's concern for the poor families a cover for his criminal interest in underfathered boys? Are the nature excursions a way of luring the boys to their deaths?

However it might be read, for Jim the story was an important one, and he recommended it to his correspondents. But critics have not been entirely certain of its artistic success. Margaret Laurence in a 'Commentary' in the *Journal of Canadian Fiction* hedges her bets: she says the story convinces her but adds that it might be questioned that a thirteen-year-old would do what this one did.[18] Ken Mitchell describes it as 'gruesome and gothic,' but says that handling this material proves, 'if nothing else, ... Sinclair Ross's continuing adaptability as a writer.'[19] I had written to ask if this story was meant to be grotesquely comic at some level, a parody of a gothic confessional or detective story. Or was it all to be taken seriously? He replied:

> As to my story *The Flowers That Killed Him*, I hung my head and stood two hours in the corner when your letter came. For yes – horrible confession – I meant it to be taken seriously. I was trying to put across the ambivalence of the boy's feelings towards his father – a dislike of his father which went a long way back, reinforced by a sense of something wrong, unhealthy, together with a kind of pity and loyalty. The way he brought off the 'execution' was a form of loyalty, so no one would know, although you might contend it was to spare himself and his mother as well.
>
> It is salutary to know how far one can be out: I meant the boy's 'flat,' unemotional way of telling the story to suggest a tremendous amount of repressed emotion. There are bits scattered here and there which I thought would serve as chinks through which the light would shine – but it adds up to what I feared when I began: patricide needs a Dostoevsky.[20]

Although he admits the story was meant to be read seriously, in the same letter Jim encourages readers to puzzle over his fiction. He tells of an Ontario university student who was held up for ridicule by his instructor because he had given a 'body-in-the-barn' explanation for the ending of 'One's a Heifer.' The instructor reportedly said she would give zero to anyone else who offered such a reading. '[But] what *was* in the stall?' asks Jim.

In late November of 1972, Jim received a visitor from Canada who would leave a vivid, unpublished account of how he was living in Málaga and of his way of hosting occasional visitors. His guest was Sheila Kieran, a forty-two-year-old writer and television producer from Toronto, a divorced mother of seven, and a close friend of the young film-maker Peter Pearson. Jim agreed to meet with Kieran because Pearson was working on a film version of *As for Me and My House.* He had already met with Pearson's co-producer and was impressed with Pearson's 1969 award-winning National Film Board feature, *The Best Damn Fiddler from Calabogie to Kaladar.* Pearson and his co-producer had hired Margaret Atwood and Graeme Gibson to prepare a screenplay from the novel, and Kate Reid was tentatively signed to play Mrs Bentley. They were in the gruelling process of trying to raise money for the film at the point when Sheila Kieran made her trip to Málaga.

Jim met her at the little airport in the afternoon, where they had Dubonnets before taking a taxi into the city. As the small hotel Jim had suggested proved to be full and it was raining heavily, they went to the nearby Hotel Málaga Palacio, where Sheila was able to get a luxurious room for approximately nine dollars. Later in the evening, she and Jim had dinner together at the hotel, and although Jim was disappointed in the food, the wine was good and Sheila felt that her prim, solitary host had relaxed a little. Next morning in her hotel room, she started writing an account of their meetings in a letter to Pearson in which she relayed what Jim had told her about his family, about the original idea for *As for Me and My House* and the importance of Philip's point of view, his own thoughts on marriage (yes, he sometimes wished he were married and had a son), and about the novel he was working on – 'the thoughts of a man as he lies in a hospital, having been shot by his wife – !'[21] Sheila and Jim met again at eleven o'clock, had lunch at a sidewalk café, and then took the bus together to Torremolinos to shop for suede jackets.

That evening they met a last time for dinner and, over a bottle of Sangre des Torros, 'got slightly and pleasantly smashed together.' During the conversation, Jim expanded further on the story he was writing – how the wounded man was an artist who had gone mad and from his dreams was fashioning a series of pictures titled, in a variation on Goya, 'The Disasters of Peace.' The story was essentially about an artist's paranoia and how society tries to be rid of such people, but he said he had little faith the story would ever get published. Jim mentioned other projects on his mind – the idea of writing Philip's diary and publishing it across the page from his wife's, the story of a small-town doctor on the eve of his retirement, and, in a sequel, the story of the old doctor's successor who comes to town and falls in love with an English war bride who, afraid others will discover their relationship, murders the young doctor. Jim also told her more about his own personal background, including the story of his birth and the midwife who passed out from drinking too much brandy. Towards midnight they went back to Sheila's room at the hotel, where she gave him some books – a copy of Margaret Atwood's newly published *Survival* and the first two volumes of Robertson Davies' Deptford trilogy, *Fifth Business* and *The Manticore.* Jim had read none of these books before. He, in turn, gave her a copy of 'The Flowers That Killed Him.' Sheila insisted they say good-bye at the hotel, that Jim not accompany her to the airport next morning, for privately she was anxious about having misplaced her passport and did not want Jim to be involved or upset should there be a problem next day.

The acquaintanceship that was established in Málaga continued by correspondence for the next six years. The immediate reason for their continuing to write concerned Jim's displeasure with the way he was being treated by McClelland and Stewart, and Sheila had promised to get him legal advice on the matter. When he had signed a contract for *Whir of Gold*, he had made McClelland and Stewart exclusive agents with world rights; he had also given them a first refusal option on his next two works. But he felt the company had made no effort to promote *Whir of Gold*, and when he learned through Alvin Goldman that it took McClelland and Stewart four months to respond to a movie 'bite,' he decided he wanted to change his contract with the company. His one bargaining chip was the copyright to *As for Me and My House*, which he had retained. Although he intensely disliked the abstract cover designs for the New Canadian Library – the latest cover for *As for Me and My House* was suggestive of Toronto City Hall – he decided that he would let McClelland and Stewart continue publishing the novel if the company would rewrite the other contract, giving Jim control of *Whir of Gold* and releasing him from the option on his next books. He was not sure, however, how far he could go, legally, in trying to acquire a new contract.[22] Sheila had sympathized with Jim over dinner and assured him that he was not alone in feeling ill-used by McClelland and Stewart. Back in Toronto, she talked to a number of her friends – Graeme Gibson, Robert Fulford, Ivor Owen (then head of Oxford University Press in Canada) – and also to her lawyer, but they all agreed that it was necessary to see a copy of the contract before solid legal advice could be offered. Jim, however, was reluctant to proceed with his plan and told Sheila in a letter that he was postponing his decision for a month or so.[23] When Sheila wrote on New Year's Eve, 1972, she had some discouraging news of another kind: Wood Gundy had turned down Peter Pearson's request for financial backing for *As for Me and My House*. The project was put on hold until another source of funding could be secured. There was talk about approaching Allan Blakeney's government in Saskatchewan.[24]

Jim's reluctance to involve Sheila Kieran in his relations with McClelland and Stewart was partly his old instinct to keep business matters to himself, but it was also an instinct to protect himself from women who might take control of his life. In Sheila's generous and passionate nature, he seems to have glimpsed the kind of woman he had created in Mrs Bentley, who in turn was someone not unlike his mother. In his letters, his sympathy for Sheila's financial and family problems (including the eventual break in her relationship with Pearson) is at war with his instinct to end the correspondence. Early in 1973, Sheila sent him a parcel of books via Toronto's Book Cellar store. He was appalled at her extravagance, knowing something of her financial plight and her many children, and he wrote to her on 21 March 1973: '... a thoughtful and warm-hearted gesture and I am sincerely grateful. However, you must not – repeat, *you must not* – do it again.' He scolded her for spending money needed for her family, and to emphasize his irritation he said he did not enjoy the one book he had read so far – Brian Moore's *The Revolution Script*. Sheila's letters tried to persuade Jim to come to Toronto and stay at her house (only Peter, and possibly Graeme Gibson, would be there for dinner, she promised), and she tried to see him on one of her trips to Europe. But Jim repeatedly found excuses not to meet again. She continued to send unwanted gifts: a sweater she had knitted for him brought a terse reply – 'I appreciate your generosity but, as I have been trying for some time to intimate, it is misplaced'[25] – and silence for the rest of the year. A bathrobe, nonetheless, followed with the promise of warm socks to come.

Jim continued the correspondence, perhaps because of Kieran's connection with Pearson, whose feature film *Paperback Hero* was shown at Cannes and was widely regarded as the best English-language film to come out of Canada to date. Jim was aware that she carried a bright torch for him, pressing friends to read his fiction, urging her many contacts in the television and publishing industries to think seriously about his work for adaptation. But he also remained sympathetic to women who were caring and emotionally needy, and though he now lived abroad in Málaga, a worldly expatriate, in situations like these he was still a Prairie boy tethered to his mother.

thirteen

Sawbones Memorial
1973–1975

March 1973 saw Jim hard at work on one of the ideas for a novel he had discussed with Sheila Kieran – the story of a Saskatchewan Prairie doctor on the
eve of his retirement. He described the project in a letter to me this way:

> ... what I'm embarked on now is something in the nature of an experiment – at
> least for me ... I'm using very plain material – I'm sure you could call it pure prai-
> rie corn - but it's the method of presenting it which interests me. Dialogue and
> some stream-of-consciousness musings – not a word of connective tissue, not a
> single 'he said' or 'she looked out the window' – nobody introduced, situations
> and characters established by the dialogue. Fairly short – no suspense, of course. I
> don't know, but I see possibilities for exploring a number of situations if I could
> develop the method. Yes, I know – I keep telling myself – sixty-five is not the age
> for experiment – but absurd as it must sound, there are things I would like to say
> and as yet I haven't found the way to say them ... Well, at least it keeps me from
> spending too much time seated with a glass in a sidewalk cafe.[1]

The manuscript would become *Sawbones Memorial,* the first of two novellas
he would write using a dramatic style in which the storyteller disappears altogether. He would later point out that the method was suggested to him by
Claude Mauriac's *Diner en ville,* although he developed it along his own lines
as suited to the western Canadian subject matter.[2] He was excited by the discipline of a new technique, quite the opposite of his expectations a year earlier when he had written to an employee at Macmillan that he no longer felt
'with it,' that at sixty-four he supposed it was 'a bit late to experiment.'[3] He
worked at the manuscript with real interest each morning until it was time for
a late lunch. The writing of a book had never before been so straightforward
or pleasurable.

In late March, Jim took a break from his desk and set out by boat on an eighteen-day trip to Morocco. He had been advised to join a tour group to see North Africa, but his instinct to travel alone, to explore the sexual subculture unnoticed, was still strong, and he made his own hotel and transportation arrangements. He went first to Tangiers and from there took a bus to Rabat and circled inland to Marrakech and Fes. The experience, he wrote to Myrna Kostash, was 'both fascinating and frustrating.'[4] He found it very difficult travelling alone because nearly all the things he wanted to see were in the old quarters, the medinas, and twenty steps inside he would find himself hopelessly lost in the maze of streets and lanes in the pushing, pulling crowds. He had been warned that it was dangerous, that he could easily be mugged and robbed, but what he found particularly difficult, he wrote to Kostash, were the beggars: 'literally by the hundreds, who don't just put out their hand but encircle you, pull at your clothes, and *follow* – there's no escape. Your coins are soon gone – putting your hand in your pocket in fact, is the worse thing you can do, they swoop down like a flock of pigeons – and then it's just a struggle to make your way out.' He found he had to hire guides, but their one concern was to take him to a store where, he guessed, they probably got a 10 per cent commission on what he purchased. He had heard stories of young male prostitutes in Morocco but could not determine at what age they began selling themselves. The boys who approached him for money on the streets were, in his eyes, still children – 'very beautiful,' he wrote to Kostash, 'fine bone structure – I suppose it's typically Arabic – and big black "liquid" eyes,' but they were children nonetheless and he had no interest in them sexually. Rather, he was haunted by their poverty and would recall years later one boy, in particular, who was lame, and who stood begging outside the hotel in Rabat, and how one day when Jim had no coins to give, the boy lurched forward and kicked him in a mixture of rage and despair.[5]

Money for beggars was no insignificant matter to Jim; he was growing ever more concerned about his own dwindling resources and made this a frequent topic in his correspondence. The Canadian dollar was rapidly losing value against the Spanish currency, and the non-resident tax was being raised from 15 per cent to 25 per cent. At the same time, the cost of living in Spain was increasing annually by about 10 per cent. He was beginning to wonder how much longer he could afford to live in Europe, enjoy his apartment on the sea, his half-bottle of wine per day, and the little trips to other parts of Europe that made life abroad so interesting and agreeable. Certainly there was no revenue to speak of from his writing: *Whir of Gold* had sold less than a thousand copies, and his earnings from the New Canadian library editions were just four and a half cents per copy. There were occasional reprint permission fees, and he lived in hope of selling film rights.

His earnings from his writings over the years were so meagre that generally he had not been able to afford to hire a typist. His increased anxiety about his pension providing enough money for him to stay on in Europe persuaded him that even now he should not pay for typing. His financial situation was also one of the reasons he gave in declining the growing number of invitations to read and speak at universities in Canada. These invitations promised to cover costs and offered him a fee (usually a modest honorarium), but when he worked it out, with visits to friends in Toronto and Montreal, and perhaps a side trip to New York, it would cost him considerably more than he would be paid.[6]

Nonetheless the literary boom in Canada interested him a great deal. From among the books that Sheila Kieran had given him, he was especially impressed with those by Robertson Davies and Margaret Atwood. After finishing *Fifth Business* and *The Manticore*, he wrote to Sheila 'I found them brilliant and engrossing and ... I can't wait for the third.'[7] He was amazed but delighted when she told him that Davies still remembered their meeting at Hart House back in 1941 and that he sent warm regards.[8] Atwood's *Survival* thesis struck home and he was immensely gratified to see his own work elevated to such prominence in her book. He was especially taken by her analysis of the passage in *As for Me and My House* where Mrs Bentley spreads out Philip's best drawings and paintings and tries to make him see their worth; he makes a deprecating remark, and she gathers them up and says the exhibition has been closed for lack of an appreciative audience. 'Exactly,' observes Atwood, with reference to that scene, and goes on to make the larger observation that for Canada's artists there was no audience yet in Canada. Atwood had sent him a copy personally inscribed 'with my admiration and that of many readers' and would continue to send him autographed copies of her works for several years. Thereafter he would say of a Canadian book, when he felt it did not meet the mark (Rudy Wiebe's *The Temptations of Big Bear*, for example), that it had lost touch with the 'survival' element at the heart of the country's experience. He liked Atwood's two novels, especially *The Edible Woman* (he thought *Surfacing* less plausible), and he thought her *Journals of Susanna Moodie* very fine poems.[9]

He was, of course, fascinated by everything that was being written about his own work. In two prominent articles, Sandra Djwa gave high praise to *As for Me and My House*, and Laurie Ricou devoted a chapter to the novel in his study of Prairie fiction titled *Vertical Man / Horizontal World* (1973). Much in Ricou's article about the metaphorical merging of external and internal landscapes rang true to his conscious artistic intentions.[10] But he wasn't sure exactly what to think of two essays that had taken a negative view of Mrs Bentley. One by Wilfred Cude made a strong case against Mrs Bentley as a decent woman and reliable narrator; the essay tries to show that Mrs Bentley is unwittingly yet systematically destroying her marriage.[11] The other essay came in the mail from John Moss. It was a manuscript chapter for his forthcoming book, *Patterns of Isolation in English-Canadian Fiction* (1974), in which he describes Mrs Bentley as a dissembler and writes that 'as she is human, she is also fallible, self-indulgent, and sometimes mean.' These readings, in a curious way, made Jim feel he was under attack. In a lengthy letter to Moss, he comes to Mrs Bentley's defence: 'You accuse her of being mean, petty, bitchy, possessive, vicious, waspish – her whimsy acid – and I feel inclined to rear up and say yes, but you, the reader, know these things about her only because *she* tells you ... it seems to me that after a humiliating afternoon it is not surprising she should have an impulse to retaliate – she is very human, neither she nor I pretend she is a saint – and she is honest and big enough to admit her vindictiveness.'[12] This was all something of a reversal. Previously it was Philip who had to be defended, and now he was inclined to argue that he felt sympathy for both of the characters, although in another letter he emphasized that he had a fairly good opinion of Philip: 'So far as I am concerned it is *his* story. I thought it might be effective having her tell it, only she took over. But to me it is his basic decency and honesty which makes him so aloof and sour and difficult.'[13] But he told Moss that, whatever the differing views, he was amazed and gratified, nonetheless, by the attention the book was receiving after the passage of so many years: 'Whatever kind of woman she is, I suppose I can conclude that at least she is very much alive.' He felt shy, however, about phrases like 'cosmic dimensions' being applied to the novel because, as he explained, he had simply been writing a small, ordinary story about two unhappy people without thoughts of cosmic irony or some larger vision. His feeling now was that 'the book ha[d] slipped away from [him] and gone its own way.' More and more the idea of a book having an independent life of its own suited him as a description of authorship.

For the first time in his career, he enjoyed the sense of an audience waiting for his next book. Although he was often puzzled by the responses to *As for Me and My House*, the attention from Canada encouraged him to feel excitement about his new writing project. Except for a short trip to Madrid in June 1973, he stayed in Málaga until the manuscript for *Sawbones* was completed. The summer was hot and muggy, but the work went well until he fell and sprained a thumb and then found typing with one hand almost impossible for a while. However, by October he felt he had made all the revisions he was going to make before showing it to a publisher. He had worked on *Sawbones* barely eight months, a record time for a book-length manuscript. It was the first time he had ever been able to work on a project from its inception without interruption, and he felt excited by the possibilities of the technique he was experimenting with and the free time he had in which to write. The only shadow cast was reflection on his age – sixty-five that year – and diminishing energies. He had read an article in one of the popular periodicals which said at about sixty or sixty-five the human brain starts losing grey cells at the alarming rate of one hundred thousand a day – a sword of Damocles, to be sure.[14] Then, in late October, he set the manuscript aside and made a long-postponed trip to England.

It was his first visit to London since he had been stationed there during the war, and he enjoyed himself thoroughly. In spite of all the changes and reconstructions after the bombing, the city was surprisingly familiar, and if he had consciously forgotten a particular location his feet seemed to know the way. For so late in the year, the weather was good – a couple of foggy days and the rest of the time pale sunshine – and the squares and parks with their plane trees turning yellow seemed especially lovely. It was not, however, a particularly good theatre season, and he went to musical events instead, enjoying Verdi's *Simon Boccanegra* and Strauss's *Elektra* at Covent Gardens. Being in London also gave him an opportunity to see films not shown in Spain, such as *Last Tango in Paris* and *The Devils*. He was especially impressed by *A Clockwork Orange* and its vision of sexual and political anarchy.[15] Jim wrote to Keath Fraser (who had recently left London for a tenure-track job at the University of Calgary) that he departed London feeling he would like to live there, but the cool weather and his back problems made a warm climate much more sensible.[16]

Back in Málaga, he read through the *Sawbones* manuscript once again, was discouraged by its smallness in size and subject matter, but decided to send it off to McClelland and Stewart nonetheless. It was accompanied by a three-page, carefully worded letter to Anna Porter, which describes something of the novel's composition history and technique, and which also discusses contractual conditions he would insist on should the company be willing to publish. He explains how he started *Sawbones* as a break from a lengthy manuscript about a wounded artist ('The Disasters of Peace' manuscript he had described to Sheila Kieran), how he had not taken the new writing very seriously, but found he enjoyed it and kept going until eight months later he had a finished work on his hands. What interested him was the technical experiment:

> The material, I'm afraid, is pure prairie corn, but the 'way' it is done may have possibilities. (You may have to read 10 pages or so before you see what I'm doing.) ... The drawback as I see it ... is that it calls for awfully *good* dialogue. Working on it I discovered how useful are all those little 'He frowned and stubbed his cigarette,' 'A strange light shone in her eyes, part fear, part passion,' how they ease the burden for the writer and help him round the corners.[17]

He is aware, he says, that by taking a leap from Copp Clark's *High School Composition* to stream of consciousness, he may risk coming down with a hard bump; but at least he enjoyed doing it, 'something unusual for me,' and in trying something avant-garde at his age, he amazed himself.

The surprising part of this letter, however, is in the uncharacteristic toughness with which he sets out terms if McClelland and Stewart agree to publish. He insists at the outset on a five-hundred-dollar advance: 'For *Whir of Gold* you gave me no advance whatever.' He also insists on a paperback edition, citing the number of Canadians familiar with his work from high-school and university reading, and demands a guarantee that there will be no changes in the manuscript to bring punctuation, syntax, etc., in line with house standards. He would not agree to McClelland and Stewart as permanent agents for the book, and he sets out elaborate restrictions on their right to publication of future works he might produce. Behind these tersely worded and stringent conditions there is a steely optimism, revealed most clearly when he outlines his plans for future books, which include a sequel to *Sawbones*, two travel books, and three other novels he has been working on, including mention for the first time of a story about the effects of a crime on a small town at the point when the criminal is to be released from jail. In a final paragraph, he gives the company three months in which to make a decision.

He did not have to wait that long. In fact, on January 2, Jack McClelland himself typed what he called 'an interim note' to let Jim know that McClelland and Stewart would very much like to publish *Sawbones Memorial*, that the company had no problem with the conditions he had set down, and that he would soon be hearing from Anna Porter, who was still on Christmas vacation. McClelland had in front of him three readers' reports, and two of these were very positive.[18] Greg Gatenby was excited and 'greatly impressed' by what he had read: 'Ross has produced another major work of fiction and it strikes [me] as nothing short of amazing that a youngster like Ross can venture off into the experimental and make it work so well. Come down with a hard bump hell! He'll be flying high and pretty if there's any justice.' Lily Miller, who had replaced Pamela Fry as senior fiction editor, was equally enthusiastic: 'It is my feeling that this novel is a great achievement for the author, and it also represents growth. He has handled a new style with general confidence and a steady hand.' She had high praise for almost every aspect of the manuscript, and her observations remain sharp and illuminating:

> The dialogue which sustains the work throughout is incisive and sprinkled with wit. The characters are deadly serious, and the wit rises from this: their fierceness to devour, their thirst for gossip, their desperate confrontations. There is very lit-

tle moralizing, yet by penetrating into his characters, giving them flesh and reality, and setting them against critical opposites, the author vividly recreates this small prairie town.

But Miller not only praises Ross's accomplishments, she suggests where transitions and clarifications are needed to help the reader, keeping in mind the challenges that such a style poses. A negative report was submitted by John Newlove, who 'was disappointed in the extreme.' He thought small-town hypocrisy was a tired theme and the writing dull and mechanical, but given Ross's reputation he urged that there be other readings of the manuscript. Jack McClelland appears to have read through the manuscript himself for, on an in-house memo to Linda McKnight, he wrote: 'I think this is a really fine work and have no hesitation in confirming the opinion of those who think we should publish.'[19] His note to Jim concluded with congratulations on a major work: 'You have charted new territory in terms of form and have done so with great skill and accomplishment.'

Jim was extremely happy to have the good news from McClelland – it was the first time he had ever received such enthusiastic praise for a manuscript – but one thing began to bother him, this praise for charting new territory in terms of form. He had, in fact, adapted the idea from a couple of experimental novels by Claude Mauriac, *Diner en ville* and *La Marquise sortit à cinq heures*, which consist of bits of conversation and private thoughts, and he began to worry that he would be exposed as a fraud if McClelland and Stewart offered his book to the public as a bold new technical experiment. So he wrote to Anna Porter and gave a detailed account of how he adapted Mauriac's technique to his Prairie town subject matter.[20] *La Marquise*, he explains, takes place at a street intersection in Paris as if a tape recorder were on the street capturing both voices and thoughts: 'Snippets of talk, of thought; people cross and recross; a couple talk and make love in a hotel bedroom; an old scholar is writing a book about the street; a homosexual dresses up to step out for the evening – you deduce all this, nothing is stated, and for a while you are flipping back desperately to see if you may have missed a clue. I lost interest and decided [with both books] it wasn't worth the effort, but still I said to myself, "Perhaps not a bad way to write a book, only why so difficult, why turn it into a puzzle?"' He had been reading Mauriac around the time the new Royal Bank building was being opened in Montreal in the 1960s, and as he observed visitors, guided tours, and staff from other branches going through the building, admiring and commenting, he thought maybe he could do something in fiction with the opening of a new building which would reveal the ambitions, rivalries, and successes as one era passed to another. The idea lay dormant for years, until he was bogged down in the novel about the wounded artist; then he tried the new form to see if it would work. He started by thinking about the opening of a new school in a small town, and eventually changed the school to a hospital. *Sawbones*, he points out, is different from Mauriac's novels in being straightforward, easy to read, not presented as a complicated puzzle. He doubts a comparison would ever be made, but anxious to be honest, he wants to make his debts known and not be put in the dock for plagiarism. Porter wrote back, amazed by such scrupulousness: 'I keep thinking of the Greek philosopher ... who wandered all over the streets of Athens with a torch in the hopes that he might one day be able to say "behold, there is an honest man."'[21]

In late January, Jim wrote two letters to Anna Porter maintaining his firm business approach to publication. In the first (23 January 1974), he said he would be willing to consider some of the suggestions Lily Miller had made for improving the manuscript, but he could not promise to make all the changes she suggested. What was more important, he would not accept anyone else's changes to what he had written. He did not mention it in the letter, but he was thinking back to the disastrous alterations he was forced to make to *The Well*; he had made up his mind he would not publish a new book if it was going to be butchered by the editors. He said he would return the manuscript by April 15. In the second letter (26 January 1974) he returned to the matter of a paperback edition. In spite of promises, McClelland and Stewart had never brought out a paperback of *Whir of Gold*, and Jim feared the same fate would await *Sawbones* unless he had it written into the contract this time. So he pressed for a clause in the contract that would guarantee by a certain date a paperback edition in the New Canadian Library. He also wanted the contract for McClelland and Stewart changed from 'exclusive' to 'non-exclusive' agents or, alternatively, 'exclusive in Canada and throughout the world for one year from date of publication, and after that non-exclusive.' He could not help dreaming about film or television prospects and wanted to remain in control of copyright.

Porter had no problem reassuring Jim that there would be no interference in the preparation of the manuscript, that he could ignore the suggestions in Miller's report if he chose.[22] The insistence on paperback publication was more problematic.[23] Malcolm Ross was still editor of the New Canadian Library, and his approval would have to be secured before the guarantee of a paperback could be written into the contract. This involved, among other things, a timing problem. McClelland and Stewart were eager to publish *Sawbones* in the fall, but waiting for Malcolm Ross to read and approve it could involve a delay. Jack McClelland was irritated by the matter and sent a memo to Porter: 'As a matter of fact if *Sawbones Memorial* bombs in hardback, I doubt that we will want to do it as a paperback. We have no indication yet that paperback publishing is a cure-all. I'm beginning to think that Sinclair Ross is becoming too bloody difficult. To hell with it.'[24] Porter apparently worded a tactful reply (although her letter has not survived), for Jim refers in a letter of 8 March 1974 to her 'promise' and Jack McClelland's 'word,' but he did not get a contractual guarantee.

After mailing off the manuscript to Porter on March 4, Jim set about catching up on his correspondence. He wrote in high spirits to Myrna Kostash about the good reception for *Sawbones* at McClelland and Stewart. It is a book about Ukrainians and 'don't you dare pan it!'[25] In similar high spirits when writing to me, he quoted from Jack McClelland's letter ('a major accomplishment ... you have charted new territory in terms of form') and ventured to suggest that he may indeed have caught the moment – 1948 in Saskatchewan – when postwar Canadian society was changing. He also thanked me for efforts I had made to find an American publisher to reissue *As for Me and My House*, concluding I must be 'a bit mad and given to biting' to make such an attempt.[26] In a more reflective but still buoyant frame of mind, Jim wrote to Bob Weaver, again quoting from McClelland's letter and admitting that he couldn't get over such a positive response. He feels like xeroxing Jack's letter, he says, and sending out copies saying, 'See what I've done!' But he also talks about a feeling of pointlessness to his life: a bachelor alone at sixty-six (he envies Bob his family) with chronic discomfort from a ruptured disc and a prostate condition, he wonders why he keeps on 'scribbling ... a sort of compulsion, I suppose.' He ironically observes that he must have guardian angels keeping watch to make sure he is not corrupted by success, and lists the number of times a film has '*nearly*' been made from one of his books. Nonetheless, he feels good about all the attention for Canadian writers and repeats again how much pleasure he took in reading new books by Davies and Atwood. Nationalism itself, however, he feels is a step backward and would caution Canadians, anxious to have a literary culture, not to end up beating a drum for the second-rate.[27]

Weaver had written asking Jim if he had any new short stories, and Jim replied that it was the novella length which interested him now. For much of 1974, he was at work on another short dramatic narrative – just dialogue and inner thoughts – not a sequel exactly to *Sawbones*, but a story about the effect on a town of a criminal being released from prison, seven years after the crime. He gave a brief account of the project to Anna Porter in the letter of March 4, predicting that it would be a little longer than *Sawbones* and that he would have it ready to show her in ten to twelve months.[28] The writing that summer seemed to go well – there were few interruptions – but in spite of the careful planning for the story he had done, he could not make the conclusion work. Something in the body of the story had failed to catch fire and propel it to a conclusion, so that he set the manuscript aside, hoping to see his way more clearly later. He wondered in letters to friends if a trip to Canada might not help him get the 'feel' of things he needed to keep working.

The one interruption of note that summer was a visit by William French, who had been sent to do an article on Sinclair Ross for the *Globe and Mail*. Actually, the interview had first been set up by Martin O'Malley, a feature writer at the newspaper with a special interest in Prairie fiction. Jim cautioned him, in a lengthy letter of 27 May 1974, that he would not prove an interesting subject: ' ... all my life I've been a bank clerk and now I'm a retired bank clerk. It's too late to become a scintillating public personality ... I hum and haw and wind up with brilliant remarks such as "Well, I suppose so – I've never given it much thought." ... In other words, you will find me an exasperating, cautious bore.'[29] O'Malley, who was eager to do the story, ignored Jim's prevarications and promised he would focus on Spain and the craft of writing. But just before O'Malley was to set out, his father died and William French was sent instead. As the senior book review editor at the *Globe and Mail*, French brought considerable prestige and importance to the task, which in turn made Jim feel anxious and upset with himself that he had acquiesced to an interview in the first place.[30]

But on July 11 he was at the airport to meet French's plane ('Mr Stanley, I presume') and, after they had taken a taxi into the city and French had checked into the Málaga Palacio Hotel, they went out to a sidewalk café for a drink, 'each probing and taking the measure of the other.'[31] 'I'm not much of a story,' Jim offered apologetically, and French replied that he was glad for an excuse to come to Spain, thinking to himself, 'He's a story all right and a damned good one, but it may take a bit of work.' French could see how wary Jim was, how terribly anxious to protect his privacy. To take the pressure off the interviews, French said he was also in Málaga to gather information for a travel article on the Costa del Sol. This seemed to put Jim more at ease, and the result was four days of exploring Málaga and the surrounding towns and countryside together and a first-rate article on Sinclair Ross for the *Globe and Mail*.

The article filled a whole page in the arts section of the Saturday paper of July 27 and was titled 'Too Good Too Soon, Ross Remains the Elusive Canadian.' The friendly trust that had been established during four days of travelling and talking together is evident in the details French was able to elicit for his article. This was the first time Jim had made public any information about his childhood (his parents' separation, his mother working as a housekeeper) or about his sometimes bitter feelings over the failure of *As for Me and My*

House. He talked with some pride about the attention the novel was currently receiving, and he even confided that the film director Ted Kotcheff, who had recently completed a very successful version of Richler's *The Apprenticeship of Duddy Kravitz*, was now interested in doing a film of *As for Me and My House*. French put it to his readers this way: '[Ross's] misfortune was that the novel was about 30 years ahead of its time. Now it would be immediately hailed as a remarkable achievement; in 1941 there was little critical apparatus in Canada to recognize its worth.' The main working interview took place in Jim's apartment one afternoon, and French worked the new information he had been given into a carefully researched account of Jim's life and career. French describes the plainly furnished apartment, the large number of books and piano recordings. The Spanish flavour of their time together is conveyed by a photograph French took of Jim at the Málaga Palacio Hotel, showing the tiled roofs of the adjacent buildings. Years later, French would remember how extremely courteous Jim was, and also how generous.[32] French had been looking for a department store in which to buy some sherry glasses; the next day when they met, Jim presented him with a half dozen *capitas*, saying he had no use for them. That made French reflect on how isolated Jim seemed to be in Málaga: not only did he not have a telephone, no one dropped by at his apartment, nor did they encounter anyone on the streets whom Jim seemed to know. "I'm a loner by nature," Jim is made to say in the article. After he read French's piece, he wrote to thank him for his 'tactful handling of the elusive Canadian.' Although he had dreaded being interviewed, he would look back thereafter on the visit from William French with pleasure and no small degree of satisfaction. Certainly, French's article was the widest public exposure he ever received during his career.

For Jim, the word 'elusive' in the title of William French's article had only one significant reference – and that was 'best-seller.' He still dreamed of writing a book that would interest and entertain a large audience, and, given the success of Canadian writers like Laurence, Atwood, Davies, and Richler, he dared hope once again that he might still pull it off, fulfilling his mother's and uncle's definition of what constituted a writer. He didn't really have such hopes for *Sawbones*, but perhaps the 'next' one ... He wrote to Myrna Kostash in August that he was reading some current best-sellers that had been translated into Spanish – books like *The Exorcist*, *The Godfather*, *The Day of the Jackel*, *The Odessa File*. It gave him good practice with the language, he said, but also: 'I rather think when you're trying to write yourself it's worth something to know what best-seller material is and how it's handled ... It's all very well to sniff and be superior but try and do it. I wish I could.'[33] He thought *The Day of the Jackel* was in fact a fine piece of suspense writing; it had him on the edge of his chair. But he was also continuing to read Lorca, who, to his taste, was the finest poet of all.

In mid-September he went to Paris for a couple of weeks but did not find it 'simpatica,' much preferring Madrid, Rome, and London.[34] On his return to Málaga in October, he took up the released criminal manuscript and tried again to push it to a satisfying conclusion, but the manuscript was becoming increasingly problematic. The following year, he wrote Kostash that it was a problem of tone. He explained it this way: 'The trouble was that the crime was serious, did a lot of damage, and my tone was becoming small-town comedy. The same thing messes up movies sometimes. I remember particularly Divorce Italian Style – hilarious most of the way, but then he kills her, and murder's not funny ...'[35]

Sawbones was published in October 1974, and it marked the only time in his career when Sinclair Ross was in the literary limelight. McClelland and Stewart gave the novel a good promotion, describing it as a major experimental fiction from one of the country's senior writers. For the initial run, 5,500 hardback copies were printed, and a striking jacket was designed for the cover – a photo of golden wheat and black sky, almost an abstract to fit Philip Bentley's definition of good art. With wide margins and generous section divisions, the book only ran to 140 pages, but as Jim wrote to Anna Porter after receiving his copies, 'it pleases both hand and eye.'[36] Robert Weaver read a piece from the novel on the CBC, and since Jim was unwilling to go on a promotional tour, McClelland and Stewart took pains to get some of the country's most influential literary figures to review the book.[37] Without exception, reviews from the likes of Margaret Atwood, Margaret Laurence, George Woodcock, and William French were overwhelmingly positive. It seemed that more than thirty years of relative neglect were being swept aside in an accolade of affection and respect for one of Canada's best writers.

The reviews were indeed generous and there were dozens of them. Fortunately a piece written for Southam News Services and syndicated in newspapers across the country was one of the most positive. The reviewer, Dave Billington, wrote that amid the din of the nationalist drums there was a soft, subtle voice speaking that was genuinely Canadian, that Sinclair Ross's new book was a gem.[38] Positive reactions to the book, however, were often diametrically opposed in describing the effect of the novel. Many viewed it as principally satire, as a work of angry social criticism. William French in the Globe and Mail wrote that 'Ross is superb at portraying small town prairie life, with all its prejudices, boredom, and malicious gossip,'[39] and Linda Sandler in the Toronto Star wrote that 'as the party unfolds the town awakens with vicious life.'[40] Jamie Portman in the Calgary Herald Magazine called the novel an impressive achievement and commended Ross for not wanting us to mourn or eulogize the Prairie community of the past: 'He is saying such communities were the scenes of terrible cruelties – a fact of day-to-day existence.' In Portman's eyes, *Sawbones Memorial* was an indictment of the sordid, destructive prejudices of small-town life.[41] Dorothy Bishop, in the *Ottawa Journal*, called it a 'prairie Peyton Place.'[42] But, in the very opposite vein, some reviewers, like George Melnyk in the *Edmonton Journal*, referred to it as 'a work of quiet nostalgia,'[43] and Karen Mulhallen in *Books in Canada* referred to 'its broad and gentle humour, its genial intelligence.'[44] In keeping with her own view of the Prairie past, Margaret Laurence in Montreal's *Gazette* saw it both ways: she wrote that 'the characters of the novel not only form the archetypal prairie town but, in their hypocrisy and cruelty and incredible generosity and open heartedness, they represent all humanity – the world seen in microcosm.' Laurence also wrote that 'the prairies of the thirties and forties are Sinclair Ross's time and place, and he has got it exactly right.'[45]

There was some praise for the novel's experimental form. Mulhallen in *Books in Canada* is especially interesting in this light because she likened the book to chamber music, in which characters are disembodied from space and time by the form, and she put *Sawbones Memorial* in the company of Faulkner's *As I Lay Dying*, Woolf's *The Waves*, and Sheila Watson's *The Double Hook*. She called it a 'rich, brilliant, and penetrating book ... a celebration.' Mulhallen also raised the issue of the new novel's status in relation to *As for Me and My House*, asserting that 'the greatest Canadian novel' award will now have to be shifted from *As for Me and My House* to *Sawbones Memorial*. Mulhallen was not alone in this opinion: George Woodcock, in *Maclean's*, and Margaret Atwood, on CBC Radio, both believed that the new novel was superior to his earlier work.[46] Atwood's review was prepared for *Sunday Supplement*, and she sent Jim a copy in the mail. (He had sent her an autographed copy in exchange for *Survival*.) She liked the form of the novel, calling it 'a remarkable achievement ... a *tour de force* ... not a word or cliché out of place ... an impeccable sense of timing.' To her it was 'a novel condensed [to the] essence of novel.' Like William French and Jamie Portman, she believed that 'few writers have shown so clearly the destructiveness of petty-minded malice, and the glee people experience in the face of the misfortune of others.' Unlike most reviewers, Atwood identified an overarching theme to the story – that of 'the nature of human evil and the evil of human nature, and the possibility of overcoming both, though in a very limited and imperfect way.' Atwood's accompanying letter to Jim continued with praise for *Sawbones*; she said the margins of her review copy were sprinkled with words like WOW, ZAP, and RIGHT, and she suggested that the 'Ladies Auxiliary' lady should be made required reading for all ladies auxiliaries. What especially pleased Jim in her letter was mention of the book's humour, which he felt was never fully appreciated by his readers. On an undated card he sent in reply, Jim wrote that her letter and review were 'the Christmas gift of my life. Feel I could step off the balcony, 12 floors up, and go right on walking all the way to Africa ...'[47]

There were, of course, a few negative reviews. Unfortunately these appeared in places where Jim had lived and still had connections. The review in Regina's *Leader-Post*, which would have been read by old school friends and by his sister's family, faulted the book for its style, arguing that readers shouldn't have to work so hard to figure out what was going on in a book. The reviewer judged the dialogue to be 'stilted and unbelievable' and the exposition of pio- neer times in Saskatchewan superficial.[48] Peter Cummings, in the *Montreal Star*, described *Sawbones* as an opaque book, difficult to read; 'one tends to get lost in the jumble of characters,' he says, none of which are sufficiently devel- oped and, except for Doc Hunter, are all 'too nasty to merit any sympathy.'[49] And the review that appeared in *Queen's Quarterly*, where Jim had such important associations, was also negative. There David Williams argued that it is really Nick Miller's story and leaving him off-stage dissipates the novel's force. Williams also pointed to 'awkward, rambling, artificial dialogue.'[50] But it was the review in the *Ottawa Citizen* that Jim found most disappointing and hurtful. It seemed to go out of its way to say negative things and reawakened all his insecurities as a writer. It consisted of the criticisms he had anticipated himself in periods when he had lost self-confidence in the project: a tedious novel ... a fragmented, unsatisfactory style ... sophomoric humour ... stereo- typed characters. The reviewer concluded that *Sawbones* should serve as a warning to other writers: '... it isn't enough to set your novel in a small Cana- dian town. It's advisable to have something new to say and the perception to say it.'[51] In typical, self-deprecating fashion, Jim referred to this review more than once in letters to friends.[52]

But the overwhelming majority of notices were positive, and Jim's feelings of accomplishment and well-being are evident in the letters he wrote for Christmas. He shows himself to be anxious about his old friends and con- cerned about their good opinion of him. (He confessed also, in a rare admis- sion, to expatriate Christmas blues.[53]) He wrote to Doris Saunders in Winnipeg, hoping she hadn't been offended when William French said in the *Globe and Mail* that there had been no local interest when *As for Me and My House* was published: '... in case you saw the article I would like to know that those were [French's] words, not mine, for remembering you and Roy and Miss Preston, how promptly you responded and how loyal you remained, I know how unfair they are.'[54] One of the reviews that had greatly pleased him appeared in the *Winnipeg Free Press* and was written by Roy St George Stubbs. Jim and Roy had lost touch with each other after Jim moved to Montreal, but Jim renewed the friendship with a Christmas card on which he wrote: 'Your review of *Sawbones Memorial* ... has given me a tremendous lift. There's no one whose good opinion of my efforts could please me more.'[55] Stubbs's review, titled 'Ross Redivivus,' rehearsed the story of the sensitive writer and the indifferent Canadian public, then went on to praise the new book highly, calling it vintage Ross – the book he had been waiting thirty-three years for. He urged his readers to each buy a copy and not lend it, so that there would be substantial sales and the kind of encouragement that Ross needed to do the best work that remained in him.[56] Stubbs's review echoed his *Saturday Night* article published back in 1941, and Jim was deeply grateful to hear his voice raised on his behalf once again. In his Christmas letter, Jim said he might be in Canada in the spring – as far west as Saskatchewan – and if so, he hoped they could see each other. He wrote to another old friend in Winnipeg, but this occasion was a sorrowful one. He had learned at Christmas that Audrey (O'Kelly) and David Peterkin's son had died, had committed suicide, and he wrote a two-page letter of sympathy to his grieving friend. In its understatement, the letter is eloquent in conveying deep, genuine feelings; he concluded by saying that 'trying to feel and understand what it must be like I find myself helpless and silent. I can only hope that your family in their need of you has helped you carry on and that now you can see your way ... I will write again.'[57] Audrey treasured the letter.

The good opinion of *Sawbones Memorial* expressed by reviewers and friends has stood the test of time. In the two novels between *As for Me and My House* and *Sawbones Memorial*, Jim had not found quite the right form or voice to give economical and compelling shape to his material. *The Well* and *Whir of Gold* are both conventional, realistic narratives that lumber slowly towards a dramatic climax. Although they contain good scenes, especially *Whir of Gold*, the style has somehow gone slack, unstrung, and their effects are considerably diminished. But the experimental dramatic form of *Sawbones*, with something like the classical unities of time and place, gives point and precision to every word in the book. The townspeople of Upward, Saskatchewan, are gathered at a party to say farewell to Doc Hunter, who is retiring after forty-five years of practice in the area, and to mark the opening of the new district hospital. The book consists of conversation among the townspeople during the evening, interspersed with memories in stream-of-consciousness form as various characters reflect alone for a moment on the past and their relationship to the doctor. As Jim frequently pointed out in his correspondence there is no connective tissue, no 'he said' or 'she smiled.' The narrative structure is the party itself, as it moves naturally to the point in the evening when refreshments are served, speeches made, and the doctor is presented with a watch to honour his retirement. The form is both organic and fragmented, yet dramatic tension is created as memories and viewpoints fall together to form a mosaic of the community and its past. The form is beautifully economical, for through its juxtapositions of fragments it suggests a whole without being at pains to describe it. Indeed, one of the central characters in the book is Nick, the new doctor and former town outcast, but he is not present at the party.

But for contemporary readers, an important appeal of *Sawbones Memorial* is that it engages us in what might loosely be described as postcolonial reasoning, for in this novel, as in *As for Me and My House*, we are forcefully reminded that there were people living in small Prairie towns who were outside the colonial, Anglo-Saxon mainstream – people from Eastern Europe, from China, as well as Aboriginal inhabitants. Jim's memories of the Myketiak brothers at the Rolling Prairie school, of the Hunchiak family in Abbey, of Wong Dong and Happy Dong in Arcola, inform this novel in important ways, although the fictional characters that might be said to embody them are, significantly, all kept off-stage; none of them – neither Nick and his Ukrainian-born parents, nor the Chinese Canadians with the confused, comic-book names, are present at the party. Marilyn Rose has shown, nonetheless, what an important part these people 'outside of history' play in Ross's fiction, how their presence and their difference interrogate the power structures portrayed in the novels, revealing the bigotry and hypocrisy of a small town.[58] Perhaps the best example of this is the fact that Doc Hunter fathers a secret heir for his practice by his Ukrainian housekeeper, Anna. Indeed, despite a matrix of English-speaking Prairie farmers and townspeople, Ross's writings, like that of contemporary fictions in the twenty-first century, are host to ethnic and racial minorities – to strangers, migrants, and mixed households.

Equally of interest in *Sawbones Memorial* is the portrayal of the gay pianist, Benny Fox, to whom Jim gave some of his own experiences – those of the boy growing up without a father, the boy made by his mother to dress differently from other boys, the boy who dreams of a career as a musician. Benny Fox has not escaped the prejudices and constraints of the small town; he lives on in Upward, playing the piano at gatherings like Doc Hunter's retirement party, a colourful, flamboyant figure, but a social misfit in a homophobic society enduring all the affects of shame. Benny and Nick (whose Ukrainian name has been changed to Miller) have been victims of bullying. Only Doc Hunter views Benny with tolerance and compassion, which inform the larger view of human nature he conveys in his 'thank you' speech near the end of the book.

Like an elder Mark Twain, the doctor berates his fellows: why, he asks, do people allow their innate goodness, visible during crises, to dissipate into everyday spite, gossip, and jealousy?

> 'A family doctor sees a lot of what's going on behind the scenes, and one of the things that has always impressed me is the enormous amount of sympathy and goodwill that springs up the moment someone is in trouble. When there's illness or death, the neighbours rush to help. No second thoughts – one question only: what can we do? They look after the children, bring food, wash clothes, sit up at night ... But then the trouble passes, the household gets reorganized, and this little burst of spontaneous kindness, instead of helping to establish new relationships, make the town an easier, happier place to live in, sputters out in the old bitterness and spite.' (128–9)

Doc Hunter continues by exhorting his listeners to set aside their ethnic bigotry and show sympathy and friendliness towards the new doctor (the 'hunky kid,' his secret son) who will be replacing him. This speech by the doctor would also turn out to be Sinclair Ross's farewell to his reading public, a simple, practical plea for tolerance and kindness.

As 1975 began, Jim was guardedly optimistic in letters to friends about the books he might yet write. He had set aside the manuscript about crime in a small town and had begun a sequel to *Sawbones Memorial*. He also had in mind a couple of 'travel' books about Greece and Spain done in the same dialogue manner as *Sawbones*. He described the main idea for these books in a letter to Myrna Kostash: 'an excursion bus visits an archeological site and the passengers talk, dull passengers chattering about food and bargains, scholarly ones discussing archeology, history, others arguing about current problems, etc. etc.'[59] In a letter to Roy St George Stubbs, he expanded on the idea, designating Crete as an especially evocative setting, where democracy, ancient and modern, could be discussed and argued by the more thoughtful travellers. Blurring the genre boundaries between fiction and travel writing seemed to have enormous possibilities in his mind, although he had to keep reminding himself that he was sixty-seven years old and probably didn't have that much time left in which to write.[60]

The sequel to *Sawbones* was titled 'Price above Rubies' (from the Book of Proverbs, 31.10: 'a virtuous woman ... her price [is] above rubies') and was in fact a story that Jim had had 'knocking around in [his] head for years.'[61] Indeed, in a letter to Grant Macdonald, as far back as 16 February 1949, he says he is thinking about a story of a sensitive young doctor, Ukrainian perhaps, cruelly mistreated in his youth, who returns to practise in his home town. He has an affair with the English wife of one of his tormentors, not so much out of love for her, as hatred for her husband. But there is no revenge or satisfaction unless the husband knows, and sensing this compulsion in her lover, the English wife in a panic kills the doctor.[62] In a letter to Anna Porter of 4 March 1974, Jim expanded on the idea for this novella:

> Probably 20/22 years later [than *Sawbones*]; the occasion, Sarah's death. Robbie, now a medical student and, to his father's chagrin, something of a hippy, not really interested in medicine, comes home for the funeral – just at the Easter break – and insensitively brings a friend – which would serve me, however, as a good way to recapitulate. He tells his friend the old stories as they filtered down to him as a child, his mother, Nick, the murder – and they both speculate. Someone at the funeral watches Caroline, poised and still beautiful, and remembers the day she saw her running up the street, screaming and spattered with blood, her dress half torn off. While Caroline recalls what really happened and the role old Sarah played in the subsequent years; while poor Duncan in his honest, not very bright way, tries again to understand; while Nellie, still sharp and shrewd, ponders the pieces and tries to arrange them; while Stanley – married now and a farmer (Duncan hurried up the marriage at the same time he 'banished' Benny) – wonders what part he and Benny may have played etc. etc. This way Nick, the most important character, would never appear on stage – throwing drama away probably; on the other hand, hovering in the background, he might be more of a 'presence.'

The question of method was still unresolved in Jim's mind, although he was leaning again to the method he used in *Sawbones*. He wrote to Porter in the same letter: 'I [have not] decided yet how to do it. A straightforward "linear" narration would be the easier way – Caroline as I now know her is articulate, sensitive and alert, and would make a good narrator; but I think it might be better, certainly more modern, broken up with the pieces laid around the reader.'

In a letter to me, written 13 November 1974, he said the original title, which he still liked, was 'Sport of Wanton Boys,' adapted from *King Lear* ('As flies to wanton boys, so are we to the gods. They kill us for their sport'). Its timeless reference seemed reinforced when he saw the film of *A Clockwork Orange*. But when he tried the title on friends, they were not very enthusiastic; accordingly, he came up with the biblical title referring to a woman's virtue which, he wrote, 'gives you a fair idea who's up to what with whom.' Yet, he adds, he hasn't given up on the original title and wonders if the two novellas might some day be brought out in one volume – two parts, *Sawbones* and *Rubies* – under the title 'Sport of Wanton Boys.' In a letter to Margaret Laurence of 14 April 1975, he explains that Robbie, like Nick, has also been bullied, which was a way of bringing the 'wanton boys' theme forward another generation. The tormenting of Robbie as a boy is another form of revenge on Duncan, one of Nick's tormentors. Jim was interested in analysing the phenomenon of bullying, which from the sidelines he had viewed with much anxiety while growing up. As a small boy on the Holden farm, he had been bullied by the Brack brothers and had learned thereafter to disappear into a crowd for self-protection. But, from the sidelines, he felt anguish for those who were victimized, whether for their size, race, or some suggestion of sexual difference. He came to understand that the tormentors were often themselves insecure, that it was a chain reaction, often involving 'sins of the fathers,' as with Duncan Gillespie and his son Robbie. Being in the army provided another vivid reminder of this unhappy aspect of human nature, and both of the war stories he published made bullying a central theme. In 'Jug and Bottle,' it led to suicide; in 'Price above Rubies,' it was to have led to murder.

Because the new story involved murder, Jim found himself in need of information regarding Canadian legal procedures. He wrote to Roy St George Stubbs, asking for legal advice and explaining the situation this way: '... a woman kills a man who assaults her – presumably attempted rape ... I want her to get off – a woman defending her honour. Under Canadian law is that possible, or, if not, what would the minimum sentence probably be?'[63] He had other questions: Where would such a trial be held in Saskatchewan, in the district courthouse or in Regina? Would bail be possible for manslaughter? If not, would the woman in custody be able to keep her child with her while waiting for trial? He was anxious to have the details correct in accordance with legal practice in 1948, the time of the murder.

He was also anxious to have correct information about the education system in Saskatchewan in the late 1960s, the time present of the novel. Would Robbie most likely study medicine in Saskatoon or Regina? Would the student's year end at Easter? Would there be examinations before the Easter break? How long is the Easter break? Would a twenty-one-year-old student, a fairly bright boy, be in third-year medicine? For answers to these questions, he wrote to writer and teacher Ken Mitchell, at the University of Regina, who had initiated a correspondence with Jim the year before.[64]

Mitchell had a passionate interest in Jim's writing and, while living for a period with his in-laws in Greece, had tried to arrange to meet Jim while he was in the Mediterranean. The meeting had not taken place, but a lively correspondence ensued, in which the two writers exchanged books and ideas about writing. Mitchell would become one of Sinclair Ross's most vocal champions and would write a valuable guide to his work. Like Margaret Laurence, he felt Ross had made Prairie writing possible for those who followed. Mitchell asked Mrs Pat Krause, who was working at the University of Saskatchewan College of Medicine, to search out and forward answers to Jim's questions. Mrs Krause was in fact a close friend of Jim's niece, Irene Gibson, Effie's daughter, and had tried, unsuccessfully, to visit Jim while she was on a holiday in Spain earlier that year. She was an aspiring writer herself and was more than happy to look up the information Jim needed. Like Sheila Kieran, she wrote Jim generous, long letters for the next few years, which included an invitation to be the 1976 guest writer at the Saskatchewan Summer School of the Arts at Fort San in the Qu'Appelle Valley.[65] Jim declined for the usual reasons – 'no experience,' 'a mumbler,' 'at 67 too late to start over' – insisting, however, that it was not because he was unsociable: 'I usually get along well with 3 or 4, but with a group, or in the presence of a tape recorder, I freeze ... I know, you say relaxed and informal, but I would worry and be edgy just the same.'[66] While she was waiting to hear from Jim, Krause wrote to the manager of marketing services at the Royal Bank in Regina, asking if the bank would put up money for a bursary to sponsor a promising Saskatchewan writer to attend the summer school at Fort San. It would be called the Royal Bank Sinclair Ross Bursary, and she outlined the reasons for giving it in Jim's name. She sent two of Jim's novels with the letter, but she did not have a reply until nearly three years later, when the manager wrote to say the letter had been misplaced, the request did not fit their guidelines, etc.[67]

The information he received from both Stubbs and Krause was critical; he had in fact made some errors in plotting out the school year for a Saskatchewan medical student and had to revise parts of the manuscript accordingly. He had told several of his correspondents during the previous year that in spring 1975 he would likely make a trip to Canada, a 'refresher course,' as he put it, in order to get information and continue writing. He was also pondering the possibility of a visit to the University of Calgary, whose head librarian, prodded by Keath Fraser, was expressing interest in purchasing any manuscripts Jim might be willing to sell. But he was now explaining that the trip was postponed, partly for reasons of health, and because the economic and political situation in Spain might necessitate his returning to live in Canada permanently once again.[68] So instead of the trip to Canada, he visited Amsterdam, which he enjoyed thoroughly. He wrote to Myrna Kostash that the weather had been wet and chilly, but he had seen the Rembrandts and Van Goghs, heard four concerts in the Concertgebauw, and indulged in all the good food – the famous Indonesian dishes, grilled salmon, and Dutch apple pie with raisins and whipped cream.[69] And to another he wrote about Amsterdam's famous sex shops, and his amusement over the banality of photographs and displays of artificial sex organs. It had been a good two weeks.[70]

But 1975 was not without frustrations and disappointments. Work on 'Price above Rubies' did not go as smoothly as it had with *Sawbones*. The gathering of the family for Sarah's funeral lacked the sharp focus for dialogue and recollections that the farewell party for Doc Hunter had provided. Robbie's storytelling to his university friend frequently excluded the other characters from the stage; there were awkward transitions. And, as he wrote to Roy St George Stubbs, there was a problem for someone his age 'getting inside a 20/21-year-old, seeing things his way and understanding his tie-ups.'[71] In addition, it was a story with a plot (the killing of Nick Miller), but the central action was more than twenty years in the past. Perhaps it was too stale; perhaps it was only lurid melodrama in the first place, with no possible public appeal.

But perhaps even more demoralizing was the fact that public interest in Sinclair Ross seemed to be quickly waning again. In a letter to Alvin Goldman, as early as 11 March 1975, he was reporting that sales for *Sawbones* were very disappointing; even with the boost of the Christmas trade, only about 2,500 copies had been sold, not even half of the print run. He was beginning to have doubts that McClelland and Stewart would make good on their word to bring out a paperback edition. During the previous fall, with so much public enthusiasm for *Sawbones* in the *Globe and Mail* and on the CBC, there had been talk of a Governor General's Award for Ross (the smart money was on Ross for *Sawbones Memorial* reported *Books in Canada*), but the award went instead to Margaret Laurence (her second) for *The Diviners*. It was William French's opinion that the failure of *Sawbones* to sell in any quantity and to win prizes was the result of Ross's refusal to do a publicity tour in Canada – to read in public, sign books, and appear on television. But that was a price higher than Jim was willing to pay.[72]

A Governor General's Award for *Sawbones* would have given him a boost (in 1941 it had gone to Alan Sullivan's now long forgotten *Three Came to Ville Marie*), but there was no question in Jim's mind that *The Diviners* was the more important book and deserved the prize that year. He had written a letter of sincere and hearty congratulations to Margaret, 5 February 1975, praising such a 'big' book and singling out her presentation of Jules Tonnerre – 'the hard, strong, wild streak [in him], contrasting with the pathetic compromises to survive.' He particularly liked the way she presented Jules's death: 'I thought it was especially fine the way [Morag] slipped out while he was still sleeping and left him to die alone. I don't know how it would be in real life, but I was so glad she respected the Indian in him and didn't hover over the ignominy of his death, humiliating him with kindness.'[73] In this observation, Jim seemed to be thinking of women, like his mother, like Mrs Bentley, and like so many of those who befriended him, who, wanting badly to be needed, smothered men with their love and attention. He had also been reading Maria Campbell's *Halfbreed*, which was set in familiar regions of northern Saskatchewan, and which moved him deeply with its account of the plight of Canada's Native people.

In a subsequent letter to Laurence of 14 April 1975, Jim revealed another one of his long-standing anxieties – finances. His old dream of making a little money from his writing had been quickened once again by the positive reception of *Sawbones*, but sales had quickly brought him back to reality. When he wrote to Laurence, he asked that in the future she not refer disparagingly in print to his forty-three years with the Royal Bank because he feared they might cut off his pension. He realized it was not likely they would do so, but the bank had been his bread and butter all his life, he says, and he did not want to be an embarrassment to his former employer.[74] In the meantime, strangely enough, Sheila Kieran was introducing herself by letter to Margaret Laurence, trying to muster her support to help persuade 'the Molson people' to award Jim their annual prize of fifteen thousand dollars: 'I fume at the idea that Ross will be well-praised when he is safely entombed when there are forms of richly-deserved recognition available now.'[75] But nothing came of Kieran's efforts, and the award that year, ironically, went to Laurence. Later that same year, Laurence wrote to Jim and suggested he apply for a short-term Canada Council grant which would provide him with funding to travel to Canada to help him write the sequel to *Sawbones Memorial*, but Jim rejected the idea, saying the sequel was written and pretty well revised. In fact, accepting money for work not done was still foreign to Jim's way of thinking, and he would continue to reject similar suggestions in the future. It was also a matter of pride. He wrote with some asperity: 'Your letter sounds, Margaret, as if what you call "the Canadian literary community" is concerned about me, and that is the last thing I want. I have my pension to live on, comfortably enough, and to get in some travelling. I'm getting along fine; nobody owes me anything. If I haven't "made it" as a writer, I have only myself to blame ... well-wishers such as you can't make it for me.'[76] The correspondence with Laurence appears to have ended with this letter, until she wrote three years later and raised the matter of a Canada Council award once again.

Although Jim was not mentioned in the Governor General's Award list there were honours of a kind proffered in 1975. In a letter to Roy St George Stubbs, he reports that the library at the University of Calgary had written with an offer to purchase his manuscripts. He says he is going to wait first to see what comes of 'Price above Rubies' before making a decision, although of course he threw out the manuscript for *As for Me and My House* years ago, 'never dreaming that a pile of scribbled-over old papers might one day be worth something.'[77] He had enjoyed a second visit with the Frasers that summer and they agreed he should wait for a good price. In the fall, he received a letter from the president of the University of Regina, asking if he would accept an honorary doctor of laws from that institution at their spring convocation. Jim declined the award, saying the honour would rest uneasily on his shoulders ('I am not a professional writer and never will be'), but that the good opinion of the people of Saskatchewan was just the tonic he needed to get along with his work on 'Price above Rubies.'[78] About the same time, John Moss wrote proposing a two-day symposium at Sir George Williams University in Montreal. He wanted to know if Jim would make an appearance at the symposium. Jim wrote back to say he was overwhelmed by the generosity of Moss's suggestion, but he declined the invitation, asking instead that Moss do him a different kind of favour – by writing to McClelland and Stewart and urging they bring out a paperback of *Sawbones*.[79] Success in Jim's eyes was still measured according to publication royalties and movie rights, not academic interest, although chance of the former had pretty much dwindled away. He had acquired a curious status, that of a failed writer held in high public esteem. It was not wholly satisfying.

fourteen

Literary Forefather
1975–1982

As for my writing career – butterflies would have been more fun. – JSR in conversation

The 'don't feel sorry for me' letter to Margaret Laurence and the silence that ensued mark Jim's gradual withdrawal from Canada's literary establishment. The poor sales for *Sawbones Memorial*, its failure to make the Governor General's Award list, and the problems he was having with 'Price above Rubies' were eroding what self-confidence he had accumulated during the last couple of years. Given his repeated failure to win a popular audience for his work, he was increasingly glad that he had remained with the bank and could now enjoy the security of his pension. In a letter to Ken Mitchell, who was tempted to give up the security of his university position, Jim reviewed the financial rewards of his career – $25 for 'A Field of Wheat,' $270 advance for *As for Me and My House*, over the years about $3,000 for the latter in the New Canadian Library – and he said he felt that pretty well explained why he stayed with the bank forty-three years. The decision was not without regrets: 'If I had cut loose I might have developed and made a good living as a writer; writing the sort of things I do, however, it's doubtful.' But he was pretty much resigned now to having, in his opinion, failed as a writer: '... what is done is done. I didn't make it and that's that.'[1]

His refusal to appear at the symposium being proposed by John Moss was explained in the same way and reflects his disappointment in both himself and his career: he won't attend, he writes, because 'apart from being a colourless old man with a poor voice who would not help things along, I don't measure up. A two-day symposium in my honour, everybody saying what a fine writer I am, while all the time, in what we might say "practical terms," I am such a dud! *Sawbones Memorial,* despite a number of favorable reviews, has sold 2,600 copies; *Whir of Gold,* 1,100. I have never been translated; apart from 3 short stories on TV, I have never been filmed. I'm not complaining; I have my own reservations about Ross; but what I would hear in Montreal, with the "facts" of my literary career staring me in my face, would have a hollow ring.' He adds that the work on the sequel to *Sawbones* has not gone well: 'I'm ready to call it a day and for the rest of the time left me try to relax and enjoy myself. Some make it, some don't. There's no use pretending. At least I can give myself an A for effort.'[2]

'Retirement,' however, had its compensations. His letters in the mid-1970s reveal two sources of pleasure beyond the day-to-day routine – his continued travels around Europe, and his correspondence with (and occasional visits from) teachers, students, and young writers. In the Málaga sunshine, the day-to-day routine was itself pleasurable enough: coffee and a newspaper on the seafront in the morning, a stretch of time at his desk, then a late lunch, an afternoon of reading or attending to correspondence, then a walk into the centre of Málaga for an evening meal. If there were concerts in the little city, they provided a welcome diversion; otherwise, he enjoyed the recordings he had collected in his apartment. For good theatre, concerts, and museums, however, he had to travel, and while he lived in Spain, he revisited the country's chief cities, especially Madrid, Toledo, and Barcelona.[3]

But he was also enjoying his role as mentor to young teachers and writers, taking that role to heart especially in relation to writers from western Canada like Ken Mitchell, Keath Fraser, and Andrew Suknaski. To each of them, he was a literary forefather whose struggle to be a writer in such barren times was both daunting and awe-inspiring. Jim liked to share his experiences when his young friends seemed to need advice or encouragement. He wrote to Ken Mitchell: 'As to the novel you're having trouble with – my own experience is that when there's a bit that doesn't seem right, that worries you, the best thing to do is cut ruthlessly; and if it's a chapter or scene that's necessary, re-write ... if something isn't *basically* right in its structure or psychology or probability, no amount of doctoring, no changes in the writing or atmosphere, will help. And I think it's for the author to decide – to trust "the feeling in his bones."'[4] In that same letter, he talks about the novels he has recently abandoned – the one about 'Disasters of Peace,' and the one about the effect of a crime on a small town – saying that when he has finished 'Rubies,' he will look them over again, because in both there are things that he likes and, being a thrifty old Scotsman, he might use the good things in another manuscript. That in fact describes something of the composition history of *Whir of Gold,* where writing from as far back as the 1940s was used in a novel published in 1970. Mitchell asked if he had ever actually thrown a manuscript away, and Jim replied that he would be ashamed to say how many, adding that in his experience if something didn't feel right, it was better to get rid of it rather than spend time and nervous energy tinkering with it. But ever modest and self-effacing, he says to Mitchell, 'My record as a writer being such a dismal one, I shouldn't take it on myself to give counsel.'[5] What Jim envied in his correspondent was youthful energy, which sometimes made him feel that any advice he might give was too cautious, the anxious mutterings of an uncertain old man.

He also warmed to the energy he felt in the letters he received from Saskatchewan poet Andrew Suknaski and envied what he perceived to be Suknaski's outgoing nature: 'I – always tied in knots – think how fortunate you are – giving yourself, seeking and accepting contacts without reserve.'[6] Jim thought highly of Suknaski's work and recommended it to others; he wrote to Roy St George Stubbs: 'I don't know anything about poetry but to me he is a fine, authentic voice';[7] and to Myrna Kostash, he wrote with uncharacteristic enthusiasm: '... his poems have so much drama in them, characters who are so real.'[8] Suknaski told Jim that As for Me and My House and the short stories were a major influence on his writing,[9] and Jim, in turn, paid close attention to Suknaski's poems, singling out individual lines for praise. He liked the anecdotal 'Wood Mountain' poems but was especially drawn to the longer family narratives in which he would have recognized a story not unlike his own. In 'Homestead,' Suknaski presents himself as the youngest son in a family brutally divided by his father's violent temper. He urged Andy to try writing a novel with this material, or a series of novels – a family chronicle – for, as he had said to Myrna Kostash and repeated to Andy, he has always felt 'that a great epic or saga is to come from the New Canadians ... from someone on the inside.'[10]

But in addition to the mentor relation, Jim seemed to cultivate a tender personal feeling for Suknaski. He wanted to see him succeed and sent him money for a second, signed, copy of Wood Mountain Poems; and in a sympathetic letter, he gave him a disarmingly open account of his own youthful vulnerability and his marginal relation to the artistic community:

> Yes, Andy, I know what you mean about certain people wearing masks. And how I know! When I was young there wasn't much of the coyote about me ... you start out starry-eyed, wanting to trust everybody ... The smart boys spot you as an easy mark and you get taken so often you begin to be suspicious of everyone. I've never mixed much with the 'literary crowd' and while it must be interesting and sometimes stimulating to rub shoulders with the good ones, I imagine there's a lot of bitchiness and friction too. Artists and writers are a thin-skinned lot, I sup-

pose that's the trouble. I'm sure I miss a lot but, especially at my age, I'm just as well to be out of things.[11]

He also seemed to take vicarious pleasure in hearing about the young poet's energetic undertakings – his publishing enterprise (he was bringing out a series of chapbooks), his travels, Canada Council grants, fishing trips, summer work at a Lake Louise hotel. It seemed like the carefree life he never had when he was a young man under his mother's watchful eye, and he wrote: 'I hope the trip to Toronto is successful and that you have a good summer in the mountains. Fishing equipment, sketchbook and a guitar – sounds wonderful.'[12] And they both liked Goya.

With both Ken Mitchell and Keath Fraser, Jim shared his troubles over the 'Price above Rubies' manuscript. He had completed the first draft by September 1975 and then launched into what he anticipated would be the 'long-drawn misery of revision.'[13] By end of December, he reported to Mitchell that the revisions were done, a good final copy had been typed, but he had misgivings: 'Readable, I think, but I wonder if it gets anywhere ... [about] a mixed-up 21-year-old and what the hell do I, nearly 68, know about today's youth and their problems.'[14] To Keath Fraser he wrote that the first draft of a manuscript was always the easiest in his experience – he let himself dream a little at that stage. The moment of truth came when he started the revisions and he was forced to realize how bad the manuscript was. He suspected, he said, that for most writers the big problem was not the manuscript as a whole, but difficult bits that never come right. He wished Keath every success in trying to write a novel.[15] He put his own manuscript aside for a couple of months, but when he looked at it again in early March, he felt it needed more work and spent several months rearranging and rewriting parts of the story, his enthusiasm for the project overshadowed by his doubt that McClelland and Stewart would be interested after the poor sales for *Sawbones*. By the end of July 1976, he had sent it off to the publishers, writing to Mitchell that he no longer knew what to think of it: 'Talk about taking risks ... It's short, crowded, and yet somehow seems sketchy, and all the talk talk talk – a lot of it is inevitably shallow.'[16]

In the meantime he had spent most of May in Greece, his first trip back since moving to Spain five years before. He admitted to Mitchell that he was still thinking he would like to write a book about Greece, although the amount of work involved was daunting. He reported a good month in that country, although everywhere seemed more crowded than he remembered, but what was particularly memorable was witnessing a two-day general strike in Athens which turned ugly and resulted in a death and some injuries. Jim ventured out to see what was happening in the streets and was quickly caught

up in the middle of it. He described for Mitchell what he called scenes of desolation: 'armoured cars, rubbish burning, barricades of billboards, oil drums,
etc. squads of police charging with their nightsticks – and using them – stones
and broken tiles flying; one of the damned teargas cannisters went twitching
and hissing inches from my feet, and as I wrote a friend on my return, you
should have seen me take to my 68-year-old legs and hightail it around the
first corner.'[17] Strangely, a similar scene repeated itself in Barcelona, where
he spent a few days in July. They left a powerful impression on him to which
he returned in his thoughts for years, epitomizing no doubt the fragile nature
of the social order as glimpsed from old age.

Jim's correspondence with Ken Mitchell accelerated in 1976 when Mitchell wrote to explain that he had proposed to McClelland and Stewart a short
book about Sinclair Ross for their Canadian Writers series. Since McClelland
and Stewart expressed interest, he hoped that Jim would give the project his
blessings. He also wrote that if Jim had reservations, he (Mitchell) would let
the project pass by, preferring their friendship and the possibility of meeting
some day.[18] Jim, in fact, was pleased with the suggestion and said he was willing to cooperate by answering questions, but he told both Mitchell and an
editor at McClelland and Stewart that he wanted to reserve the option of seeing the manuscript before its publication.[19] He had read Mitchell's proposal
to the publisher and felt his assessment of *Whir of Gold* was a little harsh, but
conceded of course that Mitchell had a right to his interpretation. Mitchell
wanted to travel to Spain at once to discuss the project with Jim in person,
but had no luck persuading McClelland and Stewart to pay the air fare. In
October of that year, he wrote to tell Jim he had recently been in Arcola in
connection with the filming of W.O. Mitchell's *Who Has Seen the Wind* and
had accidentally discovered that Jim once lived in the town. He gave Jim an
account of the house where he had once lived and told about the church and
manse which, he wrote, 'must have been the model for the house in *As for Me
and My House*'; but Jim wrote back, 'Wrong church, wrong house,' insisting
that Horizon was not patterned after Arcola.[20] He did not go on, however, to
tell him about Abbey, or give any other biographical information that Mitchell might use. He was growing wary.

That same summer, he received another letter from a teacher-scholar who
was engaged in writing a book about him. Lorraine McMullen of the University of Ottawa had a contract to write about Sinclair Ross for the Twayne
World Authors Series, and she wrote asking for information about his reading
and the books that had especially influenced him. Jim wrote back to say he was
delighted to hear someone was writing a book about him and provided
McMullen with a carefully considered list of the books and writers that
seemed important to him in retrospect. He began by saying, however, that

'influence' was a difficult matter to be precise about, that he supposed 'without our knowing it, we are influenced by everything we read.' He started reading when he was seven, he says, and was still reading, but adds: 'I can truthfully say I have never been a "disciple" of anyone. I have often been impressed by a book or author, but it has been my way to wish I could do it and pass on.' The list with commentary that he compiled for McMullen was long, beginning with the *Boy's Own* annual and the Tarzan books he was reading at ages nine and ten and concluding with his current passion for South American writers, particularly Garciá Márquez, whom he was reading in the original Spanish. The list between includes Tolstoy and Dostoevsky, Faulkner and Hemingway, and a period of reading French authors, including Sartre, Camus, Gide, Malraux, and François Mauriac (he observes how he finds it strange that someone from Saskatchewan with a Scottish-Presbyterian background should respond to the dark torments of Mauriac's Catholic world). He had mentioned Hardy in the taped interview for OISE, specifically *The Return of the Native*; what moved him, he says to McMullen, was not so much the story as the sombre mood Hardy created and the presence of the landscape in the novel. As for Canadian fiction, he had to admit he still didn't know Grove's work; he had tried to read *The Master of the Mill*, but he didn't like the style and hadn't pursued Grove any further. The one Canadian novel from the earlier period which had really impressed him was Ostenso's *Wild Geese*. In conclusion, he apologized to McMullen for his vagueness regarding influences but assured her that if she came to Spain, he would be very happy to meet and talk with her.[21]

In early 1977, Ken Mitchell and Lorraine McMullen both managed to spend time in Málaga. Mitchell arrived in February and made only a couple of pages of notes, which reflected Jim's reluctance to provide any very specific information about the small towns in which he had lived. He preferred to talk about his time in London during the war, 'the best four years of my life,' and about difficulties he had encountered over the years in getting his work published. Jim felt somewhat overwhelmed by Mitchell's 'ebullient personality' and uneasy about the research he was doing into his past.[22] Because Mitchell had made contact with his niece, Irene Gibson, he was afraid the confusion and shame of his family's past might be served up to the public at large. He confided in a letter to Keath Fraser that he hadn't been very cooperative with Mitchell.[23] He felt more relaxed with Lorraine McMullen, a reserved and soft-spoken woman, who was prepared to accept the formal, simplified account of his life and career which he had typed up in advance of her arrival. A bond of trust developed naturally between author and scholar, for McMullen was at every turn respectful of Jim's wish for privacy. As an instance, he had made clear how ill at ease he was around a tape recorder, and she had deferred to his feelings by setting it aside. McMullen was staying at Fuengirola on the outskirts of Málaga for two weeks, and Jim went out by bus several times to her hotel to have conversations, the gist of which became chapter 1 in her Twayne study. He described her to Keath Fraser as a 'warm, friendly woman' and said he enjoyed working with her on the book because she consulted him on what should be included and what omitted;[24] in letters, he made corrections and suggestions, and both were satisfied with the manuscript by the time it went to press. A few years later, he would say to Ken Mitchell that if he seemed to unbosom himself more to McMullen, it was probably because she was 'a good listener.'[25]

But before Mitchell and McMullen had arrived to do their interviews, Jim had received another blow to his pride as a writer. After keeping the 'Price above Rubies' manuscript for five months, McClelland and Stewart returned it with a flat rejection – 'not a single good word.'[26] He wrote to Doris Saunders and Roy St George Stubbs that the editors feel he is 'on the wrong track,' that he should try again, and that accordingly he was tempted to forget the whole thing, except that 'the characters keep "nagging."'[27] That spring he was suffering with infected sinuses and made up his mind to set the manuscript aside until he was feeling better.

Jim's low spirits, however, were roused again by continuing evidence of interest in his work. The year before there had been a dramatization of *Sawbones* on CBC radio, and in December 1976 CBC television had offered $1,000 for the rights to make a film of *As for Me and My House*. Jim replied, raising the price to $1,500.[28] He learned through Lorraine McMullen that McClelland and Stewart was finally bringing out a New Canadian Library paperback edition of *Sawbones* (she was writing the introduction); the University of Nebraska Press was bringing out *As for Me and My House* in their Bison paperback series (it was a 'confirmation,' he wrote, to be back in the United States);[29] and several of his short stories were being reprinted in the growing number of anthologies of Canadian writing. He also received a generous invitation that year from Rudy Wiebe (another admirer) to serve as writer-in-residence at the University of Alberta. He declined with the usual reasons of age, health problems, and lack of education, but, sensible to the honour of the invitation, he expanded a little further, stating that he felt he was no longer 'with it,' that he would probably fail to respond to the work of young writers who were doing experimental things. 'The zany and the far-out and the surrealistic,' he wrote to Wiebe, 'are probably an expression of our far-out world and deserve sympathetic consideration ... but now, alas, there are too many days when I am a short-sighted, impatient old grouch.'[30] Jim in part was thinking about his negative response to the novels by Wiebe himself. He found the much-praised *Temptations of Big Bear* a difficult, unrewarding book, and later that year he would put aside *The Scorched-Wood People* – a book about Riel no less – again finding Wiebe edifying but unreadable.[31]

Film interest in *As for Me and My House* was not without complications. Alvin Goldman, who had done much of the groundwork to interest the CBC in a production, wanted to write the script and asked Jim to make that stipulation in any contract he signed. But Jim was afraid that giving Goldman exclusive rights to the script might mean that potential producers (with their own writers) would stay clear of the project, and so he felt he had to say no to his friend's request. In the letter refusing Goldman, Jim referred to the several failures to make a film from his novel and speculated on some of the problems in the book itself, providing perhaps the clearest analysis he was ever to give of Philip Bentley:

> I rather think that *As for Me* ... is not good film material, especially today, with the pictures getting sexier and more violent. To a considerable extent, Philip is the trouble. In the book he's 'there,' brooding in the background, a presence making himself felt, but bring him onstage and he's a stick. Important: his hypocrisy is the motor which runs the book, the gnaw and anguish of having to live with himself as a liar and fraud when by nature he is frank and honest – he's in a trap – but to make telling drama from his tight-lipped silences would take an awfully good director and an awfully good actor. And if his anguish is not revealed he is just a miserable bastard who needs a good boot up his ass.[32]

Later Jim would report to Goldman that someone in England was interested in making a film, but it was still at the discussion stage and he no longer had his hopes up: 'So many have nibbled and swum away I can't believe anything will happen.'[33]

That year Jim was also asked if he would contribute an essay to *Canadian Fiction Magazine*, describing what it was like to be a writer in Canada in the 1940s and 1950s who had to make his living at a bank. Geoff Hancock was putting together a special issue on Mavis Gallant, and the latter had suggested that Hancock solicit Jim's views on what it was like trying to get published in Canada, since she had always sought markets for her own writing elsewhere. Jim was faintly insulted by the request: it seemed to imply that he could give a good account of what it was like to be a failure; moreover, Jim was not the subject of the special issue himself. He declined to write the article that Hancock suggested, saying he never thought of himself as an author who had to work in a bank, but as a bank clerk trying to do a little writing on the side. He gave Hancock an account of how little he made on selling his fiction in the 1930s and 1940s, but said he did not blame Canada – the problem was with the kind of story he wrote. There were good markets in the United States and Canada, he said, 'but what could *Chatelaine* or *The Grain Growers Guide* – or, for that matter, *Sat. Evening Post* – do with a story like "The Painted Door"?' He added, ironically, that perhaps he had received too much encouragement: '... the occasional word of approval kept me going, and I understand now I might have had a better, more satisfying life if I had put writing behind me as something that I wasn't up to and given my time to other things.'[34] The asperity of this observation can also be felt in a letter to Ken Mitchell in which he questions Mitchell's need to interview him again. If the book he is writing is a sixty- or seventy-page critical appraisal of his work for the Canadian Writers series, why does he need to meet with him – a typed-up list of questions for him to answer by mail would be better. If Mitchell and his family do arrive in Málaga, he will agree to two 'working lunches' and no more.[35] In a subsequent letter, he adds that he can't help feeling Mitchell's 'research' – two trips to Spain – is out of all proportion to the work in hand – a literary essay. Moreover, he writes, Mitchell's visit to his niece in Saskatchewan has made him suspicious of his intentions.[36]

In 1977 he enjoyed a return trip to Greece in June, but looking back in a letter to Myrna Kostash, he admits it has been 'a disappointing year. I suppose the real villain in the piece is old age as I'll be 70 in January.' But discouragement over his writing was also a factor: 'The sequel to *Sawbones* hasn't worked out, although I haven't given up yet. For my own satisfaction I think I'll *finish* it the best I can and then perhaps get on with something else.'[37] He just wished he was twenty years younger and could be part of all the creative activity in Canada. He was reading Atwood, Richler, Moore, and Engel, among others, but he was frankly puzzled at times by their success. He wrote to Doris Saunders that while he enjoyed Atwood's *Lady Oracle*, he had no idea what it was about, and that the same was true for Brian Moore's *The Great Victorian Collection*: 'Everybody is so terribly clever these days.'[38] He was even more puzzled, however, by the success of Engel's *Bear*, which had won the Governor General's Award – a disappointing book, in his opinion, because the main character, the woman, was 'ordinary' and should have been exceptional to evoke the mythical and magical dimensions of the theme. He also found the writing flat where perhaps it should have been 'poetical, incantatory, to lift the material a little.'[39] He admitted it was perhaps a case of sour old age on his part, yet he continued to be excited by the South American writers – García Márquez, Vargas Llosa, and Cortázar – especially García Márquez's *A Hundred Years of Solitude* and the more difficult *Autumn of the Patriarch* – 'an amazing performance,' in his opinion.[40]

Jim made a few last references to work on 'Price above Rubies' in letters to me and to Lorraine McMullen in late 1977 and early 1978. To me he wrote that it was an inept novel and McClelland and Stewart was right to turn it down, but nonetheless he was working on it again to see if he couldn't 'whip it into shape.' He wondered if the father-and-son relationship (Duncan Gillespie and twenty-one-year-old Robbie) might not be one of the places where he went wrong in the manuscript. But he added that 'despite my disparaging comments I still have a sneaking, stubborn feeling that there are the *makings* of a good novel in it. A matter of treatment, the right touch.'[41] To McMullen he wrote less optimistically on 15 January 1978: 'I'm working away at *Price Above Rubies* and discovering how bad I am.' He was feeling especially constrained, he said, by the all-dialogue method, the absence of description and atmospheric touches. 'At least, however, it's moving, slowly,' he reported, and reckoned that 'in a couple of months I should know whether to persist a little longer or put it away as an old man's folly.'[42] On February 5 he said to McMullen he wished the sequel to *Sawbones* was shaping up better,[43] and after that he remained silent on the subject. In later years, he said he destroyed it, along with most of his unpublished manuscripts, when he returned from Spain to Canada. The failure of the project left its mark. When McMullen asked if he had ever thought of writing an autobiography, he replied ruefully that he had indeed thought about one with the title 'Butterflies Would Have Been More Fun.'[44]

The year 1978 was pretty much uneventful, except for another trip to Greece. This time he went partly to visit with Greek friends (a couple working in Saudi Arabia and home for the holidays in Athens) and partly to check on inflation. He still toyed with the idea of returning to live in Greece again. He set out mid-July: 'a stupid time to go,' he wrote to Ken Mitchell. 'Hot and terribly crowded, hard to get reservations so I spent most of the time in Crete.'[45] The days in Crete were quiet and enjoyable, but he arrived back in Málaga feeling he was growing too old to travel, 'blistered and beat and vowing never again.'[46]

When Jim returned to his apartment in mid-August there was a letter waiting for him dated July 31 and signed by twenty of Canada's leading authors, including Margaret Laurence, Adele Wiseman, Timothy Findley, Margaret Atwood, Gabrielle Roy, Alice Munro, W.O. Mitchell, Mordecai Richler, and Robert Kroetsch. Their letter asked for Jim's permission to put his name forward for a special Canada Council grant in the Senior Arts Award category: 'We would like to be able to apply from time to time on behalf of a writer whom we feel has made an outstanding contribution to the literature of our country, for an award which would express at least in some way our gratitude for this contribution.' The letter was very flattering: '... in searching for an ideal candidate your name was the obvious choice ... You have made an enormous contribution to Canadian literature, both in your own writing and through the fact that you have been mentor (whether you realized it or not) to so many of us.'[47] But it was not a straightforward award; it was an application for one, and although the authors of the letter said they would do the paperwork and obtain letters of reference, Jim would have to complete the application forms. Nor was the award certain: 'With your name we think we have the best possible chance of success ...'

The roster of signatures was impressive, overwhelmingly so, and in the first letter he drafted (to Margaret Laurence, since her name and address were at the top of the letter), Jim said how pleased and gratified he was to be nominated by his peers for an award. But in this draft, dated 21 August 1978, he confessed to being somewhat confused: was this 'an out-and-out award, recognition for what I have already written,' or would it involve a commitment on his part to researching and writing another book? He asked Laurence for a clarification. Before sending this letter, however, he changed his mind and wrote later that same day a very different letter. He thanked Laurence for the interest and concern of his fellow writers, but said he would have to decline the offer. In what he himself described as a 'churlish' letter, he wrote:

> If the Canada Council were to extend its program to cover out-and-out awards for books already written, that is to say, for recognition, not aid, and if my name were brought forward and approved by the Selection Board, then surely an announcement would be made, a cheque mailed, and that would be it. There would be no question of references, paper work or forms to sign. I have read and re-read your letter, and every time it comes out the same: in effect I would be applying for financial aid ...[48]

Jim's pride had been hurt, and he pointed out to Laurence, as he had done three years before, that he had his pension from the Royal Bank and his living was assured. As far as writing was concerned: 'Not one damned thing stands between my typewriter and a best-selling G.G. winner but *me*. I know – poor old Ross and Mrs Bentley, we've been around such a long time and never had a G.G. – but whose fault is that? The last thing we want is Canada's writing community to feel under an obligation to arrange something by way of compensation for all those dust storms and Russian thistles.' This would have been his last letter to Laurence, but he received a letter from Timothy Findley written August 26 saying the selection committee had not yet heard from him, and so he wrote to Laurence again, this time in a more genial temper. His letter of August 21, he said, 'might have been worded more tactfully, but a re-write would not change anything essential. Sorry, I know your heart's in the right place. Just write me off as an old you-know-what.' This letter, dated 15 September, brought their correspondence to a close. He knew how ungrateful and antisocial his letters sounded and imagined his peers dismissing him as an old crank. In this low mood, he felt his writing career added up to very little and whether he wrote anything again or not made little difference.

But Jim continued to receive proof that his writing did make a difference. At a wide-reaching conference on Canadian fiction in Calgary that year, *As for Me and My House* was voted the third 'most important' novel in the country, after *The Stone Angel* and *Fifth Business*. *Sawbones Memorial* appeared in the NCL in late 1978, with an introduction that pleased him by Lorraine McMullen, and in January 1979 he received a letter from Luc Jutras of the Canada Council to say that *As for Me and My House* had been selected for translation and publication in French. Except for the radio story 'Spike,' this was the first time any of his work had been translated into French, and he was pleased at the announcement. The novel would be translated by Louis-Bertrand Raymond and published by Montreal's Les Editions Fides in 1981 with the title *Au service du Seigneur*.[49]

He was equally pleased to have in hand the Bison edition of *As for Me and My House* and wrote to me to say he was happy with both the introduction and the physical appearance of the book, with the photo of a blistered railway station on the cover.[50] He also wrote to the director of the University of Nebraska 'The book itself is attractive – easy to read and handle, with a fascinating cover – and needless to say what a satisfaction it is for me to have it return to the United States after an absence of nearly forty years.'[51] But Jim was being cautious about the novel's commercial possibilities. He had received a clipping from a Lincoln newspaper saying the publication of *As for Me and My House* was a 'coup' for University of Nebraska Press, and McClelland and Stewart reported a good notice in *Publisher's Weekly*, but he wrote to me that he was 'playing safe and expecting nothing'; he just hoped it would do well enough to justify Nebraska's faith in it.[52] Significant money for his work continued to elude him. He wrote to Lorraine McMullen: 'Somebody is interested in doing a film, English; somebody else, American. Talk, talk, but of course nobody will put up the money for such a drab, no-violence story. I wish they wouldn't tease me. It's happened several times.'[53] Thinking about money for his work reminded him again of how his mother had shaken her head one day and said: 'Why don't you write something cheerful that people will read?'[54] That opinion now seemed wholly reasonable.

Jim had almost no Canadian contacts in Málaga, only visitors, and in the previous eight years he had made very few Spanish friends. An interesting exception was a friendship with the elderly Spanish poet Jorge Guillén, who lived in the same apartment building with his wife and daughter. Jim had no previous knowledge of Guillén and by accident made the acquaintance of his middle-aged daughter when they were both making their way home on the Paseo Maritimo after a movie. She told Jim something about her father and invited him to visit at their apartment. Guillén was eighty-six and very frail, but he was interested to meet Jim because during his many years of exile from Spain he had lived for one year in Montreal, teaching at McGill during 1939–40. For his part, Jim was interested in Guillén because he had known García Lorca and could tell Jim stories of the poet whom he continued to regard as one of the world's finest writers. They exchanged signed copies of their work, and Guillén said he found *As for Me and My House* very interesting. Jim enjoyed his casual afternoon conversations with the old man but was less comfortable on formal occasions when there were literary gatherings in Guillén's apartment. He was invited to Guillén's eighty-sixth birthday party, where there was much talk of Spanish literature and the artists' struggles during the Civil War. These were self-conscious national literary events, and the apartment block where Jim and the poet lived would eventually host a plaque recording Guillén's residence there. Jim wrote to Lorraine McMullen that knowing Guillén 'makes me feel terribly small-time ...'[55]

The only Canadians Jim knew who were living in Málaga permanently were Doug Tunstell and his partner, Dallas Thorston. Jim had known Doug as far back as Winnipeg when he first met him at the student gatherings hosted by Roy Daniells. Jim was intimidated by Thorston, who had a Ph.D. from Harvard and a broad knowledge of the arts, but he enjoyed sharing the occasional lunch or dinner with the two men and meeting them for drinks in their large apartment overlooking Málaga Bay. Invariably they had news of mutual friends in Canada and interesting stories to tell from their frequent travels. At times, Jim envied them their comfortable life together, yet he could not himself imagine living as a couple with another man – his social instincts were too conventional, but even stronger at this point was his need to live alone. The youthful dream of finding the perfect friend had died long ago; the older he grew, the stronger the instinct to live alone became. He told himself that it was also the necessary condition for writing – loneliness and the desire to communicate being for him the fundamental equation.

But being alone was growing more difficult. The year 1979 was a sharp turning point in Jim's life in a negative way, for that year his health would markedly deteriorate and he would eventually be diagnosed as suffering from Parkinson's disease. In a letter to McMullen of 30 March 1979, he reported 'health problems all winter; feeling better now but still taking drugs and visiting the doctor. Want to go to Madrid and Barcelona but keep putting off till I see how things are going ...' Then in a letter to Ken Mitchell, dated 28 June 1979, in which he inquires sympathetically after the health of Ken's Greek wife (she was suffering with cancer), he describes the first visible signs of his own malady: 'I had a jar myself a few months ago – a trembling hand – which of course isn't good – and for a while I just stopped, a sort of this-is-it attitude, but I now see things differently. I've seen 2 doctors and their diagnoses conflict to some extent, but both seem to think there's a straight stretch ahead of me.' But an accurate diagnosis was slow in coming. In September he wrote to Alvin Goldman that he was suffering from vascular sclerosis, which was the reason his hand trembled. The doctor had put him on a strict diet – no coffee, tea, or wine, no salt and as little animal fat as possible – and had prescribed 'enormous quantities of pills' with the promise that he would be back to normal in two or three months. But Jim described for Alvin another more sinister experience: 'There was a terrifying month when I felt my mind slipping ... couldn't remember simple Spanish words, couldn't concentrate on a book for five minutes.'[56] But this classic symptom of Parkinson's disease still did not alert the doctor to his condition. It wasn't until he saw a neurologist late in the year that he was told he had Parkinson's disease and what he should expect for the future. He wrote to Alvin Goldman on 5 February 1980:

> I feel *fairly* well. I'm on a drug which is pretty well controlling the tremor in my hand, but I tire easily. I probably told you earlier I had vascular sclerosis, but all three doctors I saw were wrong; which is to say that for five or six months I was taking drugs which were of no help and in fact gave me headaches and nausea. My problem is Parkinson's disease. It's something you don't die of – so I believe – but you never recover from it either. The neurologist I'm seeing now assures me I won't lose my mind, although in ten years I may be somewhat forgetful. (God bless him!) Exercise, keep active and I should remain *fairly* well – all the time, of course, taking my pills.

The description of his condition was accurate as far as it went, but it omitted the more severe psychological disturbances that frequently accompany Parkinson's disease – that is, depression and paranoia. There is evidence of this beginning for Jim as early as the letter to Ken Mitchell written 28 June 1979, in which he describes his increasing anxiety over his financial situation and the state of affairs in Spain and the world generally. He writes of political unrest, strikes and bombings, and of meeting an intelligent university graduate who was a right-wing fanatic, a potential terrorist who 'scared the daylights out of me.' He also writes that the people of Spain are changing, the old courtesies disappearing and rudeness becoming a commonplace in restaurants and hotels. Illness and an overwhelming sense of insecurity determined that he should return to Canada, and so, much as he dreaded Canadian winters, he made arrangements to vacate his apartment in Málaga and fly back to Montreal at the end of March.

In the letter to Alvin Goldman written 5 February 1980, he outlined his plans for the move. He would have Iberia Airlines reserve him a room for a couple of nights at the Laurentian Hotel in Montreal while he looked for temporary lodgings in one of the rooming houses on Sherbrooke Street. From that base, he would look for an apartment in the McGill area where he used to live and then arrange to see doctors about an examination and prescriptions for drugs. The Goldmans wrote back and urged Jim to stay with them while he was getting settled in Montreal, but Jim declined their hospitality. '[M]y health being as it is, I think I had better say no. I tire easily, and when I'm out apartment hunting I may last only half an hour or so and then need to lie down and rest. So being near a bed, relatively near, is important.'[57] He did ask the Goldmans, however, to do him two favours. He would be sending his books – fourteen or fifteen cartons of them – care of their address, if they didn't mind, though he would pick them up from the post office himself. In addition, he asked Dorothy, Alvin's wife, if she would make an appointment for him to see a neurologist in the city, sometime after April 7. He warned them that when he telephoned after his arrival in Montreal they might not recognize his voice; when he was tired, Parkinson's caused him to stutter.

He had written to Ken Mitchell in January and said that he was dreading the move, but his illness had forced him to take stock and the best course seemed to be to return to Canada. He hoped to be able to look after himself for a little while longer but knew that an institution was likely in the future.[58] In March he wrote Ken again, saying his hand trembles, he loses his voice, and he staggers when walking: '... frequently I just want to lie down and turn my face to the wall.'[59] Moreover, the medication he was taking had side effects such as itchy lumps on his skin like insect bites. His hope was that doctors in Montreal could find a combination of drugs that would work for him; since he was leaving Málaga at the end of March, the Spanish doctors were not working any further on his case. In the meantime, he was sorting out and packing his things, taking it very slowly, discarding as much as he could. He had never lived as long in the same apartment building before and there was an accumulation. He invited Doug Tunstell to come by and see if there were any books he wanted among those he was discarding. In a deeply pessimistic frame of mind, Jim threw out the manuscripts for all but one of his uncompleted writing projects.[60]

In the same mood, he tried to bring most of his correspondence to an end, telling his friends it was exceedingly difficult to type or write now that he had Parkinson's disease. He continued to receive letters of interest and admiration for his work and requests to give readings. Glen Sorestad, poet and high-school teacher in Saskatoon, wrote a long letter trying to persuade Jim, as a lierary forefather, to take part in the province's seventy-fifth Anniversary celebrations; specifically he hoped Jim would agree to meet with high-school students in the province in the spring of 1980.[61] There was also a request from Philip Nixon to do a filmed interview for TV Ontario. Nixon's letter was full of high praise, ranking Jim's work in the short-story genre with that of de Maupassant and Hemingway.[62] There was a first letter of admiration from David Carpenter, who identified himself as a bachelor and fiction writer from Saskatchewan; he thought of Jim as his spiritual uncle, he said, and hoped to arrange a meeting if he got to Spain in the spring.[63] And there was a long letter from Lloyd Person in Regina, who offered Jim his home for the summer if he came to Saskatchewan.[64] To all these letters, which he kept and brought back with him to Canada, Jim sent a polite thanks for the writer's interest but explained that Parkinson's disease prevented him from accepting invitations or having company. He explained too that writing a letter was often taxing beyond his means.

But he continued to write to Ken Mitchell, who had such enthusiasm for his work and whose wife remained seriously ill. Indeed, from the vantage point of his own illness, Jim wrote with great sympathy over Roula's plight. Surgery and chemotherapy during the next two years failed to halt the progress of her disease, and she died in the summer of 1982. In the meantime, Mitchell was having trouble with the monograph he had written on Sinclair Ross: McClelland and Stewart had decided against any more titles in their Canadian Writers series, and so he had turned to a small house in Saskatchewan, Coteau Books, publishers of poetry chiefly, and found them interested in doing a textbook. They wanted, however, to embellish Mitchell's critical reading of the Ross canon with a chronology of his life, a bibliography, some photographs of the author, and a manuscript of an early story ('The Painted Door' was a preference) to be reproduced as a facsimile at the back of the book.[65] Jim supplied Mitchell with a bibliography and a few pictures (including a 1941 newspaper review of As for Me and My House that carried his photo), but he said he had no short-story manuscripts – he had always destroyed them as soon as the story was in print. Further, he flatly refused an interview, saying that nervousness made his Parkinson's symptoms worse, that he was unable to concentrate and lost his voice.[66] Mitchell was willing to forego the interview but pressed for a manuscript, even for a carbon copy of something recent, such as 'The Flowers

That Killed Him' or *Sawbones Memorial*. When he was packing for the move, Jim came upon the manuscript for the short story 'Spike,' which had not yet been published in English, and eventually sent it off to Regina.

The move to Montreal went according to plan at the beginning of April 1980, but it left Jim exhausted. To add to his misery, he could not get an appointment with a neurologist until May 20 and had to continue with the dubious medication prescribed by the doctor in Málaga. He wrote to Ken Mitchell in May that 'Parkinson's disease doesn't kill you but there are days when I think it's a pity it doesn't. No pain but always tired ...'[67] Apartment hunting had been an ordeal, and after finally choosing one on Durocher Street, he found it an intolerable place in which to live; it was just one room plus an alcove for his bed, cramped and dark, with a view of fire escapes – the very opposite of his light and airy rooms looking out on the sea in Málaga. After two months, he was able to exchange it for a brighter apartment in the same building, where he felt less hemmed in. When he finally did see a doctor, he was disappointed to learn that the prescription for drugs he was taking could not be improved.

Cheering him up was a letter from Ken Mitchell, dated July 31, inquiring about stage rights to *Sawbones Memorial*; there was a possiblity, Mitchell wrote, that he might be asked to adapt it for a Northern Lights Theatre production in Edmonton. Jim explained somewhat ruefully in reply that McClelland and Stewart had dropped *Sawbones* from their list, but as they were his agents nonetheless and held subsidiary rights, the theatre company would have to go through them.[68] Jim was extremely pleased with the thought of a stage production of *Sawbones* and tried to foster this project as best he could: he took the unusual step of writing to Lorene Wilson, who managed subsidiary rights at McClelland and Stewart, urging the publishers to be financially easy with the young theatre company,[69] and he wrote to Frank Moher, the literary manager at Northern Lights, saying that if the McClelland and Stewart fee is steep, to let him know – 'we'll work something out. *Strictly confidential.*'[70]

But the play, titled 'The Hunter Memorial,' would be cursed with the same kind of bad luck that attended so many of Jim's writing projects. Ken Mitchell was exceptionally enthusiastic. He wrote to Jim that he would swear it was the best play he had ever written, pointing out that of course the dialogue was brilliant – that was a given – but his part was to create a dramatic structure for the stage, and he felt he had done this by making the play a kind of Prairie *Our Town*, with the character of Benny Fox on stage almost the whole time, providing a musical counterpoint to the conversations.[71] There was a workshop for the play in early May of 1982 in Edmonton, overshadowed for Mitchell by his wife's final illness; from there it was to have been transferred to the Lennoxville Festival in the summer. It was Mitchell's brightest wish to have Jim in attendance – even if 'disguised as a Trappist monk,' he wrote[72] – but the festival folded before the season was over and Northern Lights Theatre had no further plans for the play. For the next several years, Mitchell tried unsuccessfully to interest a theatre in staging the play he had put together, but the response, invariably, was that the cast of fifteen characters was too large and expensive. There was a one-day workshop performance by the Saskatchewan Playwrights Centre in Regina in May 1984. A workshop at Stratford in the mid-1980s with a cast reduced to twelve was the last try.

In the early fall, he decided to make a two-week trip to New York City – 'to take my mind off my ailments' – and he reported to Ken Mitchell that he had a fairly good holiday, although at all times he made himself take it easy, because with the slightest stress his tremor got worse and he, in turn, became 'rattled' and confused. Although being in New York was pleasurable, the travelling was difficult, and he returned to his Montreal apartment feeling defeated, thinking at the same time how much he yet wanted to do, how many places to see.[73] As it turned out, this would be the last trip Jim would take that could be designated as a holiday.

In the same letter to Mitchell, he wrote that his apartment in Montreal wasn't working out, that he would have to move again in the spring. Alvin and Dorothy Goldman remembered this as a sad and turbulent time in Jim's life.[74] He was not only deteriorating physically – the characteristic shuffle of Parkinson's disease was becoming more pronounced – but he was also deteriorating mentally. In Alvin Goldman's words, 'Jim was becoming paranoid and living at cross purposes with himself, not relating to others realistically.' He believed that he was being watched and that 'they' were trying to 'get him.' He heard voices and was convinced he was being spied on and talked about, and he was determined to move as soon as he could find another apartment to his liking. He wrote to Keath Fraser that the neighbours were objecting to the sound of his typewriter, so that he had to keep his typing to a minimum.[75] He not only had enemies in his apartment building but was convinced the literary community in Canada had turned against him, and he interpreted everything – the slow proceedings over the translation of As for Me and My House, for example – as evidence that his reputation was deliberately being maligned. He had never hidden the fact of his homosexual activities, but now he imagined himself being publically reviled as a queer. For him, the term brought into focus a lifetime of being dismissed, or misunderstood. In more defiant moods, he would say, 'After I'm gone, they will dismiss me as an old queer, but they won't know the half of it.'[76]

Jim was preoccupied with antagonism towards unknown foes, but he was equally suspicious and difficult with long-time friends. During a visit with Mavis Gallant, he said he would not talk about the work he had in progress because he was afraid she would steal the idea and publish it as her own.[77] When he talked with the Goldmans, he could rationalize his paranoia as part of the disease he was coping with, but at the same time it didn't change his behaviour. They found it very hard to help. But the Goldmans, in fact, were Jim's mainstay while he was in Montreal – he saw very little of the Baxters, using ill health as an excuse. Dorothy and Alvin had him to dinner almost every week and, in general, felt responsible for his well-being. They watched in some despair as Jim moved to another apartment in February 1981, from Durocher to Ste Famille Street, and then changed his postal address to a station box number in order to elude his 'enemies.'

The year 1981 was bleak and difficult: the physical symptoms of Parkinson's grew steadily worse, particularly the tremor in his arm. It made the smallest chores, such as shaving or brushing his teeth, monumentally difficult. He no longer wanted to eat in public because he could not be sure he would be able to use his fork; he avoided meeting people because he could not rely on his voice having enough resonance to carry on a conversation. The stress of a social situation made all the symptoms worse. He continued to feel miserable from the side effects of the drugs he was taking, and the disease itself made him feel tired, worn out most of the time. He went regularly to a neurologist who had a special interest in Parkinson's, and the latter discussed with him the possibility of surgery that would reduce the tremor, but as Jim explained in a letter to Ken Mitchell there was no guarantee the operation would work and it had no effect whatsoever on the disease itself.[78] He was also increasingly miserable with an enlarged prostate. The beneficial effects of the surgery he had undergone in the early '60s ('scraping' the prostate to reduce the swelling) were long gone, and his doctor recommended complete removal of the gland to get relief. He had the second surgery in September 1981 and was able to report that the operation had been successful.[79] But to avoid social obligations when they arose or invitations – such as Geoffrey Ursell's request that he come to Regina for the launch of Ken Mitchell's *Reader's Guide* – he would continue to cite health problems in order to decline politely. In response to being besieged by his enemies, he began thinking he should move away from Montreal, perhaps as far as Vancouver, described so glowingly in letters from Keath Fraser. In a letter to Mitchell in November, he rationalized the possible move as an escape from the harsh Montreal climate.

There is evidence that Jim was still trying to do some writing during this difficult period; he would dismiss it as 'scribbling,' but in fact he was working on a manuscript with a shocking theme. A letter to Jim from Lorraine McMullen, dated 21 October 1980, refers to a work-in-progress on the subnormal, and in a letter to Keath Fraser dated 21 January 1981 there is a reference to his working on a novel about a man and his son: 'a 40 year-old widower with a 17 year-old son who has the mental age of 3.' Later he would explain that the working title of the manuscript was 'Teddy Do,' the words of a beautiful but retarded boy. It was to tell the story of a young couple who were courting within the social confines of their church, but she becomes pregnant before they marry and gives birth to a son who is mentally handicapped. The parents of the boy live unhappily, the stigma of the boy's condition somehow a visible emblem of their sexual shame in the eyes of the town. But Teddy himself is always smiling, and handsome, and eager to please. After time has passed and the unhappy mother has died, the reader is to learn that the father is a pedophile who abuses his son.[80] Jim confided to Keath Fraser some years later about the 'vile' manuscript he had burned, 'in which a father takes his retarded son in a wheelchair to a cottage at the lake, where the obliging, good-natured boy commits fellatio on him, and then later inadvertently reveals this fact to the town, by pointing to his mouth and saying (something like) "Teddy do."'[81] After the author's death, Keath Fraser would suggest that 'The Flowers That Killed Him' and the 'Teddy Do' story, the latter in verbal outline, reimagine the Philip-Steve relationship from As for Me and My House.[82] On a personal level, Jim was no doubt exploring further his dark and complicated feelings about fathers and sons, and perhaps the criminal dimension of this unpublished story reflects a degree of self-loathing the author carried within him for the homosexual aspect of his nature, for even in Spain with what Jim had viewed as its freer, more open attitudes, homosexuality was not decriminalized until 1978.

For Christmas 1981 Jim received a copy of Ken Mitchell's Sinclair Ross: A Reader's Guide. He was pleased with the book and deeply grateful for Mitchell's enthusiasm and loyalty, but his general despondency is evident in his letter of thanks: 'Things being the way they are I don't suppose much more will be written about me so your book is a gratifying send-off. It makes a drab, frustrated writing career seem a little less so ... I hope the response is good and that you won't feel your time and work have been wasted.'[83]

In his Christmas letter to Keath Fraser, he announced that he had made up his mind: he would travel to Vancouver around the middle of March, and he asked if Keath would find him a cheap hotel where he could live until he had located an apartment. He hoped that once settled he might still get in some travel – as far as San Francisco perhaps, or to the Okanagan Valley. He had old friends, Doyle and Bill Klyn, now living in the vicinity of Victoria, and he wanted to go out on the boats and see some of the coastal islands. Maybe he would even get back to Mexico again.[84] Some days he convinced himself that he could enjoy life again, that there were still interesting things to see and do, that by moving to Vancouver he wasn't just running away.

fifteen

Suicide
1982–1988

In Vancouver, Keath Fraser had offered to see what might be available in the way of apartments in the city's West End and then wrote on 1 February 1982 to say that he had rented a place for Jim on Comox Street in a building 'up against the rhododendrons of Stanley Park.'[1] It was a pleasant, one-bedroom apartment on the fifth floor (the building was thirteen years old), and it looked down on the street and to the park's tall trees. From the dining-room window there was a glimpse of English Bay, and sitting out on his balcony he would be able to hear the pock of tennis balls in the courts in Stanley Park. It reminded Fraser slightly of Jim's apartment in Málaga, although it was bigger. Fraser felt it was an enviable situation and hoped Jim would be pleased with it. He could take possession by the first of March. Jim, however, needed more time to pack his things, sell furniture, and ship his belongings west. He had fallen on a patch of ice and hurt his wrist, and as he had reported to Ken Mitchell earlier, he did 'everything in slow motion.'[2]

He had decided to travel west by train, and after saying good-bye to the Baxters and Goldmans, he left Montreal by CP Rail on March 12, arriving in Vancouver three days later. Keath met Jim at the station and would recall his short halting steps as he came along the railway platform, 'overdressed in his overcoat, tie, and a pearl-gray fedora, a little old man out of the 1930s.'[3] He took him to the Sylvia Hotel on English Bay, where he had arranged for him to stay until his furnishings arrived. They met the next day for lunch in one of the many restaurants along Denman Street, and Keath could see then how gravely altered he was from the man he had visited first in Athens, then Málaga. Not only did he seem shrunken physically and agitated by the tremors of the disease, but he was down on himself, deeply dispirited, and worried that he was becoming paranoid. Jim's furniture and books took nearly a month to arrive, so that he didn't take possession of the apartment until the second week of April, but from the beginning he was convinced the apartment wasn't going to work. In subsequent meetings for coffee or for lunch with Keath, he complained of 'noises' he was hearing and identified a woman in the apartment above his as knocking in reprimand to any noises he might be making below. Keath was not sure that Jim could live on his own and collected information about long-term-care services and private retirement homes in Vancouver. Jim's recent arrival in the city, however, was a problem; most services and care units required a year's residency in British Columbia before he was eligible. Jim wrote to Alvin Goldman that he was more or less just camping in the apartment, that his health was not good, that he felt more useless than ever. His new doctor, he said, had increased the drug he was taking, and it was giving him fits of depression.[4] In the same vein, he wrote to Ken Mitchell that he was living a restricted life: 'depressed, forgetful – oh, the hell with it.'[5]

Then one afternoon early in June, Keath found Jim 'wandering in his bedroom slippers, bruised and battered, in a sandwich shop on Denman Street.'[6] He had fallen, he said, getting out of the bath, and Keath, fearing broken bones or a concussion, called a taxi and took him to St Paul's Emergency to have him checked over. On the way to the hospital, he confided to Keath that he had decided to see a psychiatrist, that his first appointment should have been the day before, but it had been rescheduled. He was feeling 'beset, helpless.' He also spoke of euthanasia and said to Keath, 'When you don't have friends anymore, what's the point? You're young. You have friends. I don't have anybody.' The attention of the doctors at the hospital, however, revived him and X-rays showed no serious injuries, so that Keath took him back to the apartment, where he cleaned up blood in the bathroom and on the parquet floors, and sorted through blood-spattered clothes and bed linen. Jim said he had fallen – slipped in the bath – and then crawled towards his phone, before blacking out at about two in the morning. Keath brought him a rubber mat for his bathtub but afterwards wondered about a note he saw affixed inside the plastic lid of Jim's record player. He wondered too about their conversation a few days earlier in which Jim said if anything happened to him, remember to do certain things, a conversation in which Jim, uncharacteristically, thanked him for being a good friend. It wasn't until eight years later that he confessed to Keath that he had tried to end his life – 'a bottle of gin and aspirin.' Had he thrown himself from the edge of the bathtub to the floor? When he spoke of this desperate time, he said he had even tried to buy a gun, had gone out looking for one.

As he had done with the Goldmans, Jim grew dependent on the two people who had become his rescuers, one last version of the couple, the man and woman, to whom he so often attached himself; for some time, Keath and Lorraine Fraser were his only social contacts in Vancouver. He had written to me at Christmas that when he moved to Vancouver in the spring, we might meet at last. He promised at least a phone call or a note, but once in the city he found himself unable to initiate contact. A long-standing anxiety about meeting new people had increased tenfold. He had planned to visit the Klyns, who were living on the outskirts of Victoria, but kept postponing the trip to Vancouver Island. He was very comfortable, however, with Keath and Lorraine; their company created for him one final version of the family romance that can be discerned in Larsen, Sylvia, and Chris in *The Well*, in Philip, Mrs Bentley, and Paul in *As for Me and My House*, and Charlie, Mad, and Sonny in *Whir of Gold*. One might even glimpse it in 'The Painted Door.' Jim and Keath established a pattern of meeting for lunches and for long talks about writing. That summer, and until 1985, the Frasers took him to see films and sometimes to concerts at the Orpheum; they took him for picnics at the beach and invited him to their West End apartment for dinner. And sometimes they would meet Jim for dinner at restaurants in the area that he had found on his own. They created for him a haven from his 'enemies.'

The only visitor Jim entertained on his own that year after moving to Vancouver was Lorraine McMullen, who came to the city on business in April and stayed for three days at the Sylvia Hotel. They had lunch together twice, and she could see that Jim had changed a great deal as the result of his disease. He told her in their conversations that he had destroyed his unpublished manuscripts because he didn't want them to fall into the wrong hands. She recognized the paranoia and withdrawal characteristic of those with Parkinson's disease and left feeling anxious on his behalf. In her letters that summer, she tried to send good news – *As for Me and My House*, she reported, had been chosen as one of six books to launch the NCL 'classics' series – and she tried to encourage him to make contacts with other literary-minded people in the city. She urged that he phone novelist Jack Hodgins, who was in residence at the University of British Columbia that summer, and she spoke highly of Diana Brydon, also at UBC, who was writing a brief piece on him for the Profiles in Canadian Literature series being published by Dundern Press. She asked Jim if it would be all right to give his address to me and to Sandra Djwa at Simon Fraser University, as we were both eager to meet him.[7] Like Keath, Lorraine felt that Jim's reclusiveness was making his condition worse. Diana Brydon located him, and they had lunch together at a restaurant in the West End, where they discussed the brief essay she was writing.

But Jim spent most of his time alone, reading, or walking the few blocks in the vicinity of his apartment. The area afforded a few routine pleasures. He enjoyed browsing the shelves of Pauline's Bookstore on Denman Street, and watching tanned youth in bathing suits making their way to and from the beach. He took short walks along the edge of Stanley Park and frequently had lunch, sometimes dinner, at the English Bay Café, though he was always self-conscious of what he termed his Parkinson's shuffle and his frequent inability to hold a fork steady. But he enjoyed the view over the water from the café, especially sunset, and, if the restaurant was not crowded, he would linger over a second glass of wine with his meal. It was only a few short blocks back to his apartment.

He did not make the contacts that Lorraine McMullen had suggested, nor did he phone Noel Stone, a friend of Alvin Goldman. And when historian Gerald Friesen requested an interview while writing *The Canadian Prairies: A History*, Jim turned him down.[8] In September 1982 he wrote to Goldman, 'I've had lunch with someone twice since I arrived [but] no enjoyment – scared of spilling and slopping. Alone I eat a lot of fish and minced steak and frequently use my fingers.'[9] That fall, however, he became more active in trying to learn how to live with his condition. He acquired some literature from the Parkinson's Federation in Chicago and attended a symposium with a panel of American and Canadian specialists. Exercise, he learned, was terribly important – stretching and loosening exercises to fight the rigidity caused by the disease. He also joined a group therapy program for people living with Parkinson's disease; he reported to Goldman: 'For me perhaps the worst is the depression and anti-social attitudes. I have been forcing myself to go to some Group Therapy sessions which I realize are good for me – exercises, speech therapy, making contact with others, some much farther along the road, wheel-chairs, walkers, etc., but as I say, I have to force myself.'[10] One of the recommendations for speech therapy was to read poetry aloud, and he reported to Goldman that he had become absorbed in it, reading Auden, Atwood, Irving Layton, Baudelaire, and Rimbaud aloud to himself.[11]

Feeling that Jim was mentally more stable and socially more relaxed, Keath decided that fall to arrange a lunch at his apartment so that Jim could meet George Woodcock, one of his long-time admirers. He also included at the table the openly gay writer David Watmough, whose loquacity he hoped would cover any awkward moments, and David's long-time partner, Floyd St Clair. Jim said very little, never initiating any conversation except to thank Woodcock at one point for the supportive review of *Sawbones Memorial*. Most of the talk was between Woodcock and Watmough, with Keath preoccupied much of the time with the food and waitering. Woodcock later confessed he had himself been intimidated by the shy dignity of this writer he held in such high esteem, but was grateful to Keath for arranging the meeting. Jim also was warmed by the event.[12] He recognized that what he needed above all were

social activities that would 'take him out of himself,' let him forget his problems and anxieties for a while. He slept better that night.

But the following January, he wrote to Alvin saying that he was more than
ever 'becoming a recluse' – 'anti-social' – '[I] just want to turn my back.' His
paranoia seemed rational: '... the *fact* does stand out that an old man of 75 with
Parkinson's is not *wanted* anywhere.'[13] His greatest struggle from day to day
was depression and bad dreams, and while there was a medication prescribed
that gave him a sound, dreamless sleep, it left him in a fog the following day.
Accordingly, as he could not predict from day to day how he would feel, he
avoided commitments of any kind, and because of his appearance – the tremor
in his hand, shuffling steps, and the rigid expression of his face – he did not go
alone to the theatre or concerts, where he might become self-conscious.
Entertainment was limited to the occasional film playing at the movie house
on Denman Street or when he was taken to one further afield by the Frasers.
But he found movies had lost their appeal. He wrote to Alvin Goldman that
sitting through a film he got 'cramped and bored' and was no longer able to
identify with characters or project himself into their situations,[14] although
Keath Fraser would remember the keen pleasure he took in *My Dinner with
André*, a film which consists entirely of a lengthy dialogue between two men in
a New York restaurant.[15]

The one steady pleasure that remained for Jim was reading. In letters to
both Goldman and Ken Mitchell, he highly recommended Timothy Findley's
Famous Last Words,[16] and he wrote to John Gibbon that he enjoyed rereading
Hardy, F. Scott Fitzgerald, and Evelyn Waugh.[17] Other books he mentioned
in his letters during this period included Michael Ondaatje's *Running in the
Family*, Alice Munro's *Moons of Jupiter*, and Marilynne Robinson's *Housekeeping*. He described the latter as 'a book you keep thinking about' and one he
reread because it was so well written. It remained a special favourite, a book
he would continue to recommend in the years ahead.[18]

He rather enjoyed hearing from John Gibbon, the sometimes pompous
would-be intellectual he worked with at head office. His letters made no
demands on him, and they provided news of old Montreal acquaintances. Gibbon, who had retired, was taking courses in Canadian literature at McGill –
one from Alec Lucas and another from Michael Darling – and he reported the
strong enthusiasm in both courses for the works of Sinclair Ross. He thought
Lucas was a great man and splendid teacher, and sent gossip about the latter's
marriage breaking up and his fathering of a child by a much younger woman.
He also wrote of the splendid showing Mavis Gallant had made at a lecture
series at McGill and the 'disgraceful' performance, in his opinion, by Mordecai
Richler in the same series. John Gibbon was still his boastful, name-dropping

self – he recounted at length his father's importance to Canadian literature, and reminded Jim that poet Stephen Spender was best man at his sister's wedding in England years ago – but Jim came to recognize Gibbon's boasting as want of self-confidence and to see him as an amusing caricature. With reference to his bipolar condition, Gibbon confided that he too suffered severe depression at one point while still working at the bank and that he had been on medication ever since that time. He reported in one of his letters that he occasionally saw the Baxters when he went out to visit his brother in Hudson, where the Baxters were living in retirement, and that Cecil ('Lefty') Nelson from the advertising department had been killed in an automobile accident.[19]

In letters to Alvin Goldman, Jim reported the various 'nibbles' he continued to get from film-makers. An option on As for Me and My House had been taken out by Margaret Kopola ('Maggie's Movies') of Ottawa and there were sporadic reports that a film was in the works.[20] (Kopola, in fact, renewed her option until 1995, but a film never went into production during that time.) He had heard from McClelland and Stewart, continuing to act as his agent, that Norman Jewison was interested in making a film of Sawbones Memorial but dismissed the likelihood that anything would ever come of it, given Jewison's popular reputation and the number of projects he was involved in.[21] He could report, however, that film rights for short stories had been sold, and indeed during the next two years, Atlantis made short films of 'Cornet at Night,' 'One's a Heifer,' and 'The Painted Door.' Alberta film-maker Anne Wheeler directed 'One's a Heifer,' which was released in 1984. Bruce Pittman directed 'Cornet at Night' (1983) and 'The Painted Door' (1984). The latter, featuring Linda Goranson, was especially well done in terms of setting and acting, and Jim was delighted that it was nominated for an Academy Award.

In February of 1983 Jim had a visit from Ken Mitchell, who was still struggling to find a producer for 'The Hunter Memorial.' Jim marvelled at his buoyancy, given the recent death of his wife and the number of professional disappointments he had suffered. It made him reflect on his own chronic pessimism and lack of self-confidence throughout his life: perhaps he had indeed inherited his father's dour, pessimistic nature. Lorraine McMullen was in Vancouver for the month of June in 1983 and invited Jim to dinner at the apartment she was renting in the West End. In her opinion, he seemed a little more stable than the year before, both physically and psychologically.[22] Again she urged him to make contact with some of his admirers in the city; she also urged him to get a television set, something he had never owned in his life.

When I met with Lorraine McMullen during her stay in Vancouver, she suggested that I try making a connection again with Jim. The result this time was that in July he agreed we meet for lunch at the English Bay Café. We found ourselves at ease with much to talk about, and stayed at our table for at least two hours. There was only one bad moment, at the beginning, when salad arrived, and a wave of tremors made it difficult for Jim to use his fork. But a mounted policeman on a superb-looking horse drew our attention to the street and gave the meal its most memorable moment, as the eyes of the Prairie boy filled with pleasure at the spectacle passing by. The impression I carried away from that first meeting was of a small, enigmatic man whose frank, farm-boy manner was something of a mask worn habitually by a much more complicated individual. I went away thinking about the plain-spoken and mysterious American writer Paul Bowles, whose writing was similar to that of Sinclair Ross in its pitiless clarity and unrelenting exploration of the intuitive mind. I stayed in touch thereafter by telephone, although invitations to meet for lunch again, or to visit my wife and family, were declined for reasons of deteriorating health.

Jim was still battling low spirits and brooding over the failure of his life. He was shaken and demoralized by losing his wallet one day, which was located and returned (without the money) by kind visitors in the city. In August he wrote to Alvin Goldman that by age seventy-five there wasn't much to live for: '... you find yourself not just thinking what difference does it make? but really feeling it inside. Especially when you've tried to do something and realize you've failed. When it's over it's over ...' As for his social life, he lived quietly and to himself. He realized that since coming to Vancouver fifteen months ago, he hadn't so much as served a beer or a glass of wine in his apartment.[23] He had no desire to live.

The Frasers remained anxious to keep Jim's spirits up and continued to invite him to their apartment for dinner. Lorraine was a primary school-teacher, and on one of those occasions, in the spring of 1984, she introduced Jim to a colleague, a woman of Greek origins by the name of Irene Harvalias. In her late forties, with three grown children and newly separated from her husband, Harvalias was eager to meet the distinguished Canadian author, and Jim, in turn, found her a lively dinner companion and enjoyed trying to use once again some of his hard-won Greek vocabulary. There was a compatibility from the start: Irene's enthusiasm and optimistic approach to life complemented Jim's misgivings and social backwardness. She seized the opportunity Jim represented to fill a vacant place in her own life. Moreover there was a bond established by Jim's illness, for Irene's mother, in Greece, also suffered from Parkinson's disease. She began inviting Jim to her house for dinner and offered to do little chores for him that he sometimes found difficult to accomplish. The Frasers now had a baby and had bought a home in Kitsilano, so that Irene's entry in Jim's life was welcomed from their point of view. She would in fact be an increasingly important part of Jim's world up until his death.

But Jim's social life, otherwise, was limited almost entirely to his mailbox. He continued to receive interesting letters from publishers and from people who had read his fiction. Douglas Gibson, then at Macmillan, sent Jim a copy of Guy Vanderhaeghe's short-story collection *Man Descending* (1983), and Jim read the book and sent the author his congratulations. Gibson similarly sent him a copy of Roy MacGregor's *The Last Season* (1984), and Jim also sent MacGregor a word of praise. Both young writers wrote to say how much Jim's letters meant to them, since he was a writer they held in very high esteem.[24] Other writers were making public statements about Ross's enormous impact on them, which filtered back to the author. Poet Lorna Crozier wrote about first reading Sinclair Ross: 'That's when my head flew open ... I thought, Oh my God, he's writing about *my* landscape ... about the wind, the dust, the false-front stores. I think my education began then. It was the discovery of my own country.' And she lamented wryly, 'We're surely the only nation in the world that keeps its own literature a deep, dark secret.'[25] She would go on to write her own version of *As for Me and My House* from Mrs Bentley's point of view. Similarly, in 'The Moment of the Discovery of America Continues,' Robert Kroetsch wrote: '... I remember responding with shock to Ross's portrait of a marriage, a prairie town, a prairie house. He made it possible for me, by a system of contraries, to write *The Words of My Roaring* ... Ross and his characters in his town of Horizon became a generating principle ...' (4).

But hearing about these writers brought some bitter reflections; it seemed to Jim they had it so easy – government grants, editors and publishers like Gibson eager to promote their work – while he had never had any assistance. It was true that Ernest Court had encouraged him to keep writing and send out his work, but Court had no access to publishers to give him the leg up he needed. What little he had accomplished, he had done entirely on his own. His sympathies were for those who failed to achieve success in the eye of the public. In January 1984 he wrote to encourage Alvin Goldman, who was having trouble marketing his screenplays and fiction, told him not to lose faith in what he was doing: 'But I know – things move so slowly and there's the uncertainty. Also I dare say, the *fear* of building your hopes too high; it's such a letdown when a project doesn't work out.'[26]

He heard from people whose lives were not easy. Effie's daughter, Beatrice, wrote to ask whether 'The Painted Door,' which had been nominated for an Oscar, had been based on his story; she was waiting for a diagnosis for breast cancer.[27] He heard from Audrey Peterkin, whose son had committed suicide; she wrote bravely to say her daughter had been studying Jim's fiction with

Dennis Cooley, an inspiring teacher at the University of Manitoba. She also told about the books she had written and about her writing group, 'The Pen-handlers.'[28] And he had several letters from Lloyd Person in Regina, who told of his continued writing and travels despite the loss of a leg as the result of poor circulation.[29] To all of these, Jim wrote short notes, acknowledging receipt of their letters and wishing them well. He was amazed at their cour-age, although he had a certain measure of contempt for someone like Lloyd Person, a retired university professor who seemed so limited in his abilities as a writer – he wrote nostalgic sketches of a fictional Prairie town he called Minby – but who presumed to write to Jim in a familiar manner and as an equal, although they had never met. At the same time, Jim envied someone like Person who had self-confidence and who still travelled the world – Rus-sia, Romania, New York – in spite of terrific disabilities.[30]

What Jim increasingly dreaded were requests for a visit. I wanted to meet him again and to present him with a copy of a book I had written, *Major Canadian Authors*, in which he was prominently featured. Jim said he wasn't well enough to go out for lunch, and when I took the book around to his apartment, he only opened the door a crack; a trembling hand took the pack-age without speaking a word, and closed the door. It gave me a glimpse of a sparsely furnished room, but especially of how difficult his life was and how withdrawn he had become.

Robert Weaver had a similar experience. In late October 1984, he wrote to Jim to say he would be in Vancouver shortly on CBC business and planned to look him up. He found Jim in a 'pathetic' state. His surroundings were indeed spartan – a typewriter and a rented television set – and his appearance and behaviour unnatural. Bob talked, but Jim just stared without any expression on his face and 'barely said two words.'[31] Bob was anxious for his old acquain-tance and at New Year's sent a cheerful letter about the good films that had been made from Jim's stories. In early spring 1985, Doris Saunders tried to visit, but Jim would not see her. He was very aware, however, of how ungra-cious (and uncharacteristic) his behaviour was, and he was able to rally his spirits enough to send notes of apology. He wrote to thank me for the book, 'but as you can tell, it's all over for me. I have shut the door and pulled down the blinds.'[32] And to Doris Saunders he wrote on 8 April 1985: 'Have been and am frequently irrational – so we'll blame Parkinson's ... I tend to hunker down and sit it out, sometimes, I'm afraid, a bit sullen. All right. You're disap-pointed – so what else is new.' He was grateful, nonetheless, he said, for her long friendship and happy to have a letter from her. He would try to write, but found himself often 'tied in knots.' To Alan Twigg, who was preparing the reference book *Vancouver and Its Writers* and wanted to do an interview, he said: 'I would be grateful if you ignored me. You see, I have Parkinson's

Disease. I don't speak well. There are things that enter my mind to say but I don't trust myself to say them. If you came to see me, I'm afraid it might be unpleasant for you ... If you wrote about me in your book it might make some people want to visit me. And I don't want that ... I came to Vancouver about three years ago. I don't know the city well.'[33] He wondered sometimes if it was the rain and the overcast skies that made his depression seem worse.

On a night in July 1985, Jim fell again and this time broke his hip; it wasn't until past nine o'clock the next morning that he attracted the attention of the occupant in the suite below him by rapping on the floor. Keath was called to the apartment, and he accompanied Jim to Vancouver General Hospital, where the fractured hip was set and arrangements were made for extended care. Keath wondered if the fall was the result again of one of those suicidal urges that overwhelmed him. It seemed clear now that Jim could not go on living by himself. With his permission, Keath terminated the apartment rental and proceeded to clear out his things.

Jim's admission to hospital in the summer of 1985 initiated nearly eleven years of institutional care. Keath took over his correspondence. In the summer and fall of that year, Ken Mitchell was putting together a program he would call 'The Ross File' for CBC Radio in Saskatchewan and wrote to ask if Jim would be willing to do an interview to be used in the documentary. Fraser wrote to Mitchell September 27 explaining about the fall and the convalescence in hospital. The hip was mending fairly well, he reported, and Jim was starting to get around again with the help of two canes, but he had given up his apartment and was waiting for a place to come vacant in a nursing home. He reminded Mitchell that Jim's problem was not so much a broken hip as the enfeebling effects of Parkinson's. However, Fraser was able to report a positive side to Jim's life in hospital: he was eating regularly now and receiving the proper assistance to get in and out of his clothes. Moreover, he was no longer so isolated from the world.[34]

That was indeed the case, for when in the spring of 1986 he was moved to Brock Fahrni Pavilion, a new veterans wing for what was then called Shaughnessy Hospital, he had to share a room with three other men. At first Jim remained as sequestered away as possible, preferring to have the curtains drawn around his quarter-section of the room, so that he could read and listen to his radio in private. But gradually he came to enjoy the company of some of the other men living in the hospital and to make occasional use of the recreation room, which had a television, some magazines, and a piano. One of the other men in the room was Dr Jack Moscovich. He had suffered a stroke and had no conversation, but he was visited almost every day by his wife, Mary. She gradually became aware of the little man on the other side of the room, who was usually reading, and turned to him to make conversation while she paid her visit. Jim and Mary got to know each other well over the next two years, and he told her in detail about his difficult childhood, the support he had given his mother, about his years overseas. When Jim told her about his years at the Royal Bank in Montreal, Mary asked if he knew a Ms Hebb, her cousin's daughter, who had been a teller at that time. Jim remembered the young woman very clearly and was interested to learn that after she had left the bank, she had gone to law school and taken up a practice in Halifax. Mary made sure that when she brought her husband something special from home, fresh fruit, butter tarts, that there would be enough to share with Jim. Usually she found him with his curtain drawn but knew he could be tempted out with something from her kitchen.[35]

Although he was given therapy daily to help him walk again without assistance, he preferred to spend most of the day in his wheelchair – the most comfortable position for reading. That was where Ken Mitchell found him in the afternoon of 4 August 1986, when he came to see Jim and deliver a ceramic award from the Saskatchewan Arts Guild. Mitchell was in Vancouver to give a poetry reading at the Saskatchewan pavilion at Expo. As well as delivering the award, he wanted Jim to listen to a tape he had made of 'The Ross File' program that had aired earlier in the year on CBC Radio in Saskatchewan. The visit left Jim feeling upset. Although there were flattering words on the tape about Jim from interviews with Margaret Laurence and Adele Wiseman, he felt some of the information was incorrect and misleading. Mitchell, for example, persisted in identifying Arcola as the model for Horizon. Once again Jim was uneasy that someone was interviewing his old acquaintances, unearthing the often sad details of his past. But he was especially upset during Ken Mitchell's visit when the latter suggested his mother might have been warming her employers' beds as well as their kitchens. He interpreted this as a slur on the family honour, and it gnawed at him for months.

Although Parkinson's disease could not be cured, its symptoms could be alleviated by drug therapy carefully administered. Medication to control the tremors had debilitating side effects, including constipation, sleep disorders, depression, and mental confusion. While living alone, Jim had been unable to monitor his medical needs accurately, but in hospital the staff kept close watch on the effects of the drugs and created smoother transitions from day to day. Although he still felt weak and discouraged much of the time there were stretches when he was reasonably comfortable and able to take an interest again in the world around him.

He had not written to friends after breaking his hip and moving to hospital, but he still received correspondence through Keath Fraser's address, and in late 1986 Irene Harvalias volunteered to help him answer his letters. He

wrote to Dorothy and Alvin Goldman on 21 November 1986 with his characteristic irony that 'things could be worse. The food isn't bad and I still do a fair
amount of reading, although my eyes are a long way from what they used to
be. [But a] hospital, smile as one will, is a hospital.' And after reading *The Resurrection of Joseph Bourne*, he wrote a short note to its author, Jack Hodgins,
saying he enjoyed the novel but was glad he didn't have to live in a place like
Port Annie![36]

But more importantly, Irene's willingness to take dictation meant that it was
possible for him to do some creative writing again. Keath encouraged Jim to
think about the idea of writing his memoirs and drew his attention to books
like Ondaatje's *Running in the Family* to remind him of the more experimental
possibilities for organizing one's remembered experiences. He told him that his
friends John Metcalf and Leon Rooke were planning an anthology of new writing by Canadians to be published by Macmillan, and that they would welcome
a piece from a writer of Jim's stature. In his characteristically cautious and cir-
cuitous way, Jim came around to the idea. Slowly, in his head and in shorthand,
he started to make notes from his earliest memories, and he saw that the story
to be told focused around his mother. Putting her at the centre of his narrative,
he let her 'take over,' as she had done so often in his life, to tell the story of their
family and his childhood 'her way' – that is, in inflated accounts of family history and anecdotes rich in colourful detail and moral judgments. When Keath
saw that Jim was taking the project seriously, he brought over a small typewriter on which Jim tried to peck out his narrative, but the keys proved too stiff
for him to press and he eventually turned to Irene Harvalias for assistance; from
Jim's shorthand notes and from dictation, she wrote out a version in longhand
and then typed it up for Jim to read over and revise as he went along. It was a
slow, frustrating process for Jim not to be able to type himself. Irene was
extraordinarily patient and attentive, preparing the work he dictated, but she
still had a full-time job as a primary schoolteacher and was now a grandmother
and could not come to the hospital every day. But gradually, after many drafts,
a narrative of thirty manuscript pages took shape. The working title had been
'The Unreliable Narrator,' an allusion to the critics' (especially Wilfred
Cude's) view of Mrs Bentley as storyteller in his first published novel. However, as Keath Fraser has explained, he wasn't sure the allusion would be picked
up by his readers, so that when his editors at Macmillan suggested a phrase from
the narrative, he finally titled it 'Just Wind and Horses,' that summary, dismiss-
ive remark his mother made when giving her opinion of his fiction.[37]

In this tightly wrought narrative, there is no desire to sentimentalize his
memories of Kate, nor is there a wish to present her in as bleak a light as possible, but rather, as with the Bentleys in *As for Me and My House*, he wanted
to get at the complexity of character and to present her as fairly as possible.

So he tells the reader she is 'as difficult to describe as to live with' (83). He lists her negative qualities – 'domineering, unreasonable, with a sharp and sometimes reckless tongue' (96) – but then he remembers 'redemptively' how hard she worked and how determined she was that her son's life should turn out well. What is interesting are the oblique methods in this narrative, chief of which is allowing persons to speak for themselves – not just in quoted phrases or half-sentences, but in paragraph-long passages. Kate speaks at length, tracing herself back to Simon Fraser, 'the first Lord Lovat and the last man to be beheaded in the Tower of London' (83), and telling how her father, a Unitarian minister, collapsed in the pulpit and died on a day when the church was packed and he was beginning to acquire a reputation. The author also uses dialogue: between himself and his mother as he questions her about their ancestry, and between his mother and her illustrious brother, Sir John Foster Fraser, during the latter's visit to Winnipeg. He also casts in dialogue one of his parents' many quarrels, and he even creates a space for his father back in Wild Rose to say a few consoling words to the boy after the runaway accident. And he creates an echo of the neighbours' words as they gossip about Kate's extravagant ways.

But undermining the seeming authenticity of these words is the author's blunt reminder that all the characters of his narrative are gone, that what he writes is 'an old man's conversation with himself – questions and answers, the sifting of memories, guesses and surmises' (90). Similarly, he tells us that his mother exaggerated the truth shamelessly, telling 'all-out whoppers with a straight face' (96), reminding the reader that there is no truth as such, just ways of remembering. How, he wonders, should he interpret the vivid memory of his father standing behind his mother with a butcher knife to her throat? Was his father about to kill her, as it seemed to the frantic boy, or were they both just pretending, as his brother insisted? He tells us repeatedly that the attempt to write a memoir remains just that – an attempt: 'There's a lot I don't know, a lot I listened to with half an ear ... Now, trying to put it into sentences, I bridge the gaps as plausibly as I can' (86). This postmodern stance towards history, notions of truth, and storytelling also undermines any traditional account we might give of the 'prairie realist' whose best work was done in the 1930s. Here, at eighty years of age, Sinclair Ross was continuing his search for ways of telling stories that were new and responsive to the age in which he was living.

'Just Wind and Horses' was published in the spring of 1988 in *The Macmillan Anthology I*, which featured from a much younger generation such writers as Lorna Crozier, Keath Fraser, and Diane Schoemperlen. Of those included, only Norman Levine and Mavis Gallant had begun publishing before 1960. There were photographs of some of the authors by Sam Tata, including one of Jim taken in his corner of the hospital room. It was a photograph of himself that Jim disliked intensely; it presented him to the world in his wheelchair, staring stonily into the camera, his depleted existence – portable radio, a few books, towel rack, and napkins – visible for all to see. (To his chagrin an even less flattering picture from the same series appeared later on the cover of George Woodcock's 'Introduction' to *As for Me and My House* in ECW's Canadian Fiction Studies series in 1990.)

There were reviews of the anthology, however, which gave his spirits a lift, for they all singled out the Ross memoir as something special. Ken Adachi, writing for the *Toronto Star*, said up front that it was 'by far the most intriguing piece,'[38] and William French in the *Globe and Mail* called it 'a real coup.'[39] Bert Almon, reviewing the anthology for the *Canadian Book Review Annual 1988*, wrote that the Ross memoir was one of two treasures in the book,[40] but it was Janet Hamilton's observation in her review for *Quill and Quire* (June 1988) that is most to the point for she writes that 'the memoir's special gift to us is in its struggle with the problem of description.'[41] Friends wrote to congratulate Jim on taking up his pen again so successfully. He wrote to me: 'It's something of a relief to know you liked *Just Wind and Horses* – I wasn't exactly satisfied with it myself. It's hard to get people down on paper, especially when you know them well. I look forward to a visit from you, and also to a "party," as you suggest, with Lorraine [McMullen].'[42]

The warmth of public interest in 'Just Wind and Horses' encouraged him to continue thinking of ways to tell, indirectly, something of his life story. According to Keath Fraser, he had once tried to write an autobiography, piling up half an inch of manuscript before abandoning the project as too painful. Now, he felt his own life was interesting only to the degree that it involved the lives of others or was part of the drama of history. His working days at the bank in his opinion held no story of interest, and his struggles to get published while living in Winnipeg in the 1930s lacked a focus that could be narrated dramatically. The experience of going to war, however, had historical as well as personal value, and he set out once again to find a form in which he could relate obliquely a phase of his life story. Keath Fraser talked to him about a book of travel stories he was editing, to be called *Bad Trips*, and encouraged him to write something for this volume; so with Irene Harvalias's assistance again, he began a rough draft of a narrative he referred to as the 'troopship story,' an account of his trip to England with over twenty-two thousand men on the *Queen Elizabeth* in 1942, unquestionably 'the worst voyage of his life,' but which nonetheless heralded one of the best periods in his life. There was pleasure in thinking creatively about them both.

sixteen

The Order of Canada
1988–1996

Life did improve for Jim in the late 1980s, as he had hoped. Not only was he enjoying some renewed attention for his writing, but in the spring of 1988 he got a private room at the Brock Fahrni Pavilion; it would turn out to be his home space longer than any other room in which he had ever lived. Keath Fraser had stored most of Jim's belongings in the basement of his house, but he was now able to bring a few of those things to the hospital to create a more aesthetically pleasing environment for his friend. These included his desk and typewriter, a shelf unit for books, two Group of Seven prints for the wall, and a watercolour done by his Montreal friend Molly Baxter. Room 314 at the Brock Fahrni Pavilion no longer looked simply like a hospital room, but more like an artist's studio. The room, moreover, had a large window which looked out at ground level on an arboured garden that bloomed eight months of the year and where picnics and birthday parties took place in the summer months. Although it was small, room 314 was private, and Jim could now choose the degree to which he wanted to be connected to the activities of the hospital at large. Even more importantly, he could encourage friends to visit him there, knowing that there would be less chance of interruption and that he would not be disturbing the lives of others.

And he did begin to have visitors, more than he had ever had before. Keath and Lorraine's visits, usually on Saturday afternoons, were an anchor to his writing life; they brought his business mail, most of which was still directed to their address, and Keath advised him on matters connected with royalties, permissions, and copyright at McClelland and Stewart. He also shared with Jim his copies of the *New Yorker*. Keath and Lorraine often brought their son, Robin, with them, and Jim made sure he had a candy in his drawer for the boy, something purchased from the tuck shop wagon that came around in the afternoons. Irene Harvalias came in several times a week after school to help Jim answer his mail, and to bring little necessities or whimsical items that were not available anywhere in the hospital. He liked a dry Spanish sherry and specialty cheeses to have with afternoon tea. She made sure he had new clothes from time to time and took pains to find him shoes and slippers that were comfortable.

I had visited a couple of times in 1987 while Jim was still in the ward but started coming more frequently in 1988, when I saw how much more at ease and hospitable Jim felt having his own room. And one of my former students, Patricia Robertson, began appearing regularly at Jim's room. Robertson was a short-story writer whose work was being published in local magazines; she was also employed at Shaughnessy Hospital as a social worker to read to patients, etc. She was amazed to discover Sinclair Ross was one of the patients in the Brock Fahrni Pavilion and stopped at his room on a regular basis to discuss writing with this senior craftsman. Jim enjoyed her company, her English sense of humour, and her ardent desire to be a writer, and he took genuine pleasure in knowing a few years later that her collection of short stories, *City of Orphans*, had been nominated for a BC Book Prize.

For his eighty-first birthday, 22 January 1989, Irene organized a small Sunday-afternoon party in Jim's room. My wife and I brought a bottle of dry Spanish sherry, Irene brought a cake, and Lorraine McMullen, who was spending the school year teaching at the University of British Columbia, brought him something to read. At the last moment, the Frasers were unable to come, but with Irene's son Dimitri, his fiancé, and her daughter there was still a party of eight. Jim enjoyed meeting my wife, Mary-Ann, for she was someone with whom he could share his special love for horses. As the gathering came to an end there was a poignant moment when Jim said it was the first time he had ever been given a birthday party. He told how when he was a small boy his mother put those few candies and an orange saved from Christmas beside his plate at breakfast; nothing done or said otherwise. Later, when he was working in the bank, she would prepare his favourite desserts for January 22, which they would eat together alone.

One day in 1989 a young man who was working in food services at the hospital noticed something different as he passed room 314 in Brock Fahrni; certainly none of the other rooms had a desk with a typewriter, a well-stocked bookshelf, and modern art prints on the walls. The next day, when he was bringing the food trays for delivery on third floor, he paused to look at the name on the door of room 314 and was hugely surprised to read James Sinclair Ross. That was the name of the author who had written one of his favourite short stories, 'The Lamp at Noon,' and so he inquired at the desk and a nurse on duty assured him it was the writer, that he would be glad to meet him if he was interested. Andy Trapnell, the young food services employee, was indeed interested, but he felt woefully inadequate at the thought of engaging in a conversation with this esteemed man. But when he went with the nurse to say hello, he realized quickly what a gentle and socially unpretentious man this was, and he accepted Jim's invitation to look in on him again during his rounds the next day. It was the beginning of a close friendship that was sustained until the author's death. Its first flowering was a shared love of classical music; as he grew familiar with Jim's favourite composers, Andy would borrow recordings and make tapes for Jim, and they would share an hour of music together before Andy started his three to nine o'clock shifts in the afternoon. Wagner's *Parsifal* was one of the first delights; then they moved to Bach and Sibelius, and settled for a long time listening their way through much of Beethoven. His cello sonata, opus 69, moved Jim deeply, and more than once Andy noticed a tear run down his cheek as they listened to this piece. Andy taped from television a life of Beethoven, narrated by actor Peter Ustinov, and brought it to the hospital for Jim to watch.

Despite the difference in their ages (Andy was only twenty-six, Jim was eighty-one), Jim and Andy thought of themselves as soulmates. They shared a love of literature and classical music, but they also shared certain of life's handicaps: Andy's parents were separated (his mother living in Halifax, where Andy had grown up, his father living in Victoria), he had dropped out of school with a grade eleven education, and he had profound misgivings about his abilities and the future. Jim was an exceedingly sympathetic listener, and Andy began to confide in him increasingly, as a young man might turn to an older relative, an uncle or a grandfather, for advice. For Andy there was something safe and reassuring in those rooms on a dark winter afternoon when he went to work, and his greatest pleasure was to find Jim at his desk. Jim, in turn, welcomed his company because, although Andy was often troubled, he had a lively sense of humour and was a great raconteur and he could invariably cheer him up, no matter how low Jim's spirits might be. He liked to give Andy advice: when the latter described a story he would like to write some day about a boy and a veteran from the First World War, Jim shrewdly assessed that it was a big theme for Andy and suggested he try something simpler, less emotionally demanding, until he had a sure control of the craft of language. They listened to Mahler together, especially the *Kindertoten Lieder*, and said nothing in the presence of such tragic human feeling, but were comforted at least to be sharing the terrible feelings those songs expressed.

In 1989 Jim learned that there was going to be a symposium on his fiction in Ottawa the following year, organized by John Moss as part of the annual series on Canadian authors and topics. Once again his first reactions were 'I haven't published enough to make it worthwhile' and 'they will see through my work – I will be a laughing stock.'[1] Yet there was cautious pleasure in the thought that his work was considered important enough to assemble a conference of professors in the nation's capital for a two-day meeting. I had agreed to give an account for the conference of the Ross letters in selected libraries and used this occasion, accordingly, to question Jim in detail about various phases of his life, thereby initiating a process of interviews and reminiscences which would culminate in this biography. That same year, Jim received a strongly worded letter of praise for his work from John O'Connor, a professor of English at the University of Toronto. O'Connor had written to Jim a couple of times before, asking for bibliographical information about French translations and about the order in which his novels were written, but in this letter he let his enthusiasm for Jim's work show openly. On a Christmas card for 1989, Jim wrote to O'Connor: 'Your letter overwhelms me. I don't believe a word of it, and in fact I have been going around muttering "Get thee behind me." But Satan is foxy and I expect I'll be doing what he wants by the time my 82nd birthday comes around.' He told O'Connor there was little likelihood he would be going to Ottawa himself, but he welcomed the chance of a visit should O'Connor come out to Vancouver.

The conference in Ottawa, held 27 and 28 April 1990 at the National Library and the University of Ottawa, once again quickened academic interest in Sinclair Ross's work, especially in *As for Me and My House*. The novel was examined from contemporary theoretical perspectives, including feminist, reader-response, and Bakhtinian ideas in a comprehensive paper by Helen Buss titled 'Who Are You, Mrs Bentley?' and a deconstruction of the text according to its linguistic emphases and omissions in a paper by Frank Davey titled 'The Conflicting Signs of *As for Me and My House*.' There was also the reading by Marilyn Rose of the 'foreigners' in Ross's fiction along postcolonial lines and, by Charlene Diehl-Jones, a probing of *Sawbones Memorial* as a postmodern text, never fully divulging all its secrets. Jim was sent a tape of the proceedings, and though puzzled by many of the theoretical strategies on display, he enjoyed listening to the discussion of his work, especially a paper on comedy in *As for Me and My House* delivered by veteran Ross critic Wilfred Cude, and another on the humour in Ross's short fiction by David Carpenter.

When the conference was over, John O'Connor did come to Vancouver at the beginning of May for a visit, bringing news of the symposium and his own enormous enthusiasm for Jim's work. Jim had feared he would be 'all verbal thumbs and lapses' when O'Connor arrived,[2] but the initial meeting was a success, a pleasure for both parties, and O'Connor returned a second day for another long talk. Jim wrote to O'Connor on June 2 that his visit had been very important to him and that he hoped they would meet again. That day wasn't far off; O'Connor arranged to fly to Vancouver again in August. A visit in spring and one in August set a pattern that he would more or less follow for the next five years, as he researched Jim's art and life.

The year 1991 brought further public interest in Sinclair Ross as it marked fifty years since the original publication of As for Me and My House. John O'Connor discussed the book with Peter Gzowski on CBC Radio's popular *Morningside* program and then flew out to Vancouver for a little gathering in Jim's room on February 14. To mark the anniversary, Irene had a cake decorated to replicate the cover of the 1941 edition and presented Jim with a hard-to-come-by first edition. There was a telegram of congratulations from Douglas Gibson, now a senior editor at McClelland and Stewart, and good wishes from Lorraine McMullen. During the week, Liam Lacey from the *Globe and Mail* came with a photographer to interview Jim in his room, and in Saturday's paper there was a lengthy article and fine photograph celebrating 'the "cosmopolitan" prairie boy.'[3] To Jim's delight, Lacey described him as a 'youthful 83,' attractive in appearance: 'His frame looks lean and fit, his face calmly handsome, and he has the hard, steely gaze of a former military man.' The article contained some lively observations from the author, who was enjoying this public attention. He mentioned the Ottawa symposium and said he was amused to hear the academics taking themselves so seriously about his writing when he, ironically enough, had never had a university education. He wanted to set a few people straight by saying he never intended Paul to actually be Mrs Bentley's lover, and he wanted readers to know that he always felt quite sympathetic for Mrs Bentley, even though so many don't like her at all. He talked in the interview about his compulsion to keep writing – 'I feel guilty if I don't at least expose myself to a manuscript, write a few words and change a few words' – and he told Lacey about his narrative describing the voyage on the *Queen Elizabeth* in 1942. He admitted he often destroyed manuscripts that didn't please him, that he never showed anyone a work-in-progress, but that he thought this one was pretty good. To wind up the week's celebrations, Jim arranged to take Irene, John O'Connor, and Mary-Ann and me to a Greek restaurant for dinner. He travelled in a taxi outfitted with an elevator for the handicapped, and he was pleasantly surprised by how easy the procedure was. It was the first time Jim had left the hospital since he had entered five years before, but for the next three years he would look forward to similar evenings out.

As a result of the article in the *Globe and Mail*, he had a letter from Bob Savory in Winnipeg, with whom he had travelled on the troopship to England. Bob, in fact, had located a photograph of some of the men on the *Queen Elizabeth* which included a blurred image of Jim. He was pleased to have

Bob's letter – it brought him closer to the writing he was trying to do, suggesting there was an audience – and he wrote a long letter in reply, recalling the crowded conditions on that ship, the bad smells everywhere, and the challenge of climbing to the top bunk every night. Nonetheless, he wrote, 'my three and a half years in England were the best in my life.' Specifically he asked Bob if he could help him remember the kinds of food they ate on the ship – 'stews and soup and rice pudding' he supposed – but he wanted to be as accurate as possible. 'Twenty-two thousand men,' he wrote; 'there must have been a tremendous amount of eating' and, at a minimum 'twenty-two thousand bowel movements.'[4] Jim found Bob's replies helped him a great deal in reconstructing life on board ship, the words of an eyewitness, as it were. He also had a letter from Theodora Dowsley, the doctor's wife who lived in Abbey for part of the time that Kate and Jim were there. She was a widow living in West Vancouver, nearly ninety years of age, but she recalled Kate Ross with great affection and admiration and remembered 'Jimmy' playing her piano.

To mark the fiftieth anniversary of As for Me and My House, University of Toronto Press published a volume of reviews, opinions, and critical essays about the novel covering five decades. Jim enjoyed immensely reading reviews of this collection; it felt, he said, as if As for Me and My House was being reviewed for the first time. He especially liked the lengthy article by Neil Besner in the Winnipeg Free Press, where the headline caption in large letters read 'The Great Canadian Novel Looked At over 50 Years.'[5] Besner summarized the status of the novel nicely when he wrote, 'As for Me and My House has come to be seen as the first Canadian modernist classic, the first novel to succeed in two ways at once: both as a faithful rendition of small-town life on the Prairies ... and as a beautifully shaped, painstakingly crafted work of art.' It was recognition of his craft, his hard work with pencil, paper, and words that pleased Jim most. He was also immensely pleased by another review in which W.J. Keith compared As for Me and My House to Henry James's The Turn of the Screw and Joseph Conrad's Heart of Darkness, describing them as 'texts so rich in potential meaning that they respond prodigally to virtually any approach or interpretation that is applied to them.'[6]

But perhaps most interesting of all was to see in this collection, for the first time, the review written in 1941 by Robertson Davies for the Peterborough Examiner. Given Davies' subsequent status in Canadian letters, his estimate of As for Me and My House as a 'remarkable' book 'of first-rate importance,' written 'with great delicacy and sensitivity,' was gratifying indeed.[7] But the final paragraph of Davies' review, which predicts even better novels to come, reminded Jim of his failure to realize his promise as a writer. He also wondered if the exuberant praise in this review might have made a difference to him if

he had read it in 1941, might have inspired him to push on with greater conviction. As he looked back, he found it difficult to make an estimate of his life
and career; he hardly knew whether to see himself as a failure or to take pride
in what he had achieved in spite of the odds. Part of him, the emotional and
pessimistic side, felt the odds had been too great from the beginning, that like
a character in a Hardy novel he had been cursed with bad luck and had never
had 'a leg up.' His rational side told him that he probably hadn't tried hard
enough, that he should be grateful for what he had accomplished and for the
readers he had attracted. After all, the general consensus was that As for Me
and My House was one of the country's 'most important' books, and sales were
now not far from a quarter million copies.

'A wonderful talent but a failure of nerve' was Mavis Gallant's estimate of
Jim's career.[8] In May of 1992, Gallant was in Vancouver giving a reading at
Harbour Centre. She had been to Victoria to visit Doyle and Bill Klyn and
expressed an interest in seeing Jimmy Ross again. Gallant had been depressed
to see Doyle Klyn debilitated by a stroke and Bill suffering memory loss, and
she had misgivings about visiting Jim in an extended care facility. However, I
accompanied her there, and she quickly got over her revulsion at the sounds
and smells of hospital life when she found Jim in his room, with his books and
prints around him, and a warm smile and arms extended in greeting. They
kissed and hugged and re-established their friendship of the late 1940s, both
forgetting the strange time in Montreal eleven years earlier when Jim accused
Mavis of stealing his ideas. They talked about mutual friends, including the
Klyns and Mavis's ex-husband, Johnny, but mostly they talked about writing,
comparing the way they wrote, how stories started, and the way they developed. They both agreed that stories were most likely to begin with a strong
image, and it was always a mystery where it came from and why it was so
strong. Sometimes the image was something they had seen or heard ('One's a
heifer, and the other ain't'), or sometimes it seemed to invent itself. Mavis
said to Jim that for her such images always contained the trajectory of the
whole story including the ending, that style not plot was the great interest
during the writing. Jim, on the other hand, lamented that his 'images' did not
always contain the whole story, that many of his images were like seeds that
germinate but fail to grow to maturity. He told her about the many writing
projects that reached halfway and stopped, and how he finally tore them up.
He told her that recently he had started going to a 'pub' in the hospital complex with his young friend, Andy, where there was a blind man, about forty,
who played the piano in the evenings. While he played, his seventy-year-old
mother, head up high, sat by the piano and sang along with the music. 'It is
such a strong image of my own life,' said Jim, 'that I would like to do some-

thing with it in a story, but I can't see where to take it, or how it would end.'[9] He also told Mavis he was plagued by a conviction that a story should contain some kind of philosophical questioning – not just writing out what the image seemed to contain, but developing an idea latent in the image. He gave as an example the troopship story he was engaged with; one of the men in the story asks if the cosmic design really explains why we should come into and go out of this world in pain. But he is afraid always of making such philosophical speculations sound pretentious or sentimental.

They also discussed the matter of ambiguity in writing. Mavis said she dis-liked intentional ambiguity and cited European novels that create a scene of love-making without providing a social or political setting for the characters. She liked her fiction to be clear, precise, and straightforward; life was ambigu-ous and mysterious enough without making it more so – 'the writer's task is to clarify.' Jim suggested his writing was often ambiguous because he did not always understand the implications of the material he was working with; he worked often by instinct alone. He concluded that this was sometimes the strength of his work, but often its weakness – the material was often beyond his control. They both admitted to being perfectionists of sorts, polishing their stories many times over before sending them out for publication. In addition to writing, they discussed some of their other interests. Most pointed perhaps was Mavis's outspoken dislike for nature (in Banff the elk had tried to shove her off the sidewalk, she said). Jim confessed he was sentimental about nature, particularly animals, and felt there was hope for a world that was con-cerned about the environment. But Mavis countered that ecological concerns were just a fad, an evasion of real political thinking. When Jim showed Mavis a collection of Canadian stories translated into Serbo-Croatian that con-tained their work, they said they could at least agree on the fact that they should have been paid a permissions fee for their work! When the two friends parted, they wished each other 'many more stories.'

That year one more young man, who would be important in the last years of Jim's life, introduced himself at the hospital one day. His name was John Whitefoot. He had been a student at Trinity Western University, an evangel-ical Christian school in Langley, BC, but by the spring of 1992 he was working full-time for William Hoffer, a rare book dealer in Vancouver who specialized in Canadiana. Whitefoot had read *As for Me and My House* when he was a high-school student in Kitchener, Ontario, and the book had left a strong impression. When he learned from Hoffer that Sinclair Ross was still living, that Hoffer himself had visited him in a hospital in Vancouver, he was deter-mined to try to meet this author. Whitefoot was beginning to collect Cana-dian first editions, and he had a copy of *As for Me and My House* with a dust jacket in mint condition; so he set out seeking an autograph. At the hospital, Jim was not in his room; Whitefoot found him in the main lounge playing the piano, a television blaring out a soap opera at the other end of the room. After the introduction and the courtesies, Jim, who was always most at ease with the young, was happy to answer the seemingly endless string of questions that Whitefoot brought forward. Jim found himself immediately attracted to this slight, handsome youth, who had the bearing of a young actor, and decided he wanted to see him again. So after he had autographed the first edition of As for Me and My House, he gave him a copy of The Race and Other Stories, edited by Lorraine McMullen, and told him to come back again after he had read it.[10]

And return he certainly did; it was the beginning of a loving friendship on both sides. Whitefoot started visiting regularly, usually early Wednesday evenings after work, and Jim eagerly looked forward to spending an hour or two each week with this young admirer. Sometimes Whitefoot brought a friend, Steve Lutes, and they would have pizza and cokes to share with Jim in his room. Jim would tell his other visitors that he hoped 'the boys' would be coming that night. But the enormous pleasure he felt in their admiration was complicated by an erotic feeling for Whitefoot and its inevitable frustration. John Whitefoot was the last of the men whom Jim had strong feelings for, this time engaging the father-son relation from the point of view of the father. Jim sometimes pressed for some form of physical closeness, but Whitefoot turned such requests aside with light humour, and, in calmer moments, Jim himself would say to others in whom he confided, 'Why would a beautiful youth want to be touched by a loathsome old man?' Perhaps it wasn't so much the tragedy of mismatched love as the sadness of old age pining for youth, and the regrets and lost opportunities spanning the gap between. John Whitefoot was drawn to Jim by the intense admiration he felt for the writer, but he also felt the desire for a grandfatherly presence in his life – and sensing this almost at once, Jim invited him to call him 'Pop.'

The new zest for living that Jim experienced in his friendship with John Whitefoot was doubled in the summer of 1992 when it was announced that he had been made a Member of the Order of Canada. Lorraine McMullen had nominated him several times for this honour, and in 1992 her efforts were finally successful. Jim had listened to Mavis talking about her Governor General's Award for fiction and about her membership in the Order of Canada, so that he was not insensitive to the prestigious nature of this announcement. It was the kind of award he could happily accept; it did not involve lobbying on his own behalf for prizes, nor did it involve filling out forms and competing against others. There was a buzz among the staff at the hospital, which gave a great boost to Jim's sense of self-worth. The medical personnel and the maintenance staff alike congratulated Jim and told him they took pride in the fact that he was a resident in their pavilion. He received letters and notes of congratulation which, with Irene's assistance, he tried to answer. There was also a letter from Ottawa inviting him to the investiture ceremony at Rideau Hall on 21 October 1992. He and Irene toyed with the idea of trying to make the trip, but both recognized it was probably more than could be managed. In the meantime, word was circulating among local members that the governor general would be holding a series of ceremonies while on a trip to British Columbia at the end of October, and Irene persuaded Jim that he should attend one of these functions that was being held in New Westminster and be inducted into the Order by the governor general in person.

The ceremony took place on a clear late October morning in New Westminster's city hall. Jim and Irene travelled there by taxi and took their place along with dozens of others being awarded for various achievements in community service. Mary-Ann and I were also present and took photos of the event, including some motion picture footage.[11] By a curious twist, it was Sheila Kieran, working for the governor general's office, who wrote the tribute, and it was accordingly a strongly worded and deeply felt endorsement of Jim's contribution to Canadian letters. At a reception after the ceremony, the governor general, Ray Hnatyshyn, came over to congratulate Jim and say a few words informally, and Jim was heard to say to his fellow Canadian from Saskatchewan, 'Not bad for two prairie boys.' And still enjoying himself, to Mary-Ann Stouck he quipped, 'Now you will have to show me some respect.' The event was modest but tasteful, though even locally it did not become news because 26 October 1992 was also the day Canadians voted against the new deal for Confederation (the Charlottetown Accord) and the country was preoccupied with its destiny as a whole, not with the life achievement of just one of its gifted citizens. However, at the Brock Fahrni Pavilion, Irene soon had the medal and the certificate framed, and they were a 'confirmation' on the walls for others to see. For his eighty-fifth birthday in January 1993, Jim received, as a Member of the Order of Canada, letters of congratulation from the offices of the prime minister, Brian Mulroney, the leader of the opposition, Jean Chrétien, the mayor of Vancouver, Gordon Campbell, and from provincial and federal members for the hospital's riding. Jim thought, not without some remorse, how proud his mother would have been of him.

Receiving the national award made Jim think back on his life more favourably; it provided a surprising and rewarding sense of conclusion to a career that had otherwise been denied shape. He was seldom prone to nostalgia, for the past was too pitted with failure and disappointments to foster tender emotions for long; but he did think back more warmly now on his youth when, as an aspiring writer, he produced most of his best work. His larger dreams had not materialized – he was not, according to the standards of his era, a success-ful man for, as he would say, he never had a wife, owned a home, or drove a car – but those early times of aspiration and creation were themselves still intact, those days with Pegasus when his imagination lifted him up to 'the roof of life to let him see its vault and spaciousness,' and perhaps, finally, that was reward enough.

For a time, Jim's life was relatively comfortable and satisfying. His interest in his Vancouver friends and in the world at large suggested to Irene that per-haps he should have a telephone in his room; for one thing, it would make it easier for her to keep in touch with his needs on a daily basis, but it would also, she reasoned, give him a feeling of independence and connection to the world. So in the spring of 1993, she had one installed.

One of the first calls he received was a long distance message to inform him that he was being honoured again – this time with the Lifetime Award for Excellence from the Saskatchewan Arts Board. Again he was invited to attend the ceremony, but even with improved health he felt it was more than he could manage. He suggested that the awards committee contact either Ber-tha Brack Lang or his sister's family, both in Indian Head, for someone to rep-resent him at the banquet. He received a letter of congratulations from the Arts Board chair, Wayne Schmalz, dated May 13, informing him that his great-great-nephew, Shaun Miller, would accept the award at the dinner to be held that evening in the Saskatchewan Hotel in Regina. Jim dictated a letter to Irene to be sent to Schmalz, in which he said, 'Your letter makes me feel at least ten years younger. Rejuvenation is the word. It brings back memories of people who were good and kind, and the tenth [sic] of May becomes a red-let-ter day in my life.'[12] The evening was a high-profile event in Saskatchewan: the lieutenant-governor was present, and popular CBC broadcaster Knowlton Nash was master of ceremonies. The award itself consisted of a bronze bust of Saskatchewan artist Ernest Lindner, sculpted by another provincial artist, Joe Fafard. In the summer, the award was brought to Jim in person by a member of the Board, who made a fuss over him and had photographs taken of Jim and herself for the Arts Board files. Later she sent him copies for the scrapbook Irene was putting together, which included some pictures from the banquet with his nephew receiving the award. Jim took bemused pleasure in being regarded as 'the father of Saskatchewan fiction,' as one critic had phrased it.[13]

In May 1993, two young visitors introduced themselves as students from the Vancouver Film School; they said they wanted to make a short documentary film about Jim and his work and asked if, in a future visit, he would let them take some footage at the hospital. The young man, Frank Schmidt, was an international student from Switzerland and had read some of Jim's stories in a course at school that included Canadian fiction; his partner, Mairze Almas, was a Vancouver girl who had also studied some of Jim's stories in high school. They were writing up a project proposal, as part of their study at the Film School, and hoped to get Jim's cooperation. Jim was taken at once by the blonde youth from Switzerland, and although he dreaded the idea of being filmed, he wanted to encourage the young man's interest; he agreed to give it some thought and let them know on a return visit. The young pair did considerable research and outlined a film that was to include archival photos from Saskatchewan's dust bowl period, pictures of Jim when he was a boy, interviews with teachers of Jim's work, and some footage of Jim at Brock Fahrni. They brought a great deal of enthusiasm and energy to the project, and Jim enjoyed their coming and going and their desire to consult him on all aspects of the project.

The summer of 1993 was one of the happiest Jim experienced in many years. *Queen's Quarterly* published a commemorative centennial issue titled 'Sounds That Echo Still,' and 'Cornet at Night' was one of five stories that was reprinted. Other writers whose works were republished included Margaret Laurence, Margaret Atwood, Dorothy Livesay, Michael Ondaatje, Al Purdy, and George Grant. Jim was very aware of their reputations and felt it was indeed another confirmation to be included in their company. Authors wrote him notes of praise, saying how he had influenced them, and he was flattered by the wry tribute in Thomas King's novel *Green Grass, Running Water* when one of the characters describes the important books she is reading. The attention and awards he was receiving gave Jim a sense of self-worth he had never known before, a realization that he had an audience at last, and this seemed to translate into better physical health. John Whitefoot encouraged him to walk again ('We'll go dancing!'), and with concentration Jim was able to move about without a wheelchair or walker. On the spur of the moment, he decided to join John O'Connor and his daughters at Irene's townhouse for dinner, where he not only entertained everyone with his dry-humoured conversation but climbed a flight of stairs to the street unaided. Mary-Ann and I were there with the film we had taken at the Order of Canada induction, and Jim was pleased by the figure he cut in the movie. That same week, he accepted an invitation to have lunch with Mary Moscovich at her home in West Vancouver. He enjoyed her hospitality and conversation and was awed by the spaciousness and location of her waterfront home.

He also liked to think of himself hard at work that summer. He did enjoy working at the troopship story – it gave his days a purpose – but he had missed

Keath Fraser's deadlines for a short piece (*Bad Trips* was published in 1991, followed by *Worst Journeys* in 1992) and began to see his manuscript as something bigger than a personal memoir, as perhaps a novella about two Prairie boys who had set off for the war in Europe, and who had time to reflect on their past lives. He had several working titles in his head, including 'A Field Full of Mountains' from Bunyan's *Pilgrim's Progress* and 'North by Northeast.' He liked to work at his desk in the morning and have something to show Irene when she came later in the day. But if there were visitors, he was glad to let them intrude – he had no deadlines – and there were many visitors, for it was known now that he received company happily and that the supposed recluse of Canadian literature was a witty and entertaining conversationalist. There were visitors with academic interests, including Sandra Djwa, who was writing a biography of Roy Daniells, Paul Comeau, a Vancouver teacher who had published an insightful article on Jim's work in *Canadian Literature*, and Barbara Pell, who taught at Trinity Western University and knew John Whitefoot. And there were visitors like Bob Savory from Winnipeg and Gladys Olson MacLean from the Rolling Prairie District of Saskatchewan, who were hearing about Jim and wanted to visit him again. There were also pleasant afternoons spent with men living at the hospital itself, like dentist Joe Craib and his friend 'from the outside,' Frank Collier, who had been a federal judge, and Philip Headley, who did crossword puzzles and regularly borrowed Jim's dictionary to track down obscure words. One day a clue in the 'Cross Canada Crossword' read 'Author, James Sinclair ___.'

But the well-being of that summer was not to last. By September the equilibrium that had more or less held steady in the medication seemed to break down, and Jim began experiencing periods of disorientation again. His social behaviour changed radically. Whereas Jim had always been reserved and polite by nature, he became outspoken and demanding, gentleness giving way to outbursts of anger. He suspected infidelities of his friends and accused staff of stealing his belongings. He told the young woman engaged in the film project he didn't want to see her anymore, only her male partner. He challenged visitors with the information that he was a homosexual. Keath phoned Irene to see if she had noticed a change, and, in turn, Irene talked to Jim's doctor, who explained that he was needing more medication to control the Parkinson's symptoms, and the increase unfortunately was playing havoc with his 'personality' and his normal patterns of behaviour. As a result, it was no longer possible to plan things. Mary-Ann was going to take Jim out to Langley to see her horse, an Arabian whose finer points they had discussed several times, but his condition seemed too unstable to make the long drive.

Dinner at a restaurant became an unpredictable occasion; Jim might insist on leaving the table to talk with one of the waiters or with some of the other patrons rather than eating his meal.

There was a sad, confused afternoon in late September. Mavis Gallant was giving a special Sunday afternoon reading at the 1993 Vancouver Writers' Festival on Granville Island, and, with Jim's permission, John Whitefoot earlier in the summer had arranged with the organizer, Alma Lee, that Jim be in attendance in the front row during the reading. Lee was delighted at the prospect of having this famous but elusive figure present at the festival, and Jim seemed to be looking forward to making something of a public appearance and seeing Mavis again. It was arranged that everyone would meet with Mavis for something to eat after the reading. But things went badly. Lee greeted Jim and Irene warmly at the door, but when Jim saw that John Whitefoot was with his new girlfriend, Tonya Ganderton, he was upset and in an ill humour. Mavis made a dramatic appearance on stage and gave an eloquent rendering of two of her short stories, but she made no reference to the fact that her friend of forty-five years and one of Canada's most distinguished authors was seated for all to see in a wheelchair in the front row. Afterwards she said that the stage lights were in her eyes and she could not be sure if Jim was there or not. Jim was not noticed as he was wheeled out of the theatre. In the nearby restaurant there was nearly an hour's wait while Mavis signed books and talked with her fans, and when she joined the party waiting for her, she was too distracted by the attentions of the crowd to enjoy a small gathering. Jim was sullen and withdrawn, and the two friends, over large plates of cold, unappetizing food, had little to say to each other. This was the last time they would meet.

One of the biggest changes wrought by the increase in the medication was the loss of attention span. Jim would begin to read and after finishing a page would put the book down and search for something else on his shelf. The same happened if he tried to work on the troopship story; after writing a line or rephrasing a passage, he would forget the sequence and the point of the passage. The medication made him restless and irritable, and he would wheel himself out into the hall in search of distractions. Philip Headley, a man made compassionate perhaps by a life of suffering from the effects of polio, would try to calm Jim down and would fetch a nurse if he seemed in genuine distress. His room was directly across the hall from Jim's, and he would keep watch to make sure his friend was all right. Joe Craib, too, would try to help Jim get his bearings, telling stories about his boyhood in Hanna, Alberta, and about his days overseas in the army as a dental assistant. Both Craib and Headley understood Jim's importance as a writer and took pleasure in counting Jim their friend. When Andy Trapnell noticed Jim could not seem to get beyond a page or two of a book, he started reading to him in the hour before he reported for work. They both liked the Russians and read Dostoevsky (Jim's favourite) and several stories by Tolstoy, including the long novella *The Cossacks*. When Andy suggested some James Joyce one day, Jim said he was intimidated by Joyce, who was 'so damned smart,' and didn't want to be intimidated anymore. He hardly seemed to care when he was told the film project had been postponed. In fact, the project came to an end; the young couple were told at the Film School that their idea was too ambitious, and that a documentary on Sinclair Ross, properly done, would require more time and resources than their studies at the Film School would allow, regrettable advice from the point of view of literary history.

Jim's most purposeful time was spent under John Whitefoot's supervision, signing his name to a page for a chapbook of passages taken from *As for Me and My House*. Through William Hoffer, John Whitefoot had come to know Richard Spafford, a rare and used book dealer in Regina, who had a special interest in western Canadian writing. Spafford came up with the idea of a chapbook consisting of passages from *As for Me and My House*, and with Whitefoot's encouragement, Jim agreed to sign some copies. From Jim's vantage, it was a project that would keep Whitefoot coming to see him, but as it turned out, it would lead to a more ambitious undertaking before the end of the year. When Jim agreed to sign and letter twenty-six copies of the chapbook, Spafford suggested to Fraser Seeley of Fifth House, a western publishing company in Saskatoon, the idea of an autographed edition of *As for Me and My House*, one that would be expensively produced for collectors and library archives. Seeley liked the idea and arranged to come to Vancouver to discuss the project with Jim and John Whitefoot. In the meantime, Spafford distributed the chapbooks freely at the biennial meeting of the Association for Canadian Studies in the United States, held in New Orleans, November 1993.

Jim's behavioural problems grew increasingly problematic for the staff at Brock Fahrni: he was sometimes irritable and given to sinister accusations; at other times, he appeared to be hallucinating and overcome with paranoid fears. As the administration of Brock Fahrni Pavilion was shifted in the fall of 1993 to St Vincent's Hospital and staff changes ensued, Jim was convinced there was a revolution taking place, and his thoughts appeared to be vividly choreographed by scenes from the riot he witnessed in Greece in 1976. He telephoned friends to tell them of his plight and, if they were out, left messages piled up on their answering machines. He began telephoning for fast food deliveries, and his desk drawers filled with uneaten pizzas. Irene found his money, ten and twenty dollar bills, being used as bookmarks or simply hidden in corners of the room, while in the meantime he accused the staff of stealing from him. He also made public his sexual fantasies, describing himself in bondage to a tall woman who was the head administrator at Brock Fahrni, undergoing sexual punishments at her hands, he said, and telling visitors that he made love to one of the nurses on the floor – 'she was begging for it.' Some days he was found exposing himself in the hall. Jim, unknowingly, was making himself vulnerable in ways he had spent a lifetime avoiding. It was a frenetic and difficult time for Jim and for everyone involved with his care, and although the mental turbulence gradually subsided with modification in the drug therapy, it never left completely.

John Whitefoot weathered the storms of Jim's disposition and pressed him to go forward with the autographed edition of As for Me and My House. John would bring the insert pages for Jim to sign while he was there, although it did not always happen, for some days Jim refused to work, wanting to recount some of his fantasies to his young friend instead, and other days, if the medication had been reduced, his hand was too shaky to make a signature. But gradually most of the 250 copies were signed and sent back to Fraser Seeley in Saskatoon. Plans for the special edition changed during production. The original proposal was for 100 copies at a cost of two hundred dollars per volume, and Robertson Davies was to be approached to write an 'afterword,' but this proved to be more costly than the publishing house could afford.[14] Also in the planning stage was a trade paperback edition of short stories – Jim would select ten of his favourites – but McClelland and Stewart held copyright to the stories in The Lamp at Noon collection and was only willing to release three for publication by Fifth House. As Jim wanted at least six of those stories for the new collection, the idea was abandoned.

In April 1994 Jim had a phone call from Alma, Michigan, to say that his brother had died. Stuart was ninety-four. He had also suffered with Parkinson's disease for several years and experienced the same kinds of mental confusion and unrest as Jim. Stuart's death made Jim reflect on family and his lack of descendants, and he turned in thought to his sister's family. For years he had a photograph of a great-great niece on his bulletin board, a bright-eyed, attractive young woman who worked as an actress and model in Toronto. He also had a recent photograph of a great-great nephew in Indian Head, James Miller, brother of Shaun, said to be named after 'Uncle Jim.' He hoped that the boy, in his late teens, might make a trip to Vancouver to see him and toyed with the idea of sending money to pay his way, but friends cautioned that there was more responsibility to bringing a teenaged boy to Vancouver than simply paying his travel fare. Glennys Baker, one of Jim's two surviving greatnieces (who would be his heirs), spoke to Irene about the possibility of coming to Vancouver for a holiday, but she did not make the trip while Jim was alive.

As the frenzy of Jim's condition gradually subsided, it was replaced with apathy. He could no longer read or concentrate on the music from the radio and spent much of his time seated in his wheelchair staring out to the hall. Nursing and cleaning staff would turn the radio to their favourite stations, and Jim would frequently spend the day with a rock station blaring in his room. It took visitors considerable effort to engage him in conversation; his disinterest was compounded by the weakening of his voice, sometimes to an inaudible whisper. There were days when he seemed himself again, and he would sort through the books on his shelf or wheel down the hall to be part of the company in the lounge, but those days were growing fewer. Irene had the telephone discontinued, as he no longer used it, and removed the work sheets for the troopship story, as he was no longer able to work at his desk. He often had no desire to see people at all: he asked a scholar from Moscow to leave after she had been there only five minutes; and when Bill Thorne, his Win-nipeg friend when he was writing As for Me and My House, came to stay the afternoon, he signalled to Irene that he was tired, and so Thorne left after about twenty minutes. Yet he still relied on seeing Irene every other day and Keath or Lorraine on the weekends. The fluctuation in Jim's condition was apparent around the time of his eighty-seventh birthday. Visiting that day with my wife and me, he was his ironic and humorous self. When Mary-Ann observed that he had reached a wonderful age, 'Says you,' he replied with a piercing gaze. Talking about the troopship story, she asked, 'What must you have been thinking on the boat as you left Halifax harbour?' and he replied in his deadpan manner: 'I thought, I am on a boat leaving Halifax harbour.' But a few days later, I found him in a particularly distressful state. He was con-vinced again that a revolution was under way, and he had managed to get some of his clothes out of the closet and pictures and medal off the wall, and was preparing to flee.

In March 1995 the special edition of As for Me and My House was ready from Fifth House, and Jim received twenty-five copies that were designated from the outset as author's copies. Jim was pleased with the production values of the book – the maroon-coloured linen binding and slipcase with gold let-tering on the spine, the heavy, cream art paper, the wide margins and leading – although he felt there could have been a little more space at the bottom of each page. 'Nothing is ever perfect,' he said, 'although this comes very close.' This collector's edition was another of those testimonies that his writing life had not been in vain. The hundred-dollar cost of the book, however, was something he could not understand – 'It will never sell at that price,' he said, 'it will be another commercial failure.'[15] The idea of a collector's edition was at that point beyond his grasp. He wished nonetheless that his mother could see the book; certainly the price would have amazed and impressed her. But Jim's failure to remain lucid was in striking evidence one day when John Whitefoot found him in his room tearing apart one of the collector's editions, twisting the cover loose from the backing. 'The doctor says I should do something to exercise my hands,' he explained. Jim also began giving away copies of the collector's edition to anyone who happened to pass by the room. When Andy Trapnell saw what was happening, he placed the remaining undamaged copies at the back of the top shelf of his closet. Many of the other books in his library were submitted to a similar fate as he grew increasingly disoriented, some torn to pieces, others given away. His condition seemed to grow worse when, in July, Irene, now retired, moved from Vancouver to Mayne Island; she was no longer there on a regular basis to anchor Jim to everyday reality.

But in early August of 1995 there was a day that gave Jim enormous pleasure and which he continued to remember for several weeks subsequently. Except for his appearance in one of Doris Saunders's classes in 1941, Jim had refused all invitations to read and discuss his work at colleges or universities. Yet he was intensely interested not only in what critics were saying about his work, but in the ideas that it seemed to engage. For a couple of years, I had been discussing with him some of the new theories of gender and sexuality being proposed by writers like Judith Butler wherein identity is not viewed as something fixed, but always shifting and responsive to circumstances. In this light, he liked to think about his own sexual history: the constraints imposed on a Prairie boy by the rigid social codes of his era, and the expanded grasp of sexuality he had come to know in intimate relations with both men and women. He delighted in hearing stories about famous men like Laurence Olivier and Leonard Bernstein as their bisexual lives were being revealed to the public, and he liked to speculate on the sexuality of some of Canada's most famous men – Pierre Trudeau, who declared the state had no place in the bedrooms of the nation, Glenn Gould, the famous pianist, whose comportment was neurotic, epicene, and Arthur Erickson, the celebrated bachelor architect, who restlessly travelled the world.

In the summer of 1995, I taught a six-week, senior-level 'Special Studies' course at Simon Fraser University that focused exclusively on the fiction of Sinclair Ross and theoretical approaches to his writing. The twenty-three students in the seminar were amazed to think this classic author was still living and that he was domiciled nearby in a Vancouver hospital, and they grew eager to pay the author a visit. Jim's state was so fragile that it didn't seem like a very good idea, but I informed him nonetheless about the class and their interest in his work. It seemed to rouse him from his apathy that summer, and he grew curious about the students and what they were saying about his writings. Finally, a visit was arranged for Tuesday, August 8, at two o'clock in the afternoon, during the last week of the course, and the staff at Brock Fahrni were alerted that the class was coming. On that day, I found Jim eagerly anticipating his guests; he was dressed in a clean shirt and wearing his gray Harris tweed jacket, and he suggested that we take the elevator down to the lobby, where the students were waiting, and 'make an entrance.' The effect indeed was rewarding; Jim seemed to sense at once the admiration and keen interest in his audience, and in the lounge off the lobby he answered their questions and regaled them with anecdotes for nearly an hour. 'Why didn't you give Mrs Bentley a first name?' a young woman with feminist interests asked. 'I guess I just didn't apply myself,' he replied. Another asked, 'What do you think of all the new theory? There is a conference theorizing the male nipple at the University of Kalamazoo.' Jim looked around the room; then with a grin: 'How far is it to Kalamazoo?' Remembering the recent readings of his work at the Ottawa seminar, he said theory was good if it kept people reading and thinking about books. 'That's what good criticism is always for.' Then, intrigued by the sight of a young man wearing his hair in a pony tail, he turned to the student and asked if he was a girl or a guy. 'Or perhaps you are somewhere in between,' he suggested. The student was somewhat abashed and there was a brief pause. 'But you are good looking,' said Jim, 'so it doesn't matter either way.' At three o'clock, with the staff change, the lobby grew noisy and the group prepared to leave; but Jim didn't want things to break up and insisted they come upstairs to see his room, which they did in groups of five and six at a time. He showed them the remains of his library, a scrapbook Irene was keeping, and his Order of Canada medal and certificate on the wall. When I returned a few days later, Jim asked at once if I would bring the students back again; he enjoyed himself immensely, he admitted, and wished now he had talked with groups of university students before.

In November everyone noticed one of those steep declines that come suddenly to the elderly. Jim would sit now for long stretches in his wheelchair, as if in a comatose state. His mind was unusually clear during this period, but almost nothing roused his interest. He was exceedingly frail and had to be assisted to eat. Mary-Ann and I took him the usual box of cookies for Christmas, but he would only take one if it was put to his mouth. He preferred his curtains closed and said to Keath, 'I'd just like to slip away.' John Whitefoot hand fed him when he went for his evening visits, although John, now married to Tonya, was living out in Cloverdale, working and going to school again, so that he had fewer evenings to spend with Jim. Irene came over on his eighty-eighth birthday and found him in a depleted state, and Jim said to her: 'How much longer?'

It wasn't very much longer. On Sunday, the 25th of February, 1996, Jim's friends were informed by the staff at Brock Fahrni that he had collapsed that evening and had been taken to Vancouver General Hospital, where he was on intravenous feeding and antibiotics. He arrived at the General in a dehydrated state; his lungs were filled with pneumonia, and his breathing laboured. The next day, with Keath, John, Mary-Ann, and Irene at the bedside, Jim's doctor said he would not regain consciousness, and the friends present agreed that it would be best to take him off the life-support system. He was returned the next morning – Tuesday – to Brock Fahrni Pavilion, where Keath, John, Irene, and now Andy as well kept watch all day and through the night. The doctor said she had not witnessed such loyalty around a deathbed since working in a Native community in the North several years before. But when I arrived at the hospital Wednesday morning there was confusion: Jim had regained consciousness (he was smiling and trying to speak to John and Andy), and his vital organs were functioning again. Should he be taken back to the General (or possibly nearby St Vincent's) and put on intravenous to continue rehydration and the fight against infection, or should he remain at Brock Fahrni and be given morphine to relieve the pain until the fight was over? Friends were divided. The doctor's opinion was that if he lived, the quality of Jim's life would be even less than what it was before this crisis. So he remained at Brock Fahrni and was given morphine to help him sleep away the final hours. Keath returned home in the evening, but Irene, John, and Andy kept their vigil. Then Andy, who was working his shift and was overcome with exhaustion, rode his bicycle back to his apartment, where, as he entered the door, the phone was ringing and it was Irene to say that Jim died shortly after midnight. It was now Thursday, February 29, leap-year day. Andy cycled back at once and burst into uncontrollable sobbing when he came into the room. Irene went to phone the Frasers and myself and Mary-Ann. Andy and John sat talking about their dearest friend, about death and about the purpose of living, and then, eventually, Irene and Andy left, and John Whitefoot stayed the rest of the night, alone with the body, playing softly some of the music that Jim loved best. John had not left Jim's bedside since Monday.

By Friday there were notices in the papers of Jim's death and tributes on the radio. David Staines, general editor of the New Canadian Library, and Lorna Crozier, Saskatchewan writer about to publish her 'collected poems of Mrs Bentley,' spoke about Sinclair Ross on CBC's *Morningside*, and there was a deft tribute by Robert Kroetsch published in the Saturday issue of the *Globe and Mail*. A service in the Brock Fahrni chapel was scheduled for Saturday, March 2, at two o'clock in the afternoon. For days the sun had been shining radiantly, seemingly at odds with the week's events, but it seemed to shine appropriately that afternoon as Jim's friends gathered to pay their last respects. Everything at the service was simple, in keeping with his style and wishes; there was a copy of his last portrait photo on the altar table at the front of the chapel and an arrangement of flowers from the nieces and nephews in Saskatchewan and Ontario. The maple leaf Canadian flag, the Union Jack, and the Red Ensign, under which soldiers fought during the Second World War, were standing behind the altar as reminders that it was a military service. The hospital chaplain led the service and made mistakes that would have amused the deceased: 'We gather to pay honour to James Ross Sinclair ...' Pale mauve plastic flowers stood ready in case there were no real ones, and the electric organ music could have been used in the satiric presentation of any number of Sinclair Ross's small fictional towns.

But the readings and tributes by Jim's friends were sincere and moving: Mary-Ann Stouck spoke of their shared love for horses and read a passage from 'The Outlaw'; John O'Connor's son, Geoffrey, spoke on his father's behalf and read passages from As for Me and My House and 'A Day with Pegasus.' Patricia Robertson and Keath Fraser spoke of their friendship with Jim as writers, and Keath read from Sawbones Memorial. Lorraine McMullen gave a fine tribute in honour of Sinclair Ross, the writer, and Jimmy Ross, the man and her friend. Andy Trapnell read from 'The Lamp at Noon,' drawing listeners to the perfection of the prose, and also read a poem by Hermann Hesse titled 'Beim Schlafengehen' (Going to Sleep). It is the text for the third in Richard Strauss's song cycle 'Four Last Songs,' which he and Jim had often listened to together. The tributes concluded with John Whitefoot reading the one hundred and twenty-first Psalm: 'I will lift up mine eyes unto the hills, from whence cometh my help ...,' a passage from the Bible that Jim valued above others. The service ended with the playing of taps and those present placing poppies on a cross. There were about forty-five gathered in the chapel: some staff and patients from the hospital (the latter in wheelchairs), a few from the community at large, Irene and some of her family, the Frasers, a couple of students from Simon Fraser University, and a few like Bill Thorne, who had known Jim when he was a young man living in Winnipeg. There were refreshments in the Vets Lounge adjacent to the chapel, where people could meet or renew acquaintances and could talk about James Sinclair Ross, the writer and their friend. Bill Thorne grew expansive as younger people at the gathering showed an interest in his role in the writing of As for Me and My House, but by four o'clock everyone had left. Jim's remains, in the meantime, had been cremated and were being sent to Indian Head for interment as he had requested. Although he had not been back to Saskatchewan since the death of his mother, nearly forty years before, he felt it was appropriate that, as his birthplace, it should also be his final resting place.

But, of course, the Saskatchewan boy lives on in the writings of Sinclair Ross, which reach around the globe – in classes taught in a Swiss high school, in a story translated into Serbo-Croatian, or in a master's thesis written in China.[16] In Canada, his writings remain hospitable to the new ways we devise for reading literature and culture – to feminist readings and queer readings, to discussions of ethnicity and race, to studies of canon formation, and very likely to many more strategies that will follow. Almost all his writing is now in print, and one feels confident it will remain so for a long time to come.

To his biographers, Jimmy Ross told the story of his life as set forth here, but his readers can see clearly its public face in the fiction he wrote about farmers and horses, and can glimpse its private lineaments encrypted in the tangled relations of the characters in his novels. Yet, one must remember at the same time that he did not want to *express himself*; rather, like Chekhov, he wanted us to see some of the things he saw. The stark and unforgiving beauty of the prairie was one of those things, captured with all the aching loveliness of something experienced alone. He wanted us to see the society we have created and to feel uncomfortable with religion as coercive rhetoric, with our attitudes to race and ethnicity, and with our rigid constructions of gender and sexuality. He also wanted to remind us that human beings have a transforming capacity for love and kindness. But he did not presume – grade-eleven education – to teach or instruct; rather, through the evasions of Mrs Bentley in *As for Me and My House* and the unnarrated dialogues and ruminations of the townspeople in *Sawbones Memorial*, he made *us* the authors of his texts instead. As Robert Kroetsch suggested in his obituary tribute,[17] Sinclair Ross embraced his historical moment with a kind of invisibility that lets us better see ourselves and the world around us, and in so doing he taught us a new way to read.

Notes

Note: Letters from Ross (JSR) that are cited in the notes without an archival location remain in private collections. (A list of correspondents whose letters from JSR are in private collections is included in the Bibliography.)

Abbreviations

JSR   James Sinclair Ross
M&SA   McClelland and Stewart Archive
MCC   Macmillan Company Collection
MUL   McMaster University Library
NAC   National Archives of Canada / Archives nationaux du Canada
QUL   Queen's University Library
TFRBL Thomas Fisher Rare Book Library
UBCL   University of British Columbia Library
URL   University of Regina Library
USL   University of Saskatchewan Library
YUL   York University Library

1. Wild Rose

1 Mrs Clifford is described in *Footprints of Our Pioneers* [Shellbrook, SK: Wild Rose and Area History Book Committee, 1990] as a full-blooded Cree, 'a very kind and pleasant lady' (284), whose capable hands delivered many babies in the Wild Rose area. Her husband was an Englishman and a university graduate, but he had no skills for pioneer life or farming.
2 This version of Ross's birth is recorded in Ken Mitchell's 'The Ross File.'
3 JSR in conversation, 17 July 1992. A similar version can be found in notes made by Sheila Kieran, 30 Nov. 1972 and 1 Dec. 1972. She records Ross's words as fol-

lows: 'My father went to get the midwife, a half-breed named Mary Belle. My parents were teetotalers, though they kept some brandy "for medicinal purposes." Anyway, when Mary Belle arrived, my mother asked would she like a hot toddy. My father went out to feed the animals and when he got back, Mary Belle was out stiff on the floor. So I came into the world unassisted.'

4 These details were recalled in interviews with Albert Pugh, Shellbrook, SK, 28 June 1992, and Ernest Wernham, Prince Albert, SK, 29 June 1992.

5 These details and the description of the house that follows are largely taken from Ross's memoir 'Just Wind and Horses.'

6 See 'Just Wind and Horses' for a full description of the Ross homestead.

7 Dominion land grants and title certificates for this region are located in the Saskatchewan Archives Office, University of Saskatchewan.

8 Peter Ross was born in Ontario, on a farm near Owen Sound, of parents said to be from the Shetland Islands (see McMullen, *Sinclair Ross* 15), while census records for 1901 list Kate Ross as born in Ireland.

9 Ross's mother also told him about a more austere branch of Scottish ancestors on the Patterson side, Auld Kirk Cameronians, who would not light a stove on Sundays, 'drank skim milk and ate oatcakes on the Lord's Day.'

10 According to Kate Ross's account, her father died at age thirty in the pulpit in Edinburgh, but records for St Mark's Unitarian Church in that city contain no record of his death or of his having preached there.

11 See Norman Fergus Black, *History of Saskatchewan and the Northwest Territories*, 1: 394–5.

12 Mitchell, 'The Ross File.'

13 See the *Shellbrook Chronicle* for 23 Oct. 1914 and 1 May 1915.

14 Ernest Wernham, interviewed 29 June 1992. Roy Orman, interviewed by Ken Mitchell for 'The Ross File,' remembered some of the women of Wild Rose viewing Mrs Ross as 'stuck up' and wondering if she took some kind of drug. Stuart Ross, interviewed in Alma, Michigan, May 1992, provided a more benign account of his parents, emphasizing how hard they worked to make a living and what a good housekeeper his mother was.

15 Some of these details are from alternate versions of 'Just Wind and Horses,' filed with the Sinclair Ross Papers, NAC, MG 30 D369, box 1, folders 13–22.

16 The quoted passages in this paragraph are from 'Just Wind and Horses,' 95.

17 Ibid., 91.

18 Stuart Ross, interviewed in Alma, Michigan, May 1992.

2. The Housekeeper's Son

1 See the *Shellbrook Chronicle*, 16 December 1916. This item is curious because Effie was the Rosses' only daughter and there is no evidence that in 1916 they were liv-

ing in Prince Albert. Jim, who would have been nearly nine when Effie married, had no memory of attending his sister's wedding.

2 I cannot claim to know all the places where Ross and his mother lived at this time in his life. For example, he recalled their going to Kelowna, BC, where his mother worked for a time packing fruit, but school records in that area are incomplete, and according to Alan Patterson, local historian in the Okanagan Valley, those records extant do not list a James Ross in their registers.

3 The Ketcheson brothers are identified as successful farmers in Lars Larson, *Yesterday Is Gone Forever*, 153.

4 The comparison is admittedly somewhat offset by a difference of nine years. The information on Peter Ross's homestead is dated 1908, whereas the patent for pre-emption, which gives the data for Ketcheson's holdings, was registered in 1917. Land patents can be searched at the Saskatchewan Archives Office, University of Saskatchewan.

5 Emil Pederson, Abbey, SK, interviewed 13 May 1993.

6 Gladys Olson McLean, Central Butte, SK, interviewed 15 May 1993.

7 Orville Olson, Vernon, BC, interviewed 12 June 1994.

8 Information about and impressions of Nels Forfang were garnered from Douglas Bell, Riverhurst, SK, Ada McKay, Riverhurst, SK, and Gladys Olson McLean, Central Butte, SK, all interviewed 15 May 1993.

9 These recollections are from Gladys Olson McLean, Central Butte, SK, and Myrtle Doell, Chaplin, SK, both interviewed 15 May 1993.

10 *Sawbones Memorial*, 59–61.

11 *Whir of Gold*, 27–8.

12 Vesta Pickel, Regina, SK, interviewed 2 July 1992 and 18 May 1993.

13 Frank Woodbury, interviewed 7 April 1993.

14 *Stoughton Times*, 5 July 1923.

15 Ibid., 16 Aug. 1923.

16 *Indian Head News*, 28 Feb. 1924.

17 Ibid., 13 Dec. 1923 and 10 Jan. 1924.

18 Belvah Jardine Howatt, Victoria, BC, interviewed mid-February 1993.

3. Bank Clerk

1 JSR in conversation, 2 July 1993.

2 See Roy Daniells Papers, UBCL, box 4, folder 1.

3 In an essay titled '"The Child Is Father to the Manuscript": Sinclair Ross and His Women,' Lorraine McMullen holds that Catherine Ross is 'the key to the relationships between men and women in his stories and novels'

4 Harold Braaten, Abbey, SK, interviewed 28 June 1992; and Svea Pederson, Abbey, SK, interviewed 13 May 1993.

5 See John Speir, 'History of Abbey Village,' 55–7.

6 JSR in conversation, 3 June 1993.

7 Dorothy Volden, Lancer, SK, interviewed 14 May 1993.

8 An examination of Canadian Chautauqua programs from the late 1920s suggests that this group was more likely a Russian Cossack chorus, making its first Canadian tour in the summer of 1928. The advertising for the event, citing the choir's 'weird and enchanting harmony,' is curiously parallel to the author's memory. A critic is quoted as having written: 'It seemed as if we were carried into another world unlike our own, yet akin to it in human understanding. The almost uncanny power of their music gripped our hearts in a way never to be forgotten.' A collection of Chautauqua programs can be found in the Manitoba Archives, Winnipeg.

9 Dorothy Volden, Lancer, SK, interviewed 14 May 1993.

10 JSR, interviewed 22 Jan. 1991.

11 Earle Toppings, *Canadian Writers on Tape: Sinclair Ross.*

12 Lars Larson, *Yesterday Is Gone Forever*, 282.

13 Johnny 'Cross the Tracks' was suggested by Dwayne Thompson, Victoria, BC, in an interview 12 Feb. 1995.

14 Information about the Hunchiak family was provided by Dwayne Thompson, Victoria, BC, in an interview 12 Feb. 1995, and by Lena Hunchiak Campe, North Vancouver, BC, interviewed 21 Feb. 1995.

15 Bessie Cottingham, Swift Current, SK, interviewed by telephone 9 March 1995.

16 I am indebted here to John O'Connor, who located and provided me with the Washington State death certificate for Peter Ross.

17 These words remembered by JSR, 12 Feb. 1994.

18 Theodora Dowsley, interviewed 11 June 1992.

4. Musician

1 Frank Woodbury interviewed 7 April 1993.

2 See *Arcola and South of the Moose Mountains*, which provides the details of local history in the area.

3 There was a vogue in the nineteenth century for naming North American towns Arcola (there are at least five in the United States); the only thing in common between Arcola, Saskatchewan, and the location in north-eastern Italy is low, marshy ground.

4 Letter from JSR to Ken Mitchell, 18 Nov. 1976.

5 *Moose Mountain Star-Standard*, 19 Feb. 1930.

6 Correspondence with two long-time Arcola residents greatly expanded the information available about cultural life in Arcola in this period. Letters from Verna Carr, Regina, SK, are dated 9 April, 29 April, and 29 June 1994; letters from Evelyn Gordon, Arcola, SK, are dated 6 April, 3 May, and 1 June 1994.

7 *Moose Mountain Star-Standard*, 2 April 1930.

8 Ibid., 26 July 1930.

9 *Arcola and South of the Moose Mountains* and *Arcola-Kisbey Golden Heritage*.

10 *Arcola and South of the Moose Mountains*, 76.

11 Cal Ingram, interviewed in Arcola, SK, 2 July 1992. His memories of JSR are also recorded in Ken Mitchell's 'The Ross File.'

12 JSR in conversation, 2 Feb. 1994.

13 JSR in conversation, 11 Jan. 1994.

14 Ibid.

15 Dorothy Cornell's accomplishments are described in an article in the *Moose Mountain Star-Standard*, 5 Nov. 1930.

16 JSR in conversation, 11 Jan. 1994.

17 Ibid.

18 These concerts are described in the *Moose Mountain Star-Standard*, 27 May 1931.

19 See *Moose Mountain Star-Standard*, 15 July 1931.

20 Festival results were reported in the *Moose Mountain Star-Standard*, 20 April 1932.

21 Forbes Murray's activities are recorded in the issue of 28 Oct. and 18 Nov. 1931 of the *Moose Mountain Star-Standard*.

22 JSR in conversation, 3 March 1993.

23 The church was not the only judge. In *Never Going Back: A History of Queer Activism in Canada*, Tom Warner gives an exact account of the institutional construction and social oppression of homosexuality in the first half of the twentieth century. See especially the opening chapter, titled 'The Roots of Oppression,' 17–41.

24 JSR in conversation, 3 March 1993.

25 *As for Me and My House*, 81.

26 Keith Clarke died 15 May 1941 when his plane crashed in a training accident in Oxfordshire, England. Clarke was remembered by Clarence Samis, an Arcola friend living and interviewed in Vancouver, BC, 24 June 1994. Samis roomed with Clarke for one year at Wesley College but didn't feel especially close to him. He observed that Clarke 'started life with so much promise, but after university went back to Arcola and made no career for himself. His life lost momentum ... I could speculate.' Samis saw the war as a form of escape for Keith Clarke.

27 These hurtful words, attributed to his mother, were repeated several times in my conversations with JSR.

28 Tom McLellan's recollections are in a letter to Ken Mitchell dated 17 Oct. 1976 (URL, Ken Mitchell Collection).

29 The farewell party for Kate Ross is described in the *Moose Mountain Star-Standard* 8 Dec. 1932.

30 JSR in conversation, 18 July 1992.

31 This letter, in the Sinclair Ross Papers, NAC, MG 30 D369, box 1, folder 1, is in

places difficult to decipher; at seven points in this transcription, I have silently supplied a word or phrase to create a smooth-flowing text.

32 'Just Wind and Horses,' 89.

33 Ibid., 88.

34 The musical, dramatic, and social events referred to here, plus Kate Ross's return to Arcola, are reported in the *Moose Mountain Star-Standard*, 1 March 1933.

5. Winnipeg

1 A Christmas card Jim saved, sent many years later and signed 'fondly Dorothy,' suggests the connection between them never quite broke off. Jim, in his seventies, had been ill, and she wrote: 'Sorry life isn't kinder to you these years. It's such a chancey, random thing, living is. I continue to feel restored by the mountains and the simplicity of the country – so long as we can afford the cottage I'll keep positive!' It must be added here that there is no surname as part of the signature, and the card has no envelope with a return address. But the only other Dorothy he knew was married to Alvin Goldman, and both of their names would have appeared on a greeting of this kind. (Dorothy Klyn was always known as Doyle.) The Christmas card is located in the Sinclair Ross Papers, NAC, MG 30 D369, box 1, folder 5.

2 Will Conyers and the Phoenix Club were described in telephone interviews with Tora Talgoy Noyes, New Westminster, BC, 28 Oct. 1993, and Lillian Downes, Winnipeg, 29 Oct. 1993.

3 Ernest Court was described in telephone interviews with Tora Talgoy Noyes, New Westminster, BC, 28 Oct. 1993 and 18 Feb. 1994.

4 Harriet Duff-Smith was remembered by Lillian Downes, 29 Oct. 1993, as being 'rich and a little haughty.'

5 *Nash's–Pall Mall Magazine* was a conglomeration of two popular publications – *Nash's Magazine* (1909) and *Pall Mall Magazine* (1893). They were published jointly from 1914 to 1927 and known as *Nash's and Pall Mall Magazine*, separated from 1927 to 1929, then joined again as *Nash's–Pall Mall Magazine* from 1929 to 1937, at which point they were incorporated into the English *Good Housekeeping*. This confusing history has resulted in inaccurate bibliographical reporting of Ross's first story: Latham refers simply to *Nash's Magazine* when listing ' No Other Way,' and McMullen refers to *Nash's Pall-Mall Magazine*, misplacing the hyphen.

6 English novelist Somerset Maugham (1874–1965) was well known for immensely popular titles such as *Of Human Bondage* (1915) and *Cakes and Ale* (1930) Desmond MacCarthy (1877–1952) was a popular literary and dramatic critic whose *Portraits* (1931) of writers and famous people is still read today. Rebecca West (1892–1983), a leading journalist and fiction writer, considered one of the liveliest

minds of her time, is now best remembered for her reports on the Nuremberg trials (1945–6) and her astute examinations of Balkan politics.

7 'No Other Way,' *The Race and Other Stories*, 23–36.

8 See Karen Bishop, 'The Pegasus Symbol in the Childhood Stories of Sinclair Ross.'

9 This story is from an interview with Ernest Wernham, Prince Albert, SK, 29 June 1992.

10 JSR in a letter to Ken Mitchell, 1 July 1978.

11 Andrew Macphail to JSR, 10 Feb. 1935, Sinclair Ross Papers, NAC, MG 30 D369, box 1, folder 2.

12 Kirkland writes about a miserly farmhand whose life is spared as the result of a woman's death. There is some similarity in subject matter to Ross's stories, but 'As the Tree Falls' is not distinguished in style. See *Queen's Quarterly* 41.3 (Autumn 1934): 356–68.

13 'A Field of Wheat,' *The Lamp at Noon and Other Stories*, 67–76.

14 Ken Mitchell, *Sinclair Ross: A Reader's Guide*, 8.

15 An anecdote told by JSR many times in conversation. By contrast, the manager at the Portage Avenue branch of the bank was truly impressed by the story and persuaded Jim to send a copy to the editor of the *Royal Bank Magazine* at Head Office in Montreal. Jim received a letter of praise which he treasured for the rest of his life. C.P.C. Downman wrote on 18 June 1935 to say he had read the story with intense interest and sent his sincerest congratulations on such fine writing. He asked if Jim would allow the story to be reprinted in the *Royal Bank Magazine* and went on to suggest that in the future he try sending his stories to magazines like the *Atlantic Monthly*, which paid a much better price than *Queen's Quarterly*. Jim kept Downman's letter with his papers through all the moves he would make into old age.

16 'September Snow,' *The Lamp at Noon and Other Stories*, 54–61.

17 Andrew Macphail to JSR, 22 Jan. 1936, Sinclair Ross Papers, NAC, MG 30 D369, box 1, folder 2.

18 'Just Wind and Horses,' 87.

19 According to 'Just Wind and Horses,' Kate concluded that her sister-in-law was drinking too much and said to her brother: '... just between ourselves, well, the wee drappies are having their way with her. It's the first thing you notice' (89).

20 Ibid., 90.

21 The details of this meeting were recalled in a conservation with JSR, 30 Nov. 1993.

22 JSR recalled his trip to Chicago in two conversations, 6 March and 14 March 1994.

23 What was perhaps Ross's first experience of group sex remained vivid in his mem-

ory, and he gave exactly the same account to Keath Fraser. See *As for Me and My Body*, 90–1.

24 A file on the Phoenix Club, which includes pamphlets describing the club's objectives, correspondence, and newspaper articles about its activities, can be found at the Manitoba Provincial Archives, Winnipeg.

25 JSR in conversation, 10 Nov. 1993.

26 Chester Duncan, interviewed in Winnipeg with his wife, Ada, 15 June 1995.

27 *Winnipeg Free Press*, 16 April 1960, p. 10.

28 Biographies of Benjamin and Munroe can be found in *The Encyclopaedia of Music in Canada*, 110 and 896.

29 I read a copy of John Fraser's will at Somerset House, London, UK. For such information now, one contacts the Probate Department, First Avenue House, High Holborn Street, London.

30 There is a comprehensive account of gay culture in New York during the time of Jim's first visits there in George Chauncey's *Gay New York*.

31 JSR in conversation, July 1993.

32 Postcard to Harriet Duff-Smith, 15 Nov. 1938.

33 JSR in conversation, 29 March 1993.

34 'The Lamp at Noon,' *The Lamp at Noon and Other Stories*, 7–17.

35 J.C. Nelson to JSR, 29 July 1938, Ross private papers.

6. Days with Pegasus

1 'A Day with Pegasus,' *The Race and Other Stories*, 37–48.

2 'The Painted Door,' *The Lamp at Noon and Other Stories*, 93–112.

3 'Cornet at Night,' *The Lamp at Noon and Other Stories*, 29–45.

4 *Queen's Quarterly* 100 (Spring 1993): 44–65.

5 Earle Toppings, *Canadian Writers on Tape* (transcribed by John O'Connor).

6 Letter from JSR to the author, 10 Jan. 1972.

7 Myrna Kostash, 'Discovering Sinclair Ross: It's Rather Late,' 34.

8 JSR in conversation with Mavis Gallant and the author, 20 May 1992.

9 Letter from JSR to the author, 10 Jan. 1972.

10 JSR in conversation, 23 Dec. 1992.

11 Ibid.

12 Henry Bett, *Some Secrets of Style*. The book was inscribed: 'To James Sinclair Ross / From his uncle / John Foster Fraser / Jan. 1933.' Kate Ross probably brought this book with her when she returned from Britain that year.

13 Clive Bell, *Art*, 5–8, passim.

14 Ibid., 25. See D.M.R. Bentley, 'As for Me and Significant Form' for a longer commentary on the connection between Bell and *As for Me and My House*.

15 JSR in conversation, 29 Oct. 1989.

16 JSR in conversation, 27 Nov. 1989.

17 William Thorne, West Vancouver, BC, interviewed 15 Jan. 1995.

18 JSR in conversation, 12 Jan. 1995. Cultural critics today might argue that Ross's attitude to homosexuality expressed in this comment reflects an internalizing of the homophobia experienced by gay men growing up when he did.

19 JSR in conversation, 22 March 1990. A postcard from Strange to Duff-Smith dated 30 Aug. 1938 reads: 'Your party was lovely ... Mr Ross is charming, isn't he, and I'm grateful to you for the opportunity of meeting him.' She wants her husband to meet him and plans a party for everyone in the future.

20 Information about Maximilian Becker has come chiefly from a *New York Times* obituary, 5 Nov. 1992, Section D, p. 23; and from a telephone conversation with his daughter, Royce Becker, New York City, 27 April 1994.

21 Stacey Schiff, *Saint-Exupéry: A Biography*, 292.

22 Tora Talgoy Noyes, interviewed by telephone 28 Jan. 1994.

23 Details about typing the manuscript of *As for Me and My House* and about Ross's aesthetic views were given by Tora Talgoy Noyes in telephone interviews, 28 Jan., 18 Feb., and 27 Nov. 1994.

24 The correspondence between Eugene Reynal and Sinclair Ross appears not to have survived on either side. Three paragraphs (including two quoted here) are reproduced by Ross in a Guggenheim application that can be found with the Roy Daniells Papers, UBCL, box, 4, folder 1.

25 Jim was not only anxious about marketing the book in the United States but, as a modernist, was concerned to make his text as universal as possible, 'the great prairie fact' explored by Robert Thacker being that cohesive element for the literary imagination in North America.

26 Rose Feld, *New York Herald Tribune*, 23 Feb. 1941, p. 41.

7. *As for Me and My House*

1 There was a village in Saskatchewan by this name in the early part of the twentieth century. It was located roughly sixty miles south of Moose Jaw, and when a CPR branch-line reached it in 1912 and a post office was established, Horizon grew for about twenty years, boasting three grain elevators, a school, church, and several businesses. But like the 'grasshopper towns' described in the novel (127), it declined rapidly during the Depression and eventually had only ghost-town status. There is a meticulously researched article on the marketing, setting, and canonization of *As for Me and My House* that focuses on the naming of the town. See Dallas Harrison, 'Where Is (the) Horizon? Placing *As for Me and My House*.' Ross himself claimed never to have seen the actual town of Horizon, but he said its presence on the map was very suggestive when he was writing the novel.

2 Rose Feld, *New York Herald Tribune*, 23 Feb. 1941, p. 41.

3 This was the only review Ross kept for the rest of his life. Titled 'She Saves Him from Himself and from His Tragic Failure'and written by someone identified by the initials E.H., it gives a lengthy and sensitive account of the novel's characters and what happened in their lives. Ross probably appreciated most this sentence, which refers broadly to technique: 'There is something appealing about Ross's style, easy to read, naturally expressed, broken by just enough conversation and accompanied by a running account of the emotions and thoughts and dreams of the writer' (*Dayton Daily News*, 16 Feb. 1941, Section III, p. 5).

4 Marianne Hauser, 'A Man's Failure,' *New York Times Review of Books*, 2 March 1941, pp. 25, 27. Reprinted in Stouck, ed., *Five Decades*, 13–14.

5 *Springfield Republican*, 9 March 1941, p. 7e.

6 See note 4 above.

7 See note 3 above.

8 Clifton Fadiman, *New Yorker*, 22 Feb. 1941, p. 72.

9 Robertson Davies, 'As for Me and My House,' *Peterborough Examiner*, 26 April 1941, p. 4. Reprinted in Davies, *The Well-Tempered Critic*, 142–4, and in Stouck, ed., *Five Decades*, 16–18.

10 W.A. Deacon, 'Story of a Prairie Parson's Wife,' *Globe and Mail*, 26 April 1941, p. 6. Reprinted in Stouck, ed., *Five Decades*, 18–19.

11 G.B., 'Prairie Main Street,' *Winnipeg Free Press*, 12 April 1941, p. 19. Reprinted in Stouck, ed., *Five Decades*, 15–16.

12 The review in the *Vancouver Sun* appeared 12 April 1941, in the 'Sunday Supplement,' p. 4; and the review in the *Daily Province* was printed 19 April 1941, p. 6.

13 See E.K. Brown, review of *As for Me and My House*, *Canadian Forum* 21 (July 1941): 24 (reprinted in Stouck, ed., *Five Decades*, 20–1); Roy Daniells, review of *As for Me and My House*, CBC Radio, 25 Nov. 1941, in Stouck, ed., *Five Decades*, 21–4; Edward McCourt, 'Sinclair Ross,' in *The Canadian West in Fiction*, 94–9; Desmond Pacey, *Creative Writing in Canada*, 173–5.

14 For these contrasting views, see, for example, Warren Tallman, 'Wolf in the Snow,' excerpted from *Canadian Literature* 6 (Autumn 1960): 41–8, in Stouck, ed., *Five Decades*, 41–4; and Sandra Djwa, 'No Other Way: Sinclair Ross's Stories and Novels,' excerpted from *Canadian Literature* 47 (Winter 1971): 49–6, in Stouck, ed., *Five Decades*, 54–65.

15 See, for example, Stouck, 'The Mirror and the Lamp in Sinclair Ross's *As for Me and My House*,' reprinted in Stouck, ed., *Five Decades*, 95–103; and Barbara Godard, 'El Greco in Canada: Sinclair Ross's *As for Me and My House*,' reprinted in Stouck, ed., *Five Decades*, 120–37.

16 Roy Daniells, 'Introduction,' *As for Me and My House*, reprinted in Stouck, ed., *Five Decades*, 35–40.

17 Two of the strongest arguments 'against' Mrs Bentley are found in Wilfred Cude, 'Beyond Mrs Bentley: A Study of *As for Me and My House*,' reprinted in Stouck, ed., *Five Decades*, 76–95; and John Moss, '*As for Me and My House*,' in *Patterns of Isolation*, 149–65.

18 See Helen Buss, 'Who Are You, Mrs Bentley? Feminist Re-vision and Sinclair Ross's *As for Me and My House*'; Misao Dean, 'Femininity and the Real in *As for Me and My House*,' in *Practising Femininity*, 94–106; and David Stouck, 'Cross-Writing and the Unconcluded Self in Sinclair Ross's *As for Me and My House*.' An early feminist defence of Mrs Bentley can be found in Anne Hicks, 'Mrs Bentley: The Good Housewife.'

19 See David Williams, 'The "Scarlet" Rompers: Towards a New Perspective in *As for Me and My House*.'

20 Queer readings of the novel include Keath Fraser, *As for Me and My Body*, 45–66; Valerie Raoul, 'Straight or Bent: Textual/Sexual T(ri)angles in *As for Me and My House*'; Peter Dickinson, 'Sinclair Ross's "Queers,"' in *Here Is Queer*, 17–21; Terry Goldie, '"Not Precisely Gay in Tone": *As for Me and My House*,' in *Pink Snow*, 39–56; and Timothy R. Cramer, 'Questioning Sexuality in Sinclair Ross's *As for Me and My House*.' In 'On Sinclair Ross's Straight(ened) House,' Andrew Lesk argues that the pieces by Fraser, Raoul, and Cramer are based on what he calls a 'normative heterosexual understanding' of sexuality that pathologizes both Ross and his text. These three critics, he suggests, nowhere posit homosexuality as a legitimate subjectivity, nor do they reveal how Ross and his text were imbricated in the discourses of their era. Earlier essays that anticipate these readings include Richard Cavell's 'The Unspoken in Sinclair Ross's *As for Me and My House*' and Frances W. Kaye's 'Sinclair Ross's Use of George Sand and Frederic Chopin as Models for the Bentleys.'

21 For their observations on textual ambiguities produced by the effects of grammar, I am indebted to Janet Giltrow, University of British Columbia, and to Tanya Thompson. See also Giltrow, 'A Linguistic Analysis of Sample Passages from *As for Me and My House*.'

22 Jim himself described his 'expanded' ability to identify with the feelings of both sexes. For a theoretical discussion of this capacity, see Fritz Klein, *The Bisexual Option*, excerpted in Merl Storr, ed., *Bisexuality: A Critical Reader*, 38–48.

23 Homosociality refers to social bonds between persons of the same sex, such as male bonding, which may be characterized by fear and hatred of homosexuality. But Eve Sedgwick, in *Between Men*, hypothesizes a potentially unbroken continuum of desire between homosociality and homosexuality, 'a continuum whose visibility, for men, in our society, is radically disrupted' (1–2). It appears instead in symbolic form in the relations of men involving women, in which women are often viewed as property for cementing the bonds between men. Mrs Bentley, in this light,

serves as a conduit for the more important but almost invisible relationship of Paul and Philip in the novel.

24 Keath Fraser, *As for Me and My Body*, 70.

25 J.C. Nelson to JSR, 5 April 1941, Ross private papers. Nelson's letter, however, is something of a puzzle, for it refers to 'rave notices' for *As for Me and My House* that he had read in several current newspapers, but his letter is dated April 5 and at that point there were no notices in Canadian papers yet, and the American reviews had been largely indifferent.

26 Sinclair Ross Papers, NAC, MG 30 D369, box 1, folder 13.

27 Diary entry for 23 Oct. 1940, Roy Daniells Papers, UBCL, box 11, folder 19.

28 See Sandra Djwa, *Professing English: A Life of Roy Daniells*, 209–10.

29 Roy Daniells to JSR, April 1941, Sinclair Ross Papers, NAC, MG 30 D369, box 1, folder 2.

30 Edna 'Wallis' is the name Ross later gave to Doris Saunders's friend, but it was a name I was unable to verify.

31 JSR in conversation, 12 March 1992.

32 See Keath Fraser, *As for Me and My Body*, 36–7. In conversations, Ross gave a similar account of his preferred sex life to John Whitefoot. Some sexual theorists would likely posit that Ross's reluctance to be reciprocal in his relations with other men was a way of retaining his identity as a heterosexual male, since he was holding a position of power over other men (see, for example, J.M. Carrier, 'Mexican Male Bisexuality,' in Merl Storr, ed., *Bisexuality: A Critical Reader*, 75–86). But Ross was above all a man without posture and pretension, so that his stated preferences are probably best viewed as straightforward and authentic.

33 In an interview of 29 April 1994, Kenneth McCormick used this phrase to describe Max Becker.

34 Keath Fraser, *As for Me and My Body*, 67.

35 JSR to John and Harriet Duff-Smith, 19 April 1941.

36 JSR to Roy Daniells, 27 April 1941, Roy Daniells Papers, UBCL, box 3, folder 19.

37 Chester Duncan, interviewed 15 June 1995.

38 JSR in conversation, 20 March 1990.

39 Letter from JSR to the author, 30 Jan. 1979.

40 'Just Wind and Horses,' 96.

41 'Not by Rain Alone,' retitled 'Summer Thunder,' *The Lamp at Noon and Other Stories*, 46-54.

42 This memo is located with the Roy Daniells Papers, UBCL, box 3, folder 19.

43 Roy St George Stubbs, interviewed 7 Oct. 1993.

44 The story of Lovell Clark was not as firmly fixed in Ross's memory as that of others he had known. Affection for Clark in one telling was replaced by contempt in another. Most of the details recorded here emerged in conversations on 15 and

23 March 1993. Like several of Ross's male lovers, Clark later enjoyed a long and apparently happy straight marriage.

45 The typescript of the broadcast is located with the Roy Daniells Papers, UBCL, box 14, folder 5, and has been published in Stouck, ed., *Five Decades*, 21–4.

46 Roy Daniells Papers, UBCL, box 14, folder 5.

47 JSR in conversation, 10 Nov. 1993. This same anecdote occurs in a letter to Geoff Hancock, 1 Oct. 1977.

8. War Years

1 'Nell,' *The Race and Other Stories*, 49-59.

2 JSR to Doris Saunders, 25 March 1942.

3 JSR to Ralph Gustafson, 17 April and 22 May 1942, USL, Ralph Gustafson Papers.

4 JSR to Earle Birney, 29 Jan. 1942, TFRBL, Earle Birney Papers, box 16, file 18.

5 Earle Birney to JSR, 24 Feb. 1942, TFRBL, Earle Birney Papers, box 16, file 18.

6 Ibid., 3 April 1942.

7 The first of several letters from JSR to Ralph Gustafson inquiring about the publication status of 'One's a Heifer' is dated 6 June 1943 (USL, Ralph Gustafson Papers).

8 This letter is part of a proposal for a Guggenheim fellowship and can be found in the Roy Daniells Papers, UBCL, box 4, folder 1.

9 Ibid.

10 Mary Johnson, Winnipeg, interviewed 8 Oct. 1993. This occasion was also remembered vividly by Ross himself in an interview of 2 Nov. 1993.

11 Kathleen Scroggie and her father were described by Doyle and William Klyn, Saanichton, BC, interviewed August 1992.

12 Audrey O'Kelly Peterkin, Winnipeg, interviewed 8 Oct. 1993.

13 JSR in conversation, 19 May 1989. See also JSR to Ralph Gustafson, 2 Aug. 1942, USL, Ralph Gustafson Papers.

14 JSR to Ralph Gustafson, 2 Aug. 1942, USL, Ralph Gustafson Papers.

15 JSR in conversation, 19 May 1989.

16 Unpublished war memoir, not paginated, Ross private papers.

17 Ibid.

18 JSR to Audrey O'Kelly, 1 Sept. 1942.

19 JSR to Doris Saunders, 23 Oct. 1942.

20 Robert Savory, Winnipeg, interviewed 8 Oct. 1993.

21 JSR to Doris Saunders, 23 Oct. 1942.

22 JSR to Audrey O'Kelly, 1 Sept. 1942.

23 JSR to Doris Saunders, 23 Oct. 1942.

24 JSR to Audrey O'Kelly, 1 Sept. 1942.

25 JSR to Audrey O'Kelly, 20 Oct. 1942.

26 JSR to Doris Saunders, 23 Oct. 1942.

27 These lines are from a version of the war memoir that can be found with the Sinclair Ross Papers, NAC, MG 30 D369, box 1, folder 23.

28 JSR in conversation, 19 May 1989.

29 Robert Savory, Winnipeg, interviewed 8 Oct. 1993.

30 Unpublished war memoir, not paginated, Ross private papers. One of several versions of this narrative is located with the Sinclair Ross Papers, NAC. See note 27.

31 Details of the crossing and landing appear in a letter from JSR to Audrey O'Kelly, 6 Dec. 1942.

32 JSR in conversation, 20 Oct. 1989.

33 JSR to Audrey O'Kelly, 6 Dec. 1942.

34 JSR to Audrey O'Kelly, 18 March 1943.

35 JSR to Audrey O'Kelly, 6 Dec. 1942.

36 JSR to Earle Birney, 16 July 1943, TFRBL, Earle Birney Papers, box 16, file 18

37 JSR to Harriet Duff-Smith, 22 Nov. 1943.

38 JSR to Earle Birney, 26 July 1943, TFRBL, Earle Birney Papers, box 16, file 18.

39 Esther Birney recalled her husband's disappointment in that meeting and his observation that Ross was 'a colourless little man' (Esther Birney, interviewed 14 Oct. 1998).

40 See Keath Fraser, *As for Me and My Body*, 34.

41 JSR to Audrey O'Kelly, 27 Nov. 1944.

42 JSR to Audrey O'Kelly, 25 April 1945.

43 JSR to Doris Saunders, 15 Feb. 1945.

44 JSR to Audrey O'Kelly, 27 Nov. 1944.

45 JSR to Ralph Gustafson, 6 June 1943 and 29 Sept. 1943, USL, Ralph Gustafson Papers.

46 Ralph Gustafson to JSR, 19 Nov. 1943, USL, Ralph Gustafson Papers.

47 JSR to Ralph Gustafson, 4 Nov. 1944, USL, Ralph Gustafson Papers.

48 'One's a Heifer,' *The Lamp at Noon and Other Stories*, 113–28.

49 JSR in conversation, 3 April 1992.

50 In 'Something Queer Going on Here: Desire in the Short Fiction of Sinclair Ross,' Andrew Lesk argues that the indeterminacy of Ross's fiction permits a sexual reading of his young protagonists who 'begin to explore their maturing, changing, and increasingly unstable world' (129). Lesk attributes the indeterminacies in these stories to closeted homosexuality and argues specifically that the stall in 'One's a Heifer' represents a contested site of sexual secrecy.

51 'Lodging for a Night,' *Argosy* 9. 8 (August 1948): 65–76. Ross almost certainly never knew of this reprinting, which probably came about as the result of efforts made on his behalf by John Lehmann.

52 JSR to Doris Saunders, 15 Feb. 1945.
53 JSR to Audrey O'Kelly, 27 Nov. 1944.

9. Montreal

1 Military records for Staff-Sergeant James Sinclair Ross, NAC, file H-95794.
2 Ibid.
3 For a good comprehensive account of Montreal during this time period, see William Weintraub's *City Unique*.
4 See Ross's contribution to Naim Kattan's essay 'Montreal and French-Canadian Culture,' *Tamarack Review* 40 (Summer 1966): 46–7.
5 Robert K. Martin, 'Two Days in Sodom, or How Anglo-Canadian Writers Invent Their Own Quebecs,' *Body Politic* (July-Aug. 1977): 28–30.
6 See James K. Nesbitt, 'Kindness, Drive, Energy Characterized Ira Dilworth,' *Vancouver Sun*, 27 Nov. 1962, p. 13.
7 JSR in conversation, 7 Oct. 1993. Ross would never divulge the full name of this woman in case she was still living and might be 'hurt' by the story of their relationship. It is also possible that her first name was not Madeline.
8 Ibid.
9 Keath Fraser, *As for Me and My Body*, 76.
10 JSR to Grant Macdonald, 21 Sept. 1948, QUL, Grant Macdonald Papers.
11 JSR to Grant Macdonald, 31 Oct. 1948, QUL, Grant Macdonald Papers.
12 Ibid.
13 Details given here can be found in a letter from John Gray to Grant Macdonald, 29 Nov. 1948, QUL, Grant Macdonald Papers.
14 John Gray to Grant Macdonald, 10 Jan. 1949, QUL, Grant Macdonald Papers.
15 'Old Chippendale' has never been published. The only extant manuscript is with the Grant Macdonald Papers, QUL.
16 'Just Wind and Horses,' 91.
17 JSR to Grant Macdonald, 16 Feb. 1949, QUL, Grant Macdonald Papers.
18 John Gray to JSR, 2 May 1949. A copy of this letter was sent to Grant Macdonald and can be found with his papers at QUL.
19 JSR to Grant Macdonald, 12 May 1949, QUL, Grant Macdonald Papers.
20 See letter from Grant Macdonald to John Gray, 13 April 1949, QUL, Grant Macdonald Papers.
21 JSR to Grant Macdonald, 13 Jan. 1949, QUL, Grant Macdonald Papers.
22 Dorothy (Doyle) and Bill Klyn, Saanichton, BC, interviewed August 1992.
23 G.H. Clarke to JSR, 20 Oct. 1949, QUL, *Queen's Quarterly* Archive.
24 JSR to G.H. Clarke, 27 Oct. 1949, QUL, *Queen's Quarterly* Archive.
25 G.H. Clarke to JSR, 19 July 1951, QUL, *Queen's Quarterly* Archive.
26 JSR to G.H. Clarke, 31 July 1951, QUL, *Queen's Quarterly* Archive.

27 JSR to G.H. Clarke, 27 Oct. 1949, QUL, *Queen's Quarterly* Archive.

28 JSR to G.H. Clarke, 15 July 1951, QUL, *Queen's Quarterly* Archive.

29 'Jug and Bottle' is collected in *The Race and Other Stories*, 69–85.

30 See 'On Looking Back,' *Mosaic* 3 (Spring 1970): 93–4.

31 JSR to G.H. Clarke, 27 Oct. 1949, QUL, *Queen's Quarterly* Archive.

32 'The Outlaw,' *The Lamp at Noon and Other Stories,'* 18–28.

33 'The Outlaw' was read on CBC radio 21 April 1950.

34 Robert Weaver to JSR, 11 Feb. 1949, NAC, Robert Weaver Fonds.

35 Robert Weaver to JSR, 28 March 1949, NAC, Robert Weaver Fonds.

36 JSR to Robert Weaver, 11 April 1949, NAC, Robert Weaver Fonds.

37 JSR to Robert Weaver, 18 Jan. 1950, NAC, Robert Weaver Fonds.

38 'Saturday Night,' *The Race and Other Stories*, 87–97.

39 JSR to G.H. Clarke, 15 July 1951, QUL, *Queen's Quarterly* Archive.

40 Robert Weaver to JSR, 26 May 1950, NAC, Robert Weaver Fonds.

41 Robert Weaver to JSR, 11 Feb. 1952, NAC, Robert Weaver Fonds.

42 JSR to Robert Weaver, 13 Feb. 1952, NAC, Robert Weaver Fonds.

43 Ibid.

44 These anecdotes were offered by Weaver in an interview in Toronto, 9 April 1995.

45 JSR gave his account of Robert Weaver in conversation, 26 April 1995.

46 'The Runaway,' *The Lamp at Noon and Other Stories*, 77–92.

47 See David Carpenter, 'Horsey Comedy in the Short Fiction of Sinclair Ross,' in Moss, ed., *From the Heart of the Heartland*, 67–79.

48 'The Runaway' is the Sinclair Ross selection in Donna Bennett and Russell Brown's very popular textbook, *A New Anthology of Canadian Literature in English* (2002).

49 See Robert Weaver to JSR, 23 Feb. 1950, NAC, Robert Weaver Fonds.

10. *The Well*

1 JSR to John Gray, Dec. 1954. All correspondence between JSR and John Gray quoted or cited in this chapter can be found in MUL, MCC, box 130, file 10.

2 John Gray to JSR, 31 Dec. 1954.

3 JSR in conversation, 17 March 1991 and 18 May 1994.

4 The most obvious connections between *The Well* and the years Jim spent at Forfang's farm are the somewhat dour farmers with Scandinavian names and their love of horses. However, the town of Chaplin in the Rolling Prairie District might also have suggested Campkin as the name for the nearest town in the novel.

5 John Gray to J. Randall Williams III, Macmillan, New York City, 27 June 1955, MUL, MCC, box 130, file 10.

6 John Gray to JSR, 4 July 1955.

7 Kenneth McCormick, interviewed in New York City, 29 April 1994.

8 Quoted by JSR in letter to John Gray, 2 Aug. 1955.

9 See MUL, MCC, box 130, file 10.

10 JSR in conversation, 18 May 1994.

11 Janice Tyrwhitt to JSR, 9 Sept. 1955, MUL, MCC, box 130, file 10.

12 John Gray to JSR, 16 Sept. 1955.

13 JSR to John Gray (letter undated but context suggests mid-Sept. 1955).

14 John Gray to JSR, 21 Sept. 1955.

15 The contents of the letter from W.K. Wing to JSR are preserved in a letter Wing wrote to John Gray, 19 Sept. 1955, in which he recounts to Gray what he has written to Ross (MUL, MCC, box 130, file 10).

16 John Gray to JSR, 8 Dec. 1955.

17 The account here combines the author's recollection of events surrounding the revisions of *The Well* with information in a letter from JSR to John Gray, 5 May 1956. The author's memory of being coerced against his better judgment into making so many changes to *The Well* remained vivid and bitter.

18 The readers' reports are located in MUL, MCC, box 130, file 10.

19 John Gray to JSR, 26 June 1957.

20 JSR to John Gray, 29 Aug. 1957.

21 John Gray to JSR, 16 Dec. 1957.

22 Jack McClelland to Malcolm Ross, 25 Nov. 1957, MUL, M&SA, series A, box 47, file 3.

23 Jack McClelland to Malcolm Ross, 20 April 1954, MUL, M&SA, series A, box 54, file 15.

24 Malcolm Ross in conversation in Ottawa, 25 April 1981. In *Making It Real*, Robert Lecker has pointed to correspondence between Malcolm Ross and Jack McClelland as identifying another reason for the selection of *As for Me and My House* for the NCL: 'Sinclair Ross won't ask for much money' (161). Lecker, however, provides no citation for this statement.

25 JSR to Hugh Kane, 16 April 1957, MUL, M&SA, series A, box 47, file 3.

26 JSR to McClelland and Stewart editorial staff, 5 June 1957, MUL, M&SA, series Ca, box 15, file 7.

27 Roy Daniells, 'Introduction' to 1957 edition of *As for Me and My House*, vii.

28 William Hartley, 'Love and Redemption On a Prairie Farm,' *Montreal Star*, 23 Aug. 1958, p. 28.

29 Theodore Honderich, 'Farmer, Wife, and Hired Man,' *Toronto Daily Star*, 30 Aug. 1958, p. 28.

30 A.G.P., 'Canadian Novelists Turn Too Much to Theme of Sex,' *Quebec Chronicle Telegraph*, 3 Sept. 1958, p. 4.

31 Dorothy Bishop, 'A Novel of the Week,' *Ottawa Journal*, 13 Sept. 1958, p. 42.

32 JSR, 'Why My 2nd Book Came 17 Years Later,' *Toronto Daily Star*, 13 Sept. 1958, p. 32.

33 JSR in conversation, 24 Jan. 1993. It is interesting as well to note that in the 'Author's Publicity Questionnaire' that Jim filled out for Macmillan he, perhaps slyly, lists his admiration for Mauriac, Malraux, and Simenon, but not Camus, though years later he would remember Camus as the original inspiration for the novel. The questionnaire is located in MUL, MCC, box 165.

34 Kathleen Graham, *Leader-Post* (Regina), 22 Nov. 1958, p. 15.

35 Isabelle Hughes, 'Long Awaited Second Novel,' *Globe and Mail*, 20 Sept. 1958, p. 19.

36 James Scott, 'Sinclair Ross Has Forgotten Prairie Smells,' *Toronto Telegram*, 20 Sept. 1958, p. 37.

37 Ken Homer, A.M. *Chronicle*, CBC Radio, 13 Nov. 1958. The typescript of the broadcast is located in MUL, MCC, box 165.

38 H.V. Weekes, review of *The Well*, *Dalhousie Review* 38 (Winter 1959): 529–30.

39 Claude Bissell, 'Letters in Canada: Fiction,' *University of Toronto Quarterly* 28 (Summer 1959): 369–70.

40 'The Unwilling Organist,' *The Teller* [Royal Bank], Dec. 1958, pp. 12–16.

41 JSR to John Gray, 15 July 1958.

42 John Gray to JSR, 1 Aug. 1958.

43 JSR to John Gray, 10 Aug. 1958.

44 Mavis Gallant, interviewed in Vancouver, 19 May 1992.

45 This contract and all subsequent negotiations for filming *The Well* can be found in MUL, MCC, box 130, file 10.

46 JSR to Frank Upjohn, 6 June 1960, and Frank Upjohn to JSR, 8 June 1960, MUL, MCC, box 130, file 10.

47 JSR to Frank Upjohn, 19 Sept. 1960, MUL, MCC, box 130, file 10.

48 Julian Roffman to Frank Upjohn, 16 Jan. 1961, MUL, MCC, box 130, file 10.

49 Robert D. Chambers, *Sinclair Ross*, 2.

50 Lorraine McMullen, *Sinclair Ross*, 88.

51 Ken Mitchell, *Sinclair Ross: A Reader's Guide*, 58.

11. *Whir of Gold*

1 JSR to Frank Upjohn, 23 Nov. 1959, MUL, MCC, box 130, file 10.

2 This phrase from *Whir of Gold*, 3, describes Sonny's mother's words of caution that he cannot forget.

3 It could be argued that Ross's refusal to identify himself completely as a gay man was bound up in society's disapprobation of homosexuality, that bisexuality was his way of retaining partial claim to a legitimate subjectivity.

4 Molly and Bill Baxter were interviewed 19 Oct. 1993.

5 JSR in conversation, 5 Nov. 1993.

6 John Gibbon, interviewed in Montreal 20 Oct. 1993.

7 JSR to Mrs Irene Fowlie, 11 Jan. 1975, Ross private papers.

8 G.H. Clarke to JSR, 18 March 1952, QUL, Queen's Quarterly Archive.

9 JSR to Roy Daniells, 10 Dec. 1954, UBCL, Roy Daniells Papers, box 6, folder 19.

10 John Gray to JSR, 19 Oct. 1962. All correspondence between JSR and John Gray quoted or cited in this chapter can be found in MUL, MCC, box 272, file 24.

11 JSR to John Gray, 27 Nov. 1962.

12 John Gray to JSR, 10 Dec. 1962.

13 JSR to John Gray, 8 March 1966.

14 John Gray to JSR, 14 March 1966.

15 Anne Perrie to JSR, 5 May 1966, MUL, MCC, box 272, file 24.

16 J.W. Bacque to JSR, 13 June 1966, MUL, MCC, box 272, file 24.

17 The readers' reports can be found in MUL, MCC, box 272, file 24.

18 JSR to John Gray, 27 Sept. 1966.

19 John Gray to JSR, 7 Oct. 1966.

20 See Naim Kattan, 'Montreal and French-Canadian Culture.'

21 This background information about Sinclair Ross approaching McClelland and Stewart with the idea of publishing a collection of his stories is contained in a lengthy memo of 2 August 1967 written by Jack McClelland to Geoffrey Fielding, who had been assigned to the Ross story project (MUL, M&SA, CC1).

22 Jack McClelland to JSR, 26 Sept. 1967, MUL, M&SA, CC1.

23 Robert Weaver to Geoffrey Fielding, 17 Oct. 1967, MUL, M&SA, CC1.

24 Robert Weaver to Pamela Fry, 24 Nov. 1967, MUL, M&SA, CC1.

25 JSR to Robert Weaver, 22 Nov. 1967, MUL, M&SA, CC1.

26 Margaret Laurence, 'Introduction,' The Lamp at Noon and Other Stories (1968), 7; later an 'Afterword' (1988), 129.

27 Adele Wiseman's recollections of Sinclair Ross were taped for CBC Radio Saskatchewan in the mid-1980s.

28 JSR to Margaret Laurence, 4 Dec. 1966, YUL, Margaret Laurence Collection.

29 JSR to Margaret Laurence, 9 Dec. 1967, YUL, Margaret Laurence Collection. There were two points, however, on which he challenged Laurence's interpretation of his stories. In a letter to Robert Weaver of 26 Oct. 1967 (NAC, Robert Weaver Fonds), he suggested two changes to her introduction: removing the word 'old' to describe Vickers in 'One's a Heifer,' because he thought of Vickers as still being in his thirties; and removing the word 'suicide' to describe the ending of 'The Painted Door,' because he saw the husband's death as resulting from discouragement and exhaustion, not from a deliberate act to end his life.

30 Alec Lucas, interviewed in Montreal 21 Oct. 1993.

31 See Keath Fraser, As for Me and My Body, 75.

32 JSR to Ken Mitchell, 5 Feb. 1979, URL, Ken Mitchell Collection.

33 See Alan Pearson, 'James Sinclair Ross: Major Novelist with a Banking Past.'

34 JSR to Pamela Fry, 10 March 1968. All correspondence between JSR and Pamela Fry quoted or cited in this chapter can be found in MUL, M&SA, CC1.

35 JSR to Margaret Laurence, 10 Dec. 1968, YUL, Margaret Laurence Collection.

36 JSR to Pamela Fry, 1 May 1968.

37 JSR to Pamela Fry, 26 March 1969.

38 JSR to Margaret Laurence, 1 May 1969, YUL, Margaret Laurence Collection.

39 Letter with manuscript dated 10 April 1969.

40 The readers' reports for *Whir of Gold* can be found in MUL, M&SA, CC1.

41 Pamela Fry to Joseph Gaute, 19 June 1969, MUL, M&SA, CC1.

42 See, for example, Pamela Fry to JSR, 3 July 1969, and his reply, 8 July 1969.

43 JSR to Margaret Laurence, 21 Sept. 1969, YUL, Margaret Laurence Collection.

44 JSR to Doris Saunders, 2 Nov. 1969.

45 See Keath Fraser, *As for Me and My Body*, 84–5.

46 Pamela Fry to JSR, 17 Nov. 1969.

47 JSR to Pamela Fry, 12 April 1970.

48 JSR to Keath Fraser, 28 Nov. 1969.

49 Keath Fraser, *As for Me and My Body*, 10.

50 JSR to Keath Fraser, 18 Aug. 1970.

51 JSR to Keath Fraser, 14 Dec. 1970.

52 Gordon Roper, 'Letters in Canada: Fiction,' *University of Toronto Quarterly* 28 (Summer 1969): 363.

53 Ross kept a copy of this review for several years, but attempts to locate publication details have failed.

54 Letters from JSR to Doris Saunders, 30 Sept. 1969 and 2 Nov. 1969.

55 JSR to Margaret Laurence, 17 May 1970, YUL, Margaret Laurence Collection. He makes the same observations in a taped interview with Earle Toppings for OISE.

56 JSR to Pamela Fry, 10 May 1970.

57 See Keath Fraser, *As for Me and My Body*, 75.

58 JSR in conversation, 20 Oct. 1989.

59 JSR to Pamela Fry, 12 Sept. 1970.

60 Peter Sypnowich, 'A Bachelor on the Run Comes Back to Canada,' *Toronto Daily Star*, 13 Nov. 1970, p. 30.

61 See *Dear Bill: The Correspondence of William Arthur Deacon*, 216. Ross's repeated statement can be read as the evasive reply of a gay man to a question with a heterosexual assumption, but it could also be taken more literally as having some reference to his early experiences, particularly with a woman like Dorothy Cornell, for whom he definitely had special feelings.

62 Hugh Garner, 'Bamboozled by Time and Lumpen Losers,' *Globe and Mail Magazine*, 2 Jan. 1971, p. 17.

63 John W. Dafoe, 'Another Kind of Depression,' *Montreal Star*, 17 April 1971, p. 16.

64 Malcolm Foster, 'Sinclair Ross' Latest Lost in New Locale,' *Gazette* [Montreal], 12 Dec. 1970, p. 43.

65 In McMaster University's McClelland and Stewart Collection, this review, titled 'Sea of Corruption,' is attributed to Pamela Sykes, *Kingston Whig Standard*, 16 Dec. 1970, but a search of this newspaper for 1970 and 1971 has failed to locate the review.

66 Bob Ivanochko, 'Ross' Novel Whirs around Montreal,' *Windsor Star*, 30 Jan. 1971, p. 12.

67 Anne Montagnes, [no title], *Canadian Forum*, March 1971, pp. 443–4.

68 George Woodcock, 'Two Facets of Montreal Drama,' *Victoria Times Colonist*, 20 Feb. 1971, p. 18.

69 Harvard Dahlie, 'Maybe Sinclair Ross Should Have Stayed in His Small Prairie Town,' *Albertan* [Calgary], 6 March 1971, p. 8.

70 Chester Duncan, 'Not All Is Gold,' *Winnipeg Free Press*, 19 Dec. 1970, p. 14 NL.

71 JSR to Margaret Laurence, 29 Jan. 1971, YUL, Margaret Laurence Collection.

72 Susan Swan, [no title], *Toronto Telegram*, 6 Feb. 1971, p. 31.

73 Jamie Portman, 'The Big City; Lost and Lonely,' *Calgary Herald Magazine*, 24 Dec. 1970, p. 7.

74 Douglas Barbour, 'Fine Novel from a Deceptive Author,' *Edmonton Journal*, 5 March 1971, p. 60.

75 James Etherington, 'Flash of Fleeting Beauty,' *London Free Press*, 5 June 1971, p. 30.

76 JSR to Margaret Laurence, 29 Jan. 1971, YUL, Margaret Laurence Collection.

77 JSR to Alvin Goldman, 12 Jan. 1971.

78 See 'Introduction' to *The Race and Other Stories*, ed. Lorraine McMullen, 19.

12. Tourist

1 JSR to Lorraine and Keath Fraser, 24 Oct. 1970.

2 JSR to Margaret Laurence, 29 Jan. 1971, YUL, Margaret Laurence Collection.

3 JSR to Lorraine and Keath Fraser, 26 April 1971.

4 Reference to these travels can be found in JSR to John Gray, 16 Oct. 1971, MUL, MCC, box 130, file 10.

5 JSR in conversation, 17 Sept. 1995.

6 JSR to Andy Suknaski, 1 July 1975.

7 JSR to Lorraine and Keath Fraser, 16 Oct. 1971.

8 JSR in conversation, 15 July 1990.

9 Letter from JSR to the author, 29 Oct. 1971.

10 JSR to Lorraine and Keath Fraser, 29 Nov. 1971.

11 See Myrna Kostash, 'Discovering Sinclair Ross: It's Rather Late,' 33.

12 JSR to Keath Fraser, 6 May 1972.

13 JSR to Myrna Kostash, 3 June 1972, NAC, Myrna Kostash Papers.

14 Letter from JSR to the author, 20 Oct. 1972.

15 JSR to Myrna Kostash, 22 Oct. 1972, NAC, Myrna Kostash Papers.

16 Ibid.

17 'The Flowers That Killed Him,' *The Race and Other Stories*, 119–34.

18 Margaret Laurence, 'Commentary,' *Journal of Canadian Fiction* 1. 3 (Summer 1972): 74.

19 Ken Mitchell, *Sinclair Ross: A Reader's Guide*, 26.

20 Letter from JSR to the author, 19 March 1973.

21 Sheila Kieran's nine-page narrative about her visit with Sinclair Ross begins as a letter to Peter Pearson dated 30 Nov. 1972 and continues as such 1 Dec. 1972; it then drops the letter format and records in a more diary-like fashion her activities with Ross in Málaga, his conversation, and her thoughts about his personality and creative life. A copy was loaned to the author by Kieran.

22 JSR to Sheila Kieran, 30 Nov. 1972.

23 Ibid.

24 Sheila Kieran to JSR, 31 Dec. 1972.

25 JSR to Sheila Kieran, 21 Jan. 1974.

13. *Sawbones Memorial*

 1 Letter from JSR to the author, 19 March 1973.

 2 JSR to Anna Porter, 15 Jan. 1974. All correspondence between JSR and Anna Porter quoted or cited in this chapter can be found in MUL, M&SA, CC54.

 3 JSR to Ronald Paulson, 27 March 1972, MUL, MCC.

 4 JSR to Myrna Kostash, 27 June 1973, NAC, Myrna Kostash Papers.

 5 JSR in conversation, August 1989.

 6 JSR to Lloyd Person, University of Regina, 14 Feb. 1973, Ross private papers.

 7 JSR to Sheila Kieran, 11 Jan. 1973.

 8 Sheila Kieran to JSR, 31 Dec. 1972; JSR to Sheila Kieran, 11 Jan. 1973. In his letter to Kieran, Ross tells her about the Hart House lunch. This account differs from later versions in that the error regarding Dr Brown, the theologian, is recognized at once and E.K. Brown's luncheon takes place the same day. Dr Brown of the United Church is described as geniality itself, and he orders a copy of *As for Me and My House*.

 9 JSR to Myrna Kostash, 27 June 1973, NAC, Myrna Kostash Papers.

10 Ross was similarly fascinated by Dick Harrison's study in *Unnamed Country* of the prairie as an existential reflection of annihilation and unmeaning.

11 Wilfred Cude, 'Beyond Mrs Bentley: A Study of *As for Me and My House*,' *Journal of Canadian Studies* 8 (Feb. 1973): 3-18.

12 JSR to John Moss, 15 May 1973.

13 JSR to Irene Fowlie, 11 Jan. 1975, Ross private papers. Fowlie was writing a master's thesis on Ross's fiction at the University of Calgary.

14 JSR to Anna Porter, 23 Nov. 1973.

15 The return visit to London was described by JSR in a letter to the author of 30 Nov. 1973.

16 JSR to Keath Fraser, 7 Dec. 1973.

17 JSR to Anna Porter, 30 Nov. 1973.

18 The readers' reports for *Sawbones Memorial* can be found in MUL, M&SA, CC54.

19 Jack McClelland to Linda McKnight, 2 Jan. 1974, MUL, M&SA, CC54.

20 JSR to Anna Porter, 15 Jan. 1974.

21 Anna Porter to JSR, 29 Jan. 1974.

22 Anna Porter to JSR, 7 Feb. 1974.

23 Anna Porter to JSR, 27 Feb. 1974.

24 Jack McClelland to Anna Porter, 1 March 1974, MUL, M&SA, CC54.

25 JSR to Myrna Kostash, 8 March 1974, NAC, Myrna Kostash Papers.

26 Letter from JSR to the author, 19 March 1974. At a conference in the United States, I had met Alfred Knopf and his chief editor, William Koshland, and had interested them in the idea of bringing *As for Me and My House* out in a Borzoi paperback. Margaret Laurence, whose *The Diviners* they were about to publish, gave additional support. But the readers at Knopf were unanimously negative about the book's prospects in the market place and the proposal went no further.

27 JSR to Robert Weaver, 22 March 1974, NAC, Robert Weaver Fonds.

28 The manuscript he describes to Porter would be known as 'Price above Rubies.' He wrote to the author as well on the subject, 19 March 1974.

29 JSR to Martin O'Malley, 27 May 1974, Ross private papers.

30 Ross wrote of his pre-interview anxieties to Ken Mitchell (15 Aug. 1974, URL, Ken Mitchell Collection) and to the author, 13 Nov. 1974, saying to the latter '[it] pretty well spoiled at least a month for me.'

31 Quoted matter here is from William French's 'Too Good Too Soon, Ross Remains the Elusive Canadian,' *Globe and Mail*, 27 July 1974, p. 25.

32 William French, interviewed in Toronto, 20 April 1995.

33 JSR to Myrna Kostash, 27 Aug. 1974, NAC, Myrna Kostash Papers.

34 Letter from JSR to the author, 13 Nov. 1974.

35 JSR to Myrna Kostash, 10 July 1975, NAC, Myrna Kostash Papers.

36 JSR to Anna Porter, 29 Nov. 1974.

37 In conversation in November 1981, Jack McClelland mentioned to me how he urged Atwood and Laurence to 'do their best for Ross and *Sawbones*.'

38 A copy of this review titled 'The Quality of Craftsmanship,' is located with the McClelland and Stewart papers at McMaster University Library, but its ascription

to the *Winnipeg Tribune*, 16 Nov. 1974, is incorrect. I have not been able to locate a copy of this syndicated review in any of its places of publication.

39 William French, 'This One Can Stand on Its Own,' *Globe and Mail*, 26 Oct. 1974, p. 32.

40 Linda Sandler, 'Ross Turns Bigotry into Comedy,' *Toronto Star*, 29 Oct. 1974, p. F7.

41 Jamie Portman, 'Unromanticized Slice of Small Town Life,' *Calgary Herald Magazine*, 15 Nov. 1974, p. 10.

42 Dorothy Bishop, 'Prairie Peyton Place,' *Ottawa Journal*, 1 Feb. 1975, p. 40.

43 George Melnyk, 'A Work of Quiet Nostalgia on Western Canada,' *Edmonton Journal*, 28 Dec. 1974, p. 42.

44 Karen Mulhallen, 'Onward and Upward with Sinclair Ross,' *Books in Canada* 3 (Dec. 1974): 9–11.

45 Margaret Laurence, 'Sinclair Ross Looks at the Prairies, His Time and Place,' *Gazette* [Montreal], 9 Nov. 1974, p. 58.

46 George Woodcock, 'Adele Wiseman and Sinclair Ross: Return Engagements,' *Maclean's* 87 (Oct. 1974): 110; Margaret Atwood, Review of *Sawbones Memorial*, *Sunday Supplement*, CBC Radio, 15 Dec. 1974.

47 Margaret Atwood to JSR, 27 Nov. 1974, Ross private papers; and JSR to Atwood, TFRBL, Margaret Atwood Collection.

48 Roy Guay, review of *Sawbones Memorial*, *Leader Post* [Regina], 25 Oct. 1974, p. 13.

49 Peter Cummings, 'Rooted in the Prairies,' *Montreal Star*, 21 Dec. 1974, p. B-4.

50 David Williams, review of *Sawbones Memorial*, *Queen's Quarterly* 82 (Winter 1975): 641–2.

51 Wolfgang Dios, 'Small Town Portrait Full of Flaws,' *Ottawa Citizen*, 16 Nov. 1974, p. 68.

52 JSR to Sheila Kieran, 31 Dec. 1974; JSR to Alvin Goldman, 11 March 1975; and JSR to Ken Mitchell, 5 Sept. 1975, URL, Ken Mitchell Collection.

53 JSR to Margaret Laurence, 14 Dec. 1974, YUL, Margaret Laurence Collection.

54 JSR to Doris Saunders, n.d. (Christmas card for 1974).

55 JSR to Roy St George Stubbs, n.d. (Christmas card for 1974).

56 Roy St George Stubbs, 'Ross Redivivus,' *Winnipeg Free Press*, 12 Oct. 1974, p. 20.

57 JSR to Audrey Peterkin, 9 Jan. 1975.

58 Marilyn Rose, 'Sinclair Ross's "Foreigners,"' in Moss, ed., *From the Heart of the Heartland*, 91–101.

59 JSR to Myrna Kostash, 10 July 1975, NAC, Myrna Kostash Papers.

60 JSR to Roy St George Stubbs, 28 June 1975.

61 Letter from JSR to the author, 13 Nov. 1974.

62 JSR to Grant Macdonald, 16 Feb. 1949, QUL, Grant Macdonald Collection.

63 JSR to Roy St George Stubbs, 20 April 1975.

64 JSR to Ken Mitchell, 29 April 1975, URL, Ken Mitchell Collection.

65 Pat Krause to JSR, 1 Aug. 1975 and 11 Sept. 1975, URL, Ken Mitchell Collection.
66 JSR to Pat Krause, 21 Sept. 1975, Ross private papers.
67 Pat Krause to the Royal Bank, 12 Sept. 1975; bank's reply, 29 May 1978, URL, Ken Mitchell Collection.
68 Ken Glazier to JSR, 13 Dec. 1974, Ross private papers.
69 JSR to Myrna Kostash, 10 July 1975, NAC, Myrna Kostsh Papers.
70 JSR to Andy Suknaski, 1 July 1975.
71 JSR to Roy St George Stubbs, 12 Aug. 1975.
72 William French, interviewed in Toronto, April 1995.
73 JSR to Margaret Laurence, 5 Feb. 1975, YUL, Margaret Laurence Collection.
74 JSR to Margaret Laurence, 14 April 1975, YUL, Margaret Laurence Collection.
75 Sheila Kieran to Margaret Laurence, 15 Feb. 1975, YUL, Margaret Laurence Collection.
76 JSR to Margaret Laurence, 15 Dec. 1975, YUL, Margaret Laurence Collection.
77 JSR to Roy St George Stubbs, 12 Aug. 1975.
78 JSR to Dr John Archer, n.d., Ross private papers.
79 JSR to John Moss, 2 Dec. 1975.

14. Literary Forefather

1 JSR to Ken Mitchell, 29 Dec. 1975, URL, Ken Mitchell Collection.
2 JSR to John Moss, 2 Dec. 1975.
3 Reports on his travels can be found in letters he wrote to Myrna Kostash, 10 July 1975 (NAC, Myrna Kostash Papers), and Andy Suknaski, 1 July 1975.
4 JSR to Ken Mitchell, 5 Sept. 1975, URL, Ken Mitchell Collection.
5 JSR to Ken Mitchell, 11 Dec. 1975, URL, Ken Mitchell Collection.
6 JSR to Andy Suknaski, 29 March 1976.
7 JSR to Roy St George Stubbs, 28 June 1975.
8 JSR to Myrna Kostash, 10 July 1975, NAC, Myrna Kostash Papers.
9 Ross's influence on Suknaski is reported by JSR in a letter to Roy St George Stubbs, 28 June 1975.
10 JSR to Andy Suknaski, 1 July 1975.
11 JSR to Andy Suknaski, 14 Nov. 1977.
12 JSR to Andy Suknaski, 29 March 1976.
13 JSR to Andy Suknaski, 1 July 1975.
14 JSR to Ken Mitchell, 29 Dec. 1975, URL, Ken Mitchell Collection.
15 JSR to Keath Fraser, 18 Jan. 1976.
16 JSR to Ken Mitchell, 2 Aug. 1976, URL, Ken Mitchell Collection.
17 Ibid.
18 Ken Mitchell to JSR, 27 Feb. 1976, Ross private papers.

19 JSR to Ken Mitchell, 31 March 1976, URL, Ken Mitchell Collection.
20 JSR to Ken Mitchell, 18 Nov. 1976, URL, Ken Mitchell Collection.
21 JSR to Lorraine McMullen, 18 July 1976.
22 JSR in conversation, 10 March 1993.
23 JSR to Keath Fraser, 29 May 1977.
24 Ibid.
25 JSR to Ken Mitchell, 5 Aug. 1980, URL, Ken Mitchell Collection.
26 JSR to Alvin Goldman, 19 Dec. 1976.
27 JSR to Doris Saunders, 11 Jan. 1977; JSR to Roy St George Stubbs, 6 March 1977.
28 JSR to Alvin Goldman, 19 Dec. 1976.
29 Letter from JSR to the author, 5 Sept. 1977.
30 JSR to Rudy Wiebe, 1 March 1977, Ross private papers.
31 JSR in conversation, 17 June 1991.
32 JSR to Alvin Goldman, 10 May 1977.
33 JSR to Alvin Goldman, 26 Sept. 1979.
34 JSR to Geoffrey Hancock, 1 Oct. 1977, Ross private papers.
35 JSR to Ken Mitchell, 8 Oct. 1977, URL, Ken Mitchell Collection.
36 JSR to Ken Mitchell, 15 Nov. 1977, URL, Ken Mitchell Collection.
37 JSR to Myrna Kostash, n.d. [Christmas card, 1977], NAC, Myrna Kostash Papers.
38 JSR to Doris Saunders, 11 Jan. 1977.
39 JSR to Lorraine McMullen, 15 Jan. 1978.
40 JSR to Ken Mitchell, 5 July 1977, URL, Ken Mitchell Collection.
41 Letter from JSR to the author, 26 Nov. 1977.
42 JSR to Lorraine McMullen, 15 Jan. 1978.
43 JSR to Lorraine McMullen, 5 Feb. 1978.
44 Ibid.
45 JSR to Ken Mitchell, Christmas card, n.d. [1978], URL, Ken Mitchell Collection.
46 JSR to Margaret Laurence, 15 Sept. 1978, YUL, Margaret Laurence Collection.
47 This letter (Ross private papers) was typed up and sent by Margaret Laurence. The other signatories were Graeme Gibson, Sylvia Fraser, Marie-Claire Blais, Harold Horwood, Jack Ludwig, Jane Rule, Pierre Berton, June Callwood, Charles Taylor, Gwendolyn MacEwen, and Silver Donald Cameron.
48 JSR to Margaret Laurence, 21 Aug. 1978, YUL, Margaret Laurence Collection. The draft of this letter, which was not sent, is with Ross's private papers.
49 Luc Jutras to JSR, 17 Jan. 1979, Ross private papers.
50 Letter from JSR to the author, 30 Jan. 1979. I had explained that a former student, Wayne Wiens, travelling across the prairie, had taken the picture and mailed it, knowing it would make me think of the novel. 'A wonderful photograph,' wrote Ross, 'at least for prairie specialists. Rings many bells.' Certainly it made more sense than the Toronto city hall design that was then on the NCL.

51 JSR to David Gilbert, University of Nebraska Press, 2 Feb. 1979, Ross private papers.
52 Letter from JSR to the author, 30 Jan. 1979. In fact, it would take eleven years for Nebraska to sell the paperback run of five thousand copies, but it was reprinted in 1989 with a different cover -- a painting of a 'little house on the prairie' against a northern lights backdrop -- and sales were stronger, chiefly because interest in Canadian literature was beginning to increase in the United States.
53 JSR to Lorraine McMullen, 30 March 1979.
54 Letter from JSR to the author, 30 Jan. 1979.
55 JSR to Lorraine McMullen, 30 March 1979.
56 JSR to Alvin Goldman, 26 Sept. 1979.
57 JSR to Alvin and Dorothy Goldman, 19 March 1980.
58 JSR to Ken Mitchell, 7 Jan. 1980, URL, Ken Mitchell Collection.
59 JSR to Ken Mitchell, 5 March 1980, URL, Ken Mitchell Collection.
60 In conversation, repeatedly, Ross would refer to keeping one manuscript when he made his move back to Canada, but on his death no manuscript came to light among his papers.
61 Glen Sorestad to JSR, 8 Nov. 1979, Ross private papers.
62 This information comes from Philip Nixon's second letter to JSR, 3 Dec. 1979 (Ross private papers). Ross simply drew a line through the request and wrote at the top 'Parkinson's.'
63 David Carpenter to JSR, 27 Jan. 1980, Ross private papers.
64 Lloyd Person to JSR, 11 Feb. 1980, Ross private papers.
65 Ken Mitchell to JSR, 22 Feb. 1980, Ross private papers.
66 JSR to Ken Mitchell, 5 March 1980, URL, Ken Mitchell Collection.
67 JSR to Ken Mitchell, 10 May 1980, URL, Ken Mitchell Collection.
68 JSR to Ken Mitchell, 5 Aug. 1980, URL, Ken Mitchell Collection.
69 JSR to Lorene Wilson, 21 Oct. 1980, Ross private papers.
70 JSR to Frank Moher, 21 Oct. 1980, Ross private papers.
71 Ken Mitchell to JSR, 15 Dec. 1981, Ross private papers.
72 Ibid.
73 JSR to Ken Mitchell, 20 Oct. 1980, URL, Ken Mitchell Collection.
74 Alvin and Dorothy Goldman, interviewed in Montreal, 22 Oct. 1993.
75 JSR to Keath Fraser, 21 Jan. 1981.
76 JSR in conversation. When particularly despondent, he made this statement, or a variant thereof, several times in extreme old age.
77 Mavis Gallant, interviewed in Vancouver, 19 May 1992.
78 JSR to Ken Mitchell, 2 Nov. 1981, URL, Ken Mitchell Collection.
79 JSR to Geoffrey Ursell, 24 Dec. 1981, URL, Ken Mitchell Collection.
80 JSR in conversation, 23 Dec. 1991.

81 Keath Fraser, *As for Me and My Body*, 78.

82 See ibid., 78–81.

83 JSR to Ken Mitchell, 23 Dec. 1981, URL, Ken Mitchell Collection.

84 JSR to Keath Fraser, 20 Dec. 1981.

15. Suicide

1 Keath Fraser, *As for Me and My Body*, 9.

2 Hurting his wrist is referred to in a letter from Keath Fraser to JSR, 1 Feb. 1982 (Ross private papers); 'everything in slow motion' occurs in letter from JSR to Ken Mitchell, 23 Dec. 1981 (URL, Ken Mitchell Collection).

3 Keath Fraser, *As for Me and My Body*, 91.

4 JSR to Alvin Goldman, 20 April 1982.

5 JSR to Ken Mitchell, 14 April 1982, URL, Ken Mitchell Collection.

6 Keath Fraser, *As for Me and My Body*, 7. The account of a suicide attempt is taken from Fraser's memoir, 12–13, 20–1.

7 Lorraine McMullen in conversation, May 1982.

8 Gerald Friesen to JSR, 26 Nov. 1982, Ross private papers.

9 JSR to Alvin Goldman, 1 Sept. 1982.

10 JSR to Alvin Goldman, 17 Nov. 1982.

11 JSR to Alvin Goldman, 28 Jan. 1983.

12 Keath Fraser interviewed, 2 Oct. 1996. See also Fraser's *As for Me and My Body*, 67–8.

13 JSR to Alvin Goldman, 28 Jan. 1983.

14 JSR to Alvin Goldman, 26 Jan. 1984.

15 Keath Fraser, *As for Me and My Body*, 88.

16 JSR to Alvin Goldman, 1 Sept. 1982; JSR to Ken Mitchell, 24 Aug. 1982, URL, Ken Mitchell Collection.

17 This information is found in a letter from John Gibbon to JSR, 20 Oct. 1982, Ross private papers.

18 JSR to Alvin Goldman, 19 Oct. 1983, and in conversation 15 Sept. 1993.

19 John Gibbon to JSR, 1 Oct. 1982 and 25 Oct. 1982, Ross private papers.

20 JSR to Alvin Goldman, 1 April 1983.

21 JSR to Alvin Goldman, 1 Aug. 1983.

22 Lorraine McMullen in conversation, June 1983.

23 JSR to Alvin Goldman, 1 Aug. 1983.

24 Guy Vanderhaeghe to JSR, 29 Jan. 1984, Ross private papers; Roy MacGregor to JSR, 21 March 1984, Ross private papers.

25 Lorna Crozier, 'Real Truth,' 6. Her book inspired by *As for Me and My House* is titled *A Saving Grace: The Collected Poems of Mrs Bentley* (1996).

26 JSR to Alvin Goldman, 26 Jan. 1984.

27 Beatrice Obermann to JSR, n.d., Ross private papers.

28 Audrey O'Kelly Peterkin to JSR, 11 July 1984, Ross private papers.

29 Lloyd Person to JSR, 11 July, 15 Sept., and 16 Oct. 1984, Ross private papers.

30 JSR in conversation, 14 July 1995.

31 Robert Weaver interviewed 9 April 1995.

32 Letter from JSR to the author, Nov. 1984. This is quoted from memory, as the original is lost, although he uses the same metaphor of pulling down the blinds in a letter of 10 Nov. 1982.

33 Alan Twigg, *Vancouver and Its Writers*, 11.

34 Keath Fraser to Ken Mitchell, 27 Sept. 1985, URL, Ken Mitchell Collection.

35 Mary Moscovich, interviewed by telephone 23 July 1996.

36 Reported in a letter from Jack Hodgins to the author, 3 July 1997.

37 Keath Fraser, *As for Me and My Body*, 27.

38 Ken Adachi, 'Anthology Producers Try, Try, Try Again,' *Toronto Star*, 23 April 1988, p. M4.

39 William French, 'The New Harvest,' *Globe and Mail*, 30 April 1988, p. C19.

40 Bert Almon, review of *The Macmillan Anthology I*, *Canadian Book Review Annual 1988*, ed. Dean Tudor, 250–1.

41 Janet Hamilton, 'Inaugural Anthology a Positive Step for Contemporary Writing,' *Quill and Quire* 54 (June 1988): 27.

42 Letter from JSR to the author, 21 May 1988.

16. The Order of Canada

1 JSR in conversation, 23 Oct. 1989.

2 JSR to John O'Connor, 11 April 1990.

3 Liam Lacey, 'The "Cosmopolitan" Prairie Boy,' *Globe and Mail*, 16 Feb. 1991, p. C5.

4 JSR to Robert Savory, 4 March 1991, Ross private papers.

5 Neil Besner, 'The Great Canadian Novel Looked At over 50 Years,' *Winnipeg Free Press*, 2 May 1992, p. F66.

6 W.J. Keith, review of *Sinclair Ross's 'As for Me and My House': Five Decades of Criticism*, *Canadian Book Review Annual* (1991): 284.

7 Robertson Davies, review of *As for Me and My House*, reprinted in Stouck, ed., *Five Decades*, 16–18.

8 Mavis Gallant, interviewed 19 May 1992.

9 JSR and Mavis Gallant in conversation, 20 May 1992.

10 John Whitefoot, interviewed Sept. 1996.

11 To my knowledge, this is the only motion picture that was ever made of Sinclair Ross.

12 JSR to Wayne Schmalz, n.d. [1993], Ross private papers.

13 Paul Denham, 'Sinclair Ross,' 5.

14 David Carpenter, in fact, wrote a foreword for the deluxe edition, but it was not used.

15 According to Dallas Harrison's research, this was certainly the case. Harrison reports only thirty-two copies sold in the first two years. See Harrison, 'Where Is (the) Horizon?' 161–2.

16 'The Painted Door' was translated into Serbo-Croatian by Branko Gorjup as 'Obojena vrata' and published in *Antologija Kanadske Pripovijetke* (Zagreb: Nakladni Zavod Matice, 1991), 41–61; the master's thesis, on the importance of setting in the stories and novels of Sinclair Ross, was written by Gao Lanfang at Lanzhou University, China, in 1999.

17 *Globe and Mail*, 2 March 1996, p. D15.

Bibliography

A full account of primary and secondary sources until 1990 appears in David Latham's 'A Reference Guide to Sinclair Ross,' in *From the Heart of the Heartland: The Fiction of Sinclair Ross*, ed. John Moss (Ottawa: University of Ottawa Press, 1992), 125–39. Given below is an abbreviated description of primary sources, an updated account of archival materials, and a selected list of secondary sources.

I. Sinclair Ross's Published Works

Books

Each entry lists the first edition and also the most recent edition, which has served as the source of quotations for this biography. Fuller accounts of editions and reprintings are contained in chapters of the biography describing the history of each text.

As for Me and My House. New York: Reynal and Hitchcock, 1941. Toronto: McClelland and Stewart, 1989.

The Well. Toronto: Macmillan, 1958. Edmonton: University of Alberta Press, 2001.

The Lamp at Noon and Other Stories. Toronto: McClelland and Stewart, 1968; 1990.

Whir of Gold. Toronto: McClelland and Stewart, 1970. Edmonton: University of Alberta Press, 2001.

Sawbones Memorial. Toronto: McClelland and Stewart, 1974. Edmonton: University of Alberta Press, 2001.

The Race and Other Stories. Ed. Lorraine McMullen. Ottawa: University of Ottawa Press, 1982.

Short Stories

Listed here are first publications, with current printings in *The Lamp at Noon and Other Stories* (LNOS) and *The Race and Other Stories* (ROS).

'No Other Way.' *Nash's-Pall Mall Magazine* 95 (Oct. 1934): 16–17, 80–4. *ROS*, 23–36.

'A Field of Wheat.' *Queen's Quarterly* 42 (Spring 1935): 31–42. *LNOS*, 67–76.

'September Snow.' *Queen's Quarterly* 42 (Winter 1935): 451–60. *LNOS*, 54–61.

'Circus in Town.' *Queen's Quarterly* 43 (Winter 1936): 368–72. *LNOS*, 62–6.

'The Lamp at Noon.' *Queen's Quarterly* 45 (Spring 1938): 30–42. *LNOS*, 7–17.

'A Day with Pegasus.' *Queen's Quarterly* 45 (Summer 1938): 141–56. *ROS*, 37–48.

'The Painted Door.' *Queen's Quarterly* 46 (Summer 1939): 145–68. *LNOS*, 93–112.

'Cornet at Night.' *Queen's Quarterly* 46 (Winter 1939): 431–52. *LNOS*, 29–45.

'Not by Rain Alone.' *Queen's Quarterly* 48 (Spring 1941): 7–16. *LNOS* (as 'Summer Thunder'), 46–54.

'Nell.' *Manitoba Arts Review* 2 (Winter 1941): 32–40. *ROS*, 49–59.

'One's a Heifer.' *Canadian Accent.* Ed. Ralph Gustafson. Harmondsworth: Penguin, 1944, 114–28. *LNOS*, 113–28.

'Barrack Room Fiddle Tune.' *Manitoba Arts Review* 5 (Spring 1947): 12–17. *ROS*, 61–8.

'Jug and Bottle.' *Queen's Quarterly* 56 (Winter 1949): 500–21. *ROS*, 69–85.

'The Outlaw.' *Queen's Quarterly* 57 (Summer 1950): 198–210. *LNOS*, 18–28.

'Saturday Night.' *Queen's Quarterly* 58 (Autumn 1951): 387–400. *ROS*, 87–97.

'The Runaway.' *Queen's Quarterly* 59 (Autumn 1952): 323–42. *LNOS*, 77–92.

'The Unwilling Organist.' *The Teller* [Royal Bank], Dec. 1958, pp. 12–16.

'Spike.' Trans. Pierre Villon. *Liberté* 11 (mars–avril 1969): 181–97. In English in Ken Mitchell, *Sinclair Ross: A Reader's Guide.* Moose Jaw: Coteau Books, 1981, 95–107. *ROS*, 99–110.

'The Flowers That Killed Him.' *Journal of Canadian Fiction* 1 (Summer 1972): 5–10. *ROS*, 119–34.

'The Race.' *ROS*, 111–17.

Articles and Memoir

'Why My 2nd Book Came 17 Years Later.' *Toronto Daily Star*, 13 Sept. 1958, p. 32.

'Montreal and French-Canadian Culture: What They Mean to English-Canadian Novelists.' *Tamarack Review* 40 (Summer 1966): 46–7.

'On Looking Back.' *Mosaic* 3 (Spring 1970): 93–4.

'Just Wind and Horses: A Memoir.' *The Macmillan Anthology I*. Ed. John Metcalf and Leon Rooke. Toronto: Macmillan, 1988, 83–97.

II. Archives and Unpublished Manuscripts

Archives

Sinclair Ross and Irene Harvalias donated items to establish a Ross collection at the National Archives of Canada in Ottawa, but most Ross materials are still scattered throughout the country in private holdings and in the publishing archives of Macmillan and McClelland and Stewart at McMaster University.

Public Collections

McMaster University Library (MUL)
  Macmillan Company (Canada) Papers
  McClelland and Stewart Collection
National Archives of Canada (NAC)
  Myrna Kostash Papers
  Sinclair Ross Papers
  Robert Weaver Fonds
Queen's University Library (QUL)
  Grant Macdonald Collection
  Queen's Quarterly Archive
Thomas Fisher Rare Book Library, University of Toronto (TFRBL)
  Margaret Atwood Collection
  Earle Birney Collection
  W.A. Deacon Papers
University of British Columbia Library, Rare Books and Special Collections (UBCL)
  Roy Daniells Papers
University of Calgary Library (UCL)
  Rudy Wiebe Collection
University of Regina Library (URL)
  Ken Mitchell Collection
University of Saskatchewan Library (USL)
  Ralph Gustafson Collection
York University Library (YUL)
  Margaret Laurence Collection

Private Collections

In private collections there are letters to the following individuals: David Carpenter, Wilfred Cude, Harriet Duff-Smith, Keath Fraser, Alvin Goldman, Sheila Kieran, Lorraine McMullen, John Moss, John O'Connor, Audrey O'Kelly Peterkin, Roy St George Stubbs, Doris Saunders, David Stouck, and Andrew Suknaski. At present Keath Fraser is custodian of some files of Ross correspondence that have not yet been archived. Their contents, when cited in this biography, are identified as 'Ross private papers.'

Unpublished Manuscripts

'Old Chippendale' (short story), QUL, Grant Macdonald Collection

'The Troopship Story' (incomplete war memoir), NAC, Sinclair Ross Papers

III. Secondary Sources: Selected Books and Articles

Arcola and South of the Moose Mountains. Arcola, SK: Arcola Historical Committee, 1965

Arcola-Kisbey Golden Heritage. Arcola, SK: Arcola Kisbey History Book Committee, 1987.

Atwood, Margaret. *Survival: A Thematic Guide to Canadian Literature.* Toronto: Anansi Press, 1972.

Bell, Clive. *Art.* London: Chatto and Windus, 1914.

Bennett, Donna, and Russell Brown, eds. *A New Anthology of Canadian Literature in English.* Toronto: Oxford University Press, 2002.

Bentley, D.M.R. 'As for Me and Significant Form.' *Canadian Notes and Queries* 48 (1994): 18–20.

Bett, Henry. *Some Secrets of Style.* London: George Allen and Unwin, Ltd, n.d.

Bishop, Karen. 'The Pegasus Symbol in the Childhood Stories of Sinclair Ross.' *ARIEL* 16 (July 1985): 67–87.

Black, Norman Fergus. *History of Saskatchewan and the Northwest Territories.* Vol. 1. Regina: Saskatchewan Historical Company Publishers, 1913.

Brydon, Diana. 'Sinclair Ross.' *Profiles in Canadian Literature.* Ed. Jeffrey M. Heath. Vol. 3. Toronto: Dundurn Press, 1982. 97–103.

Buss, Helen. 'Who Are You, Mrs Bentley? Feminist Re-vision and Sinclair Ross's *As for Me and My House.*' *From the Heart of the Heartland: The Fiction of Sinclair Ross.* Ed. John Moss. Ottawa: University of Ottawa Press, 1992. 39–57.

Camus, Albert. *The Stranger.* New York: Alfred A. Knopf, 1946; Harmondsworth: Penguin, 1964.

Carpenter, David. 'Horsey Comedy in the Short Fiction of Sinclair Ross.' *From the Heart of the Heartland: The Fiction of Sinclair Ross.* Ed. John Moss. Ottawa: University of Ottawa Press, 1992. 67–79.

Cavell, Richard. 'The Unspoken in Sinclair Ross's *As for Me and My House.*' *Spicilegio Moderno* 14 (1980): 23–30.

Chambers, Robert D. *Sinclair Ross and Ernest Buckler.* Toronto: Copp Clark, 1975.

Chauncey, George. *Gay New York: Gender, Urban Culture, and the Making of the Gay Male World, 1890–1940.* New York: Basic Books, 1994.

Comeau, Paul. 'Sinclair Ross's Pioneer Fiction.' *Canadian Literature* 103 (Winter 1984): 174–84.

Cramer, Timothy R. 'Questioning Sexuality in Sinclair Ross's *As for Me and My House.*' *ARIEL* 30 (April 1999): 49–60.

Crozier, Lorna. 'The Real Truth, the *Poetic Truth.*' With Doris Hillis. *Prairie Fire* 6 (1985): 4–15.

Cude, Wilfred. 'Beyond Mrs Bentley: A Study of *As for Me and My House.*' *Journal of Canadian Studies* 8 (Feb. 1973): 3–18. Reprinted in *A Due Sense of Differences: An Evaluative Approach to Canadian Literature*. Washington, DC: University Press of America, 1980. 31–49.

– 'The Dark Laughter of *As for Me and My House.*' *From the Heart of the Heartland: The Fiction of Sinclair Ross*. Ed. John Moss. Ottawa: University of Ottawa Press, 1992. 59–65.

Daniells, Roy. 'Introduction.' *As for Me and My House*. Toronto: McClelland and Stewart, 1957. v–x.

Davey, Frank. 'The Conflicting Signs of *As for Me and My House.*' *From the Heart of the Heartland: The Fiction of Sinclair Ross*. Ed. John Moss. Ottawa: University of Ottawa Press, 1992. 25–37.

Davies, Robertson. *The Well-Tempered Critic: One Man's View of Theatre and Letters in Canada*. Ed. Judith Skelton Grant. Toronto: McClelland and Stewart, 1981.

Deacon, William Arthur. *Dear Bill: The Correspondence of William Arthur Deacon*. Ed. John Lennox and Michele Lacombe. Toronto: University of Toronto Press, 1988.

Dean, Misao. *Practising Femininity: Domestic Realism and the Performance of Gender in Early Canadian Fiction*. Toronto: University of Toronto Press, 1998.

Denham, Paul. 'Sinclair Ross in the Nineties.' *NeWest Review* 15 (Aug.–Sept. 1990): 5–6.

Dickinson, Peter. *Here Is Queer: Nationalisms, Sexualities, and the Literatures of Canada*. Toronto: University of Toronto Press, 1999.

Diehl-Jones, Charlene. 'Telling Secrets: Sinclair Ross's *Sawbones Memorial.*' *From the Heart of the Heartland: The Fiction of Sinclair Ross*. Ed. John Moss. Ottawa: University of Ottawa Press, 1992. 81–90.

Djwa, Sandra. 'No Other Way: Sinclair Ross's Stories and Novels.' *Canadian Literature* 47 (Winter 1971): 49–66.

– *Professing English: A Life of Roy Daniells*. Toronto: University of Toronto Press, 2002.

Footprints of Our Pioneers. Shellbrook, SK: Wild Rose and Area History Book Committee, 1990.

Fraser, Keath. *As for Me and My Body*. Toronto: ECW Press, 1997.

– 'Futility at the Pump: The Short Stories of Sinclair Ross.' *Queen's Quarterly* 77 (Spring 1970): 72–80.

French, William. 'Too Good Too Soon, Ross Remains the Elusive Canadian.' *Globe and Mail*, 27 July 1974, p. 25.

Giltrow, Janet. 'A Linguistic Analysis of Sample Passages from *As for Me and My House.*' *Sinclair Ross's 'As for Me and My House': Five Decades of Criticism*. Ed. David Stouck. Toronto: University of Toronto Press, 1991. 209–24.

Godard, Barbara. 'El Greco in Canada: Sinclair Ross's *As for Me and My House.*' *Mosaic* 14 (Spring 1981): 54–75.

Goldie, Terry. *Pink Snow: Homotextual Possibilities in Canadian Fiction*. Peterborough,

ON: Broadview Press, 2003.

Gunnars, Kristjana. 'Introduction.' *The Well*. Edmonton: University of Alberta Press, 2001. v–xviii.

Hardy, Nat. 'Introduction.' *Whir of Gold*. Edmonton: University of Alberta Press, 2001. v–xvi.

Harrison, Dallas. 'Where Is (the) Horizon? Placing *As for Me and My House*.' *Essays on Canadian Writing* 61 (Spring 1997): 142–69.

Harrison, Dick. *Unnamed Country: The Struggle for a Canadian Prairie Fiction*. Edmonton: University of Alberta Press, 1977.

Hicks, Anne. 'Mrs Bentley: The Good Housewife.' *Room of One's Own* 5 (1980): 60–7.

Kallman, Helmut, Gilles Potvin, and Kenneth Winters, eds. *Encyclopedia of Music in Canada*. 2nd ed. Toronto: University of Toronto Press, 1992.

Kattan, Naim. 'Montreal and French-Canadian Culture.' *Tamarack Review* 40 (Summer 1966): 46–7.

Kaye, Frances. 'Sinclair Ross's Use of George Sand and Frederic Chopin as Models for the Bentleys.' *Essays on Canadian Writing* 33 (Fall 1988): 100–11.

Kostash, Myrna. 'Discovering Sinclair Ross: It's Rather Late.' *Saturday Night* 87 (July 1972): 33–7.

Kroetsch, Robert. 'Afterword.' *As for Me and My House*. Toronto: McClelland and Stewart, 1989. 217–21.

– 'The Moment of the Discovery of America Continues.' *The Lovely Treachery of Words: Essays Selected and New*. Toronto: Oxford University Press, 1989. 1–20.

Lacey, Liam. 'The "Cosmopolitan" Prairie Boy.' *Globe and Mail*, 16 Feb. 1991, p. C5.

Larson, Lars. *Yesterday Is Gone Forever*. Abbey, SK, 1973.

Lecker, Robert. *Making It Real: The Canonization of English-Canadian Literature*. Concord, ON: Anansi Press, 1995.

Lesk, Andrew. 'On Sinclair Ross's Straight(ened) House.' *English Studies in Canada* 28 (March 2002): 65–90.

– 'Something Queer Going on Here: Desire in the Short Fiction of Sinclair Ross.' *Essays on Canadian Writing* 61 (Spring 1997): 129–41.

Martin, Robert K. 'Two Days in Sodom, or How Anglo-Canadian Writers Invent Their Own Quebecs.' *Body Politic* (July–Aug. 1977): 28–30.

McCourt, Edward. *The Canadian West in Fiction*. Toronto: Ryerson Press, 1949.

McMullen, Lorraine. '"The Child Is Father to the Manuscript": Sinclair Ross and His Women.' *Ilha Do Desterro: A Journal of English Language, Literatures in English and Cultural Studies* 31.1 (1994): 87–102.

– 'Introduction.' *Sawbones Memorial*. Toronto: McClelland and Stewart, 1978. 5–11.

– *Sinclair Ross*. Boston: Twayne, 1979.

Mitchell, Ken. 'Introduction.' *Sawbones Memorial*. Edmonton: University of Alberta

Press, 2001. v–xii.

– 'The Ross File.' *Ambience*. CBC Radio, 6 July 1986.

– *Sinclair Ross: A Reader's Guide*. Moose Jaw: Coteau Books, 1981.

Moss, John. *Patterns of Isolation in English-Canadian Fiction*. Toronto: McClelland and Stewart, 1974.

– ed. *From the Heart of the Heartland: The Fiction of Sinclair Ross*. Ottawa: University of Ottawa Press, 1992.

New, W.H. 'Sinclair Ross's Ambivalent World.' *Canadian Literature* 40 (Spring 1969): 26–32. Reprinted in *Articulating West: Essays on Purpose and Form in Modern Canadian Literature*. Toronto: new press, 1972. 60–7.

Pacey, Desmond. *Creative Writing in Canada*. Toronto: Ryerson Press, 1952.

Pearson, Alan. 'James Sinclair Ross: Major Novelist with a Banking Past,' *Montrealer* 42 (March 1968): 18–19.

Raoul, Valerie. 'Straight or Bent: Textual/Sexual T(ri)angles in *As for Me and My House*.' *Canadian Literature* 156 (Spring 1998): 13–28.

Ricou, Laurie. 'The Prairie Internalized: The Fiction of Sinclair Ross.' *Vertical Man / Horizontal World: Man and Landscape in Canadian Prairie Fiction*. Vancouver: University of British Columbia Press, 1973. 81–94.

Rose, Marilyn. 'Sinclair Ross's "Foreigners."' *From the Heart of the Heartland: The Fiction of Sinclair Ross*. Ed. John Moss. Ottawa: University of Ottawa Press, 1992. 91–101.

St George Stubbs, Roy. 'Presenting Sinclair Ross.' *Saturday Night*, 9 Aug. 1941, p. 17.

Schiff, Stacey. *Saint-Exupéry: A Biography*. New York: Alfred A. Knopf, 1994.

Sedgwick, Eve Kosofsky. *Between Men: English Literature and Male Homosocial Desire*. New York: Columbia University Press, 1985. (Reprinted with new preface, 1993.)

Speir, John. 'History of Abbey Village.' *Memories of Yesteryear: Rural Municipality of Miry Creek No. 229, 1913–1963*. Saskatoon: Modern Press, 1963.

Storr, Merl, ed. *Bisexuality: A Critical Reader*. New York: Routledge, 1999.

Stouck, David. 'Cross-Writing and the Unconcluded Self in Sinclair Ross's *As for Me and My House*.' *Western American Literature* 34.4 (Winter 2000): 434–47. Reprinted in *Articulating Gender*. Ed. Anjali Bhelande and Mala Pandurang. Delhi: Pencraft International, 2000. 171–82.

– 'Introduction.' *As for Me and My House*. Lincoln: University of Nebraska Press, 1978. v–xiii.

– 'The Mirror and the Lamp in Sinclair Ross's *As for Me and My House*.' *Mosaic* 7 (Winter 1974): 141–50.

– ed. *Sinclair Ross's 'As for Me and My House': Five Decades of Criticism*. Toronto: University of Toronto Press, 1991.

Sypnowich, Peter. 'A Bachelor on the Run Comes Back to Canada.' *Toronto Star*, 13 Nov. 1970, p. 30.

Tallman, Warren. 'Wolf in the Snow.' *Canadian Literature* 5 (Summer 1960): 7–20, and *Canadian Literature* 6 (Autumn 1960): 41–8.

Thacker, Robert. 'A Complex of Possibilities: Prairie as Home Place.' *The Great Prairie Fact and Literary Imagination*. Albuquerque: University of New Mexico Press, 1989.

Toppings, Earle. *Canadian Writers on Tape: Mordecai Richler / Sinclair Ross*. Toronto: Ontario Institute for Studies in Education, 1971.

Twigg, Alan, *Vancouver and Its Writers*. Madeira Park, BC: Harbour Publishing, 1986.

Warner, Tom. *Never Going Back: A History of Queer Activism in Canada*. Toronto: University of Toronto Press, 2002.

Weintraub, William. *City Unique: Montreal Days and Nights in the 1940s and '50s*. Toronto: McClelland and Stewart, 1996.

Williams, David. 'The "Scarlet" Rompers: Towards a New Perspective in *As for Me and My House*.' *Canadian Literature* 103 (Winter 1984): 166–74.

Illustration Credits

Royal Bank Corporate Archives: Sinclair Ross publicity photo, 1941; Ross at Royal Bank head office, 1962.

Saskatchewan Archives Board: Saskatchewan dust storm, R-A4665.

National Archives of Canada: Ross in Málaga, Spain, PA188033.

Private Collections: James Sinclair Ross and his mother, ca. 1910 (courtesy of Doris Saunders); skating party in Indian Head, 1915 (courtesy of Margaret and Donald Price); Rolling Prairie District schoolhouse (courtesy of Myrtle Doell); Hunchiak family (courtesy of Lena Campe); United Church in Abbey, SK (author's photo); Arcola, SK (courtesy of Vesta Pickel); Dorothy Cornell (courtesy of John O'Connor); Keith Clarke (*Moose Mountain Star-Standard*); Ross on horseback (Ross collection); dust jacket for *As for Me and My House* (courtesy of John Whitefoot); Catherine Fraser Ross, n.d. (courtesy of Margaret and Donald Price); letter to Grant Macdonald (courtesy of Queen's University Library); Doyle Klyn (courtesy of Doyle Klyn); Ross with the Baxters (courtesy of the Baxter family); Sinclair Ross publicity photo, 1958 (Ross collection, photograph by William Notman & Son); Sinclair Ross, Vancouver, 1982 (Schiffer Photography, Ross collection); Sinclair Ross and Keath Fraser (courtesy of Keath Fraser, photograph by Sam Tata); Sinclair Ross and Mavis Gallant (author's photo); Order of Canada photo (Ross collection); last photograph of Sinclair Ross (Ross collection, photograph by Peter Henderson). Unless otherwise indicated, photographers for these private collections are unknown.

Index

Abbey, SK, 12–14, 24, 26–40 *passim*, 43, 77, 81, 90, 96, 112, 176, 246, 281
Adachi, Ken, 275
Adams, Hughie, 23–4, 38
Albertan (Calgary), 204
Algeria, 162
Allen, Ralph, 163, 165, 166
Almas, Mairze, 287
Almon, Bert, 275
Alstad, John 'Arndt,' 18, 19
Amsterdam, 238–9
Anderson, Marian, 85
Anderson, Nellie, 72, 83–4, 101, 123
Andre Deutsch (publisher), 170
Arcola, SK, 22, 42–68 *passim*, 69, 81, 84, 112, 176, 246, 272, 302n3
Arcola and South of the Moose Mountains, 302n2
Argosy (magazine), 138
Athens, 193, 194–208 *passim*, 245, 251, 262
Atlantic Monthly, 66, 75, 91, 101, 104, 305n15
Atlantis Films, 94, 96, 137, 267
Atwood, Margaret, 77, 221, 227, 229, 230, 231–2, 250, 251, 265, 287; *The Edible Woman*, 204, 221; *Journals of Susanna Moodie*, 221; *Lady Oracle*, 250; *Surfacing*, 221; *Survival*, 216, 221
Aubert, Helen, 85–6
Auden, W.H., 265
Auld Kirk Cameronians, 300n9
Ayles, Joe, 69–70

Bach, Johann Sebastian, 54, 128; *The Well-Tempered Clavier*, 54, 56
Bacque, James Watson, 187
Bad Trips (travel anthology), 275, 288
Barbour, Douglas, 205
Barcelona, 208–12, 213, 243, 255
Baudelaire, Charles, 265
Baxter, Bill, 176, 181, 182, 183, 188, 193, 194, 260, 262, 267
Baxter, Molly, 176, 181, 183, 188, 194, 260, 262, 267, 276
Becker, Maximilian, 103, 104–5, 115, 121, 123, 127, 134, 136, 155, 160, 162, 168, 169, 170, 186, 307n20
Becker, Royce, 307n20
Beethoven, Ludwig van, 31, 58
Bell, Clive, 99
Bell, Douglas, 301n8
Benjamin, Arthur, 86–7, 117; *The Devil*

Take Her, 86; 'Jamaican Rhumba,' 86; *Prima Donna*, 86
Bentley, D.M.R., 306n14
Bernstein, Leonard, 293
Berton, Pierre, 163, 165, 324n47
Besner, Neil, 281
Best, Marshall, 170
Bible, 27, 34, 95, 235, 296
Billington, Dave, 230
Bird family (Arcola), 44
Birney, Earle, 116, 125, 133–4, 136, 157, 202; *David and Other Poems*, 125
Birney, Esther, 312n39
Bishop, Dorothy, 174, 175, 231
Bishop, Karen, 74
Bissell, Claude T., 176
Black, Norman Fergus: *History of Saskatchewan and the Northwest Territories*, 300n11
Blais, Marie-Claire, 324n47
Blakeney, Allan, 217
Blatty, William Peter: *The Exorcist*, 229
Books in Canada, 231, 239
Borges, Jorge Luis, 163
Bowen, Cecily, 31
Bowen, Wilfred, 31, 38
Bowles, Paul, 213, 268; *The Sheltering Sky*, 213
Boynton-Coffey, W.J., 48, 68
Boy's Own, 247
Braaten brothers (Abbey), 36
Brack, Bertha. *See* Lang, Bertha Brack
Brodersen, George, 114
Brown, Dr (theologian), 116, 320n8
Brown, E.K., 109, 115, 116
Brydon, Diana, 264
Bunyan, John: *Pilgrim's Progress*, 288
Buss, Helen, 279

Cabri, SK, 33

Caldwell, Erskine: *Tobacco Road*, 82
Calgary Herald, 205, 230
Callaghan, Morley, ix, 144, 173; *Such Is My Beloved*, 173
Callwood, June, 324n47
Cameron, Silver Donald, 324n47
Campbell, Dorothy, 53, 68
Campbell, Gordon, 285
Campbell, Maria: *Halfbreed*, 240
Campe, Lena Hunchaik, 302n14
Campkin, Grace, 25
Camus, Albert, 162, 172, 180, 247, 316n33; *The Stranger*, 162, 180
Canadian Accent, 136
Canadian Authors Association, 102, 131, 184
Canadian Fiction Magazine, 249
Canadian Forum, 204
Canadian Literature, 199, 288
Carpenter, David, 158–60, 257, 279
Carr, Emily, 141
Carr, Verna, 302n6
Carrier, J.M., 310
Carter, Dyson, 121, 122; *Night of Flame*, 121
Cavell, Richard, 309n20
CBC: radio, 96, 123, 126, 141, 143, 149, 154–5, 158, 175, 184, 190, 192–3, 230, 231, 248, 270, 271, 272, 280, 295; television, 94, 96, 150, 178, 192, 212
CBC Times, 184
Chambers, Robert D., 179–80
Chaminade, Cécile: 'Autumn,' 52
Chaplin, SK, 15, 314n4
Chatelaine, 72, 250
Chautauqua, 33, 44, 47, 302n8
Chekhov, Anton, 297
Chesterton, G.K., 163
Chicago, 81–2, 209

China, 234, 297
Chopin, Frédéric, 37, 66, 309n20
Chotem, Neil, 143
Chrétien, Jean, 285
Clark, Lovell, 122, 127, 140, 191–2, 310–11n44
Clarke, George Herbert, 151, 153, 155, 158, 185
Clarke, Keith, 50–1, 52–76 passim, 303n26
Clarke family (Arcola), 50, 51
Clay, Charles, 131; Young Voyageur, 131
Clifford, Mary Belle, 3, 299n1, 300n3
Clockwork Orange (film), 223, 236
Collier, Frank, 288
Comeau, Paul, 288
Conrad, Joseph: Heart of Darkness, 281
Conyers, Will, 71–2, 84
Cooley, Dennis, 270
Cornell, Dorothy, 45–58 passim, 68, 69, 70, 76, 119, 177, 193, 304n1, 318n61
Cornell family (Arcola), 49, 53, 58
Cortázar, Julio, 250
Coteau Books (publisher), 257
Cottingham, Bessie, 38
Court, Ernest, 72, 73, 75, 83, 91, 103–4, 123, 269
Coutts, George, 44, 50
Coward, Noel: Blithe Spirit, 133; In Which We Serve (film), 133
Craib, Joseph, 288, 289
Cramer, Timothy, 309n20
Crozier, Lorna, 269, 274, 295; A Saving Grace: The Collected Poems of Mrs Bentley, 326n25
Cude, Wilfred, 221, 273, 279, 309n17
Cummings, Peter, 232
Currie, Josephine, 87

Dafoe, John, 126, 204

Dahlie, Harvard, 204–5
Dalhousie Review, 176
Daniells, Roy, 109–27 passim, 139, 141, 173, 185, 192, 199–200, 232, 254, 288
Darling, Michael, 266
Davey, Frank, 279
Davies, Robertson, 109, 116, 146, 149, 163, 216, 221, 227, 229, 281, 291; Eros at Breakfast, 149; Fifth Business, 216, 221, 253; Fortune My Foe, 146; The Manticore, 216
Deacon, W.A., 109, 117, 175
Dean, Misao, 309n18
de Gaulle, Charles, 134
de la Roche, Mazo, 144, 149
Depression (1930s), 47–8, 54–5, 58–9, 61, 82, 83, 107, 110, 112, 119
Devils (film), 223
Dickinson, Peter, 111, 309n20
Diehl-Jones, Charlene, 279
Dilworth, Ira, 114, 117, 141, 149
Divorce Italian Style (film), 230
Djwa, Sandra, 221, 264, 288
Dobbs, Kildare, 165
Doell, Myrtle, 301n9
Dong brothers (Arcola), 43, 234
Dostoevsky, Fyodor, 131, 215, 247, 290; The Brothers Karamazov, 131
Downes, Lillian, 304n4
Downman, C.P.C., 305n15
Dowsley, Theodora, 39, 281
Drainie, John, 154
Dryden, ON, 142
Duff-Smith, Harriet, 72, 75, 101, 112, 123, 134, 304n4, 307n19
Duncan, Chester, 85, 117, 118, 205

Easton, Stuart C., 117
Edinburgh, 63, 65, 112, 149
Edmonds, Miss (teacher), 17, 32

Edmonds, WA, 38
Edmonds, Walter, 126
Edmonton, 258
Edmonton Journal, 205, 231
El Greco, 209
Eliot, George: *Mill on the Floss*, 27; *Silas Marner*, 70
Eliot, T.S., 134
Elmo, Ann, 103, 115, 121
Elwick, Ada, 86, 117
Engel, Marian: *Bear*, 250
Erickson, Arthur, 293
Etherington, Agnes, 145
Etherington, James, 205

Fadiman, Clifton, 108
Fafard, Joe, 286
Farrell, James, 187
Faulkner, William, 159–60, 247; *As I Lay Dying*, 231
Feld, Rose, 106, 108
Fenton, James, 44
Fielding, Geoffrey, 189, 317n21
Fifth House (publisher), 290–2
Findley, Timothy, 251, 252; *Famous Last Words*, 266
Finlay family (Arcola), 44
Fitzgerald, Edward: *The Rubaiyat of Omar Khayyam*, 40
Fitzgerald, F. Scott, 155, 266
Flagstad, Kirstin, 89
Flaubert, Gustave: *Madame Bovary*, 132
Flin Flon, MB, 60
Footprints of Our Pioneers, 299n1
Forbes, Bill, 27
Forester, C.S., 138
Forfang, Nels, 15–18, 20, 21, 63, 77, 162, 180, 314n4
Forsyth, Frederick: *The Day of the Jackal*, 229; *The Odessa File*, 229

Foster, Malcolm, 204
Fowlie, Irene, 321n13
Fraser, Clara, 88, 90
Fraser, Constance, 62, 64, 66, 67, 78–80, 87, 305n19
Fraser, Helen Mary Lawrence, 87
Fraser, John (maternal grandfather), 5, 112–13, 300n10
Fraser, Sir John Foster Fraser (maternal uncle), 5, 20, 62, 63, 64, 65–7, 78–80, 87, 88, 99, 120, 157, 274, 306n12; *Canada As It Is*, 79; *Round the World on a Wheel*, 78
Fraser, Keath, x, xiii, 117, 135, 143, 192, 197, 199, 202, 208, 209, 210, 211, 223, 238, 243, 245, 247–8, 259, 261, 262–96 *passim*, 309n20
Fraser, Lorraine, xiii, 199, 202, 208, 209, 263–4, 268, 276, 292
Fraser, Robin, 276
Fraser, Simon (Lord Lovat), 5, 274
Fraser, Stuart (maternal uncle), 5, 88, 90
Fraser, Sylvia, 324n47
Fraser, Theodore (maternal uncle), 5, 66
French, William, 228, 230, 231, 232, 239, 275
Freud, Sigmund, 61, 171, 182, 214
Friesen, Gerald, 265
Fry, Pamela, 189, 194–204, 206, 224
Fry, Roger, 99
Frye, Northrop, 116–17
Fulford, Robert, 211, 217

Gallant, Johnny, 150, 184, 282
Gallant, Mavis, 150, 161, 177, 184, 193–4, 249, 259–60, 266, 274, 282–3, 284, 289
Ganderton, Tonya, 289, 294
Gao, Lanfang, 328n16
García Márquez, Gabriel, 247, 250;

Autumn of the Patriarch, 250; *One Hundred Years of Solitude*, 250
Garner, Hugh, 204, 207
Gaskell, Eric, 131
Gatenby, Greg, 224
Gaute, Joseph, 196
Gazette (Montreal), 204, 231
Gibbon, Edward: *Decline and Fall of the Roman Empire*, 40
Gibbon, John, 183–4, 266–7
Gibbon, John, Sr, 184; *Canadian Mosaic*, 184
Gibson, Douglas, 269, 280
Gibson, Graeme, 204, 216, 217, 218, 232, 324n47
Gibson, Irene Price (niece), 172, 238, 247
Gide, André, 247
Gielgud, John, 136
Gill, Isabel, 60, 65, 69
Gill, William, 58, 60
Giltrow, Janet, 309n21
Glasgow, 65
Globe and Mail, 109, 117, 175, 204, 228, 230, 232, 239, 275, 280
Godard, Barbara, 209
Godfrey, David: *New Ancestors*, 204
Gogol, Nikolai: 'The Overcoat,' 184
Goldie, Terry, 309n20
Goldman, Alvin, 191, 194, 195, 206, 217, 249, 255–73 *passim*
Goldman, Dorothy, 256, 259–60, 262
Goranson, Linda, 94, 267
Gordon, Evelyn, 302n6
Gorjup, Branko, 328n16
Gould, Glenn, 293
Governor General's Award, 239, 240, 242, 250, 252, 284
Goya, Francisco, 209, 216
Graham, Kathleen, 175

Grainger, Percy: 'Country Gardens,' 37, 125, 128
Grain Growers Guide, 250
Grant, George, 287
Gray, Antoinette, 146
Gray, John, 144, 146–7, 148–9, 154, 155, 161–88 *passim*, 190
Greek Islands, 195, 197, 199, 235, 251
Grove, Frederick Philip, 139–40; *Master of the Mill*, 247; *Over Prairie Trails*, 173
Guillén, Jorge, 254
Gunnars, Kristjana, 180
Gunther, John: *Inside Europe*, 132
Gustafson, Ralph, 125, 136, 138
Gzowski, Peter, 280

Haliburton, Thomas Chandler, 173
Halifax, 132, 272, 278, 292
Hamilton, Janet, 275
Hampshire, Cyril, 44, 54, 56–7
Hancock, Geoff, 249
Hanna, Matilda, 43
Harcourt Brace (publisher), 161, 166
Hardy, Nat, 207
Hardy, Thomas, 153, 247, 266, 282; *Return of the Native*, 247
Harland, Henry: *The Cardinal's Snuff Box*, 67
Harmsworth Universal Encyclopedia, 140
Harper's (publisher), 169
Harrap and Company (publisher), 196
Harrison, Dallas, 328n15
Harrison, Dick, 320n10
Hartley, William, 174
Harvalias, Dimitri, 277
Harvalias, Irene, xiii, 268, 272–97 *passim*
Hauser, Marianne, 108
Haydn, Josef: 'Gypsy Rondo,' 31

Hayes, Helen, 89
Hayman, Mac, 27, 94
Headley, Philip, 288, 289
Heaslip, Miss (Royal Bank, Winnipeg), 122
Hebb, Ms (Royal Bank, Montreal), 272
Hemingway, Ernest, 121, 132, 247, 257; *For Whom the Bell Tolls*, 132
Henry, O., 94, 137
Herbert, Victor: 'O Sweet Mystery of Life,' 125
Herolett, Maurice: *Little Novels of Italy*, 67
Hess, Dame Myra, 135
Hesse, Hermann: 'Beim Schlafengehen,' 296
Hicks, Anne, 309n20
Hill, Walter, 11
Hitchcock, Curtice N., 105, 126
Hnatyshyn, Ray, 285
Hodgins, Jack, 264, 273; *The Resurrection of Joseph Bourne*, 273
Hoffer, William, 283, 290
Holden family (Indian Head), 11
Holm, Celeste, 150
Holmes, Andrew, 5
Holmes, Jessie Patterson Fraser (maternal grandmother), 5, 112
Holmes, Thomas, 5
Holt, Sir Herbert, 69
Holt (publisher), 170
Homer, Ken, 175
Honderich, Theodore, 174
Hopper, Mrs John, 64
Horizon, SK, 307n1
Horwood, Harold, 324n47
Howard, Mrs Bert, 46, 68
Howard, Rev. Bert, 46, 53, 61, 68, 112, 113
Howatt, Belvah, 25

Hughes, Isabelle, 175
Hughes, Richard, 121
Hunchiak, Anna, 36–7, 234
Hunchiak, Frank, 36–7, 234
Hunchiak, Nick, 36–7, 234
Hutner, Meyer, 179

Ibsen, Henrik: *Hedda Gabler*, 133; *Peer Gynt*, 83
Indian Head, SK, 10–12, 21, 24–5, 27, 31, 32, 38, 48, 61, 64, 138, 143, 166, 286, 296
Indian Head News, 24
Ingram, Cal, 49, 64–5
Istanbul, 197

James, Henry: *The Turn of the Screw*, 281
Jewison, Norman, 267
Johnson, Mary, 127–8
Jones, D.G., 210
Journal of Canadian Fiction, 209, 214, 215
Joyce, James, 290
Jutras, Luc, 253

Kane, Hugh, 173, 196
Kapola, Margaret, 267
Karsh, Yousef, 176: *Portraits of Greatness*, 176
Kattan, Naim, 169, 188
Kaye, Frances, 309n20
Keith, W.J., 281
Kelowna, BC, 301n2
Kennedy, Dennis, 30
Kerr, Ellie, 42, 68
Ketcheson, Eva, 26–7
Ketcheson, Sid, 12–15, 24–5, 26–7, 33, 38, 94, 124, 154, 180
Keynes, Maynard, 135

Kieran, Sheila, 215–18, 219, 221, 238, 240, 285, 299n3, 320nn21, 8

King, Thomas: *Green Grass, Running Water*, 287

Kingston, ON, 145, 146–7, 158

Kinsey, Alfred: *Sexual Behavior in the Human Male*, 51, 182

Kipling, Rudyard, 78

Kirkland, Hal B., 76, 305n12

Kisby, SK, 44

Klein, Fritz, 309n22

Klyn, Dorothy (Doyle), 149–50, 157, 181, 184, 188, 194, 261, 264, 282

Klyn, William, 149, 181, 184, 188, 194, 261, 264, 282

Knopf, Alfred A., 321n26

Koshland, William, 321n26

Kostash, Myrna, 97, 210–12, 213–14, 220, 227, 229, 230, 235, 238, 244, 250

Kotcheff, Ted, 229

Kozak, Carl, 36

Kozak, Johnny, 36

Krause, Pat, 238

Kreisler, Fritz, 85

Kroetsch, Robert, 163, 204, 210, 251, 269, 295, 297; *The Studhorse Man*, 204; *The Words of My Roaring*, 269

Lacey, Liam, 280

Lac La Ronge, SK, 6

Lake Katepwa, SK, 61

Lake Winnipeg, 98, 100, 127

Lancer, SK, 36, 40–1, 43, 137

Lang, Bertha Brack, 11, 286

Larson, Lars, 36

Last Tango in Paris (film), 223

Lathan, David, 329

Lauder, Sir Harry, 20

Laurence, Margaret, 163, 189, 190–1, 194–208 passim, 215, 229, 230, 231, 237, 238, 239, 242, 251–2, 272, 287, 317n29, 321n26, 324n47; *The Diviners*, 239–40, 321n26; *A Jest of God*, 190, 191; *The Stone Angel*, 191, 253

Layton, Irving, 265

Leacock, Stephen, 77, 173, 184; *Literary Lapses*, 173

Leader, SK, 30, 40

Leader-Post, 175, 232

Lean, David: *In Which We Serve* (film), 133

Le Carré, John, 163, 312n51

Lecker, Robert, 315n24

Lee, Alma, 289

Lehmann, John, 134; *New Writing*, 134, 135

Leoncavallo, Ruggero: *I pagliacci*, 18

Leschetizky, Theodor, 37, 45

Lesk, Andrew, 309n20, 312n50

Levine, Maurice, 38

Levine, Norman, 274

Levine family (Abbey), 38

Liberté (magazine), 193

Liberty (magazine), 32, 71

Lindner, Ernest, 286

Livesay, Dorothy, 287

Livingston family (Indian Head), 11

London, UK, 65, 66, 67, 78, 80, 133–8 passim, 183, 193, 199, 223, 230, 247

London Free Press, 205

Longfellow, Henry Wadsworth, 22, 160

Lorca, Federico García, 213, 230, 254

Lucas, Alec, 191–2, 266

Lucas, Koula, 191–2

Ludwig, Jack, 324n47

Lutes, Steve, 284

McAllister, D.E., 28, 39

Macbeth, Madge, 131; *The Kinder Bees, The Land of Afternoon, Shackles*, 131

MacCarthy, Desmond, 73, 304n6
McClelland, Jack, 157, 172–3, 189, 191, 196, 224, 225, 226–7, 317n21, 321n37
McClelland and Stewart (publisher), 92, 108, 109, 194–258 passim, 267, 276, 280, 291, 317n21
McClung, Nellie, 37
McCormick, Elizabeth, 89, 115
McCormick, Kenneth, 89, 115, 134, 163, 310n33
McCourt, Edward, 109, 110
Macdonald, Fred, 34
Macdonald, Grant, 145–9, 235
Macdonald, Lettie, 34–5
McDougall, Colin: The Execution, 178
MacEwen, Gwendolyn, 324n47
McGill University, 184, 191, 192, 194, 254, 256, 266
MacGregor, Roy, 269; The Last Season 269
McKay, Ada, 301n8
McKenzie family (Indian Head), 24
McKnight, Linda, 225
Maclean's, 32–3, 71, 155, 165–6, 168, 231
McLellan, Tom, 62–3, 65, 67
MacLennan, Hugh, ix, 146, 169, 202; Two Solitudes, 146
McLeod (Lancer), 41, 137
Macmillan Anthology I, 274
Macmillan Company (publisher), 144, 161–88 passim, 190
McMullen, Lorraine, 246–7, 248, 251, 253, 254, 260, 264, 265, 267, 275, 277, 280, 284, 296, 301n3
Macphail, Alexander, 75, 94, 96, 106
Macphail, Sir Andrew, 75–6, 78, 116, 151; Essays on Puritanism, 75; The Master's Wife, 75

Macpherson, Leroy, 71, 90
McVeigh, Ruth, 18
Madeline (Montreal friend), 142, 143, 313n7
Madrid, 209, 222, 230, 243, 255
Mahler, Gustav, 278; Kindertoten Lieder, 278
Málaga, 213–56 passim, 262
Malraux, André, 247, 316n33
Mandel, Eli: Trio, 169
Manitoba Arts Review, 124, 144
Martin, Robert K., 141
Maugham, Somerset, 73, 304n6
Maupassant, Guy de, 257
Mauriac, Claude, 219, 225, 226, 247, 316n33; Diner en ville, 219, 225; La Marquise sortit à cinq heures, 225
May, Ruth (Bendukov), 169
Maynard, Max, 141
Melchior, Lauritz, 89
Melnyk, George, 231
Men's Musical Club (Winnipeg), 84, 85, 86
Menuhin, Yehudi, 85
Merrick, Leonard, 67
Metcalf, John, 273
Mexico, 178, 181, 188, 191, 208, 261
Millard, Mrs Frank, 34
Miller, James (great-great nephew), 291
Miller, Lily, 224–5, 226
Miller, Shaun (great-great nephew), 286
Milne, Kathleen, 39, 172
Milton, John, 113
Minneapolis, 52, 79, 80, 81
Miscampbell (Abbey), 28
Miscellany of Tales and Essays, 77
Mitchell, Ken, 77, 158, 180, 193, 210, 215, 237–8, 242–72 passim, 299n2; Sinclair Ross: A Reader's Guide, 193, 246, 257, 260, 261

Mitchell, Roula, 255, 257, 267
Mitchell, W.O., 22, 145, 146, 163, 165, 251; *Vanishing Point*, 166; *Who Has Seen the Wind*, 146, 246
Modern Canadian Stories (1966), 190
Moher, Frank, 258
Montagnes, Anne, 204
Montreal, 64, 67, 140–94 *passim*, 221, 225, 243, 254, 256–61, 266, 271
Montrealer, 193
Montreal Standard, 149, 150
Montreal Star, 174, 204
Moore, Brian, 163, 218, 250; *The Great Victorian Collection*, 250; *The Revolution Script*, 218
Moore, Mavor, 178
Moose Jaw, SK, 39, 167, 171–2
Moose Mountain Star-Standard, 44, 45, 64
Morgan, Jane, 150
Morocco, 220
Morrow (publisher), 168, 169, 170
Mosaic, 200
Moscovich, Jack, 271
Moscovich, Mary, 271–2, 287
Moss, John, 209, 222, 241, 242, 278, 309n17
Moszkowski, Moritz: 'Spanish Caprice,' 53
Mulhallen, Karen, 231
Mulholland, Mrs (Rolling Prairie District), 17, 18
Mulroney, Brian, 285
Munro, Alice, 158, 251; *Moons of Jupiter*, 266
Munroe, Lorne, 86
Murison, Mrs J. (Arcola), 64
Murray, Forbes, 59–60, 61, 65, 69, 112, 113
Myketiak brothers (Rolling Prairie District), 20, 36, 234

Nash, Knowlton, 286
Nash, Ogden, 138
Nash's–Pall Mall Magazine, 73, 304n5
National Film Board of Canada, 96, 184, 192
Nelson, J. Cecil, 91, 111, 176, 182–3, 267, 310n25
New, W.H., 110, 199
New Canadian Library (McClelland and Stewart), 109, 119, 170, 172–4, 189, 191, 195, 217, 220, 226, 242, 248, 264
Newlove, John, 225
Newman, Peter, 163
New Westminster, BC, 140, 285
New York City, 87–90, 102, 104, 107, 115, 121, 141, 161, 163, 169, 170, 185, 193, 221, 259
New Yorker, 75, 108, 276
New York Herald Tribune, 106, 108
New York Times Review of Books, 108
Nixon, Philip, 257
Norrona (newspaper), 72, 103

Obermann, Beatrice (great niece), 172, 269
O'Connor, Geoffrey, 296
O'Connor, John, x, 279, 280, 287, 296, 302n16
Odets, Clifford, 187
Okanagan Valley, BC, 261, 301n2
O'Kelly, Audrey (Peterkin), 128, 130, 131–2, 133, 135, 138, 200, 233, 269
O'Kelly family (Winnipeg), 128, 132
Olivier, Laurence, 136, 293
Olson, Gladys (MacLean), 18, 288, 301nn8, 9
Olson family (Rolling Prairie District), 15, 16, 18
O'Malley, Martin, 228

Ondaatje, Michael: *Running in the Family*, 266, 273, 287
Ontario Institute for Studies in Education (OISE), 202, 247
Order of Canada, 284–5, 287, 294
Orman, Roy, 300n14
Ostenso, Martha, 32, 102; *Wild Geese*, 32, 102, 247
Ottawa, 67, 129–32, 133, 176, 278, 279, 280, 285, 294
Ottawa Citizen, 232
Ottawa Journal, 174, 231
Owen, Ivor, 217
Oxbow, SK, 150

Pacey, Desmond, 109, 115
Palestrina, Giovanni Pierluigi da, 53
Palliser Triangle, 13, 29, 43
Paris, 193, 230
Parker, Theodore, 5, 113
Patterson, Alan, 301n2
Patterson, Carol, 45, 56, 68
Patterson, Jessie. *See* Holmes, Jessie Patterson Fraser
Patterson family (Arcola), 65
Pearson, Peter, 203, 215–18, 320n21; *The Best Damn Fiddler from Calabogie to Kaladar*, 216; *Paperback Hero*, 218
Pederson, Svea, 172
Pell, Barbara, 288
Penhandlers (Winnipeg), 123, 136, 270
Perrie, Anne, 186–7
Person, Lloyd, 257, 270
Peterborough Examiner, 109, 281
Peterkin, Audrey. *See* O'Kelly, Audrey
Peterkin, David, 233
Peterson, Eric, 94
Phoenix Club (Winnipeg), 72, 83–4, 91, 101, 103–4, 112, 123, 306n24
Pickel, Enid, 21, 22, 23

Pickel, Vesta, 21, 22
Pickel, Weldon Umberto, 21–2, 23, 32
Pictorial Review, 32
Pinza, Ezio, 85
Pittman, Bruce, 94, 96, 267
Pons, Lily, 85
Pooley, Constance (Rolling Prairie District), 17, 20, 31, 32
Porter, Anna, 201, 223, 225, 226, 227, 230, 236
Portman, James, 205, 230–1
Powys, T.F., 138
Pratt, E.J., 77, 115, 116, 149
Preston, Miss (Winnipeg), 98, 118, 120, 232
Price, Effie Ross (sister), 6, 8, 10, 24, 31, 38, 48, 61, 64, 90, 138, 143, 166–7, 172, 238, 300–1n1
Price, Matthew, 11
Prince Albert, SK, 3, 5, 6, 11, 15, 63, 66
Princes Risborough, UK, 66
Province (Vancouver), 109, 175
Puccini, Giacomo: *Madama Butterfly*, 84
Pugh, Albert, 300n4
Puzo, Mario: *The Godfather*, 229

Quarterly Review (London), 76
Quebec Chronicle Telegraph, 174
Queen's Quarterly, 75–81 passim, 91, 94, 96, 98, 113, 119, 124, 151–60 passim, 185, 199, 232, 287, 305n15
Queen's University, 145, 192
Quill and Quire, 275

Rachmaninoff, Sergei, 37, 85
Radcliffe, Madge (Abbey), 35–6
Radcliffe, Tex (Abbey), 36
Radcliffe, Walter (Abbey), 36
Raoul, Valerie, 309n20

Raymond, Louis-Bertrand: *Au service du Seigneur*, 253

Regina, 10, 39, 43, 44, 53, 56, 65, 66, 99, 257, 258, 259

Regina College, 50, 56

Regina Conservatory of Music, 44, 52, 53–4

Reid, Kate, 204, 216

Rembrandt, 238

Reynal, Eugene, 105, 108, 115–16, 123, 126, 307n24

Reynal and Hitchcock (publisher), 105, 106, 121, 123, 125, 127

Reynolds, Roy, 71, 90

Richler, Mordecai, 202, 229; *The Apprenticeship of Duddy Kravitz*, 229, 250, 251, 266

Ricou, Laurie, 221

Riel, Louis, 126

Riley, Edna, 114, 118, 122, 310n10

Rimbaud, Arthur, 265

Riverhurst, SK, 15, 16, 17, 20, 31

Roberts, Charles G.D., 116

Roberts, Kenneth, 126

Robertson, Patricia, 277, 296; *City of Orphans*, 277

Robins, John D., 116; *A Pocketful of Canada*, 116

Robinson, Marilynne: *Housekeeping*, 266

Roffman, Julian, 177–9

Rolling Prairie District, SK, 15–21, 59, 77, 288, 314n4

Rome, 230

Rooke, Leon, 273

Roper, Gordon, 200

Rose, Marilyn, 234, 279

Ross, Catherine (Kate) Moir Foster Fraser (mother), 3–9, 10–128 *passim*, 132, 138, 140, 142, 143, 147–8, 150, 166–7, 171–2, 191, 271, 272, 273–4, 285, 292–3, 300n3, 301n3

Ross, Effie (sister). *See* Price, Effie Ross

Ross, James Sinclair: ancestry, 5; apprentice writing, 32, 55, 57, 62, 66, 71; bank employment, 28–9, 142–3, 182–4; birth, 3; bisexuality, 41, 51, 60, 182; death, 295; education, 9, 11, 14, 18–20, 21–2, 23, 24–5, 26, 35; on friendship, 23–4, 38, 50–1; illness, 12, 90, 135, 147, 182, 194, 206, 254–5, 254–97 (Parkinson's disease); interviewed, 120–2, 153, 193, 202, 203, 228, 257; music, 22, 28, 30–1, 37–8, 40, 42–58; painting, 17, 31–2, 39, 66; on religion, 47, 135–6; sexual experience, 11–12, 19–20, 23, 41, 49, 52, 60, 82, 84, 87, 88–9, 115, 182, 213; war experience, 128–38; on writing style and structure, 99, 151, 282–3
WORKS:
Books:
– *As for Me and My House*, 23, 24, 27–47 *passim*, 55, 58, 60, 92, 96–101, 103–6, 107–23, 124, 126, 130, 136, 138, 139, 143, 147, 152, 155, 156, 157, 162, 170, 172–3, 175, 176, 177, 183, 184, 185, 189, 192, 196, 197, 199, 200, 203–4, 209–17 *passim*, 221–2, 227, 228–9, 231, 232, 234, 241–9 *passim*, 253–69 *passim*, 273, 279–84 *passim*, 290, 291, 296, 315n24, 320n8, 321n26
– *The Lamp at Noon and Other Stories*, 92–3, 189, 191, 194, 199–200, 291; 'Circus in Town,' 71, 96; 'Cornet at Night,' 27, 92, 94–6, 97, 137, 184, 207, 267, 287; 'A Field of Wheat,' 75, 76–7, 79, 80, 81, 123, 147, 155,

242; 'The Lamp at Noon,' 90–1, 94,
137, 189, 277, 296; 'Not by Rain
Alone,' 119, 199 (Part I: 'Summer
Thunder,' 119; Part II: 'September
Snow,' 62, 77–8, 93, 119); 'One's a
Heifer,' 92, 125, 136–8, 147, 149,
155, 189, 207, 215, 267, 317n29;
'The Outlaw,' 14, 58, 154, 155,
185, 186, 296; 'The Painted Door,'
74, 92, 93–4, 96, 137, 192, 250,
257, 264, 267, 269, 317n29,
328n16; 'The Runaway,' 147, 149,
155, 158–60
– The Race and Other Stories, 284;
'Barrack Room Fiddle Tune,' 129,
144, 151; 'A Day with Pegasus,' 92–
3, 94, 96, 189, 207, 296; 'The Flowers That Killed Him,' 23, 209, 214–
15, 217, 257; 'Jug and Bottle,' 74,
132, 144, 147, 151–3, 162, 237;
'Nell,' 124; 'No Other Way,' 72–4,
124; 'Saturday Night,' 58, 151,
155–6 ; 'Spike,' 192–3, 253, 258
– Sawbones Memorial, 18, 19, 20, 25,
31, 35, 36, 156, 219–36, 239, 242,
243, 245, 248, 250, 253, 258, 265,
267, 279, 296
– The Well, 20, 75, 161–80, 183, 185,
186, 192, 206, 226, 233, 264,
314n4, 315n17
– Whir of Gold, 19, 31, 58, 142, 185–
8, 195–207, 217, 220, 224, 226,
233, 243, 246, 264, 316n2
Essays and Memoir:
'Just Wind and Horses,' 7, 11, 14, 21,
29, 64, 112–13, 172, 274–5; 'Montreal and French-Canadian Culture,' 313; 'On Looking Back,' 200;
'Why My 2nd Book Came 17 Years
Later,' 174, 185

Short Stories:
'The Unwilling Organist' (uncol-
lected), 176; 'Old Chippendale'
(unpublished), 147–8
Unpublished Manuscripts (presumed
destroyed):
'The Call of the Canvas,' 32, 71; 'Day
Coach to Wageneria,' 28, 123, 124–
5, 126, 127, 131, 133, 143, 175,
207; 'Disasters of Peace,' 216, 223,
243; 'Price above Rubies,' 194,
235–41, 242, 243, 245, 249, 250–1;
'Sonny and Mad,' 185; 'Sport of
Wanton Boys,' 236–7; 'Teddy Do,'
261; 'The Wife of Peter Guy,' 57,
67, 71, 97, 101, 104, 105; 'A World
of Good,' 156
Unpublished Memoir:
'The Troopship Story,' 129, 132, 275,
280, 283, 287, 289, 292
Ross, Malcolm, 109, 172–3, 189, 226
Ross, Peter Sinclair (father), 3–9, 13,
15, 38–9, 61, 146, 148, 300nn3, 8
Ross, Stuart (brother), 6, 8, 13, 61, 172,
274, 291, 300n14
Ross, William, 114, 127
Roth, Philip: Portnoy's Complaint, 195
Roy, Gabrielle, 84, 251
Royal Bank of Canada, 28, 31, 42, 43,
48, 49, 69, 109, 112, 139, 190, 225,
238, 240, 252, 271
Rule, Jane, 324n47

St Clair, Floyd, 265
Saint-Exupéry, Antoine de, 103
St George Stubbs, Roy, 120–1, 122, 233,
235, 237–8, 241, 244, 248; Lawyers
and Laymen of Western Canada, 120;
Men in Khaki: Four Regiments of Manitoba, 120

Salvatore, 197–8

Salverson, Laura Goodman, 118, 120, 122; *Confessions of an Immigrant's Daughter*, 118; *The Viking Heart*, 117, 140

Samis, Clarence, 303n26

Sand, George, 309n20

Sand Hills Region, SK, 40, 137

Sandler, Linda, 230

Sandwell, B.K., 184

Sartre, Jean-Paul, 247

Saskatoon, 290, 291

Saturday Evening Post, 134, 250

Saturday Night, 33, 71, 117, 120, 184, 210–11, 233

Saunders, Doris, 114, 117, 122, 124, 125, 129–39 *passim*, 158, 167, 191, 194, 197–8, 200, 232, 248, 250, 270, 293

Savory, Robert, 130, 132, 280–1, 288

Schamp, Cornelia, 28

Schellenberg, August, 94

Schiff, Stacey, 103

Schlass, Ruth, 113

Schmalz, Wayne, 286

Schmidt, Frank, 287

Schoemperlen, Diane, 274

Schubert, Franz: 'Military March,' 53

Scott, F.R., 169

Scott, James, 175

Scroggie, Kathleen, 128, 149, 150

Sedgwick, Eve: *Between Men*, 309–10n23

Seeley, Fraser, 290, 291

Shakespeare, William: *As You Like It*, 27; *Hamlet*, 136; *King Lear*, 136, 236; *The Merchant of Venice*, 133; *Richard III*, 136

Shaw, George Bernard: *Heartbreak House*, 133

Shellbrook, SK, 3

Shellbrook Chronicle, 6, 8, 11

Sillitoe, Alan, 163

Simenon, Georges, 103, 316n33

Simon Fraser University, 210, 264, 296

Sir George Williams University, 241

Sitwell, Sir Osbert, 147

Soles, Mrs (Wild Rose), 6, 74

Sorestad, Glen, 257

Southampton, 63

Spafford, Richard, 290

Spender, Stephen, 267

Springfield Republican, 108

Staines, David, 295

Stead, R.J.C.: *Grain*, 140

Stendhal: *Le Rouge et le noir*, 185

Stephens, Donald, 210

Stevenson, Robert Louis, 67

Stone, Dr (Arcola), 43, 58

Stone, Mrs (Arcola), 43, 57, 62, 67

Stone, Noel, 265

Story (American magazine), 116, 125, 133, 136

Stouck, David: *Major Canadian Authors*, 270

Stouck, Mary-Ann, 277, 280, 285, 287, 288, 294, 295, 296

Stoughton, SK, 21–4, 38, 56

Stoughton Times, 23

Strange, Harry, 102

Strange, Kathleen, 101–3, 115, 126, 307n19; *With the West in Her Eyes*, 101, 102, 103

Strauss, Richard, 223, 296

Stringer, Arthur: *The Prairie Child*, *The Prairie Mother*, *The Prairie Wife*, 97

Stringer, Mrs (Lancer), 40

Sturgess, Marie, 57

Suknaski, Andrew, 243, 244

Sullivan, Alan: *Three Came to Ville Marie*, 239

Swan, Susan, 205
Swift Current, SK, 27, 30, 33, 34
Swinn, Charlie, 143
Sykes, Pamela, 204
Sypnowich, Peter, 203

Talgoy, Magnus, 72, 103
Talgoy, Tora, 72, 103–4, 127, 138, 140, 172
Tallman, Warren, 185, 210
Tata, Sam, 275
Taylor, Charles, 324n47
Teller (previously the *Royal Bank Magazine*), 176–7, 305n15
Tennyson, Lord Alfred, 22
Thacker, Robert, 307n25
Thomas, Lillian Benyon, 84, 123
Thompson, Dwayne, 302nn13, 14
Thompson, Ernest, 62
Thompson, Meredith, 114
Thompson, Tanya, 309n21
Thomson, Tom, 32
Thorne, William, 98–101, 292, 296
Thorolfson, Frank, 85, 86
Thorolfson, Irene, 85, 86
Thorston, Dallas, 254
Thurber, James, 138
Toledo, 209, 243
Tolstoy, Leo, 247, 290; *The Cossacks*, 290
Toppings, Earle, 153, 202
Toronto, 67, 115–17, 158, 186, 202–3, 218, 221
Toronto Conservatory of Music, 44, 45, 54, 57
Toronto Daily Star, 174, 203, 275
Toronto Telegram, 175, 205
Torremolinos, 213, 216
Trapnell, Andy, xiii, 277, 282, 289–90, 293, 295, 296

Trinity Western University, 283, 288
Trudeau, Pierre Elliott, 293
Tunstell, Douglas, 114, 192, 254, 256
Turgenev, Ivan: *A Month in the Country*, 133
Turks and Caicos Islands, 120
Turnbull, Gael: *Trio*, 169
Twain, Mark, 77, 123, 235
Twigg, Alan, 270–1
Twigg, Mabel (Arcola), 46
Tyrwhitt, Janice, 165, 166

Union Bank (Royal Bank of Canada), 28, 31
United Church of Canada, 33–5, 36, 37–8, 40, 45, 46, 61, 68, 97, 176
United College (Winnipeg), 98
University of Alberta Press, 180
University of British Columbia, 264, 277
University of Calgary, 223, 238, 240
University of London (UK), 199
University of Manitoba, 50, 53, 85, 101, 113, 115, 139, 140, 191, 270
University of Nebraska Press, 248, 253, 325n52
University of New Brunswick, 192
University of Ottawa, 246
University of Regina, 241
University of Saskatchewan, 58
University of Toronto, 115, 158, 192, 200, 279
University of Toronto Press, 281
University of Toronto Quarterly, 176, 200
Upjohn, Frank, 155, 164, 169, 178, 179, 182
Ursell, Geoffrey, 260
Ustinov, Peter, 278

Vancouver, 140, 210, 260, 261, 262–96 *passim*

Vancouver Island, 113, 264
Vancouver Sun, 109, 175
Vanderhaeghe, Guy, 210; *Man Descending*, 269
Van Gogh, Vincent, 238
Van Herk, Aritha, 210
Vargas Llosa, Mario, 250
Verdi, Giuseppi: *Simon Boccanegra*, 223
Victoria, BC, 261, 278, 282
Victoria Times Colonist, 204
Viking (publisher), 170
Villon, Pierre, 193
Viney, Frank, 34
von Logau, Friedrich, 160

Wagner, Richard, 28, 89; *Parsifal*, 278
Warner, Tom: *Never Going Back*, 303n23
Watmough, David, 265
Watson, Sheila: *The Double Hook*, 231
Watt, Margaret, 49, 50
Waugh, Evelyn, 266
Weaver, Emily P., 157
Weaver, Robert, 154–5, 156, 157–8, 189, 192, 196, 227, 230, 270, 317n29
Webb, Phyllis, 169; *Even Your Right Eye*, 169; *Trio*, 169
Weekend Magazine, 150
Weekes, H.V., 176
Weintraub, William: *City Unique*, 313n3
Wells, H.G.: *The Outline of History*, 40
Wernham, Ernest, 6, 8, 300nn4, 14
Wesley College (Winnipeg), 50, 56
West, Rebecca, 73, 304–5n6
Weyburn, SK, 37
Wheeler, Anne, 138, 267
Whitefoot, John, xiii, 283–4, 287–95 passim, 310n32
Whitman family (Arcola), 43

Wiebe, Rudy, 210, 248; *The Scorched-Wood People*, 249; *The Temptations of Big Bear*, 221, 248
Wilder, Thornton: *Our Town*, 258
Wild Rose, SK, 6–14 passim, 59, 71, 74, 121, 147, 274
Williams, David, 232, 309n19
Williams, Oscar, 134
Willmar, SK, 46
Wilson, Ethel, 145, 158, 169
Wilson, Lorene, 258
Windsor Star, 204, 206
Wing, Willis K., 163–4, 165–6, 168, 169
Winnipeg, 29, 51, 52, 54, 57, 61, 62, 66, 68, 69–129 passim, 130, 138, 139, 140, 141, 142, 149, 150, 166, 190, 191, 192, 200, 209, 274, 280, 288
Winnipeg Free Press, 109, 126, 131, 190, 205, 233, 281
Winnipeg Tribune, 72, 104
Wiseman, Adele, 163, 190, 191, 251, 272; *The Sacrifice*, 191
Woodbury, Frank, 22, 42, 44–5, 46, 52–4, 55–6, 58, 60, 68, 69
Woodbury, Gladys Waters, 53, 65
Woodcock, George, 158, 184, 204, 230, 231, 265, 275; *A Choice of Critics*, 184
Woodsworth, J.S., 83
Woolf, Virginia: *To the Lighthouse*, 131; *The Waves*, 231
Worst Journeys, 288
Worth family (Abbey), 34, 38
Wright, Richard B., 187; *Clara Callan*, ix

Yeast family (Abbey), 35
Youngblud, W.F., 46, 57, 68
Youngblud, Mrs W.F., 46
Young Men's Musical Club (Winnipeg), 85, 86, 87, 143